Open Economy Macroeconomics

Professor Rødseth here provides a broad survey of open economy macro-economics within a unified framework. This upper-level textbook reviews the theories employed by ministries of finance, central banks and financial institutions which form the basis for most quantitative models of open econo-mies. It also points out the limitations of these theories and gives an update on recent research. The emphasis is on how the nature of the markets for foreign exchange and for exports and imports sets the stage for government policy and determines the macroeconomic effects of external and internal shocks. Particular attention is paid to the relations between short- and long-run equilibria and the long-run consequences of national policies. Short-run wage rigidities play a key role, and models with wage bargaining are compared to more traditional formulations. Exchange rate policy and the transmission of shocks are discussed from both a national and an interna-tional perspective.[*]

ASBJØRN RØDSETH is Professor of Economics at the University of Oslo. He has for many years advised the Norwegian Ministry of Finance and the central bank on economic modelling. He is vice-chairman of the board of the Banking, Insurance and Securities Commission of Norway. He has been an academic visitor at Yale University, London School of Economics, Stanford University and the Institute for International Economic Studies at Stockholm University.

[*]Answers to exercises and other supplementary material are available at
<www.cup.cam.ac.uk>.

Open Economy Macroeconomics

Asbjørn Rødseth

UNIVERSITY OF OSLO

PUBLISHED BY THE PRESS SYNDICATE OF THE UNIVERSITY OF CAMBRIDGE
The Pitt Building, Trumpington Street, Cambridge, United Kingdom

CAMBRIDGE UNIVERSITY PRESS
The Edinburgh Building, Cambridge CB2 2RU, UK   http://www.cup.cam.ac.uk
40 West 20th Street, New York, NY 10011-4211, USA   http://www.cup.org
10 Stamford Road, Oakleigh, Melbourne 3166, Australia
Ruiz de Alarcón 13, 28014 Madrid, Spain

First published 2000

Printed in the United Kingdom at the University Press, Cambridge

Typeface Utopia   System 3B2

A catalogue record for this book is available from the British Library

Library of Congress Cataloguing in Publication data
Rødseth, Asbjørn.
Open economy macroeconomics / Asbjørn Rødseth.
      p.   cm.
Includes bibliographical references.
ISBN 0 521 78304 6 – ISBN 0 521 78874 9 (pbk.)
1. Macroeconomics. I. Title.
HB172.5.R63 200080-023023
339–dc21

ISBN 0 521 78304 6   hardback
ISBN 0 521 78874 9   paperback

Contents

Figures

Tables

Preface

This text is based on notes from lectures held for master students at the University of Oslo. Selected sections have also been used for third-year undergraduates in Oslo, for PhD students in Finland and for master students at the Norwegian University of Science and Technology. This also describes the intended audience of the book which is advanced students, primarily at the masters level. I have in mind both students who will later practise economics in government, finance and industry and those who want to become researchers. Compared to other advanced texts, I have given more weight to the first group, but it should also give PhD students a good background for ventures into the journal literature. Subsets of the book suitable for third- or fourth-year undergraduates can be selected in a number of different ways; some suggestions are given on the book's homepage www.cup.cam.ac.uk, which also contains suggested answers to the exercises.

Over the years I have benefited from comments from those with whom I have taught open economy macroeconomics: Christian Riis, Bent Vale, Birger Vikøren, Espen Frøyland and Ragnar Nymoen. I am also grateful for comments on earlier versions from Steinar Holden, Kai Leitemo, Halvor Mehlum, Jørn Rattsø, Jon Strand, Ragnar Torvik, Atle Seierstad and Knut Sydsæter, and from a large number of students in Oslo and Helsinki. Sveinung Skjesol drew the originals of the graphs and has provided me with excellent assistance in so many ways. Lately, his job has been taken over by Jens Festervoll who continues in the same good spirit. Thanks also to Helen Viland and Inger Lande.

List of standard symbols

Volumes

Y output (income)

C private consumption (or consumption function)

I private real investment (or investment function)

G government consumption and real investment

X net exports (or net export function)

T net taxes and transfers

W financial wealth

N employment

K stock of real capital

Financial assets, nominal values

M money (domestic currency)

B bonds (interest bearing assets in domestic currency)

F foreign currency (interest bearing assets in foreign currency)

Prices, interest rates

P price

W wage rate

E exchange rate, domestic currency per unit of foreign currency

ω real wage

Π real price (price divided by wage rate)

R real exchange rate, relative price of foreign in terms of domestically produced goods

i nominal interest rate

ρ real interest rate

Functions

m (real) money demand function

f (real) demand function for foreign currency

b (real) demand function for domestic bonds

Miscellaneous

e rate of depreciation ($\dot{E}/E$)

r risk premium on domestic relative to foreign bonds

τ tax rate

Subscripts

p private

g government

*   foreign

t traded goods industry

n non-traded goods industry

e expected value

Introduction

I.1 The field

An economy is 'open' when it trades with other countries in goods, services and financial assets. Today, with few if any exceptions, all countries are open. Thus, it may seem odd to have a special branch of economics that is labelled 'open economy macroeconomics'.[1]

It is customary to see economics as divided in two main branches, microeconomics and macroeconomics. Personally I prefer a classification where at the top level there is general economic theory (most of that now classified as 'microeconomics'); this is highly abstract and provides us with a tool-kit that we use in a number of applied fields, macroeconomics being one. Macroeconomics tries to explain the behaviour of certain economy-wide aggregates (GDP, the price level, the current account, etc.), and takes a particular interest in aggregative aspects of fiscal and monetary policy. Ultimately one is then interested in open economies. However, in order to explain the relevant aggregates we need to study a large number of behavioural mechanisms that take part in their determination: consumption demand, investment demand, wage-setting, expectations formation, etc. In the end we try to integrate these mechanisms into a common framework, a model, which explains the aggregates. Different branches of macroeconomics focus on different mechanisms that should ultimately be woven into the same picture. In open economy macroeconomics the focus is on the behavioural mechanisms that are specifically and most directly related to international trade in goods, services and financial assets.

This means that in open economy macroeconomics we try to explain the same economy-wide aggregates as in all of macroeconomics, but the focus is on the international side: capital movements, exports and imports, exchange rates. In other areas, such as savings behaviour, investment demand and wage formation, we have to be more brief. We still try to keep these aspects in the picture, but the discussion of them must remain at a more superficial level. This is not to be regretted; when we go beyond the level of introductory macroeconomics, we have to narrow the focus, otherwise we are stuck at the same elementary level. At the same time we must provide a framework of the complete picture in order to see how the parts fit in: the interplay between the different mechanisms is the core of macroeconomics.

International macroeconomics is another name for the field. However, the main perspective in the present book is that of a single country and its relations with the

1

rest of the world. In many instances we assume that the country in focus is 'small' relative to the world economy. This is no great limitation; all the countries we usually speak of as 'large' – with one possible exception, the United States – are small enough relative to the total world economy. Besides, much of the analysis is relevant also for 'large' countries with only minor qualifications. Towards the end of the book we also look at how countries interact in the world economy.

Interest in the field has surged in recent years. Several events have contributed: large swings in exchange rates between the major currencies; spectacular currency crises in Asia, Europe and Latin America, and the abandonment of fixed exchange rates by some countries; the formation of monetary union in Europe and the spread of the currency board system in other parts of the world; persistent trade imbalances – for example between the United States and Japan; the debt crisis in developing countries. There has been an underlying tendency to increased openness to trade that has helped to put the international aspects at the forefront.

I.2 The book

The book gives a broad survey of the field of open economy macroeconomics within a unified framework. It reviews theories that are used by good practitioners in ministries of finance, central banks, international organizations and financial institutions, and that form the basis for most quantitative models of open economies. It also points out the limitations of these theories and guides the reader to recent research.

The book differs from other texts on several counts. Some advanced textbooks focus primarily on the most recent theoretical developments. However, the field has a core of theories and models which have been with us for a while, and which has not been made redundant by the recent research. It is usually to these theories that both practitioners and researchers turn when faced with practical policy problems or when making forecasts. This book gives an update on recent research, but the material in it has primarily been selected to satisfy the needs of the applied economist.

The unity in the exposition is obtained by consistently applying a stock equilibrium approach to the foreign exchange market. Capital movements are seen as portfolio shifts, not as gradual flows. All elements in the models are well known from the literature, but the way they are joined together has required some research. Too often, textbooks present a succession of disjunct models in their original versions without replacing obsolete parts. My approach is to present models that are as updated as possible given the constraint that the technical level should not be too demanding. For example, some well known conclusions from the original Mundell–Fleming models fall apart if expectations are not static and if capital movements are seen as portfolio shifts: still, these conclusions are often repeated as truths. The exposition here starts from an updated version.

The book has three parts. Part 1, chapters 1–4, focuses on the financial markets in open economies, and especially on the foreign exchange market. It explains, mostly in a partial equilibrium setting, how exchange rates, interest rates and capital movements between currencies are determined. Chapter 1 provides a basic model of the foreign exchange market and introduces key concepts. It argues that how investors divide their portfolios between different currencies is a key factor in exchange rate determination. Chapter 2 goes more deeply into the reasons behind the portfolio choices that are made, and takes a look at the empirical evidence about capital mobility. Chapter 3 extends the model to allow a broader discussion of monetary policy. It explores different options for monetary and exchange rate policy, and the consequences of these for the workings of the financial markets. The emphasis is on the determination of interest rates and exchange rates and the consequences of high capital mobility. Expected future exchange rates play a key role in the determination of the present exchange rate, and this is, of course, included in the models of chapters 1–3. In chapter 4 we ask (not for the last time) how such expectations can be formed on a rational basis. It is then necessary to extend the model to include the real side of the economy, and as a first example of this a simple general equilibrium model based on the monetary approach to exchange rate determination is presented.

Part 2 of the book, chapters 5–8, integrates the financial and the real side of the economy more fully. These chapters explore the determination of output, employment, the current account, the foreign debt and the rate of inflation. They are organized according to the assumptions made about the structure of the goods market in relation to international trade.

In chapter 5 we look at an 'extremely open economy'. This means that all goods are traded internationally. The same goods are produced at home and abroad, and they are sold in competitive markets where the law of one price applies. In chapter 6 the home country is specialized in the production of *home goods* that are imperfect substitutes for the *foreign goods* produced abroad. Both goods are traded internationally, but the market for home goods is limited, and the foreign currency price of home goods is affected by domestic supply and demand. In chapter 7 there are two sets of goods. *Traded goods* can be exported or imported at given world market prices like the goods in chapter 5. *Non-traded* goods are neither exported nor imported. Their prices are determined in a closed domestic market.

The three chapters are complementary. In actual economies we usually find examples of all three market structures together. In chapter 8 we compare the three approaches, present some empirical evidence and look at the implications of various forms of monopolistic competition. A common presumption in the four chapters is that wages (or prices) are rigid in the short run, but flexible in the long run, and some evidence on this is also presented in chapter 8. Throughout the chapters wage equations based on modern theories of union wage bargaining are considered in addition to traditional augmented Phillips curves.

Space considerations prevent us from discussing every important substantive issue for each assumption about market structure (and it would be boring, too). The solution has been a certain division of labour between the four chapters. Chapter 5 is the most comprehensive. The simple market structure there makes it relatively easy to analyse the full time path from short- to long-run equilibrium. The current account and the foreign debt are given much attention in this chapter; it is simple to give an integrated treatment of their dynamics together with the dynamics of the exchange rate, the wage level and the capital stock. The market structures in chapters 6 and 7 open up for short-run effects of aggregate demand on output and employment and, hence, these are more in focus there, including a discussion of short-run effects of fiscal and monetary policy. Chapter 6 explores the long-run dynamics of aggregate demand: fixed and flexible exchange rates are compared throughout. In chapter 7 there is more focus on supply-side dynamics and supply-side policy. The broader survey of the issue of market structure in chapter 8 should make it possible to see how the elements from the preceding chapters can be integrated in a more complete model. I have not presented such a general model, however, because in my view it would be too complicated to learn much from, except if implemented as a quantitative simulation model with estimated equations.

Part 3 of the book consists of two separate chapters. In chapter 9 the perspective is changed from that of a single country to the world economy. Major subjects are the international monetary system, the transmission of the effects of shocks throughout the world economy and the potential gains from international policy cooperation. Chapter 10 reverts to the single-country perspective and discusses exchange rate policy in a small open economy, including the issue of speculative attacks. Although the perspective is different, chapters 9 and 10 have in common that they attempt to compare alternative exchange rate regimes.

The book gives equal emphasis to fixed and floating exchange rates. This reflects the fact that both systems are practised by a large number of countries, and that different systems have been in vogue at different times.

One limitation is that the analysis pertains mainly to economies where international trade in goods and financial assets is not heavily regulated. Some restrictions on trade can be accommodated easily – for example, tariffs, prohibitions on imports or exports of certain goods, the exclusion of some investors from certain asset markets. However, there must be a substantial volume of trade that is free to respond to changes in incentives. Similarly, some investors must be free to move substantial amounts of capital across borders and between currencies. The trend in recent years has been towards increased trade liberalization. However, there are still countries where foreign transactions are so heavily regulated that the analysis in this book needs important qualifications.

While relatively free trade is assumed, people in this book do not move across borders (neither as workers, nor as consumers). Making them mobile would hardly change the main thrust of the conclusions as long as there are some mobility costs. However, in some cases migration may be quantitatively important.

I.3 The approach

The text is applied economic theory. Empirical results on some key relationships are surveyed briefly. Among them are results related to capital mobility, import and export demand and purchasing power parity (PPP). In accord with the focus on open economy macroeconomics, there is no attempt to survey empirical evidence that is not directly related to international relations. Ideally the theory should be illustrated with examples taken from actual historical episodes and current policy discussions. However, for the advanced student it is more important to have a broad treatment of the theory within the same covers. A large number of articles and books provide good examples, and some are referred to later. Any teacher will doubtlessly find a number of other examples which are suited to his or her audience.[2]

A recent trend in open economy macroeconomics has been the application of intertemporal general equilibrium models based on explicit utility and profit maximization. This has produced many useful insights. Yet the analysis in this book in many places starts with assumed behavioural functions. The reason is twofold: (1) It allows us to focus on the main driving forces, to avoid unnecessary detail and to be a bit agnostic about what lies behind the observed behaviour. (2) It is simpler, meaning greater pedagogical efficiency: the reader can obtain more economic insight with less effort. Naturally, I have used explicit utility or profit maximization whenever I found it useful for the exposition, and I have tried to take account of insights from the intertemporal approach.[3]

My approach is, I believe, the same that Krugman (1995) argues strongly in favour of as a 'workable guide' to answer a wide range of questions in open economy macroeconomics. It is telling that many of those who devote much energy to models with maximizing agents often come down to quite simplistic models with assumed behavioural functions when they discuss policy questions.[4]

Some academic economists have apparently issued a ban on models that do not start from explicit utility maximization. It is hard to see that this ban is justified. All models are simplifications; in order to tackle the technical difficulties in models that start from explicit utility maximization, one often has to make extreme simplifications. Even if one believes that economic behaviour can always be described as utility maximization, this does not mean that particular models of utility maximization *a priori* have greater claim to truth than models where we start with behavioural functions. Progress in economic science is probably best promoted by openness to different approaches. An approach that has proved to be useful empirically should not be discarded on the grounds that it does not satisfy the methodological requirement that everything should be derived explicitly from utility maximization. For a philosophically inspired defence by an economist of the approach to macroeconomics that is taken here, see Mayer (1993).

I.4 Prerequisites

As with most other advanced texts in economics, this book requires familiarity with differential calculus. In several places systems of differential equations in two unknown time functions are analysed (notably sections 5.5, 5.8–5.9, 6.6–6.7 and 7.5). Hence, for these parts some knowledge of the qualitative theory for such systems is desirable. All the necessary results are contained in appendix A (p. 353). The book draws heavily on microeconomic theory, especially in sections 5.7–5.9, chapter 7 and sections 8.2–8.5, where microeconomics at the intermediate level is needed. Within macroeconomics the book is reasonably self-contained. A basic course in macroeconomics should suffice if the reader has sufficient training in mathematics and microeconomics. Each chapter is also reasonably self-contained. However, section 3.1 is a prerequisite for later sections on imperfect capital mobility (sections 5.4–5.5 and 6.2–6.4). An overview of the notation that is used is given on p. xii.

Part 1

Financial markets

1   The foreign exchange market

This chapter gives a first description of how the exchange rate and the foreign exchange reserves of a country are determined. We assume that the country is 'small', which in this context means just that foreign interest rates are given exogenously. The country may still be able to influence the interest rate on assets denominated in its own currency. A central topic is how far this influence goes, and what the consequences are of setting interest rates which deviate from those abroad. More details of the plan for the chapter are given towards the end of section 1.1, after we have introduced some basic concepts.

1.1 Some basic concepts

An exchange rate is the price of one currency in terms of another. In most of the chapters of this book we focus on a single country, and abstract from the fact that the rest of the world consists of many countries with different currencies. When we speak of the 'exchange rate', it is then the price of the single foreign currency in terms of the currency of the country in focus. As a shorthand we shall often refer to the foreign currency as dollars, and the domestic currency as kroner. The exchange rate is then the price of dollars in kroner.

As other prices, the price of foreign exchange is determined in a market. We can divide the participants in the foreign exchange market in two groups: the central authorities (central bank and central government) in our country on the one hand, and the general public at home and abroad on the other. (We come to the foreign central authorities later.) Normally we assume that the general public are price takers in the foreign exchange market. The trade of each is too small to have a significant influence on the price. It is different with the central authorities. Their actions in the foreign exchange market are coordinated through the central bank, and they may be large enough to influence the price of foreign exchange.

In figure 1.1 the curve depicted as S shows how the public's net supply of foreign currency depends on the exchange rate. Among the public there are some who want to sell foreign currency and some who want to buy. The net supply is the difference between the amounts that the public wants to sell and to buy. As is usual in economics, net supply is drawn as an increasing function of the price. We return to this assumption shortly.

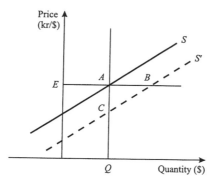

Figure 1.1 Equilibrium in the foreign exchange market.

The price that will prevail in the market depends on how much foreign currency the central bank decides to buy. If the central bank buys the quantity Q, the usual market forces produce an equilibrium at the intersection between supply and demand, A, where the price is E.

The units of measurement on the quantity axis need a comment. Until some years ago most theories of the foreign exchange market looked upon the supply of foreign currency as a *flow* that was to be measured in units of foreign currency per unit of time – e.g. in dollars per year. These theories tended to assume that a major part of the supply and demand for foreign currency arose from the needs of importers and exporters. The former needed foreign currency to pay for their imports, and the latter needed to convert foreign currency earnings into domestic currency which could be used to pay the domestic factors of production. Exports and imports are measured per unit of time – i.e. they are flows.

Today, however, most trade in foreign currency is *capital movements*. Foreign currency is bought and sold in order to change the composition of asset portfolios. Large stocks of wealth can be shifted from one currency to another literally in seconds. In accord with this most modern theories of the foreign exchange market look upon the supply of foreign currency as a *stock* supply. The unit of measurement for quantity is then simply units of foreign currency – e.g. dollars (not dollars per unit of time). This is the modern approach that we shall pursue. In the stock approach the supply of foreign currency at a moment in time is determined by how the public decides to invest its wealth at this moment. Thus, the supply curve in figure 1.1 is a result of decisions by (domestic and foreign) private investors on how much of their wealth they want to keep in foreign currency at this moment. When the supply curve is increasing, it means that if the price of foreign currency is higher, the investors want to have smaller net holdings of assets denominated in foreign currency, and, thus, immediately offer more foreign currency to the central bank.

The quantity Q is the net amount of foreign currency held by the central authorities. It consists of the official *foreign exchange reserve* minus the debt that the central authorities have incurred in foreign currency. For simplicity, we sometimes speak of the net amount of foreign currency assets held by the central authorities as the 'foreign exchange reserve'. When the authorities buy or sell foreign exchange, this is called *intervention.*

The central bank can pursue different strategies in the foreign exchange market. One important alternative is *fixed exchange rates.* Then the central bank sets a target exchange rate, which may be equal to E in figure 1.1. The central bank buys or sells as much foreign currency as is necessary to keep the exchange rate at E. In figure 1.1 this turns out to be the quantity Q. With fixed exchange rates, price is the exogenous policy variable, and quantity follows endogenously, determined by the supply in the market.

The opposite is *floating exchange rates*, when the quantity purchased is the exogenous policy variable, and the price follows from the market. The central bank sets Q, and E follows. The distinction between fixed and floating rates that we make here is thus a distinction according to which variable – price or quantity – the central bank uses as its decision variable.

The distinction between fixed and floating rates is sometimes described as a distinction between 'administratively determined' and 'market determined' exchange rates. This is somewhat misleading; a better analogy is a monopolistic supplier of a commodity who can use either price or quantity as her decision variable.

The difference between fixed and floating rates is not as fundamental as it may first seem. In both cases the central bank has to choose among points that are on the supply curve for foreign currency. All points on the supply curve can be reached by using either price or quantity as the decision variable. Irrespective of which variable is the decision variable, the central bank can be more or less active in the foreign exchange market. When the exchange rate is fixed, we distinguish between a *permanently fixed* rate and an *adjustable* rate. When the exchange rate is floating, we distinguish between a *clean* and a *managed* float. In the former case the central bank is supposed to be completely passive and never buy or sell foreign exchange. The quantity Q that it possesses is kept constant 'forever'. In a managed float Q is adjusted now and then. An adjustable fixed rate and a managed float may be used in such a way as to yield the same combination of Q and E. There is a greater difference between a permanent fix and a clean float.

The difference between fixed and floating rates is brought out more clearly when we look at a shift in the supply curve, as from S to S' in figure 1.1. If the exchange rate is fixed, the new equilibrium is at point B, where the price is unchanged and the foreign exchange reserves have increased. If the exchange rate is floating, the new equilibrium is at C, where reserves are unchanged and the price of foreign currency has fallen. These are the immediate consequences. If the central bank wishes, it can then adjust its policy and reach any point it wants to on the new supply curve.

When the price of foreign currency goes down, as in the example just discussed, we say that the domestic currency *appreciates*. It has increased in value relative to the foreign currency. If the price of foreign currency goes up, we say that the domestic currency *depreciates*. When the authorities change a fixed exchange rate, the corresponding terms are *revalue* and *devalue*.

Figure 1.1 gives the first example of a convention that is used throughout the book:

> *Curves that apply before a shift are drawn smooth. Curves that apply only after the shift are broken. When there is no risk of ambiguity, the curves after the shift are not labelled.*

In general, the shape and position of the supply curve depends on the public's expectations about government policy. Different exchange rate systems may entail different supply curves. The common supply curve drawn in figure 1.1 serves only to make clear the principal distinction between fixed and floating rates.

Figure 1.1 may be illustrative, but by itself it does not say much. We have to ask what is behind the supply curve: What kind of behaviour? Why does the curve slope upwards? What can cause it to shift? Section 1.2 describes an accounting framework which can be used as a basis for discussing the demand and supply of foreign currencies. Section 1.3 describes the motives behind the public's demand for different currencies. In section 1.4 we put the pieces together in a model of the equilibrium in the foreign exchange market at a moment of time. This gives us opportunity to discuss the important concept of *capital mobility* and the relationship between interest rates and exchange rates in section 1.5. There we examine to what extent it is possible for a small open economy to keep interest rates different from those abroad. Section 1.6 brings in the current account of the balance of payments. Finally, in section 1.7, we discuss the forward market for foreign exchange.

1.2 The balance sheet

For our purpose it is convenient to divide the economy into three sectors:

- Domestic government (subscript g)
- Domestic private (subscript p)
- Foreign (subscript $*$).

The domestic government sector includes the central government and the central bank. The domestic private sector comprises all other domestic sectors. For convenience, we refer to the central authorities interchangeably as the government and as the central bank, depending on which branch of policy we are discussing.

In order to keep the discussion down to the essentials, we distinguish between just two types of assets:

- Kroner assets – i.e. assets denominated in the domestic currency

Table 1.1 *Net financial assets, by sector*

| | Sector | | | |
Assets	Government	Private	Foreign	Sum
Kroner assets	B_g	B_p	B_*	0
Dollar assets	F_g	F_p	F_*	0
Sum in kr	$B_g + EF_g$	$B_p + EF_p$	$B_* + EF_*$	0

- Dollar assets – i.e. assets denominated in foreign currency.

In table 1.1 we have written down the financial balance sheet of this economy at a point in time. The new symbols are:

B_i = Net kroner assets of sector i ($i = g, p, *$)
F_i = Net dollar assets of sector i ($i = g, p, *$)

'Net assets' means assets minus liabilities. Kroner assets are measured in kroner and dollar assets in dollars.

Since we are looking at financial assets only, one agent's asset is the liability of another. If, for example, the government has borrowed 1 billion kroner from the private sector, it appears as +1 billion kroner in B_p and −1 billion kroner in B_g. The value of each financial asset appears with a plus sign in the accounts of one agent and a minus sign in the account of another. Thus, when we add together the net assets of all sectors in each currency, the sums must be zero:

$$B_g + B_p + B_* = 0 \tag{1.1}$$

and

$$F_g + F_p + F_* = 0 \tag{1.2}$$

Each sector's financial wealth is the sum of the net assets the sector has in different currencies. Measured in kroner the financial wealth of the different sectors is thus

$$B_i + EF_i \quad i = g, p, *$$

We shall be more interested in its real value: nominal wealth deflated by the appropriate price level. Let

P = domestic price level measured in kroner
P_* = foreign price level measured in dollars

Then the real financial wealth of the two domestic sectors is

$$W_i = \frac{B_i + EF_i}{P} \quad i = g, p \tag{1.3}$$

and that of the foreign sector is:

$$W_* = \frac{(B_*/E) + F_*}{P_*} \tag{1.4}$$

In (1.4) the numerator is foreign financial wealth measured in dollars. W_* is the same as our *foreign debt*. Note that foreign debt and debt denominated in foreign currencies are two entirely different concepts.

When measured in the same units, the net financial wealth of all sectors must of course add up to zero, as indicated in the last line of table 1.1. This means that

$$W_g + W_p + \frac{EP_*}{P} W_* = 0$$

From (1.2), it follows that the net foreign exchange holdings of the domestic government is

$$F_g = -F_* - F_p$$

or the negative of the net holdings of the two other sectors. Thus the supply of foreign currency towards the domestic central bank is the negative of the net demand for foreign currency from the other sectors. Clearly, the supply of foreign currency to the central bank will be determined by how much wealth the other sectors own, and by how they decide to distribute this between currencies.

The net financial wealth of a sector can change in two ways:

- through net investment in financial assets; if a sector's savings exceeds its investments in real capital, it has to invest the remainder in financial assets
- through revaluations – i.e. through changes in the prices of assets already held.

Saving and investment in real capital are flows with dimensions per unit of time. Only with the passage of time will the discrepancy between savings and real investment add up to sums which are significant compared to the total existing stock of assets. Thus, when we look at short time periods, as one day, or – in the extreme – one moment, we can regard the stock of financial wealth as predetermined except for the changes that occur because of revaluations.

For any period we can write down financial balance sheets at both the beginning and at the end of the period. Think of a period which is short enough for the discrepancies between saving and real investment over the period to be insignificant, and assume that all trades during the period takes place at a single price. Then the net financial wealth of each sector is the same both at the beginning and the end of the period. If we distinguish beginning-of-period stocks by an extra subscript 0, we can write

$$B_i + EF_i = B_{i0} + EF_{i0} \quad i = g, p, * \tag{1.5}$$

or

$$B_i - B_{i0} + E(F_i - F_{i0}) = 0 \quad i = g, p, *$$

Purchases of one currency have to be paid for by sales of another. Within a short period investors can redistribute their financial wealth between currencies; the total, however, is given. Its nominal value can change only with the exchange rate, its real value only with the exchange rate and the price level.

Later we use continuous time – i.e. the limiting case where the length of the market period is just one moment. Still we can think of the initial stocks as given as the moment is entered. Then the agents can redistribute their stocks momentarily.

1.3 The demand for currencies

How do private investors decide how much to invest in each currency? Obviously they will be interested in the rate of return that they achieve on their investments. Let

i = the kroner rate of interest

i_* = the dollar rate of interest

e = the rate of depreciation ($e = \dot{E}/E$, where, as usual, a dot over a variable means its derivative with respect to time)

Then the rate of return on investing in kroner is i. The kroner rate of return on investing in dollars is $i_* + e$, since in addition to the dollar interest rate the investor gets an extra return if the dollar increases in value relative to the krone. Obviously the highest return is obtained by investing in kroner if $i > i_* + e$, in dollars if $i < i_* + e$. It is easily seen that the same condition applies for someone who is interested in the dollar return. When $i < i_* + e$, it even pays to borrow kroner and invest in dollars.

However, investors cannot know what the rate of depreciation will be. Instead they have to form an opinion of how likely different rates of depreciation are.

If investors base their decisions on expected returns only, and if all investors have the same expectations, we have *perfect capital mobility* between currencies. If we denote expectations with a subscript e, the expected return from investing in kroner is i, and the expected return from investing in dollars is $i_* + e_e$. With perfect capital mobility, if $i > i_* + e_e$, everybody wants to invest all their wealth in kroner, and borrow dollars to invest even more in kroner. If $i < i_* + e_e$, they do the opposite: borrow kroner and invest in dollars. As long as $i \neq i_* + e_e$, there will be only lenders in the market for one currency, and only borrowers in the market for the other. Equilibrium in the asset markets can be achieved only if

$$i = i_* + e_e \tag{1.6}$$

When this condition holds, we have *uncovered interest rate parity*. This must always be the case when capital mobility is perfect.

Capital mobility between currencies can also be *imperfect*. This means that desired portfolios may contain both currencies in finite amounts even if uncovered interest rate parity does not hold. We can list four main reasons for this:

Exchange rate risk and risk aversion

Investors cannot know what the rate of depreciation will be. Risk averse investors are willing to forgo some expected return in order to reduce uncertainty. The way to reduce uncertainty is to divide the portfolio between the different currencies. Suppose the highest expected return is in dollars. If an investor puts all his money in dollars, he may suffer a heavy loss if the dollar depreciates more than expected. If instead he leaves some of his money in kroner, he will get a smaller expected return, but he will also suffer a smaller loss if the dollar depreciates more than expected. These arguments about risk and return are developed at length in chapter 2.

Differing expectations

As long as there is uncertainty about the future of the exchange rate, there is also room for different opinions. Some investors may expect the highest return on dollars, others on kroner. If they do not care about risk, the former group invests its wealth in dollars, the latter in kroner. The aggregate portfolio then contains both currencies. If we allow the investors to borrow, those in the first group want to borrow kroner to invest more than their total wealth in dollars. Those in the second group do the opposite. However, such borrowing will be limited because of the possibility of bankruptcy. The investors will have to borrow from people with expectations that differ from their own. If you believe for sure that kroner gives the highest return, you limit your lending to someone who bets on dollars giving the highest return. According to your belief, if the borrower has borrowed too many kroner, he is certain to go bankrupt. Endogenous credit rationing thus ensures that the net private demand for each currency is finite (positive or negative) as long as some investors believe that the highest return is in kroner and some that the highest return is in dollars.

Transaction costs and liquidity

It is costly to change money between currencies. Depending on where they trade and pay taxes, people need one or the other currency for transaction purposes. As is well known from standard discussions of the demand for money, they may then forgo some interest in order to economize on transaction costs. Even if expected returns in dollars are higher, a risk neutral investor may keep some balances in kroner in order to settle transactions that have to be made in kroner. Participating in the foreign exchange market may entail some fixed costs (e.g. costs of collecting information). These costs may keep small investors out of the market altogether.

Exchange controls

These are government regulations intended to have a direct impact on the supply of foreign currency. They may prohibit certain groups of investors from lending or borrowing foreign currency, set quantitative limits on the investments or take more subtle forms.

In this book the standard assumption is that expected return and risk are the only concerns of the investors. There are goods reasons for this focus. A large number of countries have abolished all or nearly all exchange controls. This includes all the industrialized and a large number of developing countries. As argued in chapter 2, the analysis can easily be adapted to cases where exchange controls exclude some groups from the foreign exchange market. In countries with well developed credit markets liquidity can be obtained by borrowing money. What is important in the foreign exchange market is the *net* demand for each currency. In chapter 3 we argue that this is not much affected by transaction needs when credit markets are well developed and not heavily regulated.

In the present chapter we assume more specifically that the domestic public's real demand for foreign currency is a function of its financial wealth, W_p, and the expected rate of return differential, $r = i - i_* - e_e$:

$$\frac{EF_p}{P} = f(r, W_p) \quad \text{where} \quad 0 < f_W < 1 \quad \text{and} \quad f_r < 0 \tag{1.7}$$

r is called the *risk premium* on kroner. It tells how much extra the investors get paid over the expected return on dollars to take the risk of investing in kroner. The risk premium may of course be negative.

The remainder of the public's financial wealth must be invested in kroner. Thus the demand for kroner is

$$\frac{B_p}{P} = W_p - f(r, W_p) \tag{1.8}$$

A higher risk premium in favour of kroner means that the expected return on kroner has increased relative to the expected return on dollars. Investors will then find it worthwhile to move more of their portfolios from dollars to kroner, even if this increases risk. Thus the demand for dollars depends negatively on the risk premium on kroner ($f_r < 0$), while the demand for kroner depends positively on the risk premium.

The assumption that $0 < f_W < 1$ means that if wealth increases by, say, 1 billion kroner, the public invests some of its extra wealth in kroner and some in dollars. It is not obvious that these shares should always be between zero and one. If the expected return on dollars is sufficiently higher than on kroner, investors may want to borrow kroner in order to invest more than their total financial wealth in dollars. When they get richer, they may want to borrow even more kroner in order to increase their dollar investments more than their financial wealth. The assumption that $0 < f_W < 1$ precludes this. The assumption thus limits speculative investments.

The functional form, f, must depend on the amount of uncertainty that the investors perceive, and their attitudes towards risk. We return to this subject in chapter 2.

For the foreign sector we assume similar demand functions. From their point of view kroner is the foreign currency, and their demand for kroner is in real terms

$$\frac{B_*}{EP_*} = b(r, W_*) \quad \text{where} \quad 0 < b_W < 1 \quad \text{and} \quad b_r > 0 \tag{1.9}$$

The corresponding demand function for dollar assets is

$$\frac{F_*}{P_*} = W_* - b(r, W_*) \tag{1.10}$$

Formally our demand functions are based on the assumption that all agents have the same expectations e_e. However, the demand functions may be reinterpreted in such a way that they also cover the case of differing expectations. Then we must think of e_e as the average over all investors of the expected rate of depreciation. Behind the functional form f must be the distribution of expectations around e_e among the investors. When r increases, it means that some investors tip from seeing dollars to seeing kroner as the most profitable investment – and, hence, the demand for dollars declines. However, with differing expectations we have a serious aggregation problem when there is an increase in wealth. The effect on asset demands clearly depends on whose wealth is increased: those who believe in the dollar, or those who do not. This would complicate the formal analysis, but qualitatively most of our conclusions would probably be the same.

1.4 A simple portfolio model

We now have the main elements ready to set up a simple portfolio model for the determination of the exchange rate and the foreign exchange reserves.[5] Even if this means some repetition, we rewrite all the necessary equations here. They are

$$W_p = \frac{B_{p0} + EF_{p0}}{P} \tag{1.11}$$

$$W_* = \frac{B_{*0}/E + F_{*0}}{P_*} \tag{1.12}$$

$$r = i - i_* - e_e \tag{1.13}$$

$$e_e = e_e(E) \tag{1.14}$$

$$\frac{EF_p}{P} = f(r, W_p) \tag{1.15}$$

$$\frac{F_*}{P_*} = W_* - b(r, W_*) \tag{1.16}$$

$$F_g + F_p + F_* = 0 \tag{1.17}$$

Equations (1.11) and (1.12) define financial wealth as the value of the initial stocks. Equation (1.13) defines the risk premium. Equation (1.14) just says that expected depreciation depends on today's exchange rate. We return to this shortly. Equations (1.15) and (1.16) are the two demand functions for foreign currency. Equation (1.17) is the equilibrium condition for the foreign exchange market. The net demands of all sectors added together must sum to zero.

The seven equations determine seven variables. They are W_p, W_*, F_p, F_*, r, e_e and, in the case of floating exchange rates E – or, in the case of fixed exchange rates F_g. When the exchange rate is floating, F_g is exogenous; when the exchange rate is fixed, E is exogenous. The remaining exogenous variables are P, P_*, i and i_*. In addition B_{p0}, F_{p0}, B_{*0} and F_{*0} are predetermined.

The list of exogenous variables needs some explanation. The small country assumption makes P_* and i_* exogenous. P will be endogenized in later chapters, but for the moment we look upon it as predetermined. We assume that the domestic interest rate i is set exogenously by the central bank. The central bank stands ready to lend or borrow money at this interest rate as the public demands.

We are now ready to continue the discussion of exchange rate determination from section 1.1. There we drew an upward-sloping supply curve for foreign currency. We can now examine the slope of the supply curve as it appears in the simple portfolio model. As already explained in section 1.2, the supply of foreign currency to the domestic central bank is the negative of the net demands for foreign currency by the other sectors, or

$$F_g = -F_p - F_*$$

If we insert in this first from (1.15) and (1.16), and then from (1.11)–(1.14), we get

$$\begin{aligned}
F_g &= -\frac{P}{E}f(r, W_p) - P_*[W_* - b(r, W_*)] \\
&= -\frac{P}{E}f\left(i - i_* - e_e(E), \frac{B_{p0} + EF_{p0}}{P}\right) \\
&\quad - P_*\left[\frac{B_{*0}/E + F_{*0}}{P_*} - b\left(i - i_* - e_e(E), \frac{B_{*0}/E + F_{*0}}{P_*}\right)\right]
\end{aligned} \tag{1.18}$$

We can see that E has two types of effects. It changes the real value of existing stocks of assets, and it changes expected depreciation. By differentiating we find that the slope of the supply curve is

$$\frac{\partial F_g}{\partial E} = \frac{1}{E}\left[F_p - f_W F_{p0} + (1 - b_W)(B_{*0}/E)\right] + \left[(P/E)f_r - P_* b_r\right]e_e'$$

As is standard practice in portfolio models, we compute the derivative at the initial equilibrium – i.e. where $F_p = F_{p0}$ and $B_* = B_{*0}$. The expression can then be simplified to

$$\frac{\partial F_g}{\partial E} = \frac{P}{E^2}\gamma - \frac{P}{E}\kappa e'_e \tag{1.19}$$

where

$$\gamma = (1 - f_W)\frac{EF_{p0}}{P} + (1 - b_W)\frac{B_{*0}}{P}, \quad \text{and} \quad \kappa = -f_r + \frac{EP_*}{P}b_r > 0$$

Thus the effect of the exchange rate on the supply of foreign currency can be split into two main components:

- *The portfolio composition effect* measured by γ. When the domestic currency is depreciated, all foreign currency assets increase in value relative to domestic currency assets. This changes both the wealth distribution between sectors and the value distribution of each sector's portfolio on the two currencies. As a result investors will rebalance their portfolios, and this is the portfolio composition effect.
- *The expectations effect*, measured by $-\kappa e'_e$. A depreciation may change expectations about future depreciation. This changes the risk premium, which again changes the demand for foreign currency. How strongly the real demand for foreign currency reacts to the risk premium is measured by κ.

It is not obvious that $\partial F_g / \partial E$ is positive. Consider first the portfolio composition effect. If the domestic public has positive net foreign currency assets ($F_{p0} > 0$), it is made richer by a depreciation. If $0 < f_W < 1$, it wants to invest some of its increased wealth in foreign currency, and some in kroner. However, the immediate effect of the depreciation is to increase the value of the foreign currency the private sector already possesses by the same amount as the increase in wealth. After the depreciation, the public then wants to reduce its holdings of foreign currency and buy kroner. Thus, if both $F_{p0} > 0$ and $f_W < 1$, the wealth effect means that a depreciation lowers the domestic public's demand for foreign currency. This contributes through the first term in (1.19) to a positive slope of the supply curve. It will contribute to a negative slope if either assumption is violated – i.e. if the public has foreign currency debts ($F_{p0} < 0$) or if there is excessive speculation ($f_W > 1$).

A symmetric statement can be made about the portfolio composition effect on foreigners. If foreigners have positive holdings of our currency ($B_{*0} > 0$), they *lose* from a depreciation. If $0 < b_W < 1$, they want to spread the reduction in wealth on kroner and dollar assets. However, the immediate effect of the depreciation is to reduce the value of the kroner assets they already possess by the same amount as the reduction in wealth. After the depreciation, the foreigners then want to reduce their holdings of foreign currency and buy kroner. Thus, if both $B_{*0} > 0$ and $b_W < 1$, the portfolio composition effect means that a depreciation lowers the foreign public's demand for foreign currency, and this contributes to a positive slope of the supply curve (cf. (1.19)).

Another way of looking at the portfolio composition effects is: suppose the public at home and abroad hold positive amounts of both currencies. A depreciation of the domestic currency means that the value share of domestic currency in all portfolios decreases. When $0 < f_W < 1$ and $0 < b_W < 1$, the public responds to this by selling some foreign currency to increase the share of kroner again. In this way, they keep the portfolio diversified and hedge against further changes in the exchange rate in one direction or the other.

Now to the expectations effect in (1.19). Its sign clearly depends on the sign of e_e'. We can define three cases:

- *Regressive expectations*, $e_e' < 0$. A depreciation now lowers the expected future depreciation.
- *Extrapolative expectations*, $e_e' > 0$. A depreciation now increases expected future depreciation.
- *Constant expectations*, $e_e' = 0$. A depreciation now has no effect on expected future depreciation.

Only in the case of regressive expectations is the expectations effect in (1.19) positive. If expectations are regressive, a depreciation of kroner now leads to a decrease in the expected future return on dollars. The private investors then move some of their portfolio from dollars to kroner, and thus offer more dollars to the central bank.

There is no general answer to whether expectations are regressive or extrapolative. An often used example of an e_e function is

$$e_e = \alpha \frac{E_e - E}{E} \tag{1.20}$$

where E_e is an expected future equilibrium exchange rate and the constant α is the expected speed of convergence towards the equilibrium. If E_e is independent of E, expectations in this example are regressive ($e_e' = -\alpha E_e / E^2 < 0$). More generally, if the expected future *level* of the exchange rate is independent of the present level, this tends to make expectations regressive. The reason is that the higher the present exchange rate, the more the exchange rate must fall from today's level in order to reach the expected future level. A depreciation beyond the expected future level now, implies an expected future appreciation. As (1.20) reveals, it is sufficient for this argument that E_e depends less than proportionally on E. For the period of floating surveys of exchange rate expectations have produced some evidence that they tend to be regressive when the horizon is not too short (see Takagi, 1991).

In a fixed rate system a devaluation usually changes the expected future exchange rate. Suppose, however, that e_e were positive before the devaluation. Immediately after the devaluation there is often little reason to expect another. Thus, e_e may become equal to zero after the devaluation. An increase in E has then led to a fall in e_e, as with regressive expectations. However, the devaluation may make people think that the government has become more prone to devalue. If that is the case, expected depreciation may soon rise again.

Expectations are a subjective entity, but they should depend on the factors which determine the future exchange rate. The slope of the supply curve may depend on government policy giving people reason to have regressive expectations. In chapter 4, we present more sophisticated models of expected depreciation where the e_e function is derived, not postulated.

Our discussion of the slope of the supply curve can be summarized like this: a set of sufficient conditions for the supply curve to be increasing is

$$F_{p0} > 0, \quad B_{*0} > 0, \quad f_W < 1, \quad b_W < 1, \quad e'_e < 0 \tag{1.21}$$

These conditions can sometimes be violated. The public at home or abroad may have net debts in the other currency. There may be excessive speculation. Expectations may be extrapolative. Even if one condition is violated, the total effect of a depreciation may still be positive. However, we cannot exclude *a priori* that the supply curve slopes downwards. In some countries the private sector has borrowed heavily in foreign currencies, and large deviations from interest rate parity may lead to excessive speculation.

If the supply curve is falling, the foreign exchange market is unstable. Fixed exchange rates, or some degree of exchange rate management, must then be preferred in order to avoid chaos in the market.

Since the slope of the supply curve is in general not decided, it is also possible that the supply curve is bending several times, as in figure 1.2. Then we have multiple equilibria with floating rates. In figure 1.2 there are three of them, two stable (A and C) and one unstable (B).

In the sequel we assume that the supply curve slopes upwards everywhere, and that there is thus just one equilibrium. This case completely dominates the literature. Then exchange rates and reserves are determined as described in section 1.1. We have just given a somewhat deeper explanation for the supply curve, and learned more about

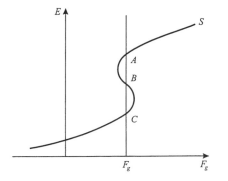

Figure 1.2 Multiple equilibria.

variables which can shift it. In section 1.5 we take a closer look at the effects of interest rates and of exchange rate expectations, and discuss the consequences of deviating from uncovered interest rate parity. Before that, however, there are two matters which deserve comment: the kroner market and the foreign central bank.

The market for kroner is a mirror image of the market for foreign currency. When one is in equilibrium, the other must also be in equilibrium. Corresponding to the supply of foreign currency there is a demand for kroner from the domestic central bank, which is given by

$$-B_g = B_p + B_*$$
$$= P[W_p - f(r, W_p)] + EP_*b(r, W_*)$$

(1.18a)

If we differentiate this with respect to E, we find that when conditions (1.21) are satisfied, the demand curve slopes upwards, as in the right-hand panel of figure 1.3. When the exchange rate is depreciated, the public supply more dollars to the central bank. As a mirror image of that, they demand more kroner from the central bank. The fact that the demand curve for kroner slopes upwards is not so surprising when we remember that E is the inverse of the price of kroner. The central bank's net supply of kroner is $-B_g$, the net amount of kroner that it borrows from the public (or, if you prefer, the net kroner claims that the public has on the central bank).

Equation (1.18a) can also be interpreted as the equilibrium condition for the kroner market. It is equivalent to the equilibrium condition for the foreign exchange market (1.18). Just insert in (1.18a) for B_g and B_* from the balance equations (1.4), and use the definitional equations from section 1.2 a couple of times, and you have (1.18). This shows that when the foreign exchange market is in equilibrium, the kroner market is also in equilibrium. We here see an example of Walras' law: when there are n markets and $n - 1$ of them are in equilibrium, the nth market must also be in equilibrium.

In figure 1.3 we have illustrated how a positive shift in the supply of foreign currency affects the two markets. We may think of the shift as caused by a rise in the kroner interest rate. The public moves some of its portfolio from dollars to kroner. This means that they demand more kroner from the central bank – i.e. they increase their kroner deposits or reduce their borrowing of kroner from the central bank. Corresponding to

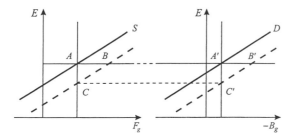

Figure 1.3 The relationship between the markets for foreign currency and for kroner.

the increased supply of foreign currency there is an increased demand for kroner of the same amount. If the exchange rate is fixed, the central bank's net kroner debt increases by the same amount as the foreign exchange reserves increases – i.e. the equilibrium moves from A and A' to B and B'. If the exchange rate is floating and the central bank does not intervene in the foreign exchange market, both its net kroner and its net dollar assets are constant. The new equilibrium is where the new supply and demand curves intersect with the vertical lines marking the given quantities (points C and C'). Whether we look at the kroner market or the foreign exchange market, the new equilibrium exchange rate is the same, since the equilibrium conditions are equivalent.

Now to the foreign central bank. An exchange rate is a relative price between two currencies (or between one currency and a basket of other currencies). In a world with two currencies there must be two central banks, but there can be only one exchange rate. Clearly, both countries cannot fix the exchange rate independently. When we have discussed fixed exchange rates, we have so far assumed that the exchange rate is set unilaterally by the domestic central bank, and that the domestic central bank alone undertakes to intervene in the foreign exchange market. This assumption is retained until chapter 9, where we discuss different ways of organizing the international monetary system and of dividing responsibilities between countries.

1.5 Capital mobility, interest rates and expectations

Suppose there is an increase in the domestic interest rate. This will lead investors to sell some dollars and invest more of their wealth in kroner. Thus, the supply curve for dollars shifts to the right. As we saw in figure 1.1, this leads to an increase in the foreign exchange reserves if the exchange rate is fixed, and to an appreciation if it is floating. The same obviously happens if there is a fall in the foreign interest rate, or if there is an exogenous reduction in the expected rate of depreciation.

From (1.18), the effect of the interest rate on the supply of foreign currency is

$$\frac{\partial F_g}{\partial i} = -\frac{P}{E}f_r + P_*b_r = \frac{P}{E}\left[-f_r + \frac{EP_*}{P}b_r\right] = \frac{P}{E}\kappa > 0 \tag{1.22}$$

$\kappa = -f_r + (EP_*/P)b_r$, which we already encountered in section 1.4, is a measure of the *degree of capital mobility* between the two currencies. A high degree of capital mobility means that differences in expected return have a strong effect on the supply of foreign currency. Generally we expect the degree of capital mobility to be high if investors have little risk aversion, or if there is not much exchange rate risk; this is explained in chapter 2.

In the present section we look at the consequences for the foreign exchange market and for interest rate policy of different degrees of capital mobility. What does the degree of capital mobility mean for the effects of interest rates, expectations and central bank interventions? To what extent does high capital mobility restrict the options the central bank has when setting interest rates? Throughout we assume that expectations are regressive ($e'_e < 0$) and that the portfolio composition effect has the usual sign ($\gamma > 0$).

Floating exchange rates

We have already seen that the slope of the supply curve for foreign currency, (1.19), depends on κ. A high degree of capital mobility means a flat supply curve (high $\partial F_g / \partial E$). An immediate effect of this is that a purchase of a given amount of foreign currency by the central bank has a small effect on the exchange rate. Thus, interventions lose some of their effect when capital mobility is high. Algebraically we find the effect of F_g on E by differentiating the equilibrium condition (1.18) with respect to these two variables. This yields

$$dF_g = \frac{\partial F_g}{\partial E} dE$$

or

$$\frac{dE}{dF_g} = \frac{1}{\frac{\partial F_g}{\partial E}} = \frac{1}{(P/E^2)\gamma - (P/E)\kappa e'_e} > 0 \tag{1.23}$$

(cf. (1.19)). We recognize the portfolio composition effect and the expectations effect in the denominator. When the central bank buys foreign currency, it drives up the price. As the price increases, investors sell foreign currency, partly because they rebalance their portfolios and partly because they expect the price of foreign currency to increase less in the future. In this way, equilibrium is restored at a higher E. The more investors are willing to sell when the price goes up, the smaller the price increase. From (1.23) we can see that dE/dF_g declines with an increase in κ. The reason is that when expectations are regressive, high capital mobility means that investors react to a small price increase by selling large amounts of foreign currency. Obviously, strongly regressive expectations (a high $|e'_e|$) reduce the effect of an intervention on today's exchange rate in the same way as high capital mobility does.

With perfect capital mobility the simple portfolio model of section 1.4 collapses, because we do not have separate demand functions for each currency. Instead, the exchange rate is determined by the interest parity condition $i = i_* + e_e(E)$, which in this case becomes the equilibrium condition for the foreign exchange market. This means that the supply curve for foreign currency in figure 1.1 is horizontal at the exchange rate determined by the interest parity condition: F_g has no effect on E. The same happens, of course, when κ goes to infinity. The supply curve defined by (1.18) becomes horizontal, and interventions cease to have an effect on E. In (1.23) dE/dF_g approaches zero.

The effect on E of an increase in i depends on κ for two reasons. First, the direct impact of an increase in i on the supply of foreign currency is by definition greater when capital mobility is high. Second, the supply curve is flatter when capital mobility

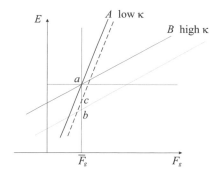

Figure 1.4 The effect on E of an increase in i for different degrees of capital mobility.

is high. This is illustrated in figure 1.4 where the curve marked B represents higher capital mobility than A. The initial equilibrium is at a. With high capital mobility an increase in i results in a large rightward shift of the supply curve. However, because of the different slopes of the curves, it is not immediately obvious in which case the effect on E is strongest. It is thus not obvious whether the new equilibrium with high capital mobility b, is above or below the new equilibrium with low capital mobility, c. Here it is helpful to differentiate the equilibrium condition (1.18) in order to find the derivative of E with respect to i. This yields

$$dF_g = \frac{\partial F_g}{\partial E}\, dE + \frac{\partial F_g}{\partial i}\, di = 0$$

or (cf. (1.19) and (1.22)):

$$\frac{dE}{di} = -\frac{\dfrac{\partial F_g}{\partial i}}{\dfrac{\partial F_g}{\partial E}} = -\frac{\kappa}{\gamma/E - \kappa e_e'} = -\frac{1}{\gamma/(\kappa E) - e_e'} < 0 \tag{1.24}$$

The denominator is positive whenever the supply curve slopes upward.

The absolute value of dE/di is increasing in the degree of capital mobility. Thus, the interest rate has a stronger effect on the exchange rate when capital mobility is high, as figure 1.4 also illustrates. When κ goes to infinity, the effect of the interest rate on the exchange rate goes to $1/e_e'$. This is, of course, the same effect as we get by differentiating the equilibrium condition under perfect capital mobility, $i = i_* + e_e(E)$. Thus, when expectations are regressive, there is an upper limit to the effect of the interest rate on the exchange rate.

The higher the level of $|e_e'|$, the smaller the effect of the interest rate on the exchange rate according to (1.24). If, on the contrary, $|e_e'|$ is close to zero while capital mobility is high, the exchange rate becomes very sensitive to interest rates. The market is then close to being unstable in the sense discussed in section 1.4. Shifts in the expected rate of depreciation work in the same way as changes in interest rates. Thus, they too have greater effect on E when capital mobility is high.

The importance of exchange rate expectations can be illustrated with an example. Interpret the model as a period model. Let E_e be the exchange rate expected to prevail next period. Then the expected rate of depreciation from this period to the next is

$$e_e = \frac{E_e - E}{E} \qquad\qquad (1.25)$$

Obviously, these expectations are regressive when E_e is constant. Assume first perfect capital mobility. Insert (1.25) in the interest rate parity condition and solve for the equilibrium exchange rate. You then get

$$E = \frac{E_e}{1 + i - i_*}$$

Thus, this period's exchange rate is proportional to the exchange rate expected for next period. The factor of proportionality depends on the interest rate differential $i - i_*$. If interest rates are close to each other, the deviation from the expected exchange rate for next period will be small. If the domestic interest rate is above the foreign interest rate, we must have an expected depreciation, and this requires that E is lower than E_e.

Suppose the exchange rate one year from now is expected to be 100, and this is not affected by today's interest rates. Then if $i = i_*$ and capital mobility is perfect, the formula above tells us that the exchange rate today will also be 100. If we raise the domestic one-year interest rate 1 per cent above the foreign rate, today's exchange rate will be 99. If we make the differential 10 per cent, today's exchange rate will be 91. It is not uncommon that a floating exchange rate moves by more than 10 per cent in a few weeks. Small changes in interest rates will not stop such movements unless investors revise their expectations of exchange rates one year ahead. Thus, compared to expectations interest rates may seem relatively unimportant.

If capital mobility is imperfect, the effects of interest rates are even smaller. However, the effect of E_e is also less than proportional.[6]

The above discussion assumes that the function $e_e(E)$ is independent of current policies as represented by F_g and i. However, if current policies give signals about future policies, they may affect expected future exchange rates directly and hence shift the e_e function. Such signalling effects come in addition to the more direct effects discussed above. Dominguez and Frankel (1993a) analyse a number of cases where interventions have been used in attempts to influence the exchange rates between the major currencies (yen, mark, dollars) after they became floating in the early 1970s. The evidence that they had much direct effect seems weak. This is consistent with the view that capital mobility was high. However, the authors claim that in some instances the interventions had important signalling effects. One explanation may be that they gave signals about future interest rates and, hence, affected expected future exchange rates that way. Be that as it may, it is obviously important to examine how investors can form rational expectations about future exchange rates. This topic is best treated after we have gained some understanding of the effects of exchange rates on the real economy and on inflation.

Fixed exchange rates

As we already know, the supply of foreign currency to the central bank is an increasing function of the risk premium, r. When the exchange rate is fixed, the foreign exchange reserve is then also an increasing function of the risk premium. Two examples are shown in figure 1.5, where the steeper curve corresponds to the lower degree of capital mobility. When κ goes to infinity, the 'supply curve' in figure 1.5 approaches a horizontal line. Presumably this is located at $r = 0$, which means that as κ goes to infinity, the economy approaches perfect capital mobility.

The central bank can choose the size of the risk premium by varying the interest rate. However, it has to accept the ensuing changes in the level of reserves. These can be large if capital mobility is high. If the central bank sets the interest rate too low, it risks running out of reserves. In principle it can then borrow foreign currency in order to satisfy the demands of the other sectors. However, there will be limits to how much the central bank (or its government) can borrow, especially in the very short run. Thus there may be a lower limit for the interest rate below which the central bank is unable to accommodate the ensuing demand for foreign currency.

Even if the central bank does not run out of reserves, it may be costly to set interest rates which deviate from interest rate parity. The reason is that if the interest rate differential is large, the central bank inevitably ends up as borrower in the market with high expected returns, and as lender in the market with low expected returns. Let p be the domestic rate of inflation ($p = \dot{P}/P$). Then, the real return on the central bank's portfolio is

$$(i - p)B_g + (i_* + e - p)EF_g$$

From (1.5) $EF_g = B_{g0} + EF_{g0} - B_g$. By inserting this we find that the real return is

$$(i_* + e - p)(B_{g0} + EF_{g0}) + (i - i_* - e)B_g$$

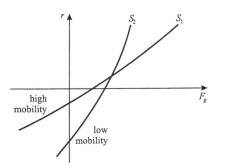

Figure 1.5 Risk premium and reserves.

The first term tells what the return on the central bank's portfolio is if there is *ex post* interest rate parity ($i = i_* + e$). Our interest is in the last term where i comes in. This term is the product of the *ex post* rate of return differential and the outstanding stock of domestic currency assets.

Suppose first that $e = e_e$. In this case *ex post* and *ex ante* rates of return are the same. If the central bank sets the domestic interest rate high, making the differential $i - i_* - e$ strongly positive, the public chooses to have large kroner assets. The central bank then has to accept large kroner deposits. It becomes a net debtor in kroner, which means that B_g is negative. The product $(i - i_* - e)B_g$ is negative, and contributes negatively to the overall return of the central bank. The reason for the loss is that the central bank has to reinvest the kroner, for which it pays a high interest rate, in the alternative asset, which is dollars with a low rate of return. If capital mobility is high, the loss can be substantial.

If, on the other hand, the central bank sets a low interest rate, making $i - i_* - e$ strongly negative, the public wants to borrow kroner. B_g becomes positive. Again the product $(i - i_* - e)B_g$ is negative. Whether the central bank makes interest rates deviate in one direction or the other, it ends up as the loser. The only way this can be avoided is through a surprise change in parity ($e \neq e_e$). If the central bank first induces an unsuspecting public to invest heavily in kroner, and then devalues, the central bank naturally gains.

Setting $i = i_* + e_e$ does not necessarily maximize the return of the central bank even when $e = e_e$. Nor should profit maximization be the bank's purpose. The desirability of deviating from interest rate parity must be judged on macroeconomic grounds. However, eventual revenue losses must be part of the consideration; if capital mobility is high, they constitute a powerful argument against large deviations.

We have little quantitative knowledge of the relationship between the risk premium and the foreign currency reserves. Probably the relationship depends on time and place, as the underlying circumstances determine the degree of capital mobility. The relationship could be as in figure 1.6. Close to interest rate parity there is an interval over which the central bank can vary the risk premium without causing too large

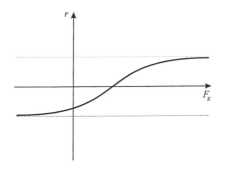

Figure 1.6 Risk premium and reserves: an example.

capital movements. However, when the premium becomes larger in absolute value, the degree of capital mobility also increases. If the central bank makes the premium too big, it leads to capital movements which are unmanageably large and prohibitively expensive to accommodate. Thus, the central bank has to keep the risk premium within a limited interval around zero if it wants to keep the exchange rate fixed.

One way of thinking about the limits in figure 1.6 is: there is some probability for a devaluation, but an upper limit on its eventual size. If the krone interest rate is high enough, one can be sure of making money by borrowing dollars and lending kroner. Then there is no limit to the supply of foreign currency to the central bank. There is also some probability that the krone will be revalued, but an upper limit to how much. Thus, when the krone interest rate is low enough, one can be sure of making a profit by borrowing kroner and lending dollars. The rate of return differential must not be so large that one or the other currency is a sure bet; this point is further elaborated in section 2.4.

The higher capital mobility is, the smaller the interval is within which the interest rate differential must be kept. In the extreme it collapses to a single line where $r = 0$. This is the case of perfect capital mobility, where interest rate parity must hold continuously.

In section 1.1 we defined a fixed exchange rate as a case where E is set by an exogenous policy decision and F_g is used to keep E at the targeted level. However, it follows from the equilibrium condition for the foreign exchange market (1.18) that E may be kept at a pre-assigned level by varying either F_g, i or both. We still speak of a fixed exchange rate. The upshot of the above discussion is that when capital mobility is high, the central bank in practice cannot rely on F_g alone, but has to use i. This is a consequence of what we saw with floating exchange rates – namely, that interventions lose some of their effect when capital mobility is high. When capital mobility is perfect, there is only one interest rate which is compatible with a fixed exchange rate – namely, $i = i_* + e_e(E)$. Interventions are of no use.

It is often necessary to defend a fixed exchange rate against expectations of devaluation or revaluation. The role interventions and interest rates can play in these two cases are somewhat different.

Suppose that initially $e_e = 0$ and $i = i_*$. Then e_e increases, which means there is a downward pressure on the domestic currency. The central bank can avoid losing reserves by raising i by the same amount as e_e. Then $r = i - i_* - e_e$ is kept constant, and the demand for foreign exchange is unaffected. A more common response has been to set the interest rate higher than abroad, but lower than the expected return on foreign currency $(i_* < i < i_* + e_e)$. Since this means that r goes down, the foreign exchange reserves decline. Whether the central bank loses or gains on this reshuffling of portfolios depends on whether it succeeds in defending the exchange rate. If $e = 0$, the central bank gains, since it bought kroner, which had the high interest rate, and sold dollars, which had the low interest rate. More generally, if $e < i - i_*$, the central bank gains. If $e > i - i_*$, the speculators, who sold kroner, gain.

When a revaluation is expected ($e_e < 0$), the central bank is not in danger of running out of reserves. It is free to supply as much of the domestic currency as the public wants. Defending the exchange rate may thus seem easier than when $e_e > 0$. However, a defence with the interest rate as the only weapon may be difficult. If $i_* + e_e < 0$, keeping $r = 0$ requires a negative i, which is impossible.

The interest rate differential that is required to compensate for an expected parity change can be quite large. Suppose there is a 10 per cent probability of a 10 per cent devaluation within one month. Then the expected devaluation over the month is 1 per cent, which corresponds to an interest rate differential of 12 per cent per annum. This means that the domestic one-month interest rate must exceed the foreign interest rate by 12 per cent in order to compensate for the expected depreciation. If the probability of the devaluation increases to 50 per cent, the expected rate of depreciation over the next month is 5 per cent corresponding to an interest differential of 60 per cent (or 79.6 per cent when compounded). If a 10 per cent devaluation is expected within the next few days, the required differential in overnight interest rates may be several hundred per cent. There are examples of countries which have used overnight interest rates of over 500 per cent in attempts to fend off devaluations.

The defensive actions of the central bank may themselves influence expectations. An increase in i may reduce aggregate demand and, hence, inflation. There may then be less reason to fear a devaluation and, thus, a downward shift in e_e may result. This effect, which is not included in our formal model, seems to make the interest rate a more effective tool for fixing the exchange rate. However, if interest rates are kept very high for some period of time, they will have a devastating effect on the economy, perhaps precipitating a financial crisis. Thus, while moderately high interest rates may act as a positive signal, very high interest rates may be taken as a sign that the central bank soon has to give in, and thus they may actually increase speculative pressures.[7] How soon high interest rates cause serious financial trouble may depend on to what extent the interest rates on existing loans are affected by the current market rates. Countries where most loans have interest rates that are fixed for relatively long periods may be in a better position to use high interest rates as a defence against speculative attacks.

If people learn that the central bank has used the bulk of its reserves, this may also reinforce devaluation expectations and lead to further reserve losses. When there are no exchange controls, it is hardly possible for a small country acting alone to keep the exchange rate fixed unless the public is fairly confident that the currency will not be devalued. Experience still shows that exchange rates can be kept fixed for considerable periods of time. Speculative pressures caused by increased fear of devaluation (or occasionally fear of revaluation) happen from time to time, but can often be handled by a combination of interventions and interest rate policy. However, at times the central bank loses control. We get a 'currency crisis' where the pressure on the central bank escalates as the public realizes that the bank's defence is not sustainable. In sections 5.6 and 10.2 we look at some important reasons why fixed exchange rates are exposed to speculative attacks.

One option for a country exposed to speculative pressure is to follow a *restoration rule*. This means that when pressures get too strong, it allows the exchange rate to float, but continues to use interest rates and interventions in order to gradually bring the exchange rate back to its old level. If practised repeatedly, a restoration rule may tie the expected long-run exchange rate to the official parity and reduce speculative pressures.

1.6 The current account and the government surplus

As mentioned in section 1.1, we use the stock approach to the foreign exchange market. This does not mean that the current account is unimportant. We shall now give a sketch of how it comes into the picture. The main channel is through changes over time in the distribution of financial wealth between foreign and domestic sectors. The government surplus changes the distribution of financial wealth between the government and the private sector in much the same way as the current account surplus changes the distribution between the foreign and the domestic sectors. Thus, it is natural to discuss the effects of these two surpluses together.

We use the symbols D and D_g for the volumes of, respectively, the current account surplus and the government surplus. We assume that the volumes are measured by deflating the nominal kroner values by the domestic price index P. It is useful to recall that the current account surplus, D, is defined as the sum of the trade surplus (or export surplus), net transfers and net property income from abroad The government surplus, D_g, is defined as net transfer payments to the government (taxes less transfers to the public) plus net property income and minus government purchases of goods and services. However, from elementary national accounting we also know that the current account surplus is equal to the difference between national savings and real investment, and that the government surplus is equal to the difference between government savings and government real investment.

In section 1.2 we defined the net financial wealth of the three sectors. Their time rates of change are related to the two surpluses by the definitional relations:

$$\dot{W}_p = D - D_g + e\frac{EF_p}{P} - pW_p$$

$$\dot{W}_g = D_g + e\frac{EF_g}{P} - pW_g \tag{1.26}$$

$$\dot{W}_* = -\frac{PD}{EP_*} - e\frac{B_*}{EP_*} - p_*W_*$$

p_* is the foreign rate of inflation – i.e. $p_* = \dot{P}/P$.[8] In section 1.2 we mentioned that the net financial wealth of each sector can change in two ways: through net financial investment (i.e. through savings in excess of real investment), and through revaluations of existing assets. This is brought out in (1.26), where the excess of savings over real investment for the three sectors is respectively $D - D_g$, D_g and $-D$. In addition to these terms comes the revaluation of the existing assets. What we should note is how the two surpluses contribute to the redistribution of financial wealth over time. We could have introduced the symbol $D_p = D - D_g$ for the 'private surplus' to make the equations more symmetric and make clear that $D = D_p + D_g$.

Equation (1.26) presumes that P and E are differentiable functions of time. At moments when these variables make discrete jumps, real financial wealth also jumps. At such moments the time rates of change are not defined.

From (1.18) the supply of foreign currency is

$$F_g = -\frac{P}{E}f(r, W_p) - P_*[W_* - b(r, W_*)] \tag{1.27}$$

Assume that P, E, P_* and r are constant. By differentiating (1.27) with respect to time, we find then that the time rate of change of the supply of foreign currency is

$$\dot{F}_g = -\frac{P}{E}f_W \dot{W}_p - P_*(1 - b_W)\dot{W}_*$$

If we insert in this from (1.26) with $e = p = p_* = 0$, we get

$$\dot{F}_g = \frac{P}{E}(1 - b_W - f_W)D + \frac{P}{E}f_W D_g \tag{1.28}$$

For a given level of the government surplus, a surplus on the current account increases the supply of foreign currency if $1 - f_W > b_W$ – i.e. if domestic investors invest more of a marginal increase in wealth in kroner assets than do foreign investors. This seems a reasonable assumption. When it is true, a country with a surplus will, everything else being constant, experience a gradual shift in the supply curve for foreign currency, as shown in figure 1.7. Under fixed exchange rates a surplus country will experience a gradual increase in its foreign currency reserves. Under floating rates it will experience a gradual appreciation. In both cases it takes time for the shift to become large enough

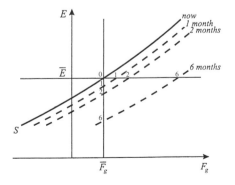

Figure 1.7 The effect over time of a current account surplus.

to have a significant effect. However, we should not take figure 1.7 as the final word on the effect of the current account on a floating exchange rate, since a gradual appreciation contradicts the assumption we made about all prices being constant.

For a given current account surplus, a surplus on the government budget leads in (1.28) to a gradual increase in the supply of foreign currency if $f_W > 0$. Suppose the current account is balanced. Then the counterpart to the government surplus is a gradual decline in private financial wealth, which makes private investors sell some of their foreign currency assets. Conversely, even if the current account is balanced, a government which runs a deficit will experience a gradual decline in its net foreign exchange reserves. The reason is that private financial wealth is growing, and when $f_W > 0$ the private investors want to invest some of that increased wealth in foreign currency. Even in a country which has a surplus on the current account, the central bank may observe a gradual decline in the net foreign exchange reserves if the government's budget deficit is large enough.

The above results should be compared to the traditional distinction between the current account and the capital account of the balance of payments. The overall balance of payments is usually defined as the change in official reserves – i.e. as $E\dot{F}_g$ when measured in domestic currency. Since $F_g = -F_p - F_*$,

$$E\dot{F}_g = -E\dot{F}_p - E\dot{F}_*$$

Since a current account surplus has to be invested somehow, $PD = -\dot{B}_* - E\dot{F}_*$. This yields $E\dot{F}_* = -PD - \dot{B}_*$, and after this has been inserted

$$E\dot{F}_g = PD + \dot{B}_* - E\dot{F}_p \tag{1.29}$$

The first term on the right-hand side is the current account surplus. The two other terms together form the private capital account surplus. It consists of the increase in the amount of kroner held by foreign residents minus the increase in the amount of foreign currency held by domestic residents. Thus, the traditional distinction between the current account and the capital account can be made within our framework of definitions.

We learned above that a current account surplus by itself normally leads to changes in the amount of foreign currency held by domestic residents, and in the amount of domestic currency held by foreign residents. As (1.28) showed, these may make the impact of a current account surplus on the overall balance of payments considerably smaller than it appears from (1.29). The current account has consequences for the capital account.

The discussion above suffices to give a first impression of how surpluses on the current account and on the government budget gradually change the equilibrium in the foreign exchange market. However, most of the discussion was carried out under the assumption that all prices were constant, and that the risk premium was constant. It was also partial in that we did not discuss how the current account and the government surplus are determined, and how they may be interconnected. In chapter 5 we return to the effect of the current account on the foreign exchange market in less restrictive settings.

1.7 The forward market and covered interest rate parity

The exchange rate we have discussed so far is the *spot* rate, the price of foreign currency delivered and paid for today. We can write the spot exchange rate on day t as E_t.

Most economies also have a forward market for foreign exchange. In the forward market agents agree today to exchange currencies at some future date at a price and in an amount agreed on today. The price of foreign exchange in this market needs to be dated both by time of contract and time of delivery. Thus, the *forward exchange rate* $\mathcal{F}_{t,\tau}$ is the price of foreign currency agreed on day t in contracts which are executed at day τ $(\tau > t)$.

Forward contracts can be used by agents who want to avoid exchange rate risk. An exporter who expects a payment in dollars three months from now can sell the dollars in the three-months-forward market. He then knows how many kroner he will receive in three months. Similarly, an importer who has to pay a given dollar amount three months from now can protect himself from exchange rate risk by buying the dollars in the forward market now.

Forward contracts are not the only way of protecting oneself against exchange rate risk. Another possibility is to use the spot market. The importer we just mentioned may buy the necessary amount of dollars in the spot market immediately and keep them in a bank account until he needs them. He must then ask himself where it is cheapest to buy protection against exchange rate risk: in the forward market or in the spot market. We shall look at this question in terms of the one-period-forward market where the exchange rate is $\mathcal{F}_{t,t+1}$. The period length is arbitrary; it may be interpreted as one month, three months or any other relevant interval.

Suppose I need one dollar next period. If I buy it on the forward market, the cost to me next period is

$$\mathcal{F}_{t,t+1} \text{ kroner}$$

If instead I use the spot market, I can do with buying $1/(1 + i_*)$ dollars now (i_* is the per period interest rate). When interest is added next period, I then have one dollar. In order to get $1/(1 + i_*)$ dollars now, I have to pay $E_t/(1 + i_*)$ kroner now. Suppose I borrow these. Then next period I have to pay back the loan with interest – i.e. I have to pay

$$(1 + i)E_t/(1 + i_*) \text{ kroner}$$

We now have two alternatives which both give me one dollar next period in return for a payment in kroner made next period, but determined today. If one alternative is cheaper than the other, everyone who wants to buy dollars for next period will use the cheapest alternative. All sellers, however, will want to use the most expensive alternative. Equilibrium in both the spot and the forward market is thus possible only when both alternatives cost the same – i.e. when

$$\mathcal{F}_{t,t+1} = E_t \frac{1+i}{1+i_*} \tag{1.30}$$

An equivalent way of writing this condition is

$$i = \frac{\mathcal{F}_{t,t+1}}{E_t}(1+i_*) - 1 \tag{1.31}$$

It is sometimes called the *forward parity condition*. It relates the two interest rates and the spot and forward exchange rates.

The left-hand side of the forward parity condition (1.31) tells how many kroner I have to pay in interest next period if I borrow one krone from this period to the next. An alternative is to borrow dollars, buy kroner in the spot market now and at the same time buy enough dollars in the forward market to make the repayment next period. This is called a *currency swap*. In order to get one krone now I need to borrow $1/E_t$ dollars. Next period I then have to pay $(1+i_*)/E_t$ dollars. Buying these in the forward market costs me $\mathcal{F}_{t,t+1}(1+i_*)/E_t$ kroner. This is the amount of kroner I have to pay next period in order to get one krone now. Thus, the kroner rate of interest which I implicitly pay on this currency swap is $\mathcal{F}_{t,t+1}(1+i_*)/E_t - 1$, which is the right-hand side of (1.31).

The forward parity condition thus tells that the cost of borrowing kroner should be the same irrespective of whether one borrows in the ordinary way or uses a currency swap. In both cases we get one krone now, and we pay the same amount of kroner next year. There is no exchange rate risk involved in either alternative, and the law of one price must apply.

Condition (1.31) is also called *covered interest rate parity*, since it says that in equilibrium it should cost the same to borrow kroner directly, or to borrow dollars, convert to kroner and cover the exchange rate risk in the forward market. The name immediately raises the question: what is the relationship between covered interest parity, discussed here, and uncovered interest rate parity, discussed on p. 15? In discrete time the condition for uncovered interest rate parity can be written

$$i = \frac{E_{t+1}^e}{E_t}(1+i_*) - 1 \tag{1.32}$$

where E_{t+1}^e is today's expectation of next period's exchange rate. If we invest in kroner, the expected rate of return is i. For one krone we can now get $1/E_t$ dollars, which gives us $(1+i_*)/E_t$ dollars next period. The expected value of this in kroner is $E_{t+1}^e(1+i_*)/E_t$, and by subtracting the initial investment of 1, we get the expected rate of return from a dollar investment, which is the right-hand side of (1.32).[9]

By comparing (1.32) and (1.31) we observe that covered and uncovered interest rate parity are equivalent if $\mathcal{F}_{t,t+1} = E_{t+1}^e$ – i.e. if the forward exchange rate is equal to the expected future spot rate. In general, we cannot expect this to happen. Except by accident, uncovered interest rate parity holds only when there is perfect capital mobility. Among other things, this requires risk neutrality or absence of exchange rate risk. Forward parity is an equilibrium condition which equates the rates of return on two investments with identical risk characteristics. It holds irrespective of attitudes to exchange rate risk. The forward exchange rate is equal to the expected future exchange rate only when there is no risk premium in the interest rate.

Covered interest rate parity does not hold in all circumstances, however. Obviously the transactions involved in swaps must not be subject to exchange controls. The credit risk (risk of default of one of the contracting parties) must not differ between the swap and the ordinary loan contract. Since there are more parties involved in a swap, this is not always the case. Transaction costs will also differ between swaps and ordinary loans. This gives some scope for minor deviations from covered interest rate parity (see Baille and McMahon, 1989). However, if there are no exchange controls, and if we are interested in the foreign exchange market from the macroeconomic point of view, we probably make no great error by assuming that forward parity holds continuously. de Vries (1994, p. 353) states as one of his 'stylised facts' that covered interest rate parity holds for all major traded currencies. However, Frankel (1993, ch. 2) gives some striking examples of countries which had large deviations from forward parity until exchange controls were abolished. From then on forward parity holds as a close approximation. Frankel found substantial deviations from forward parity for some OECD countries well into the 1980s (e.g. an average deviation of 1.7 percentage points for France), indicating that capital controls were still important then. Among the developing countries in his study forward parity holds for some, while capital controls create very large deviations for others. Levich (1985, pp. 1026–8) gives some nuances, but the impression there too is that forward parity holds as a close approximation when exchange controls are not too tight.

The forward parity condition is often presented in a simplified form. It is common to define the *forward premium* as $fp = (\mathcal{F}_{t,t+1} - E_t)/E_t$. Then $\mathcal{F}_{t,t+1}/E_t$ is the same as $1 + fp$, and we can write condition (1.31) as

$$i = (1 + fp)(1 + i_*) - 1 = i_* + fp + fp \cdot i_*$$

The product $fp \cdot i_*$ tends to be a small number if the period in question is not too long. Thus a good approximation to covered interest parity is that

$$i = i_* + fp \tag{1.33}$$

i.e. the kroner interest rate equals the dollar interest rate plus the forward premium on dollars.

Forward parity means that we can neglect the forward market for the rest of this book. The owner of a forward contract has a claim in one currency and a liability in another. If I have bought one dollar in the one period forward market, I have a claim in dollars and a liability in kroner. The present dollar value of the dollar claim is $1/(1 + i_*)$.

The present kroner value of the kroner liability is $\mathcal{F}_{t,t+1}/(1+i)$. In this way all forward contracts can be translated to assets and liabilities in the currencies involved, and we can include these in our accounts of the net assets each sector holds in each currency. Forward parity ensures that investors with the same currency distribution of their net assets get the same return on their portfolios irrespective of whether their portfolios include forward contracts or not. Thus, there is no need for explicit treatment of the forward market. We can translate all positions in the forward market into positions in the underlying currencies and proceed from there. If we want to determine the forward exchange rate, we can simply use the forward parity condition (1.30) after we have determined the interest rates and the exchange rates.

Exercises

1. (a) What is the effect of an increase in the foreign interest rate i_* on the exchange rate E and the foreign exchange reserves F_g when the exchange rate is fixed and when it is floating? How does the degree of capital mobility affect the result? (b) What is the effect of the increase in i_* on the real value of the country's net foreign debt and on the net holdings of foreign currency assets of all domestic sectors taken together?

2. The central bank can keep the exchange rate fixed either by buying or selling foreign exchange (interventions) or by adjusting the interest rate. Which variables in the simple portfolio model will you treat as exogenous and endogenous in each case? In each case, what are the effects on the foreign exchange reserves and on the domestic interest rate of an exogenous increase in the expected rate of depreciation e_e?

3. Suppose that $F_{p0} < 0$ and $B_{p0} < 0$. (Thus the domestic private sector is a net debtor.) Discuss what this means for the stability of the foreign exchange market.

4. Suppose the exchange rate is fixed. An amount of wealth ΔW is transferred from the foreign sector to the domestic private sector. What is the effect on the foreign exchange reserves of the domestic country? What is the corresponding effect on B_g? If instead the transfer ΔW is from the government to the domestic private sector, what then are the effects?

5 The spot exchange rate is 100. The one-year-forward rate is 102. The domestic interest rate is 10 per cent per year, the foreign interest rate is 7.5 per cent per year. How large is the deviation from covered interest rate parity? (Do the calculation as accurately as possible.) If one wants to borrow the domestic currency, which is cheaper: to do this directly or through a swap?

6. An investor owns 2 million dollars and 10 million kroner. She has sold 1 million dollars on a one-year-forward contract against kroner. What are her present net positions in dollars and kroner? Assume that the kroner interest rate

is 8 per cent, the dollar interest rate is 6 per cent, the spot exchange rate is 6 kr/$ and forward parity holds.

7. Suppose the exchange rate is fixed. Derive the interest rate i which maximizes the real return of the central bank when actual and expected depreciation are equal. What is the condition for $i = i_* + e$ to give the maximum return?

8. The government's net foreign currency assets ('net reserves'), F_g, is the difference between official (gross) reserves, F_R and the government's foreign currency debt, F_D – i.e. $F_g = F_R - F_D$. If the government wants to keep the exchange rate fixed, there are limits to how low official reserves can become. Suppose the exchange rate is fixed and all prices are constant. (a) The government has a deficit X, while the current account is balanced. The government does not want F_R to decline, and it does not want to change the interest rate. How much foreign currency does it have to borrow per year in order to achieve this? (b) Suppose instead that the government does not borrow foreign currency. By how much will it then have to increase the interest rate in order to avoid a decline in official reserves? (c) Suppose that in addition to the government deficit, X, there is also a current account deficit of the same size X. How does this change the answers to (a) and (b)?

9. Mention some reasons why γ on p. 20 may be negative. If $\gamma < 0$, but the supply curve still has a positive slope, what can you then say about the connection between κ and the effect of interest rates on exchange rates?

2 Portfolio choice, risk premia and capital mobility

In chapter 1 we postulated a demand function for foreign currency. In this chapter we derive foreign currency demand from maximizing behaviour and give a brief survey of empirical evidence. The choice of portfolio composition when rates of return are risky has been studied extensively in the theory of finance. In economics expected utility maximization is the dominating theory of choice under uncertainty. However, in finance, the general state-preference theory has given few useful results. A large part of the theory of finance therefore uses 'mean–variance theory', which is compatible with expected utility maximization only when special assumptions are satisfied.[10]

In the first two sections of this chapter we apply mean–variance analysis. In section 2.1 we derive the demand functions for foreign currency, and in section 2.2 we go on to discuss market equilibrium. This approach is chosen because it is effective in demonstrating which factors must be important for currency demand. In section 2.3 the validity of the mean–variance model is discussed together with some possible extensions. In section 2.4 we give an example of how expected utility maximization can be applied to a case where mean–variance analysis may not be adequate. Section 2.5 contains a brief summary of some empirical research on capital mobility between currencies and the related issue of exchange rate expectations.

Capital mobility between currencies is just one aspect of capital mobility. The general issue is to what extent capital flows between countries and currencies respond to differences in expected returns. Another aspect of this is whether capital movements are permitted to equalize across different countries the interest rates on assets denominated in the same currency. This subject was treated in section 1.7 on covered interest rate parity. Yet another aspect is the mobility of equity capital and the extent to which investors have the same return requirements for real investments in different countries.

2.1 Mean–variance analysis and the demand for foreign currency

This section shows how mean–variance analysis can be used to derive a domestic investor's demand for assets denominated in foreign and domestic currency.[11]

The budget constraint of a domestic investor is

$$\frac{B}{P} + \frac{EF}{P} = \frac{B_0}{P} + \frac{EF_0}{P} = W \tag{2.1}$$

where

B = Domestic currency assets
F = Foreign currency assets
E = Exchange rate
W = Financial wealth
P = Price level
Subscript 0 signifies initial stocks. It is assumed that $W > 0$.

The share of his financial wealth which the investor chooses to hold in foreign currency assets is

$$f = \frac{EF}{PW} \tag{2.2}$$

In the sequel f is treated as the basic choice variable. After f has been chosen, the two asset demands can be computed as $F = fPW/E$ and $B = (1 - f)PW$ (cf. (2.1)).

In mean–variance analysis it is assumed that the investor maximizes a utility function:

$$U = E(\pi) - \frac{1}{2}R\,\mathrm{var}(\pi) \tag{2.3}$$

where E is the expectations operator, π is the real rate of return on the portfolio, and $R > 0$ the coefficient of relative risk aversion. The investor wants a high expected return, and he dislikes risk. The higher R is, the more expected return he is willing to sacrifice in order to reduce risk. Risk is here measured by the variance of the return. Risk comes in because the rates of depreciation and inflation are uncertain. We disregard default risk and other forms of risk.

Before we maximize (2.3), we need to calculate the expected rate of return and its variance. Let

i = domestic currency rate of interest
i_* = foreign currency rate of interest
e = rate of depreciation ($\dot{E}/E$)
p = rate of inflation ($\dot{P}/P$)

The real returns on investments in domestic and foreign currency assets are, respectively, $i - p$ and $i_* + e - p$. Thus, the real rate of return on the chosen portfolio is

$$\pi = (1 - f)(i - p) + f(i_* + e - p) = (1 - f)i + f(i_* + e) - p \tag{2.4}$$

e and p are stochastic variables. Denote their expected values by μ_e and μ_p, their variances and covariances by σ_{ee}, σ_{pp} and σ_{ep}. Then, by the rules for expectations and variances of linear combinations of stochastic variables,

$$E(\pi) = (1 - f)i + f(i_* + \mu_e) - \mu_p \tag{2.5}$$

$$\mathrm{var}(\pi) = f^2 \sigma_{ee} + \sigma_{pp} - 2f\sigma_{ep} \tag{2.6}$$

The first-order condition for maximization of (2.3) is

$$\frac{dU}{df} = \frac{dE(\pi)}{df} - \frac{1}{2}R\frac{d\mathrm{var}(\pi)}{df} = 0 \tag{2.7}$$

The derivatives involved are easily calculated from (2.5) and (2.6). When the resulting equation is solved for f, we get

$$f = \frac{\sigma_{ep}}{\sigma_{ee}} + \frac{1}{R\sigma_{ee}}(i_* + \mu_e - i) \tag{2.8}$$

As can be easily checked, the second-order condition is satisfied, and the optimal share of foreign currency is thus given by (2.8). The resulting demand function for foreign currency has the same arguments as the one that was postulated in chapter 1.

The optimal f can be written as a sum of two terms: $f = f_M + f_S$, where $f_M = \sigma_{ep}/\sigma_{ee}$ and $f_S = (1/R\sigma_{ee})(i_* + \mu_e - i)$. This means that the optimal portfolio can be seen as a sum of two portfolios. The first is called the *minimum-variance portfolio*, since f_M is the share of foreign currency which minimizes the variance (2.6). It consists of $f_M W$ invested in foreign currency assets and $(1 - f_M)W$ in domestic currency. The second is called the *speculative portfolio*. It consists of $f_S W$ in foreign currency assets and $-f_S W$ in domestic currency. We need to discuss both components.

The minimum-variance portfolio

Since the *real* rate of return on both assets is uncertain, the investor has no risk-free alternative. Exchange rate risk does not necessarily mean that it is safer to invest in the home currency. The minimum-variance portfolio is as close to safety as the investor can come. It defines the diversification which minimizes risk. Normally one would expect a positive correlation between inflation and depreciation. Then, by investing a positive amount in foreign currency, the investor hedges against domestic inflation.

In order to understand what determines the composition of the minimum-variance portfolio, it is useful to look at some special cases. Suppose that we have relative purchasing power parity[12] in the sense that the rate of depreciation is equal to the discrepancy between the two inflation rates – i.e. $e = p - p_*$. Then the two real rates of return are $i - p$ and $i_* - p_*$. If one also assumes that the two inflation rates are uncorrelated, then standard rules for computing variances and covariances give $\sigma_{ee} = \sigma_{pp} + \sigma_{p_*p_*}$ and $\sigma_{ep} = \sigma_{pp}$. Thus, the share of foreign currency in the minimum-variance portfolio is

$$f_M = \sigma_{pp}/(\sigma_{p_*p_*} + \sigma_{pp})$$

and the share of the domestic currency is

$$1 - f_M = \sigma_{p_*p_*}/(\sigma_{p_*p_*} + \sigma_{pp})$$

In order to minimize variance the investor should divide his portfolio in inverse proportion to the variance in inflation in the two countries. The more uncertainty about home country inflation, the more it is prudent to invest in foreign currency. If there is no uncertainty about the inflation rate in one currency, the investor has a risk-free alternative. If he wants to minimize risk, he should then invest his whole portfolio in that currency.

Note that in the example the shares are symmetric. If inflation rates are reversed between the two countries, the portfolio shares of the two currencies are also reversed. There is no preference for the home currency.

At the other extreme from purchasing power parity (PPP) is the assumption that exchange rates are entirely uncorrelated with prices ($\sigma_{ep} = 0$). In this case, investing in foreign currency just adds extra risk, as can be seen from (2.6). It is not possible to hedge against domestic inflation by investing in foreign currency. The minimum-variance portfolio contains no foreign currency.

In the intermediate case, where $\sigma_{ep} > 0$ while purchasing power parity does not hold, the share of each currency in the minimum-variance portfolio is between zero and one. The further we are from purchasing power parity and the more predictable domestic inflation is, the larger is the share of domestic currency. Deviations from purchasing power parity create a preference for the home currency in the minimum-variance portfolio. This justifies the assumption made in section 1.6 that (on the margin) domestic residents invest more of their wealth in domestic currency than do foreigners.

The speculative portfolio

Recall that the share of foreign currency in the speculative portfolio is $f_S = -r/R\sigma_{ee}$, where $r = i - i_* - \mu_e$ is the risk premium in favour of the domestic currency. As in chapter 1, an increase in r reduces the demand for foreign currency. The effect is stronger the lower R and σ_{ee} are. Thus, *high risk aversion and high exchange rate risk mean low capital mobility*. The more unpredictable the exchange rate is, the smaller is the effect of interest rates on the portfolio composition. Perfect capital mobility prevails when there is either no exchange rate risk ($\sigma_{ee} = 0$) or no risk aversion ($R = 0$).

A numerical example may illustrate what the order of magnitude may be for the coefficient in front of the risk premium. Estimates of the degree of relative risk aversion for investors in financial markets have often been around 2. Based on observations at the end of each month from 1972 to 1993, the variance of the rate of depreciation of the French franc relative to the US dollar was 0.0011. This yields a value of $1/R\sigma_{ee}$ of 454. Since we measure interest rates per year, not per month, this figure divided by 12 gives us the effect of a change in the interest rate. Thus, the crucial figure is $454/12 = 38$. It tells us that an increase in the risk premium of 0.01 per year (one percentage point) leads to a reduction of the share of foreign currency in the portfolio by 0.38 (38 percentage points). Obviously, small changes in the risk premium can have large effects on the portfolio composition if the degree of relative risk aversion is not higher than 2.

If the investors believe that $e = p - p_*$, then $\mu_e = \mu_p - \mu_{p_*}$. The higher the expected inflation rate is in a country, the less investors will hold of that currency in the speculative part of their portfolios.

While there is good reason to believe that $0 \leq f_M < 1$, the sign of f_S depends on the sign of r and no restriction is implied on its absolute value. Thus, when r differs from zero, we cannot exclude that f is outside the range $[0, 1]$. As we saw in section 1.4, this may have consequences for the stability of the foreign exchange market. σ_{ee} measures the exchange rate risk that is perceived by investors. This perception can sometimes shift dramatically as, for example, when the Danish referendum in 1992 raised new doubts about the plans for monetary unification in Europe. Suppose a country with a fixed exchange rate has used a positive risk premium to attract large speculative investments to the domestic currency. If σ_{ee} increases, this could then lead to a large outflow from the domestic currency and a corresponding loss of foreign exchange reserves as the speculative portfolios are reduced. This can happen even if μ_e is the same as before. This yields an extra argument for keeping interest rates close to parity. Deviations from uncovered interest rate parity may destabilize the foreign exchange market, especially when there is a change in the perceived exchange rate risk.

Generalization to several currencies

The model above is easily generalized to more than two currencies (see, for example, Branson and Henderson, 1985). The main results are as above. There is one important difference, however. When there are only two currencies, they have to be substitutes – i.e. if the expected rate of return on one currency is increased, the demand for the other currency goes down. When there are more currencies, some of them may be complements – i.e. the demand for one currency may go up as the expected rate of return on another currency increases. This can happen when the exchange rates of the two currencies are negatively correlated. Then one currency may serve as a hedge for an investment in the other.

A practical example may involve a home country which produces just enough oil to cover its own consumption, and two foreign countries: one an oil exporter and one an oil importer. The two exchange rates may be negatively correlated because of the different impact of an oil price shock. A prudent investor may then find it optimal to hedge an investment in the oil exporter by also investing in the oil importer's currency. An increase in the interest rate in the oil exporting country may then lead the investor to increase his demand for the currencies of both the oil importer and the oil exporter.

The effect of an equal-sized increase in all foreign interest rates will still be positive, and equivalent to the effect of a decline in the domestic interest rate.

Empirical applications

There have been several attempts at calculating the optimal currency composition of portfolios based on observed variances and covariances and observed returns (see de Macedo, Goldstein and Meerschwam, 1984, for an example). Such calculations tend to imply that the share of domestic currency in the minimum-variance portfolios should be close to 100 per cent. In the calculations by de Macedo, Goldstein and Meerschwam (1984), it varies between 87 and 105 per cent in a sample of eight countries. This reflects that the correlations between depreciation and inflation are low in quarterly data. The results are in accord with the preference for domestic currency shown by most investors. However, the use of quarterly data may lead to an underestimation of the gains from currency diversification. If inflation follows depreciation with a lag, it may be wise to invest in foreign currency to hedge against domestic inflation, even if the short-run correlation between depreciation and inflation is low.

The published studies focus on developed countries with fairly low and stable inflation rates. A similar calculation for an Argentinian investor considering US dollars as the only alternative to the peso shows a minimum-variance portfolio containing only 14 per cent pesos and 86 per cent US dollars based on yearly data from 1977 to 1990 when Argentina had high inflation. (The same calculation for Germany over the same period results in 91 per cent marks, 9 per cent dollars.) The phenomenon that dollars take over as the standard currency for long-term debt contracts is well known from many high-inflation countries. It is part of a wider phenomenon called *dollarization*, which is when a foreign currency takes over one or more of the functions of money. Here it is as a store of value, but it may also take over as a medium of exchange or a standard of value (see Calvo, 1996, ch. 8).

If we are willing to assume a certain degree of risk aversion, the calculations of de Macedo, Goldstein and Meerschwam (1984) also provide estimates of the degree of capital mobility. The estimated degree of capital mobility is somewhat higher than in the example we gave for the franc. If we again use the data for Argentina and Germany we find that $1/\sigma_{ee}$ was 1.06 for the former 52 for the latter, which means that with the same degree of risk aversion, capital mobility should have been 50 times higher for Germany than Argentina.

Some authors have gone one step further and estimated the mean–variance model based on observations of the actual portfolio composition.[13] One example is Frankel's (1982) study of five major currencies for the period 1973–80. He used historical variances and covariances, while exchange rate expectations and the degree of risk aversion were estimated from the actual portfolio composition. Frankel was unable to reject perfect capital mobility ($R = 0$), nor could he reject $R = 2$. For $R = 2$ he gave estimates of $1/R\sigma_{ee}$ in the range from 210 down to 30 per year, meaning that a change in the own interest rate of 0.01 changes the portfolio share of the currency by between 2.1 and 0.3. Again the impression is that mean–variance models predict a high degree of capital mobility, unless the degree of relative risk aversion is considerably higher than 2.

However, the degree of capital mobility, as defined in chapter 1, depends in the present model not only on $1/R\sigma_{ee}$, but also on the wealth to be invested W. It is often assumed implicitly that all private holders of wealth are active foreign exchange speculators. In many countries a cursory examination is enough to show that this is not true. One reason may be that there are fixed transaction costs which keep small investors out. More important than fees and commissions are probably the time costs of keeping informed about the outlook for future exchange rate developments. There is also the risk of being taken advantage of by more professional market participants. This adds to the pure exchange rate risk. One may conceive of a model where the population is divided in two, one group of exchange rate speculators and one group which never speculates. Then it is the wealth of the speculators together with their R and σ_{ee} which determines the degree of capital mobility. The speculators may actually be changing their portfolio shares dramatically in response to relatively small differences in expected returns. Still, the effect on the aggregate portfolio composition may be small.

A division of the population into those who speculate and those who do not is unlikely to be stable. Everybody is probably a potential speculator if the ratio of expected return to risk appears high enough. Then even small investors may find it worthwhile to incur the fixed costs. If we look at a small country, the fixed information costs are probably higher on average for foreign than domestic investors. Even fairly large foreign investors may normally stay away. But if they are alerted by special events – for example, dramatic movements in interest rates, exchange rates or reserves – they may find it worthwhile to move in. Capital mobility can increase when the risk premium gets high, because more investors find it worthwhile to participate in the market.

The model of chapter 1 is valid also if large groups of wealth owners stay out of the foreign exchange market entirely. This lowers the degree of capital mobility and perhaps also the share of an increase in wealth that is invested in foreign currency, but the demand function for foreign currency is not fundamentally altered. This also shows that the model is able to cover cases where exchange controls exclude certain groups from the foreign exchange market. The same goes for cases where there are quantitative limits on the amounts that may be invested.

When f is outside the interval $[0, 1]$, the investor is borrowing one currency to invest in the other. He may then go bankrupt if the currency he has borrowed appreciates sufficiently. Thus, there is a risk for the creditor, and creditors usually limit the amount of credit that they extend to speculators. This means that each speculator can only choose an f in a limited range. Buyers of forward contracts are usually required to make margin payments which are a certain percentage of their implicit debt. The amount of wealth they have available for margin payments then limits how much they can speculate. Credit constraints limit the amount of speculation.

In most countries there are restrictions on the currency positions that banks and other financial intermediaries can take. These are motivated by prudential concerns, and can be found in countries which have abolished all capital controls. In the European Union insurance companies are required to cover 80 per cent of their obligations in one currency by assets in the same currency. In several of the member countries banks' open positions in foreign currencies are limited to a certain fraction of their net worth. While small investors may stay out of the market because of large transaction costs, many large institutional investors have their foreign exchange speculation limited by regulation.

2.2 The equilibrium risk premium

This section describes the market equilibrium which arises when investors in both countries behave according to the mean–variance rules derived in section 2.1. In particular, we study the relationship between risk, interest rates and exchange rates. In order to make the exposition as simple as possible, we assume that all private investors in both countries are net lenders ($W > 0$). The main results would be unchanged if we also permitted some of them to be net debtors.

We use the same symbols as in chapter 1. The balance sheet is the same as in section 1.2 and the model is the same as in section 1.4. The only difference is that we replace the postulated portfolio demand functions of chapter 1 with the more specific demand functions derived in section 2.1.

The demand for foreign currency by domestic residents is from (2.8):

$$F_p = fPW_p/E = \left[\frac{\sigma_{ep}}{\sigma_{ee}} - \frac{r}{R\sigma_{ee}}\right] PW_p/E \tag{2.9}$$

By analogy to (2.8) the share which foreigners invest in what from their point of view is 'foreign' currency is

$$b = \frac{-\sigma_{ep*}}{\sigma_{ee}} + \frac{r}{R\sigma_{ee}}$$

The reason for the minus sign in front of σ_{ep_*} is that we still measure the exchange rate from the point of view of the home country. A depreciation of the domestic currency is the same as an appreciation of the foreign currency.

Since the residual share $1 - b$ is invested in foreign currency, the demand for foreign currency by foreign residents is

$$F_* = (1 - b)P_*W_* = \left[1 + \frac{\sigma_{ep*}}{\sigma_{ee}} - \frac{r}{R\sigma_{ee}}\right] P_*W_* \tag{2.10}$$

Equilibrium in the market for foreign currency is characterized by

$$F_p + F_* + F_g = 0 \tag{2.11}$$

By inserting the two demand functions (2.9) and (2.10), and using the budget equations ((1.3) and (1.4) in chapter 1) we find that the equilibrium condition can be written

$$F_g = -fPW_p/E - (1-b)P_*W_*$$

$$= -\left(\frac{\sigma_{ep}}{\sigma_{ee}}\right)\left(\frac{B_{p0}}{E} + F_{p0}\right) - \left(1 + \frac{\sigma_{ep*}}{\sigma_{ee}}\right)\left(\frac{B_{*0}}{E} + F_{*0}\right)$$

$$+ \frac{r}{R\sigma_{ee}}\left(\frac{B_p^0 + B_*^0}{E} + F_{p0} + F_*^0\right) \tag{2.12}$$

The right-hand side of (2.12) is the supply of foreign currency to the central bank. If the exchange rate is floating, F_g is exogenous, and (2.12) implicitly determines the exchange rate. If the exchange rate is fixed, (2.12) determines the amount of intervention that the central bank has to undertake.

The supply of foreign currency to the central bank is the negative of the two minimum-variance portfolios plus a speculative portfolio. As in chapter 1, it depends positively on the risk premium. By differentiating (2.12) one finds that the supply curve slopes upwards if, and only if,

$$\frac{\partial F_g}{\partial E} = f\frac{B_{p0}}{E^2} + (1-b)\frac{B_{*0}}{E^2} > 0 \tag{2.13}$$

This is the condition for a positive portfolio composition effect (cf. γ in (1.19) in section 1.4). Since there is nothing new to say about the expectations effect, we assume for simplicity that μ_e is constant. Condition (2.13) is always satisfied whenever both groups of investors keep positive amounts of both currencies.

In section 1.6 we saw that a current account surplus raises the supply of foreign currency gradually over time if a transfer of financial wealth from the foreign to the domestic public raises the supply of foreign currency. A transfer of wealth has no effect on the speculative portfolio. Thus a transfer of wealth from abroad increases the supply of foreign currency to the central bank if the share of foreign currency is higher in the minimum-variance portfolios of foreign than of domestic residents – i.e. if

$$1 + \frac{\sigma_{ep*}}{\sigma_{ee}} > \frac{\sigma_{ep}}{\sigma_{ee}} \tag{2.14}$$

In section 2.1 we argued that if there is purchasing power parity the optimal portfolio shares are independent of the country of residence, which means that (2.14) holds with equality instead of inequality. A transfer of wealth then has no effect on the supply of foreign currency and, thus, a current account surplus does not change the supply of foreign currency over time. In section 2.1 we also argued that deviations from purchasing power parity create a preference for the home currency. Domestic residents then hold a larger share of domestic currency than foreign investors. This seems to be a fairly innocent assumption.

The equilibrium condition (2.12) defines a relationship between the foreign exchange reserves, the exchange rate and the risk premium. Formally, the equation can be written with any one of the three variables on the left-hand side. The solution with the risk premium on the left-hand side gives an interesting perspective. Equation (2.12) can be written in simplified form as

$$F_g = -f_M \frac{PW_p}{E} - (1 - b_M)P_*W_* + \frac{r}{R\sigma_{ee}}\left(\frac{PW_p}{E} + P_*W_*\right)$$

When we solve this for r, we get

$$r = R\sigma_{ee}\left[\frac{f_M PW_p + (1 - b_M)EP_*W_*}{PW_p + EP_*W_*} - \frac{-EF_g}{PW_p + EP_*W_*}\right]$$

or, after adding and subtracting 1 inside the brackets,

$$r = R\sigma_{ee}(\bar{b} - \bar{b}_M) \tag{2.15}$$

where

$$\bar{b} = 1 - \frac{-EF_g}{PW_p + EP_*W_*} = 1 - \frac{E(F_p + F_*)}{PW_p + EP_*W_*}$$

and

$$\bar{b}_M = 1 - \frac{f_M PW_p + (1 - b_M)EP_*W_*}{PW_p + EP_*W_*}$$

are the market averages of the shares of domestic currency in, respectively, the actual and the minimum-variance portfolios. The difference between these two measures the extent to which private investors are taking more exchange rate risk than the minimum they can get away with. The equilibrium risk premium is thus a product of three terms: the degree of risk aversion (R), the exchange rate risk (σ_{ee}) and the extent to which private investors are excessively exposed to this risk ($\bar{b} - \bar{b}_M$). If $\bar{b} = \bar{b}_M$ the risk premium is zero. If $\bar{b} > \bar{b}_M$, the market is 'oversupplied' with the domestic currency and the risk premium has to be positive. The market portfolio available for private investors is, of course, a mirror image of the portfolio held by the authorities.

Equation (2.15) always holds in equilibrium. This means that the risk premium can always be decomposed in the three terms just mentioned. However, it may be misleading to say that (2.15) determines the risk premium. It is just another way of writing the equilibrium condition. By definition $r = i - \mu_e - i_*$. If i_* and μ_e are exogenous, and if the domestic central bank sets i exogenously, the risk premium is determined by the central bank when it sets the interest rate. The equilibrium condition, which can be written equivalently as (2.12) or (2.15), determines either F_g or E, depending on whether the exchange rate is fixed or floating. However, if the central bank aims to keep both F_g and E fixed, (2.15) tells us what interest rate the central bank has to set. Only when the central bank uses the interest rate instead of interventions in order to peg the exchange rate can (2.15) be said to determine the risk premium.

Note that the risk premium can be positive or negative for any currency. It all depends on which portfolio composition the public is offered. If the authorities want private investors to hold more domestic currency than in their minimum-variance portfolios, the authorities have to pay a positive risk premium. One implication is that if a government borrows heavily in the domestic currency, it must be prepared to pay a positive risk premium in the domestic interest rate. If the government borrows in foreign currency instead, the risk premium in the domestic interest rate could be negative. Heavy borrowing in the domestic currency could also induce expectations of further depreciation. These expectations must be compensated by higher interest rates, but that is not part of the risk premium. We return to these issues in chapter 5.

It is important to know whether the risk premium can be large enough to be of macroeconomic significance. In the example of the franc that we used in section 2.1, $\sigma_{ee} = 0.0011$, or 0.0132 when we multiply by 12 to make the figure comparable to interest rates computed per year. If we also assume $R = 2$, the product of the first two components of the risk premium is 0.0264 (2.6 per cent per annum). This gives some indication of the levels of risk premia that are possible. If the two portfolio shares in the third term are between zero and one, 0.0264 is an upper limit for the risk premium. In general the shares are not constrained to be between zero and one, and it is possible to imagine even higher risk premia. A higher degree of relative risk aversion will, of course, also allow higher risk premia.

2.3 Further discussion of the mean–variance model and extensions

This section discusses briefly some shortcomings of the mean–variance model, some alternatives to it and some possible extensions.

Relation to expected utility maximization

The modern theory of behaviour under uncertainty does not start with the mean–variance utility function (2.3). Instead one assumes that the investor maximizes the expected utility of her life-time consumption path. This is consistent with the maximization of (2.3) at every moment if two assumptions are satisfied: (1) Preferences are time-separable and the instantaneous utility function has constant relative risk aversion. (2) The prices P and E follow a so-called Wiener process (also known as Brownian motion). This means that the instantaneous rates of depreciation and inflation, p and e, are jointly normally distributed and independent over time. Expectations, variances and covariances must be constant. The survey by Branson and Henderson (1985) provides further details (see also Dumas, 1994).

The assumptions about the distribution of p and e are questionable. The price level normally responds to the exchange rate with a lag. This means that we do not have independence over time. If the exchange rate is fixed, but allowed to vary within a band, the expected future rate of depreciation must depend on where in the band the exchange rate is now (see section 3.4). This creates another dependence over time. Furthermore, the distribution of the rate of depreciation is sometimes highly asymmetric, because the public knows the direction of an eventual parity change. Mean–variance analysis may be particularly inadequate then. This is the reason that we use expected utility theory in section 2.4 to look at a case where the distribution of the exchange rate is asymmetric.

In the mean–variance model the probability distribution of the rate of depreciation is given exogenously, while the level of the exchange rate is determined endogenously. For those who insist on model-consistent expectations it is then a natural step to demand that the assumed probability distribution is replaced by a distribution that is generated by the model. The uncertainty in the exchange rate should then be traced to the underlying uncertainty in the exogenous factors that determine the exchange rate. In the most ambitious version of this research programme complete dynamic general equilibrium models are constructed where the exchange rate uncertainty is related to underlying shocks in technology, preferences or policy. The disadvantage is that the model gets complicated, and one often has to make rather extreme simplifying assumptions in order to come up with any conclusions. A good introduction is Obstfeld and Rogoff (1996). For examples see Lucas (1982) and Sibert (1989), for surveys Dumas (1994) or Lewis (1995).

Simple general equilibrium models easily run into empirical problems. It is difficult to reproduce something which resembles actual paths of consumption and of returns to foreign exchange investments unless one assumes extremely high degrees of relative risk aversion (see Backus, Gregory and Telmer, 1993; Dumas, 1994, p. 331).

Even if from a theoretical point of view there are objections to mean–variance analysis, it is highly suggestive of the factors that are important in determining the demand for foreign currency. The final test is not whether the theory can be derived from maximization of intertemporal expected utility, but how well it describes the actual behaviour of investors.

Real capital and negative financial wealth

Investors usually invest in both real and financial assets. Some invest more than their total wealth in real capital, which means they have negative financial wealth. The above model is inadequate in these cases. A net borrower is interested in a low, not a high, expected real rate of interest on his loan portfolio.

It is fairly simple to extend the model to include real capital as a third asset. The simplest case is when the real return on capital is uncorrelated with the rates of inflation and depreciation. Maximization of the same kind of preference function as in section 2.1 then leads to a demand function for foreign currency which can be written

$$\frac{EF}{P} = \frac{\sigma_{ep}}{\sigma_{ee}} W - \frac{r}{R\sigma_{ee}} (W + K) \tag{2.16}$$

where K is real capital and, as before, W is financial wealth. Thus, $W + K$ is total wealth. For a solvent investor $W + K > 0$, while W may be negative. The result is the same as before with one exception: the basis for the speculative portfolio is total wealth, not financial wealth alone. It is the investor's total wealth that forms the basis for his risk taking. An increase in r reduces the demand for foreign currency irrespective of whether W is positive or negative as long as $W + K$ is positive. When r goes up, a net borrower, who has $W < 0$, borrows less in domestic currency and more in foreign currency. The proceeds of new foreign currency loans are used to repay domestic currency loans. The net supply of foreign currency to the central bank then increases in the same way as when a net lender sells foreign currency and buys domestic currency.

Investors who are net borrowers are likely to have negative net positions in each currency. For them the portfolio composition effect works in the 'wrong' direction when E changes. However, since governments are usually large net debtors, private investors must on average be net lenders.

Firms' demand for foreign currency

In many countries firms are large holders of foreign currency assets and debts. This fact might lead one to expect that there is a large literature on firms' currency demand. However, this is not the case.[14] A main reason is that the finance theory which has been applied to the foreign exchange market is usually based on assumptions which lead to the Modigliani–Miller theorem (see Copeland and Weston, 1988). This says that the firm's financing decisions are irrelevant. Whatever the firm does of borrowing and lending in different currencies, the owners can undo by taking opposite positions themselves. In the end the preferences of the owners decide the aggregate net demands for currencies. The focus has thus been on the ultimate holders of wealth.

Imagine a firm based in a small country selling its output in a competitive international market. Its revenues measured in foreign currency are independent of the exchange rate. This is almost as if the firm owns an asset denominated in foreign currency: the expected net revenues from sales to the world market. The firm's operating expenditures are paid in domestic currency. If these are not immediately affected by a devaluation, it is as if the firm has a liability in domestic currency. The firm may reduce its exposure to exchange rate risk by matching these implicit assets and liabilities with opposite positions in its financial portfolio. This means that the firm does its borrowing in foreign currency and makes some investments in domestic currency assets. If it does not, the firm's owners may consider doing so privately.[15]

A firm which sells its product in a domestic market protected from international competition does not have the same motive for borrowing abroad. Thus we would expect firms in the non-traded sectors to finance their capital stock by borrowing in the domestic currency.

Whether the above considerations are important for the portfolio demand in the aggregate depends on how close we are to a Modigliani–Miller world. One assumption behind the Modigliani–Miller theorem is that firms cannot go bankrupt.

A related issue is the consequences for the foreign exchange market of equity investments across borders. If a foreigner buys domestic equity, and finances the purchase by drawing on foreign currency assets, that increases the supply of foreign currency. If he finances some of the purchase by borrowing the domestic currency, the effect on the supply of foreign currency is smaller. How much exchange rate risk the investor takes must in principle still be governed by considerations such as those we discussed in section 2.1, but covariances with the return on equities now also become relevant. Following Solnik (1974) there is a large literature on how to compose an optimal international portfolio of equities and interest bearing claims (see Copeland and Weston, 1988, ch. 22; Dumas, 1994; or Lewis, 1995). One robust conclusion, 'the home bias puzzle', is that actual portfolios are too concentrated on equities from the investors' home countries. There are large unexploited gains from diversifying internationally in equity and then using positions in foreign currency to hedge against the associated exchange rate risk. This means that an American investor who buys shares in Europe should finance part of the purchase by borrowing euros if his real returns on the shares depend positively on the price of euros in terms of dollars. In that way, if the euro depreciates, his loss on the shares is (partly) offset by his gain on the loan.

The investment horizon

In section 2.1 we did not say anything about the length of the period for which the investment was made. However, as already hinted at, the period length matters for empirical applications of the model. Suppose all interest rates, inflation rates and rates of depreciation are measured per year. Then if we estimate σ_{ee} by the observed variance of the rate of depreciation, we typically tend to get lower estimates as we extend the investment period. This means that the estimated degree of capital mobility depends strongly on which investment horizon is chosen. Another observation is that the correlation between inflation and depreciation is virtually zero if the horizon is short, and increases with the length of the horizon.

We are again in an area where apparently there has not been much research, and are left to make conjectures. Suppose we have a certain amount of money that we are going to spend domestically one month from now. Over that month the correlation between inflation and depreciation is zero, and the safe option is to invest the whole amount in domestic currency. Furthermore, σ_{ee} is relatively high, which means that even if there is an expected return differential in favour of foreign currency, the optimal share of foreign currency in the portfolio would still be relatively small. If the investment period is closer to a year, the minimum-variance portfolio still consists mainly of domestic currency, but should respond more strongly to the expected rate of return differential. This seems to indicate that there is a connection between the demand for foreign exchange and liquidity preference. The question is really whether investors are averse to uncertainty about the returns over the next month or over a longer period. If the relevant period is very short, the response to changes in expected return may be small.

More accurate approximation of the risk premium

The expressions we have used for expected returns are approximations. Take as an example a domestic investor who buys foreign currency. In discrete time the exact expression for his real rate of return is

$$(1 + i_*)\frac{E_{t+1}}{E_t}\frac{P_t}{P_{t+1}} - 1 = (1 + i_*)(1 + e)/(1 + p) - 1$$

This is approximated first by using the fact that $1/(1 + p) \approx 1 - p$ for small p. The approximate rate of return is then

$$(1 + i_*)(1 + e)(1 - p) - 1 = i_* + e - p + i_*e - i_*p - ep - i_*ep \tag{2.17}$$

Another approximation is then made by neglecting the product terms on the grounds that they are products of numbers which themselves are small if the period we look at is short. In particular, this would seem to be justified if we go to the limit and assume continuous time. The approximate rate of return is then $i_* + e - p$, which has expected value $i_* + \mu_e - \mu_p$. This is the expression that our analysis has been based on. Similar approximations have been used for the other rates of return. However, an approximation is necessarily inaccurate, and in the present case it leads to two errors that need to be mentioned. The problems are related to the fact that we approximate first and then take expectations.

If we take expectations of the right-hand side in (2.17), we find that the expected return is $i_* + (1 + i_*)[\mu_e - \mu_p - \sigma_{ep} + \mu_e\mu_p]$. When the period we look at is short, the error we make by replacing $1 + i_*$ with 1 and neglecting the term $\mu_e\mu_p$ is small. However, it may be dangerous to neglect σ_{ep}. Suppose $\sigma_{ep} > 0$. Then, this contributes negatively to the expected return on foreign currency for a domestic investor. The reason is that when foreign assets give a high nominal return, inflation is also likely to be high. This reduces the expected real returns. Indeed, if E_{t+1} and P_{t+1} always vary in the same proportion, there is no real gain from a depreciation. Thus, as pointed out by Krugman (1981), we should probably express the risk premium as $r = i - i_* - \mu_e + \sigma_{ep}$. The equation for the share of foreign currency (2.8) is then changed to:

$$f = \frac{\sigma_{ep}}{\sigma_{ee}} + \frac{1}{R\sigma_{ee}}(i_* + \mu_e - \sigma_{ep} - i) \tag{2.18}$$

Earlier we have seen that a high covariance between e and p increases the share of foreign currency in the minimum-variance portfolio. It now reduces the share of foreign currency in the speculative portfolio. The net result depends on the degree of relative risk aversion.

Siegel's paradox

With the approximations we used earlier, the risk premium is the same for foreign and domestic investors. However, the exact expressions differ. One reason is that the covariance between inflation and depreciation need not be the same for the two countries. Another reason has to do with the fact that $E(1/E) \neq 1/E(E)$. This leads to a systematic bias in favour of investing abroad.

In order to see what is involved, assume that prices are constant. This means we can focus on nominal returns. By the same reasoning as above, the risk premium from the point of view of a domestic investor is then $r = i - i_* - \mu_e - i_* \mu_e$, where the last term can be neglected. For a foreign investor the rate of return on an investment in our currency is

$$(1 + i)\frac{E_t}{E_{t+1}} - 1 = (1 + i)\frac{1}{1 + e} - 1$$

Earlier we have used the approximation $i - \mu_e$. However, if we stick to the exact expression, the risk premium from the point of view of a foreign investor is $r_* = (1 + i)\,E[1/(1 + e)] - 1 - i_*$. Not only does this differ from r. It can be shown that r_* systematically tends to be greater than r. Suppose for simplicity that $i = i_* = \mu_e = 0$. Then $r = 0$, while $r_* = E[1/(1 + e)] - 1$. From Jensen's inequality in mathematical statistics we know that $E[1/(1 + e)] > 1/E(1 + e)$. Hence,

$$r_* > \frac{1}{E(1 + e)} - 1 = \frac{1}{1 + \mu_e} - 1 = \frac{1}{1} - 1 = 0$$

Thus, Jensen's inequality in this case is enough to make $r_* > r$. This effect will be present also in the more general case. It means that the expected return on the domestic currency tends to look more favourable from the point of view of foreign than of domestic investors. There is an inherent attraction in investing abroad. This paradox was first recognized by Siegel (1972).

Several authors have claimed that *Siegel's paradox* is unimportant, because empirically the difference between $E[1/(1 + e)]$ and $1/E(1 + e)$ (and between r and r_*) is small. However, Sinn (1989) and Aboudi and Thon (1993) have pointed out that when $R = 1$ the difference is of the same order of magnitude as the risk premium itself. They showed, under fairly general assumptions about preferences and exchange rate distributions, that if $R < 1$, an interval for i exists where domestic investors prefer to invest all their wealth in foreign currency, while foreign investors would invest all their wealth in the domestic currency. It has been argued that Siegel's paradox shows that capital mobility cannot be perfect. If expectations differ because of Jensen's inequality, and investors consider only expected returns, no equilibrium exists. Risk aversion then seems necessary for the existence of equilibrium. However, nobody has provided empirical support for the strong aversion against one's own currency that Siegel's paradox implies. Both Sinn and Aboudi and Thon assumed that the price level was non-stochastic, and thus uncorrelated with the exchange rate. The paradox disappears if there is always purchasing power parity.

2.4 Expected utility maximization: an example

As mentioned in section 2.3, compatibility of mean–variance analysis with expected utility theory requires that the rate of depreciation is normally distributed. When the exchange rate is fixed, investors are often quite certain of the direction of an eventual parity change. Since the normal distribution is symmetric around the mean, it may then give a poor description of the actual distribution. One purpose of the present section is to illustrate how the asymmetry of the distribution of returns affects the demand for foreign currency. We do this by means of an example which is chosen for its analytical tractability rather than for its generality.

Assume that the investor maximizes expected utility

$$E[U] = E[\ln(W)] \tag{2.19}$$

where $U = \ln(W)$ is utility and W is end-of-period wealth. The utility function is logarithmic, which means that the degree of relative risk aversion is equal to 1. End-of-period wealth is

$$\begin{aligned} W &= W_0\big[(1-f)(1+i)+f(1+i_*)(1+e)\big]/(1+p) \\ &= W_0\big[(1+i)-f\Delta\big]/(1+p) \end{aligned} \tag{2.20}$$

where

$$\Delta = (1+i)-(1+i_*)(1+e)$$

is the rate of return differential in favour of domestic currency.

Let there be two outcomes for e: $e = a$ with probability Π and $e = b$ with probability $1 - \Pi$. Assume, without loss of generality, that $a > b$. Assume that the domestic interest rate is in the interval

$$(1+i_*)(1+b)-1 < i < (1+i_*)(1+a)-1 \tag{2.21}$$

If i were below the lower limit, the rate of return would be higher in foreign than in domestic currency irrespective of the outcome for the exchange rate. One then gets a sure gain from borrowing unlimited amounts of domestic currency to invest in foreign currency. If i were above the higher limit, the reverse is true. Equilibrium is possible only if i is in the interval described by (2.21). We encountered a similar case in connection with figure 1.6 (p. 29).

From (2.19) and (2.20) we can calculate expected utility, which is

$$E[U] = \ln W_0 + \Pi \ln[(1+i) - f\Delta_a] + (1-\Pi)\ln[(1+i) - f\Delta_b] - \mathrm{E}\ln(1+p)$$

(2.22)

where Δ_a and Δ_b are the values of Δ when we insert, respectively, $e = a$ and $e = b$. Note that the rate of inflation appears only in an additive term at the end. This is independent of f, and thus we do not need to specify the distribution of p in order to derive the optimal f. The choice of currency composition is independent of the distribution of the rate of inflation. This is a special property of the logarithmic utility function.[16]

The first-order condition for a maximum of (2.22) is

$$\frac{d\mathrm{E}(U)}{df} = -\Pi\frac{\Delta_a}{(1+i) - f\Delta_a} - (1-\Pi)\frac{\Delta_b}{(1+i) - f\Delta_b} = 0$$

When this is solved for f, we get the optimal share of foreign currency

$$f = (1+i)\frac{\Pi\Delta_a + (1-\Pi)\Delta_b}{\Delta_a\Delta_b}$$

(2.23)

If we insert for Δ_a and Δ_b and take account of that $\mathrm{E}e = \Pi a + (1-\Pi)b$, we find that the numerator is the same as the risk premium $r = (1+i) - (1+i_*)(1+\mathrm{E}e)$. Thus, we can write the optimal portfolio share as

$$f = (1+i)\frac{r}{\Delta_a\Delta_b}$$

(2.24)

This resembles (2.18) with $R = 1$. The product $\Delta_a\Delta_b$ is a measure of exchange rate variability, although it is not the variance. Because i is in the interval described by (2.21), $\Delta_a < 0$ and $\Delta_b > 0$. Hence, $\Delta_a\Delta_b < 0$. An increase in r reduces f.

At the point where there is interest rate parity the two expressions (2.24) and (2.18) can be made even more similar. A straightforward calculation shows that when $r = 0$

$$\Delta_a\Delta_b = -\Pi(1-\Pi)(a-b)^2/(1+\mathrm{E}e) = -\mathrm{var}(e)/(1+\mathrm{E}e)$$

Hence, at this point the degree of capital mobility in (2.24) is indeed inversely proportional to the variance of the exchange rate. The extra terms $1+i$ and $1+\mathrm{E}e$ relative to (2.18) are there because we now use discrete time and avoid approximations.

Equation (2.24) produces a complex non-linear relation between the domestic interest rate and the share of foreign currency in the portfolio. Figures 2.1 and 2.2 give two examples. Figure 2.1 shows a symmetric case where there is an equal probability of 5 per cent depreciation and 5 per cent appreciation. Figure 2.2 shows an asymmetric case where there is a 10 per cent chance of a devaluation by 10 per cent. Otherwise the exchange rate stays unchanged. The period length is taken to be three months, and the foreign interest rate is 5 per cent per annum in both examples.

In figure 2.1 interest rate parity means that i is also 5 per cent. The interest rate has to stay in the interval $(-0.1525, 0.2525)$. Roughly this is interest parity plus/minus 4 times the maximum size of the possible depreciation/appreciation (5 per cent). We

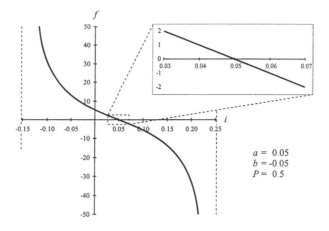

Figure 2.1 The relationship between the domestic interest
rate and the portfolio share of foreign currency: a
symmetric example.

multiply by 4 since the period is one quarter and interest rates are quoted per year. The
global picture should be compared to figure 1.6. The interest rate can be varied in a
wide range around interest rate parity without capital mobility going beyond all limits.
However, capital mobility increases as we move away from interest rate parity in both
directions (in the sense that the effect of i on f increases). If the amount of wealth
available for speculation is high, deviations from interest rate parity of more than 1 or 2
per cent may cause capital movements that are difficult to handle. The close-up shows
that as the interest rate goes from 1 per cent below parity to 1 per cent above parity, the
portfolio share of foreign currency is reduced from +1 to −1. A higher degree of risk

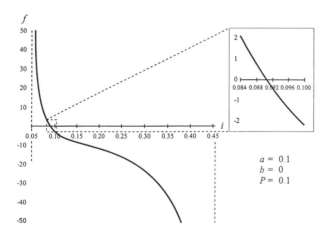

Figure 2.2 The relationship between the domestic interest
rate and the portfolio share of foreign currency: an
asymmetric example.

aversion would produce a similar curve with the same asymptotes. However, it would be uniformly less steep than the curve in figure 2.1.

In figure 2.2 the expected rate of depreciation is 1 per cent (an 0.1 probability for a devaluation times an eventual devaluation size of 0.1). Thus, interest rate parity means that i is equal to 9 per cent (5 per cent foreign interest rate plus an expected rate of depreciation per year of 4 times 1 per cent). The interest rate has to stay in the interval (0.05, 0.455). Since there is no chance of an appreciation, the domestic interest rate must always stay above the foreign interest rate. The demand curve has the same general shape as in figure 2.1, but it is highly asymmetric. If the starting point is at interest rate parity, a reduction in the interest rate has a stronger effect than an increase. The close-up shows, however, that this difference may be rather modest in the relevant range. The degree of capital mobility is not modest, however. If the interest rate is raised from 0.087 to 0.094, f declines from $+1$ to -1.

The examples in this section have illustrated four points: (1) Even if the rate of depreciation does not conform to the normal distribution, the degree of capital mobility is inversely related to the variance of the exchange rate. (2) If the range of variation for the exchange rate is limited, this limits the possible range of variation for the interest rate. (3) Capital mobility increases as one moves away from interest rate parity towards eventual limits on the interest rates. (4) Asymmetries in the probability distribution of the rate of depreciation mean that changes in the interest rate away from parity have stronger effects in one direction than in the other.

The numerical examples may give the impression that the degree of capital mobility is very high. The variances of the exchange rate in the examples are of an order of magnitude often observed in quarterly data. However, one should not jump to conclusions from these simple examples. A higher risk aversion makes a difference.

2.5 The degree of capital mobility between currencies

The focus in this chapter has been on how risk and risk aversion determine the degree of capital mobility between currencies. Some of the examples may have given the impression that capital mobility is close to perfect. However, in the empirical literature there are hundreds of tests of perfect capital mobility, and the great majority have led to rejections.

Most tests of perfect capital mobility test for uncovered interest rate parity. The parity equation can be written:

$$e_e = i - i_*$$

It is common to assume that expectations are 'rational' in the sense that the expected rate of depreciation is equal to the actual rate of depreciation plus a random error term, u – i.e.

$$e = e_e + u$$

where u has expectation zero and is uncorrelated with the interest rate differential. Then

$$e = i - i_* + u$$

and perfect capital mobility is tested by estimating

$$e = a + b(i - i_*) + u \qquad (2.25)$$

where a and b are parameters to be determined. Strictly speaking perfect capital mobility should mean that $a = 0$ and $b = 1$. Because of Siegel's paradox, it is usually only the test for $b = 1$ which is emphasized. The hypothesis that $b = 1$ is almost always rejected. In fact, most estimates of b have been below 0 for floating exchange rates (Froot and Thaler, 1990). The book by Hodrick (1987) provides a good review of different tests as well as the author's own estimations. There are useful surveys by Levich (1985), MacDonald and Taylor (1992), de Vries (1994) and most recently by Lewis (1995) and Taylor (1995). Another useful source is Baille and McMahon (1989, chs. 6–7).

There are at least two common explanations for the almost universal rejection of $b = 1$. One is that there is a varying risk premium, the other that expectations are not rational. If there were a constant risk premium, that would show up as $a \neq 0$, not as $b < 1$. A third, more technical, explanation is that expectations have included a small probability for some 'large' event which did not materialize during the period of observation. The best example may be that there has been some probability for a large devaluation, but it did not take place until after the sample period. This is called the 'peso problem'.

This chapter has been about the risk premium. As mentioned, the estimated deviations from interest rate parity tend to be quite large. One question, which follows from our earlier discussion in this chapter, is whether the observed deviations are too large to be explained as risk premia with a reasonable degree of risk aversion. If there is a risk premium, $e_e = i - i_* - r$ and r depends on the relative supply of assets denominated in the different currencies (see (2.15)). In principle it is possible to test for a risk premium by including relative assets supplies (and possibly also different measures of exchange rate and inflation risk) in (2.25). In spite of many attempts, it has been difficult to find evidence for the existence of substantial risk premia in this way. According to Lewis (1995) a main problem is that there is not enough variation in relative asset supplies to account for significant variation in r. However, what constitutes large variations in asset supplies depends on the amount of wealth that is available for foreign exchange speculation, as discussed in section 2.1.

The alternative explanation for the rejection of $b = 1$ was that expectations are not rational. In section 1.7 we showed that perfect capital mobility together with *covered* interest rate parity means that the forward exchange rate is equal to the future spot rate. In other words, the expected rate of depreciation is equal to the forward premium, which again is equal to the interest rate differential. In (2.25) the interest rate differential is often replaced by the forward premium, and the test is described as a test of whether the forward rate is an unbiased predictor of the future spot rate. When there is a peso problem, there is an undue rejection, because the rare, large event did not happen during the sample. The forward rate appears to be a biased predictor because the observation period in a sense is too short.

The essence of the definition of rational expectations applied here is that expectational errors should be uncorrelated with the interest differential $i - i_*$. The interest rates are known at the time of prediction. If the expectational error is systematically correlated with $i - i_*$, it means that an information available has not been efficiently used when making the prediction.[17] However, if the economic structures generating the data have changed, as when major countries went from fixed to floating exchange rates in the early 1970s, it may be difficult to know how to use the information efficiently. Rational expectations, in the sense of expectations being unbiased predictors of future exchange rates, are best seen as an equilibrium condition for a learning process. If the environment is stable, people should learn to make predictions of recurrent phenomena without making systematic errors. In real life, the environment is changing. The ongoing learning process may then account for some of the apparent deviation from uncovered interest rate parity which is observed when we replace expected with actual depreciation (see Lewis, 1989).

Support for the hypothesis that expectations are not unbiased predictors of future exchange rates also comes from surveys of the expectations of foreign exchange traders. When using survey data instead of actual depreciation to measure expectations, Froot and Frankel (1989) are in most cases unable to reject $b = 1$. However, they also find evidence of a substantial risk premium in the interest rate differential between US dollars and German Marks. This appeared to be constant over the estimation period. Dominguez and Frankel (1993b), using survey data for a longer period, found evidence of a risk premium that varies with relative assets supplies just as mean–variance theory predicts. Thus, the latest results based on survey data indicate that the rejection of $a = 0$ and $b = 1$ in (2.25) is caused both by a risk premium and non-rational expectations.

Survey respondents appear to have heterogeneous expectations – for example, one study reports a high–low range of 15.2 per cent on a forecast of the exchange rate six months ahead (Frankel and Froot, 1990). If this is representative, heterogeneity of expectations could be more important than risk aversion for the degree of capital mobility. A 15 per cent difference in exchange rate expectations over six months means that there is a 30 per cent range for the interest rate in which the investors will be divided; some expecting the highest return in one currency, and some in the other. Even if all investors were risk neutral, heterogeneous expectations would create a relationship between the interest rate and relative asset demands comparable to that created by risk aversion. If the environment is stable, learning may gradually reduce heterogeneity. Then capital mobility may increase over time.

Finally, we should not forget that until recently capital controls were in effect in most countries. Furthermore, for small investors the transaction costs of entering the foreign exchange market are still relatively high. This includes the risk of getting unfair deals from better informed professionals in a market where there has been little time to build up reputation. For good reasons, many small investors have never considered investing in foreign currency. This may change over time as financial institutions develop better services for the new market created by deregulation.

Exercises

1. In the model of section 2.1, suppose that p and p_* are correlated. How would this affect the minimum-variance portfolio?
2. In the model of section 2.1, suppose $e = p - p_* + x$, where x is uncorrelated with both p and p_* and can be interpreted as a kind of noise in the foreign exchange market. The level of noise is measured by the variance σ_{xx}. How does the level of noise affect the composition of the portfolio?
3. Suppose $\sigma_{ep} = \sigma_{ep_*} = 0$. What does this mean for $\bar{b}_M$? Reinterpret (2.15) in the light of this. What is the condition for the risk premium to be positive?
4. In the mean–variance model, show that

$$f_M = \rho_{ep}\sqrt{\frac{\sigma_{pp}}{\sigma_{ee}}}$$

where ρ_{ep} is the coefficient of correlation between e and p. Comment on what this means for the size of f_M. Discuss the effect of an increase in σ_{ee} on f.

3 Money

In chapters 1 and 2 there were just two financial assets: one denominated in domestic currency, one denominated in foreign currency, and both interest bearing. This precluded a discussion of monetary policy proper. The interest rate was treated as an exogenous policy instrument. In the present chapter we also allow the central bank to make policy through adjusting the quantity of money. Nominal interest rates are then determined endogenously.

In section 3.1 we extend the simple portfolio model from section 1.4 to include money.[18] The model allows us to discuss various strategies for monetary policy in the open economy. It is used in later chapters as a representation of the financial side of the economy. In section 3.2 we take a closer look at the demand for money. This leads to a discussion of competition between currencies and the use of foreign currency for transaction purposes. In section 3.3 we extend the portfolio model further by including banks and wind up with some conclusions about money supply targets. The final section (3.4) looks at the role of foreign exchange reserves when the exchange rate is fixed and at two variants of fixed rate systems: currency boards and target zones.

3.1 A portfolio model with money

We now allow for two assets denominated in each currency: one interest bearing called *bonds*, and one more liquid with zero interest called *money*. In order to make the model as simple as possible, we assume that foreigners hold only foreign currency denominated assets, and that domestic residents do not hold foreign money. The structure of the balance sheet is summarized in table 3.1, where M is the quantity of money and B is the (net) quantity of kroner bonds. The purpose of the present section is to discuss how the interest rate on domestic bonds, i, is determined when M or B is the policy instrument, and to discuss the relationship between interest rates and the foreign exchange market in this case.

The equations of the model are:

$$(M + B + EF_p)/P = (M_0 + B_0 + EF_{p0})/P = W_p \tag{3.1}$$

$$(-M - B + EF_g)/P = (-M_0 - B_0 + EF_{g0})/P = W_g \tag{3.2}$$

$$F_*/P_* = F_{*0}/P_* = W_* \tag{3.3}$$

Table 3.1 *Financial balances*

Asset	Sector			
	Private	Government	Foreign	Sum
Money (kr)	M	$-M$	0	0
Kr bonds	B	$-B$	0	0
$ assets	F_p	F_g	F_*	0
Net assets	$M + B + EF_p$	$EF_g - M - B$	EF_*	0

$$r = i - i_* - e_e \tag{3.4}$$

$$e_e = e_e(E), \qquad e_e' < 0 \tag{3.5}$$

$$\frac{M}{P} = m(i, Y), \quad m_i < 0, \quad m_Y > 0 \tag{3.6}$$

$$\frac{B}{P} = W_p - f(r, W_p) - m(i, Y) \tag{3.7}$$

$$\frac{EF_p}{P} = f(r, W_p), \quad f_r < 0, \quad 0 < f_W < 1 \tag{3.8}$$

$$F_p + F_g + F_* = 0 \tag{3.9}$$

Equations (3.1)–(3.3) are the budget constraints that the new allocation of assets must satisfy. As usual, the subscript 0 indicates initial values. The last equalities in (3.1)–(3.4) define financial wealth. Note that because foreigners are excluded from the kroner market by assumption, $F_* = F_{*0}$. Equation (3.4) defines the risk premium, while (3.5) describes regressive expectations. Then follow the three asset demand equations of the private sector ((3.6)–(3.8)) and the equilibrium condition for the foreign exchange market (3.9).

The asset demands need some explanation. The 'kroner bonds' in the model, like the foreign currency assets, have a fixed price and a variable interest rate (like ordinary bank deposits). Perhaps a better term would have been 'kroner debt certificates' or 'kroner loans'. Ordinary bonds with a fixed interest rate and a variable price could be added to the menu of assets without changing the conclusions. However, the existence of kroner assets with a variable interest rate is important. The investor knows with certainty the kroner return he receives if he invests in kroner bonds. It is equal to the kroner interest rate, which is always positive. If he invests in 'money', he receives no interest. Kroner bonds give the investor the same exchange rate and inflation risk as kroner money. This means that kroner bonds dominate kroner money as a store of wealth. The only reason to hold kroner money is that it saves transaction costs.

Since money and kroner bonds entail the same risk, the alternative cost of holding money in liquid form is simply the nominal kroner interest rate. Presumably the investor optimizes his money holdings by trading off interest forgone against transaction costs saved. On the margin the rate of return on kroner money must then be equal to the rate of return on kroner bonds; only in the first case the return is in the form of transaction costs saved, in the second case in the form of interest. The investor's choice problem is analysed further in section 3.2.

We can think of the composition of the portfolio as being decided in two steps. In the first step the portfolio is divided between assets denominated in domestic and foreign currency. In the second step the investor decides how to divide his total kroner assets between money and bonds. In the first step the investor decides how much exchange rate risk to assume. As in chapters 1 and 2, this choice depends in (3.8) on the risk premium and on wealth. The investor can take for granted that on the margin the return on kroner is the same irrespective of whether they are invested in money or bonds. In the second step the decision depends on transaction needs and on the kroner interest rate i. This means that we can write the demand function for money in the standard form (3.6) where the gross domestic product Y measures the volume of transactions. Since money is held only for transaction purposes, the demand for money does not depend on wealth. The demand for kroner bonds in (3.7) is the residual between the total demand for kroner assets and the demand for money. If it is negative, the public gets kroner liquidity by borrowing kroner.

The model has twelve equations. Only ten are independent. The portfolio demand equations (3.6)–(3.8) naturally add up to satisfy the budget constraint in (3.1). Any one of these equations can thus be derived from the other three. The first part of (3.3) can be derived by adding (3.1) and (3.2) and then taking account of the fact that $F_p + F_g + F_* = F_{p0} + F_{g0} + F_{*0} = 0$ by definition.

The model will be used to determine ten variables. Which ten depends on which variables the central bank uses as policy instruments. However, some variables can be classified as exogenous or endogenous irrespective of policy regime. They are:

Endogenous: $W_p, W_g, W_*, F_*, F_p, r, e_e$

Exogenous: i_*, Y, P, P_*

Predetermined: $M_0, B_0, F_{p_0}, F_{g_0}, F_{*0}$

The exogeneity of Y and P is provisional. The model of the financial markets here is a building block in later models where Y and P are endogenous. The endogeneity of F_* and W_* is more formal than real because of (3.3). The remaining variables are the candidates for being policy instruments: i, E, M, B and F_g. Two of them have to be exogenous, three endogenous. There are ten different ways of choosing two exogenous variables from a list of five candidates. Each choice constitutes a policy regime.

In the present section we report results on six policy regimes which are summarized in table 3.2. As before, we look at both fixed exchange rates (E exogenous) and floating exchange rates (F_g exogenous). In each case we look at three different strategies the central bank can have in the domestic financial markets (i, M or B exogenous).

Regimes I and IV, where the interest rate is exogenous, were discussed extensively in chapter 1. In these regimes both M and B are endogenous. This means that the central

Table 3.2 *Exogenous and endogenous variables in six policy regimes*

Regime		Exogenous	Endogenous
Fixed exchange rate:			
I	Fixed interest rate	E, i	F_g, M, B
II	No sterilization	E, B	F_g, M, i
III	Full sterilization	E, M	F_g, B, i
Floating exchange rate:			
IV	Fixed interest rate	F_g, i	E, M, B
V	No sterilization	F_g, B	E, M, i
VI	Full sterilization	F_g, M	E, B, i

bank stands ready to borrow and lend domestic currency at a given interest rate. Thus, M and B are determined by the private sector's demand for money and bonds given by (3.6) and (3.7). This is just an appendix to the model of chapter 1 with no implications for the foreign exchange market. Hence, there is no need for a new discussion of regimes I and IV here, but in some places we report the results from these regimes for comparison.

In a closed economy it is immaterial whether M or B is the exogenous policy variable. The two are linked through the balance sheet of the central bank (3.2). In a closed economy $F_g = 0$, and when M is decided, B is also decided. It is common in texts on closed economies to assume that the central bank determines M, but it makes no difference if we assume that it determines B instead. In an open economy this is no longer true, because the balance sheet includes a third variable, F_g. Then it may matter whether M or B is exogenous. This is the reason why we include two new regimes for monetary policy, one with B and one with M exogenous.

The term 'sterilization' needs an explanation. As a starting point we can note that a purchase of an asset must still be paid for with equal value of another asset. By rearranging (3.2) we get

$$(M - M_0) + (B - B_0) - E(F_g - F_{g0}) = 0$$

or after a change of notation

$$dM + dB - EdF_g = 0$$

This is the same as

$$dM = EdF_g - dB \tag{3.10}$$

which says that the change in the supply of money is equal to the central bank's purchases of foreign currency plus its purchases of domestic bonds (the negative of its sales). The two terms on the right-hand side are usually labelled the foreign and domestic components of the money supply, respectively. With a fixed exchange rate investors are free to exchange foreign currency for domestic money. These trades determine the money supply. Thus a natural starting point for the analysis of monetary policy under fixed exchange rates is regime II, where B is exogenous and M endogenous.

However, the central bank can use dB to counteract the changes in the money supply which follow from interventions in the foreign exchange market (EdF_g). This is called *sterilizing* the inflow of foreign currency. The degree of sterilization is defined as $s = dB/EdF_g$. Complete sterilization occurs when $s = 1$. This is our regime III, where the money supply is exogenous. Complete sterilization means that the effect on the money supply of exchange market interventions is fully offset by operations in the domestic bond market.

When the exchange rate is floating, the central bank is not obliged to change foreign currency into domestic money and vice versa. As long as $dF_g = 0$, keeping B constant is equivalent to keeping M constant. When the central bank does not intervene in the foreign exchange market, regimes V and VI are identical. Just as in a closed economy, it does not matter whether M or B is exogenous. When two of the three variables on the central bank's balance sheet have been decided exogenously, the third follows immediately. Thus, it is immaterial which pair we chose to be exogenous. Regimes V and VI differ only on the occasions when the central bank intervenes in the foreign exchange market – i.e. when F_g is changed exogenously.

The upshot of all this is that our discussion in the present section will be focussed on three different cases: fixed exchange rate without sterilization (regime II), fixed exchange rate with full sterilization (regime III) and floating exchange rates with either M or B exogenous (regimes V and VI, which are equivalent).

What about the four remaining regimes that are not in table 3.1? One is inconsistent with the money demand function (M and i exogenous), one nobody has found interesting (i and B exogenous) and one is equivalent to regimes V and VI (M and B exogenous). Thus, the only interesting case that has been left out is the regime where F_g and E are exogenous. This regime, where the interest rate is used to keep the exchange rate fixed, was touched upon in section 1.5. Its consequences for the money and bond markets are left for the reader to resolve.

Solving the model

Our model has three markets. However, there are only two prices: E and i. This is no problem, as we can show that if two of the three markets are cleared, then the third is also cleared. Thus Walras' law applies. In order to see this, it is convenient to rewrite the budget equations (3.1)–(3.3) as

$$M^d + B^d + EF_p^d = PW_p$$
$$-M^s - B^s + EF_g^d = PW_g \quad\quad (3.11)$$
$$EF_*^d = EP_*W_*$$

where superscripts d and s denote demand and supply. If we add the three equations together we get

$$(M^d - M^s) + (B^d - B^s) + E(F_g^d + F_p^d + F_*^d) = PW_g + PW_p + EP_*W_* = 0$$

where the last equality follows by definition. The left-hand side is the sum of excess demand in all three markets. Since this is equal to zero, equilibrium in two of the markets implies that there is also equilibrium in the third. If we want to determine E and i, it is sufficient to look at two of the markets. We shall now see how we can first find the solution for the interest rate and then for the exchange rate or the foreign exchange reserves. When these key variables have been determined, the rest follows easily.

In regimes III and VI, M is exogenous. The equilibrium condition for the money market is the familiar

$$M = Pm(i, Y) \tag{3.12}$$

Since i is the only endogenous variable in this equation, (3.12) determines i. A picture of the money market in these regimes is given in figure 3.1. The vertical line $\bar{M}$ represents the exogenous money supply. Money demand, M^d, is a downward-sloping function of the interest rate. The equilibrium interest rate is where the demand curve intersects with $\bar{M}$.

As already noted, regimes V and VI are identical as long as F_g is constant. Thus, even if M is formally endogenous in regime V, we can still use figure 3.1 as a picture of how the interest rate is determined in this regime. There is a constant money supply, and equilibrium is where this meets the money demand curve. The money supply changes only if the central bank intervenes by changing B or F_g, which are both exogenous.

The odd case is regime II where the exchange rate is fixed and the central bank does not sterilize. E and B are exogenous. In this case, it is convenient to use the equilibrium condition for the market for domestic bonds to determine the interest rate.[19] We get this equilibrium condition by inserting (3.1), (3.4) and (3.5) in (3.7). The result is

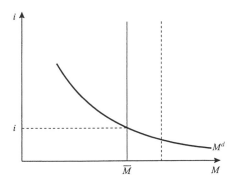

Figure 3.1 Interest rate determination in Regimes III, V, and VI.

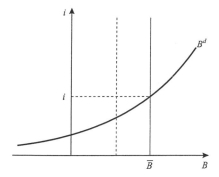

Figure 3.2 Interest rate determination
in Regime II.

$$\frac{B}{P} = \frac{M_0 + B_0 + EF_{p0}}{P} - f\left(i - i_* - e_e(E), \frac{M_0 + B_0 + EF_{p0}}{P}\right) - m(i, Y) \qquad (3.13)$$

Figure 3.2 pictures the equilibrium. There is a given supply, $\bar{B}$, of domestic currency bonds determined by the central bank/government. The demand for domestic currency bonds, B^d (given by the right-hand side of (3.13)), is an increasing function of the interest rate. When i goes up, the public reduces its holdings of both domestic money and foreign bonds. The counterpart is an increased demand for domestic bonds. The interest rate is determined by the intersection of the demand curve and $\bar{B}$.

A difference between the equilibrium conditions (3.12) and (3.13) is that in the latter the foreign interest rate, exchange rate expectations and private wealth enter as arguments. Through e_e and W_p the interest rate also depends on the exchange rate. Sterilization insulates the domestic interest rate from disturbances in the foreign exchange market. With a fixed exchange rate and no sterilization such disturbances have a direct effect on the interest rate. We return to this difference later.

Now to the foreign exchange market. By inserting (3.8) in (3.9) we find that the equilibrium condition is

$$F_g = -F_{*0} - \frac{P}{E}f\left(i - i_* - e_e(E), \frac{M_0 + B_0 + EF_{p0}}{P}\right) \qquad (3.14)$$

Since i has already been determined, this equation determines F_g when the exchange rate is fixed, E when it is floating. The right-hand side of (3.14) is the supply of foreign currency to the central bank, which we discussed in chapter 1. For a given i, the slope of the supply curve is (cf. (1.18), p. 19)

$$\frac{\partial F_g}{\partial E} = \frac{F_{p0}}{E}(1 - f_W) + \frac{P}{E}f_r e'_e > 0 \qquad (3.15)$$

We assume that $F_{p0} > 0$. Together with the assumptions made when we introduced the model this ensures that both the portfolio composition effect and the expectations

Table 3.3 *Signs of multipliers: fixed exchange rate*

	Regime I				Regime II				Regime III			
	dM	dB	dF_p	dF_g	di	dM	dF_p	dF_g	di	dB	dF_p	dF_g
di	−	+	−	+								
dB					+	−	−	+				
dM									−	−	+	−
di_*	0	−	+	−	+	−	+	−	0	−	+	−
dY	+	−	0	0	+	+	−	+	+	+	−	+
dP^1	+	−	0	0	+	+	−	+	+	+	−	+
dE	0	+	−	+	−	+	−	+	0	+	−	+
dF_*^2	0	−	−	−	+	−	−	−	0	−	−	−

Notes: 1 The signs are for the special case that $f(r, W_p) = \bar{f}(r)W_p$.
2 It is assumed that $dW_g = 0$, which implies that $dW_p = -EdF_*/P < 0$.

Table 3.4 *Signs of multipliers: floating exchange rate*

		Regime IV			Regimes V and VI	
		dE	dM	dB	dE	di
di		−	−	+		
dM	$(dB = -dM)$				+	
dF_g		+	0	+		
dF_g	$(dB = EdF_g)$				+	0
dF_g	$(dM = EdF_g)$				+	−
di_*		+	0	0	+	0
dY		0	+	−	−	+
dP^1		0	+	−	−	+
dF_*	$(dW_p = -EdF_*/P)$	+	0	−	+	0

Note: 1 The signs are for the special case that $f(r, W_p) = \bar{f}(r)W_p$.

effect are positive and that the supply curve has a positive slope. Since the interest rate has already been determined, we can then exploit the results from chapter 1.

The next step is to find the effects of changes in the exogenous variables. A summary is given in tables 3.3 and 3.4, which also include regimes I and III for comparison. There is not enough space to go through all elements in the tables. Thus, we first focus on the main topic of this chapter, monetary policy. Next we give two examples of the effects of other exogenous variables. When deriving the effects of exogenous variables, remember the sequence we went through when solving the model: first the interest rate, then the exchange rate or the foreign exchange reserves.

Before we go on, the last line of tables 3.3 and 3.4 needs explanation. Since foreigners do not hold kroner, F_* is the foreign debt. The line shows the effect of a transfer of wealth from the domestic private sector to foreigners. It can be also be interpreted as the effect of a current account deficit, and should be compared to the results in section 1.6.

Monetary policy with a fixed exchange rate: the difference between sterilization and non-sterilization

The natural starting point for the discussion is regime II without sterilization. An expansionary monetary policy means that the central bank buys bonds from the public and in this way increases the money supply. The supply of bonds, B, is reduced. The supply line in figure 3.2 shifts to the left, and we can see that the result is a decline in the interest rate. From differentiating (3.13) the effect on the interest rate of a purchase of bonds is

$$-\frac{di}{dB} = \frac{1}{Pf_r + Pm_i} < 0 \qquad\qquad (3.16)$$

The minus sign in front is because an increase in B means that the government sells bonds to the public and thereby reduces the money supply. Thus di/dB measures the effect of a monetary *contraction*, and we need to reverse the sign to get the effect of a monetary *expansion*.

The interest rate is the link from monetary policy to the foreign exchange market. The fall in the interest rate which results from an expansionary monetary policy induces a capital outflow, and the result is a reduction in the foreign exchange reserves.

The reduced interest rate also makes people demand more money. Thus, the money supply increases, since it is determined by the public's demand for money. However, the final increase in the money supply differs from the amount of money that the central bank initially circulated by buying the extra bonds. In other words: $dM \neq -dB$. The reason is that people use some of the extra money to buy foreign currency. That is how the foreign exchange reserves come to decrease and, as can be seen from (3.10), this reduces the money supply.

More formally, by differentiating (3.6) and (3.14) with respect to i and then inserting for di/dB from (3.16) we find that the effects on the quantity of money and on the foreign exchange reserves of an expansionary open market operation are

$$0 < -\frac{dM}{dB} = -Pm_i \frac{di}{dB} = \frac{m_i}{f_r + m_i} < 1 \qquad\qquad (3.17)$$

and

$$-1 < -E \frac{dF_g}{dB} = Pf_r \frac{di}{dB} = -\frac{f_r}{f_r + m_i} < 0 \qquad\qquad (3.18)$$

Observe that both dM/dB and EdF_g/dB are smaller than one in absolute value. The original increase in the money supply is partly, and only partly, offset by the ensuing outflow of capital.

Suppose the central bank purchases bonds for 1 billion kroner. The first purchase results, as we have just seen, in a capital outflow, which reverses some of the initial increase in the money supply. Sterilization means that the central bank responds by buying more bonds and raising the money supply again. Complete sterilization means that it continues to buy bonds until it has finally succeeded in raising the money supply by 1 billion kroner without further capital outflows taking place.

In regime III (full sterilization) an exogenous increase in M shifts the money supply line in figure 3.1 to the right. By differentiating the equilibrium condition (3.12) we find that the effect on the interest rate is

$$\frac{di}{dM} = \frac{1}{Pm_i} < 0 \tag{3.19}$$

Note that the multiplier in (3.19) is greater in absolute value than the one in (3.16). The reason why the decline in the interest rate is greater is that the final increase in the money supply is greater when there is sterilization. The initial purchase of domestic bonds is followed by more purchases as the central bank sterilizes the ensuing out-flows of foreign exchange.

The effects on the stock of bonds and on the foreign currency reserves are from (3.7) and (3.14), respectively

$$\frac{dB}{dM} = \frac{dB}{di}\frac{di}{dM} = -\frac{f_r + m_i}{m_i} < -1 \tag{3.20}$$

$$\frac{dF_g}{dM} = \frac{dF_g}{di}\frac{di}{dM} = -\frac{1}{E}\frac{f_r}{m_i} < 0 \tag{3.21}$$

That dB/dM is below -1 means that in order to increase the quantity of money by 1 billion kroner, the central bank has to buy domestic bonds for more than 1 billion kroner. The extra purchases are necessary to offset the capital outflow given by (3.21).

It is evident from (3.16)–(3.21) that the effects of monetary policy depend on the degree of capital mobility as measured by $|f_r|$. Again we can focus first on the case with no sterilization. According to (3.16), a high degree of capital mobility means that monetary policy has but a small effect on the interest rate. As the degree of capital mobility goes to infinity, the effect of monetary policy on the interest rate goes to zero. In figure 3.2 high capital mobility means a flat demand curve for domestic bonds. When the degree of capital mobility goes to infinity, the demand curve approaches a horizontal line at $i = i_* + e_e$.

A small effect on the interest rate also means a small final effect on the quantity of money, as can be seen from (3.17). The counterpart is the effect on the foreign exchange reserves. From (3.18) we observe that the greater the degree of capital mobility, the greater is the effect on the foreign exchange reserves. Higher capital mobility means that more of the initial decrease in the money supply is offset by the ensuing capital movements. When the degree of capital mobility goes to infinity, dF_g/dB goes to $1/E$. This means that the whole of the initial decrease in the money supply is offset by the increase in the foreign exchange reserves. When people are indifferent between holding domestic and foreign bonds, attempts at increasing their holdings of domestic bonds only result in them exchanging domestic bonds for foreign bonds. Since they are indifferent, they need no change in the interest rate to be induced to do so, and the domestic money supply remains unaffected. The increase in the foreign component of the money supply is equal to the reduction in the domestic component.

When the central bank sterilizes completely, the effect of a change in M on the interest rate is independent of the degree of capital mobility, as we can see from (3.19). Apparently monetary policy works as in the closed economy. This is only apparently, however. We observe from (3.20) and (3.21) that the stronger capital mobility is, the stronger are the effects on B and F_g. If capital mobility is high, an expansionary monetary policy leads to a large loss of foreign exchange reserves. When the degree of capital mobility goes to infinity, the effect on the foreign exchange reserves of a change in the money supply also goes to infinity. The same is true about the effect of any variable which shifts the demand for money, and thus changes interest rates. This shows that *complete sterilization is impossible if capital mobility is perfect.* Another way of putting this is that *the central bank of a small open economy with perfect capital mobility and a fixed exchange rate is not able to control the money supply.*

Complete sterilization means that the central bank tries to take control of the interest rate in an open economy. It runs into difficulties when capital mobility is high in the same way as an independent interest rate policy does (see section 1.5). Even with moderate degrees of capital mobility, sterilization requires that the central bank has large reserves of foreign currency.

Monetary policy with a floating exchange rate: sterilized and unsterilized interventions

When the exchange rate is floating, an increase in the money supply $(dM > 0)$ created by a domestic open market operation $(dB = -dM)$ means that the equilibrium interest rate is lowered (cf. (3.12)). This in turn lowers the supply of foreign currency and leads to a depreciation of the exchange rate. The basic story is the same as told in section 1.5 about the effect of a change in interest rates. We have just added a story about how the interest rate is determined.

An intervention in the foreign exchange market can be either *sterilized* $(dB = dF_g, dM = 0$, regime VI) or *unsterilized* $(dM = dF_g, dB = 0$, regime V). A sterilized intervention does not affect the money supply and, thus, leaves the domestic interest rate unchanged. The interventions we discussed in section 1.5 were sterilized interventions since the interest rate was held constant. We learned there that a purchase of foreign currency leads to a depreciation of the domestic currency, and that the effect is smaller when capital mobility is high.

   If the central bank buys foreign currency for 1 billion kroner and allows the money supply to increase by 1 billion kroner, this is an example of an unsterilized intervention. It reduces the interest rate. Thus, a purchase of foreign currency which is not sterilized leads to even more depreciation than if the intervention had been sterilized. While sterilized interventions lose their force when capital mobility is high, unsterilized interventions remain effective since they change the interest rate. As we saw in section 1.5, when capital mobility is perfect interventions have no effect unless the interest rate is also changed.

   Edison (1993) and Dominguez and Frankel (1993a) survey the literature on the effects of interventions. The latter also contains some interesting case studies. The overall conclusion, shared by Obstfeld (1995b), is that there is little evidence that sterilized interventions between the major currencies have had any effects except as signals about future interest rate policy (see also section 1.5). However, the evidence against perfect capital mobility referred to in section 2.5 indicates that sufficiently large interventions might have an effect, and Dominguez and Frankel (1993b) find that interventions have worked not just as a signal, but also through changing the portfolio composition.

The effects of exogenous shocks: two examples

   The two examples we shall focus are the effects of Y and i_*. The results are typical of what happens when shocks emanate from, respectively, the money market and the foreign exchange market.

   The effect of an increase in the volume of transactions, Y, on the interest rate is of central interest in chapter 6, where the present model of the financial markets is integrated with a model of how Y is determined. In regimes III, V and VI the relation between Y and i is given by the equilibrium condition for the money market (3.6). By implicit differentiation of this we get the familiar result that

$$\text{in regimes III, V and VI:} \quad \frac{di}{dY} = -\frac{m_Y}{m_i} > 0$$

In regime II the relationship between Y and i is given by (3.13), which is the equilibrium condition for the bond market. By differentiating (3.13) we find that the effect of Y on i is

$$\text{in regime II:} \quad \frac{di}{dY} = -\frac{m_Y}{f_r + m_i} > 0$$

As in the regimes where M is exogenous, the effect is positive. Increased transaction needs reduce the demand for domestic bonds by the same amount as they increase the demand for money. In figure 3.2 the bond demand curve shifts to the left. Since B is given, there is an excess supply of bonds at the initial interest rate. Sellers of bonds have to offer higher interest rates until equilibrium is restored with an increased i. However, the effect of Y on i is smaller in regime II than in regime III, as can be seen from the extra term in the denominator. In other words, an increase in the volume of transactions has a smaller effect on the domestic interest rate when the exchange rate is fixed and there is no sterilization, than in the regimes where the money supply is kept constant. The reason is that when the central bank does not sterilize, some of the increased money demand is satisfied by increased money supply. The increase in the money supply takes place because the increase in i induces the public to sell foreign currency to the central bank.

An increase in Y has no direct effect on the foreign exchange market. However, it has an indirect effect through the interest rate. As usual, when the domestic interest rate goes up, it leads to an increase in foreign exchange reserves under fixed rates, and an appreciation under floating rates. Since the effect on the interest rate is smaller, the effect of Y on F_g under fixed rates is smaller when there is no sterilization.

Now to the effect of an increase in i_*. Since i_* does not enter the money demand function, the only regime where it can have an effect on the domestic interest rate is regime II: fixed exchange rate and no sterilization. In this regime an increase in the foreign interest rate raises the domestic interest rate. By differentiating the equilibrium condition (3.13) we find that

$$0 < \frac{di}{di_*} = \frac{f_r}{f_r + m_i} < 1$$

An increase in the foreign interest rate reduces the demand for domestic bonds. The supply of domestic bonds is constant. The domestic interest rate must then increase in order to balance demand and supply. However, when the domestic interest rate is increased, people move from both foreign bonds and money into domestic bonds. Since some of the increased bond demand can come from reduced money balances, it is not necessary to raise the domestic interest rate quite as much as the foreign interest rate. However, we can see from the expression for di/di_* that if the degree of capital mobility is large relative to the interest sensitivity of the demand for money, the effect of i_* on i is close to being one to one.

As long as the domestic interest rate is constant, an increase in the foreign interest rate raises the public's demand for foreign currency and leads either to depreciation or to loss of foreign exchange reserves, in the same way as discussed in chapter 1. The increase in the domestic interest rate in regime II dampens the loss of foreign exchange reserves relative to regimes I and III. However, since the increase in the domestic interest rate is smaller than the increase in the foreign interest rate, the risk premium is reduced, and the net effect is after all a loss of reserves.

Some final remarks

As we have seen, the exchange rate and the foreign exchange reserves are determined in the same way in the extended portfolio model as in the simple portfolio model of chapter 1. What is new in this chapter is that we allow interest rates to be determined in different ways depending on the monetary policy regime. Irrespective of regime capital mobility sets limits for what can be done with monetary policy.

If the central bank keeps the money supply constant, then the domestic interest rate is insulated against disturbances from the foreign exchange market. Foreign variables do not enter the money market equilibrium condition (3.12). In practice, a policy of sheltering the domestic interest rate completely against foreign influences is possible only when capital mobility is limited or the exchange rate is floating. With a fixed exchange rate and no sterilization the interest rate is subject to both foreign and domestic influences.

It should be emphasized that the insulation result depends critically on the assumption that decisions about liquidity and currency composition can be separated. In portfolio models where money is held not just for transaction purposes, money demand may depend on wealth and on the expected rate of return on foreign currency investments. Then there is a direct connection from the foreign interest rate and the exchange rate to the money market, and sterilization does not insulate the interest rate against foreign influences (see Branson and Henderson, 1985). Because the separation assumption is so important, we look at its foundation in section 3.2. In section 3.3 we shall see that when there are banks, the separation result need not hold in the aggregate, even if individuals can separate their decisions.

Above, perfect capital mobility was seen as the limiting case when $|f_r|$ goes to infinity. However, since this special case plays a central role in later chapters, it is useful to be more explicit about how the equation system (3.1)–(3.9) is transformed then. Perfect capital mobility means that investors are indifferent as to whether they hold kroner bonds or dollar bonds as long as they give the same expected return. Thus, separate demand functions for foreign and domestic bonds do not exist. The money demand function (3.6) still applies, but the demand functions for the two other assets (3.7) and (3.8) have to be dropped. Instead we can write down a single demand function for bonds (domestic and foreign) which is just wealth minus money demand. In this way we lose one equation, but that is replaced by the interest parity condition $r = 0$, which is an equilibrium condition under perfect capital mobility.

The upshot is that the essentials of interest rate and exchange rate determination can be summarized in two equations:

$$\frac{M}{P} = m(i, Y) \tag{3.22}$$

$$i = i_* + e_e(E) \tag{3.23}$$

i.e. the demand function for money and the interest parity condition. Under fixed exchange rates the interest parity condition determines i. This means, as we have seen before, that regimes I and III (interest rate control and complete sterilization) are impossible under perfect capital mobility. Since the interest rate is determined by interest rate parity, the quantity of money has to be determined by demand. Otherwise the equilibrium condition for the money market cannot be satisfied.

With a floating exchange rate the central bank can always control the money supply. With an exogenous money supply the domestic interest rate is determined by the equilibrium condition for the money market (3.22), while the exchange rate is determined by the interest parity condition (3.23), as explained in chapter 1. Sterilized intervention does not appear in (3.22) and (3.23), and thus has no effect on the exchange rate or the interest rate. The public is indifferent and accepts the changed portfolio composition without any price change.

Sometimes it is said that money demand determines the foreign exchange reserves when capital mobility is perfect and the exchange rate is fixed. This presupposes that B is fixed. However, since the central bank can change the reserves without any effect on E, it seems more appropriate to say that the central bank sets the level of reserves that it wants.

In the beginning of this section the exogenous policy variables were thought of as instruments under direct control of the authorities. However, there is another possible interpretation. They may be thought of as *operational targets* for the central bank. If M is an operational target, it means that whatever the instruments are, they are used in such a way as to make M equal to an exogenously specified level. We may think of decision making in monetary policy as taking place at two levels. The top level sets the operational targets, the lower level the actual instruments. If the lower level is able to meet the operational targets with sufficient accuracy, we need not worry about exactly what goes on there. Since our models are simplified descriptions of reality, it may be a matter of taste whether we call an exogenous policy variable an instrument or an operational target.

In principle it should be possible for the central bank to control the composition of its balance sheet directly. The composition is decided when two of the three variables M, B and F_g have been decided. It may then seem natural to regard the composition of the balance sheet as the instrument. When E or i are set exogenously, these are operational targets that tie up the use of the instruments. The instruments then have to be endogenous. Part of what we have done above is then to describe how the financial markets react to exogenous shocks when the behaviour of the central bank is described by different operational targets.

It may seem difficult for the central bank to have direct control over the two market prices i and E. However, it can come close to controlling the short-run interest rate by setting its own lending and deposits rates. Thus, given that the model is a simplification, there is nothing wrong with regarding, for example, i and F_g as instruments under direct control. What we cannot do is choose the exogenous variables, whether they are interpreted as instruments or operational targets, in such a way that they are incon-sistent with the behaviour of the private sector. This is the reason that we cannot choose both M and E or both E and i as exogenous when capital mobility is perfect.

3.2 Money demand and currency substitution

In this section we take a closer look at money demand in the open economy. We shall also see how our model has to be modified if foreign money is used for transaction purposes alongside the domestic variety. We stick to the case where money is held only for transaction purposes.

In section 2.1 we derived the optimal currency composition of a portfolio of interest bearing assets. We can extend this analysis to derive the optimal portfolio composition when domestic money is on the menu of assets. Let the real quantity of money be $m = M/P$. Money gives no interest, but it gives a return in the form of saved transaction costs. This cost saving, s (measured in real terms), must be a function of the transaction needs, measured by Y, and the real quantity of money m. Thus, we can write the return from holding money as $s = s(Y, m)$. This function is akin to a production function, and presumably s is increasing and concave in m.

As in section 2.1, let the share of the portfolio invested in foreign bonds be f. The share invested in domestic money is m/W. The share invested in domestic bonds must then be $1 - f - m/W$. The real rate of return on the whole portfolio is then

$$\pi = (1 - f - m/W)(i - p) + f(i_* + e - p) + s(Y, m)/W - (m/W)p$$

The first two terms are the real returns on domestic and foreign bonds. The last two terms are the real returns from the money holdings. They consist of the saved transaction costs minus the loss due to inflation. By rearranging terms the real rate of return can be written as

$$\pi = [(1 - f)(i - p) + f(i_* + e - p)] + [s(Y, m)/W - (m/W)i] = \pi_1 + \pi_2 \qquad (3.24)$$

where π_1 and π_2 are equal to the first and second bracket, respectively. There are two choice variables, f and m. π_1 depends only on f, π_2 only on m. Suppose, as in section 2.1, that the objective function of the investor is to maximize

$$U = \mathrm{E}(\pi) - \frac{1}{2}R \operatorname{var}(\pi)$$

Since π_2 is non-stochastic (it does not depend on the two stochastic variables e and p), the utility function can be written

$$U = \mathrm{E}(\pi_1) + \pi_2 - \frac{1}{2}R \operatorname{var}(\pi_1)$$

Thus, the problem of choosing the optimal combination of f and m can be separated into two independent problems: The first is to find the optimal currency composition of the portfolio. This is the problem we solved in section 2.1, by maximizing what is here

$$E(\pi_1) - \frac{1}{2} R \, \text{var}(\pi_1)$$

The second problem is to find the optimal degree of liquidity, and this is solved by maximizing π_2, the return from money holdings. In the definition of π_2 the nominal interest rate plays the role as the alternative cost of liquidity services.

By differentiating $\pi_2 = [s(Y, m) - mi]/W$ with respect to m we get the first-order condition for optimum m:

$$s_m(Y, m) = i$$

the marginal return in the form of saved transaction costs should equal the alternative cost, i – or in other words: on the margin kroner bonds and money should give the same kroner return. This equation can be solved for the money demand, m, as a function of Y and i. The solution is a standard money demand function:

$$\frac{M}{P} = m(i, Y)$$

The usual signs of the derivatives also follow provided we make the natural assumption that $s_{mY} > 0$ – i.e. that a larger volume of transactions increases the amount of transaction costs saved by a marginal increase in the quantity of money.[20]

Our derivation of money demand is based on some assumptions that are worth making explicit:

- The volume of transactions for which kroner liquidity is needed is independent of wealth
- Investors can borrow and lend kroner at the same interest rate
- In real terms the transaction costs saved are independent of the realized values of the stochastic variables e and p.

If any of these assumptions are violated, the optimal m and f can in principle no longer be chosen separately. However, it is difficult to see that the last point can be of much practical importance. I have seen no practical suggestion for how one should use the foreign exchange market to hedge against uncertainty in transaction cost.

The first two assumptions are potentially more important. If there is a margin between kroner borrowing and lending rates, different investors have different marginal costs of liquidity. For certain values of the exogenous variables the investor will choose to have a share of kroner bonds equal to zero – i.e. to be neither lender nor borrower. The marginal return on money, s_m, must then be somewhere between kroner borrowing and lending rates. On the margin, the alternative to holding foreign currency is then to increase kroner liquidity, not to buy kroner bonds. This means that money demand comes to depend on i_*, on W and on exchange rate expectations and uncertainty. A marginal increase in wealth will be divided between foreign bonds and domestic money, while domestic bonds get no part. How important the problem is depends on the size of the margin between borrowing and lending rates, and on how many investors choose to be neither lender nor borrower in kroner bonds.

The problem is most likely to arise in economies where financial markets are under-developed and many investors are subject to credit rationing. If the domestic interest rate is kept low, and the exchange rate tends to depreciate, investors may want to keep all their financial wealth in foreign currency, and to borrow kroner if possible. If there is credit rationing, the alternative to holding domestic money in transaction balances is then to hold more foreign currency. For a risk neutral investor the alternative cost of liquidity is then the expected return on foreign currency. If the investor is risk averse, his money demand will depend on i_*, e_e and on exchange rate risk.

Currency substitution

So far, we have assumed that only domestic currency is used for transaction purposes. Sometimes two or more currencies circulate in the same country. We use the term 'currency substitution' when different currencies can substitute for each other as a means of transaction.[21] We shall analyse the demand for money when there are two parallel currencies in the same way as we just analysed money demand when only one currency was used for transaction purposes. We shall also describe the market equilibrium. Then we shall look at the deeper questions of which currency to use, and why more than one currency may be used in transactions.

Let the quantity of foreign money held by a domestic investor be N. The real quantity is $n = EN/P$. Suppose that the transaction costs saved by holding quantities m and n of money in the two currencies are $s = s(Y, m, n)$, where s is increasing and concave in m and n. By the same reasoning as above, we can show that the decisions about currency composition and about liquidity within each currency can be separated (see Stulz, 1984) – i.e. the decisions can be taken in two steps. The optimal money demand is found by maximizing

$$s(Y, m, n) - im - i_* n$$

where the two nominal interest rates are the opportunity costs of liquidity in each currency. The first-order conditions for a maximum are

$$s_m(Y, m, n) = i$$

$$s_n(Y, m, n) = i_*$$

With suitable regularity conditions on the s function this gives us demand functions for the two currencies

$$\frac{M}{P} = m(i, i_*, Y), \quad m_i < 0, \quad m_{i*} > 0, \quad m_Y > 0 \tag{3.25}$$

$$\frac{EN}{P} = n(i, i_*, Y), \quad n_i > 0, \quad n_{i*} < 0, \quad n_Y > 0 \tag{3.26}$$

The two currencies are substitutes also in the sense that the two cross-derivatives, n_i and m_{i_*}, are positive. As before, the total demand for the domestic currency is $W_p - f(r, W_p)$, for the foreign currency $f(r, W_p)$. By subtracting the amounts which according to (3.25) and (3.26) are held in liquid form, we get the demands for the two types of bonds:

$$\frac{B}{P} = W_p - f(r, W_p) - m(i, i_*, Y) \tag{3.27}$$

$$\frac{EF_p}{P} = f(r, W_p) - n(i, i_*, Y) \tag{3.28}$$

Our main interest is in how currency substitution changes the equilibrium conditions in the money market and the foreign exchange market. For the money market, the answer is simple. The only change is that the foreign interest rate is now an argument in the demand function for domestic money. An increase in i_* raises the demand for domestic money. If the supply of money is fixed, the result is an increase also in the domestic interest rate. The extent of the increase depends on how close substitutes the two currencies are for transaction purposes.

When it comes to the foreign exchange market, we must remember that net foreign debt is no longer F_*, but $F_* - N$. The net foreign debt measured in foreign currency is given by past history. Thus $F_* - N = F_0$, where F_0 is determined by the past. As before, the equilibrium demands for foreign bonds have to satisfy

$$F_g + F_p + F_* = 0$$

If we insert from (3.28) and from $F_* = F_0 + N$, we get the equilibrium condition

$$F_g + (P/E)f(r, W_p) - (P/E)n(i, i_*, Y) + F_0 + N = 0$$

Since foreign bonds can presumably be freely exchanged with foreign money, the demand for foreign money is always satisfied. This means that $N = (P/E)n(i, i_*, Y)$, and that the equilibrium condition for the foreign exchange market can be simplified to

$$F_g + (P/E)f(r, W_p) + F_0 = 0 \tag{3.29}$$

Thus, we end up with exactly the same equilibrium condition as before. Currency substitution does not change the equation which determines the exchange rate or the foreign exchange reserves. However, it does provide another channel for the influence of the foreign interest rate on the domestic interest rate in policy regimes where M or B are exogenous. In these regimes an increase in the foreign interest rate leads, because of currency substitution, to a (stronger) increase in the domestic interest rate, and this dampens the effect of the foreign interest rate on the foreign exchange market.

Which currency to use?

As any introduction to the theory of money explains, money is useful because it overcomes the problem of 'double coincidence of wants'. The whole point of singling out one object as money is that the same object shall be acceptable as a means of exchange in many transactions. Transaction costs and impediments to trade should be at their lowest if one money is used in all transactions. This speaks for standardizing the choice of money.

Which currency will be chosen for transaction purposes? From the point of view of the individual, the alternative cost of liquidity is the nominal interest rate. This speaks for choosing the currency with the lowest nominal interest rate. Suppose all transactions are carried out in the currency with the lowest interest rate. Then no group of private agents has any incentive to start using other currencies. To keep other currencies in transaction balances is more costly in terms of interest forgone. If we have perfect capital mobility, the country which appreciates the most has the lowest interest rate. There is then a stable equilibrium where the same currency is used for transaction purposes everywhere – namely, the currency of the country which tends to have the lowest inflation and to appreciate the most.

However, government may want to prevent this equilibrium. Formally, the money stock is a liability of the central bank. It can be seen as an interest-free loan from the public. If the government did not have this interest-free loan, it would have to sell bonds and pay interest instead. Thus, the monopoly on printing money gives the government an income iM/P, which is called *seigniorage*.

If the private sector chooses to hold its cash balances in foreign currency, the domestic government loses seigniorage. In order to protect their seigniorage revenue governments normally insist on using the domestic currency in most transactions they are involved in. In a modern economy, where almost every citizen has some transactions with the government (e.g. tax payments), this is a strong coordinating force towards using the domestic currency as the standard means of transaction. Governments may also use the law to promote the use of the domestic currency in transactions between private citizens.

Suppose the domestic currency is established as the universal means of exchange in transactions between domestic citizens. If the domestic interest rate is above the foreign interest rate, small groups of private individuals may have an incentive to agree to use foreign currency for transactions between them, because liquidity is cheaper in foreign currency. However, there are well known economies of scale in managing cash balances. If the same amount of transaction costs are going to be saved when the cash balances are split between two currencies, it is necessary to keep higher total cash balances – in particular, if the transactions in foreign currency are infrequent. Thus the exclusive use of domestic currency in domestic transactions may be a locally stable equilibrium in the sense that no *small* group has an incentive to break out even if the foreign interest rate is lower.

Since there are strong arguments for corner solutions where only one currency is used for domestic transactions, one may ask whether the smooth currency substitution in the 'production function' $s = s(Y, m, n)$ is a reasonable description of reality. The best way of defending it is probably to say that it applies to cases where the domestic currency is clearly inferior, but where its use is upheld by the government. A certain minimum use of both currencies may then be ensured, and the s function may be concave from the point of view of the individual even though it is not concave for the society as a whole.

The theory of currency substitution is sometimes said to be in conflict with *Gresham's law.* 'Bad money drives good money out of circulation.' One explanation for this empirical phenomenon is that an individual who can choose to pay with either of two currencies in his possession will pay with the depreciating currency and keep the other.[22] Only if the seller does not accept the depreciating currency will the buyer pay with the other. However, the law often obliges the seller to accept the domestic money. The reason why Gresham's law is not in conflict with currency substitution is that it is a statement about the velocity of circulation and not about the stock demand for money. What it says is that the depreciating currency circulates more rapidly. Individuals may still hold larger stocks of the appreciating currency: carry mainly US dollars for transaction purposes, but spend whatever you have of the depreciating local currency first.

The currency substitution model above assumes that exchange rate uncertainty is controlled by adjusting the currency distribution of interest bearing assets. In practice it is impossible to carry out this balancing every time cash balances change. If the domestic price level is reasonably stable, while the exchange rate is not completely fixed, using foreign currency in transactions necessarily adds to the risks the individual faces. This may be an extra argument for sticking to the domestic currency. If, on the other hand, domestic currency prices are highly volatile, and the real purchasing power of foreign currency is more stable, this speaks for keeping more of the transaction balances in foreign currency.

Other views on currency substitution

Our discussion of currency substitution has been embedded in a portfolio model where there were interest bearing alternatives in both currencies. Early models of currency substitution (see, for example, Calvo and Rodriguez, 1977) often assumed that there were no interest bearing alternatives. Then the choice of liquidity and of currency composition cannot be separated. This approach leads to models which are similar to the simple portfolio model in section 1.4, but with both interest rates set to zero. In other words, the expected rate of return differential is equal to the expected rate of depreciation. This kind of model may be relevant for economies without developed financial markets, but it is misleading for more developed economies.

So far, we have focused on currency substitution going on inside the domestic economy. Some countries must of course be in the reverse position: their currency is held in transaction balances by the citizens of other countries. For good reasons, it is usually the currencies of large countries with relatively low inflation and low interest rates which are used for this purpose. The money markets in these countries will be affected by interest rates, activity levels and other conditions in foreign countries.

In modern economies interest bearing bank accounts are as important means of transaction as are bank notes. In section 3.3 we shall see how banks can be included in the portfolio model. When money pays interest, the alternative cost of liquidity is reduced. This also limits the incentives for using foreign currency in domestic transactions. Currency substitution thus seems to be most relevant in countries with a high nominal interest rate, much inflation uncertainty and underdeveloped financial markets. de Vries (1994) states as one of his 'stylized facts' from empirical studies of exchange rates that the elasticity of currency substitution is not very high.

In section 2.1 we argued that in countries with high and variable inflation minimum-variance portfolios often contain a large share of foreign currency. In the absence of credit controls the economy is *dollarized*. There is little incentive to develop markets for loans denominated in the domestic currency. With no domestic bond market, money and foreign assets are the only alternatives. In this case, the private sector's demand for foreign currency is equal to its financial wealth minus its demand for money. The latter depends on the expected nominal return on foreign currency (where the rate of depreciation is the main component), on exchange rate risk and on transaction needs. An increase in output, Y, then has a direct negative effect on the private demand for foreign currency and a corresponding positive effect on the supply of foreign currency to the central bank.

3.3 Banks

Banks hold money in reserve to meet withdrawals of deposits and to meet legal reserve requirements. Their money demand is related to the volume of bank liabilities. If bank assets or liabilities are alternatives to foreign currency assets, the demand for bank reserves may indirectly depend on the expected return on such assets. This creates a new link from the foreign exchange market to the demand for money.

In the foreign exchange market banks mainly act as middlemen and arbitrageurs. Banks' total assets and liabilities are usually large relative to their own capital. If the currency composition on the two sides does not match, banks may easily lose their own capital when exchange rates change. Thus, banks are usually reluctant to take on much exchange rate risk, and their open positions in the foreign exchange market are often constrained by prudential regulations (e.g. extra capital requirements on uncovered positions).[23] To the extent that banks have a net demand for foreign currency different from zero, this is not fundamentally different from when other agents take

Table 3.5 *A balance sheet with banks*

Asset	Private	Bank	Government	Foreign	Sum
			Sector		
Money (kr)	M_p	M_b	$-M$	0	0
Demand deposits (kr)	D	$-D$	0	0	0
Loans (kr)	$-L$	L	0	0	0
Kr bonds	B_p	B_b	B_g	0	0
$ bonds	F_p	0	F_g	F_*	0
Financial wealth (kr)	W_p	0	W_g	EF_*	0

open positions. Thus, if banks are brought into the model of section 3.1, the main change is in the money market.

In table 3.5 the balance sheet from table 3.1 has been extended to include a banking sector. The private sector is divided in its bank and non-bank parts with subscripts b and p, respectively. There are two new assets: bank deposits, D and bank loans, L, both denominated in domestic currency. The banks' net holdings of foreign currency denominated assets is assumed to be zero. For simplicity, we have normalized the two price levels to one, and the net wealth of the banks to zero.

Banks take deposits from the public, make loans and keep reserves in the form of central bank money. Bank deposits are distinguished from kroner bonds by being more liquid. Both have variable interest rates. If deposits exceed bank loans plus bank reserves, the remainder is invested in bonds. If loans exceed deposits minus bank reserves, the banks sell bonds to finance the extra loans. Thus, B_b can have either sign.

The demand for bank reserves may be heavily influenced by the exact nature of legal reserve requirements, which vary between countries. For illustrative purposes we assume here that banks keep reserves in a fixed proportion $0 < \xi < 1$ to their total liabilities. If the banks are lenders in the bond market, their total liabilities are D, and their demand for money is

$$M_b = \xi D \tag{3.30}$$

If the banks are borrowers in the bond market ($B_b < 0$), their total liabilities are $D - B_b$ and their demand for money is

$$M_b = \xi(D - B_b)$$

From table 3.5 the balance sheet equation of the banks is $D - B_b = L + M_b$. Thus, the demand for bank reserves when $B_b < 0$ can also be written

$$M_b = \xi(L + M_b)$$

or

$$M_b = \frac{\xi}{1-\xi} L = \xi_L L \qquad\qquad (3.31)$$

This shows that a reserve requirement ξ on total liabilities $(D - B_b)$ is equivalent to a reserve requirement $\xi_L = \xi/(1-\xi)$ on bank lending (L) when $B_b < 0$.

Since there are two new assets in the model, there are also two new markets. However, if the markets for bank loans and deposits are competitive and the marginal costs of providing loans and deposits are constant, the interest rates on deposits and loans, i_D and i_L, are determined by simple arbitrage conditions. Suppose $B_b < 0$. If a bank lends one krone extra, it has to borrow $(1 + \xi_L)$ kroner to finance the loan and the accompanying reserve requirement. Marginal funds are obtained from the bond market. Thus, the funding cost of the loan is $i(1 + \xi_L)$, where, as before, i is the interest rate on bonds. The banks have an additional cost per krone of loans, c_L. Competition in the market for bank loans means that $i_L = i(1 + \xi_L) + c_L$. Similarly, if a bank gets one krone extra in deposits, it can reduce its borrowing in the bond market by one krone, and thereby save the interest i. With a proportional cost, c_D, related to deposits the equilibrium deposit rate is then $i_D = i - c_D$. Given these interest rates, banks accept the deposits offered to them and grant the loans which are demanded. (Presumably loans which have been screened out because they are too risky do not count as demand.) Thus, the problem of finding an equilibrium boils down to determining the two prices i and E and, as before, it is sufficient to consider the money market and the foreign exchange market. The same is true if $B_b > 0$, but then the arbitrage conditions are changed to $i_L = i + c_L$ and $i_D = (1 - \xi)i - c_D$ since the reserve requirement then falls on deposits.

Since $i_D < i$, deposits are dominated by bonds as a store of wealth in the same way as money is. We can separate the decisions about liquidity and about exposure to exchange rate risk in the same way as in section 3.2. This means that we can use the same equilibrium condition for the foreign exchange market as before, and the public's demand for central bank money is as before

$$M_p = m(i, Y), \quad m_i < 0, \quad m_Y > 0 \qquad\qquad (3.32)$$

The alternative cost of liquidity in the form of central bank money may vary from agent to agent depending on whether the alternative is deposits, bonds or bank loans. However, since all the relevant interest rates are increasing functions of i, M_p is still decreasing in i.

Total money demand depends also on the demand for bank reserves, and thus it differs between the two cases that we distinguished above. The most interesting case is when $B_b < 0$ and $M_b = \xi_L L$. Since $i_L > i$, borrowers prefer bonds to bank loans. However, borrowing in the bond market may be possible only for the banks, the government and large firms with a first-class credit rating. Other borrowers may have to take bank loans. For them an alternative to bank loans denominated in domestic currency may be bank loans denominated in foreign currency. The borrowers at the bank adjust their kroner liquidity by borrowing more or less kroner. The demand for bank loans denominated in domestic currency is then similar to the demand for domestic bonds, and can be written

$$L = l(i, r, Y, W_p), \quad l_i < 0, \ l_r < 0, \ l_Y > 0 \tag{3.33}$$

i has a negative effect on the demand for bank loans as the borrowers economize on liquidity. Note that an increase in i raises the interest rate margin between deposits and loans since it increases the cost of keeping bank reserves. r has a negative effect on loan demand as borrowers switch to foreign currency loans when domestic currency loans become more expensive. An increase in Y raises loan demand, because some investors borrow to raise their liquidity when transaction needs are higher. In the wealth argument in the demand function we should really distinguish between the borrowers who have access to the bond market and those who have not, but this is not important for our conclusions.

The equilibrium condition for the money market when M is exogenous can now be written

$$M = m(i, Y) + \xi_L l(i, i - i_* - e_e, Y, W_p) \tag{3.34}$$

Through the demand for bank loans and bank reserves money demand here depends on the foreign exchange market represented by i_* and e_e, and also on wealth, which depends on E. Unlike in section 3.1 the interest rate is directly influenced by the foreign exchange market even if M is kept constant.

The total money demand in (3.34) depends positively on Y and negatively on i, as before. An increase in i_* raises money demand because it raises the demand for bank reserves. Hence, if the exchange rate is fixed and the central bank sterilizes, the domestic interest rate now responds positively to the foreign interest rate. Sterilization no longer insulates the domestic interest rate. By differentiating (3.34) we find that

$$\frac{di}{di_*} = \frac{\xi_L l_r}{m_i + \xi_L(l_i + l_r)}$$

which is between zero and one, and likely to be modest if ξ_L is not too large.

With a floating exchange rate, (3.34) and (3.14) must be solved simultaneously for i and E. Under standard assumptions, foreign exchange market equilibrium (3.14) defines a negative relation between the interest rate and the exchange rate. This is drawn as the FF curve in figure 3.3. In general, the slope of the relation between i and E defined by money market equilibrium (3.34) – the MM curve in figure 3.3 – is ambiguous, because the effect of E on money demand is ambiguous. The reason for this ambiguity is that an increase in E has two opposing effects on money demand: (1) e_e declines, r increases, borrowers shift to foreign currency loans and the demand for bank reserves goes down. (2) If borrowers have borrowed positive amounts of both currencies, the share of foreign currency in the loan portfolio initially increases. Borrowers rebalance their portfolios by reducing their foreign currency borrowing and increasing their domestic currency borrowing. This increases the demand for

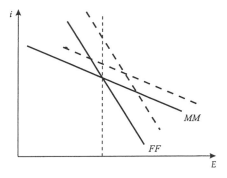

Figure 3.3 Simultaneous equilibrium in the markets for foreign exchange and money.

bank reserves. Thus, the expectations effect and the portfolio balance effect work in opposite directions. The downward slope assumed in figure 3.3 corresponds to the case where the expectations effect dominate. In that case an increase in E lowers money demand, and hence leads to lower interest rates. In general we cannot tell which curve is the steeper. Most likely, however, it is the FF curve. This will be the case if the exchange rate has a comparatively strong influence on the demand for foreign exchange, and the interest rate a comparatively strong influence on the demand for money.

An increase in i_* shifts both curves in figure 3.3 upward – i.e. for a given E, a higher i is required to sustain equilibrium in both the foreign exchange and the money market. The shift in the FF curve is the greater. Equilibrium in the foreign exchange market is preserved at the initial E if the increase in i is equal to the increase in i_*. A smaller increase in i is sufficient to preserve equilibrium in the money market, since i reduces money demand not only through r but also directly (cf. (3.34)). As we see from figure 3.3, the net result of an increase in i_* is a depreciation. The only thing we can say about i is that it does not increase more than i_*. Theoretically it may even fall. If the MM curve slopes upward, we get the same result, except that the possibility of a fall in i is excluded. The main point is that the demand for bank reserves can create a positive relationship between the domestic and foreign interest rates also under floating exchange rates.

The case where banks are net lenders in the bond market ($B_b > 0$) is less different from what we have encountered earlier. The demand for bank reserves is then $M_b = \xi D$. Because deposits are dominated by bonds as a store of wealth, and because all relevant alternative costs depend on i, we can write the demand for deposits as

$$D = d(i, Y), \quad d_Y > 0 \tag{3.35}$$

Here the sign of d_i is in doubt. Suppose there is an increase in i. On the one hand, it then becomes more expensive to keep liquidity in cash rather than in deposits. This tends to increase the demand for deposits. On the other hand, the margin between bank loans and deposits and between deposits and bonds increases because of the increased costs of bank reserves. This reduces the demand for deposits. The equilibrium condition for the money market is now

$$M = m(i, Y) + \xi d(i, Y) \tag{3.36}$$

which is independent of i_*, E and e_e. As long as the overall effect of i on money demand is negative, nothing has changed qualitatively from section 3.1. A more detailed analysis should probably take account of the fact that ξ usually depends negatively on i for reasons explained in, for example, Tobin (1982), and when this is taken account of there is less reason to worry that the overall effect of i on money demand is positive.

Instead of using the supply of base money, $M0 = M = M_p + M_b$, as an operational target, the central bank may target broader measures of money supply like $M1 = M_p + D$ or $M2 = M_p + D - B_b$ (assuming $B_b < 0$). In the model here the demand for $M1$ is independent of i_* and E. Thus targeting $M1$, unlike targeting $M0$, insulates the interest rate from foreign influences. In fact it leads us back to a model which is equivalent to that of section 3.1 with exogenous money supply. Targeting $M2$ is equivalent to targeting L, since these are proportional. Since the demand for L depends among other things on i_* and E this again means giving foreign variables influence on i. From this it may seem that those who argue for a monetary target as a means to independence in monetary policy should opt for an $M1$ target, although in practice it may be difficult to distinguish between $M1$ and $M2$.

However, the above cases are merely examples of how the existence of financial intermediaries may change the money market. With different institutional assumptions one can create other examples. The main point from the present section is thus that one should pay appropriate attention to the institutional structure of the country one is studying.

Goodhart (1994) argues that central banks are unable to control the money supply in any case. One reason is that there are large short-run fluctuations in the demand for cash and for bank reserves. Some of them are foreseeable, related to dates for tax payments and seasonal shopping, some are more unpredictable. Relative to these fluctuations the interest elasticity of money demand is small. Thus, the central bank has to accommodate them, or else it risks creating a liquidity crisis in the banking system. What the central bank can do is set the interest rates at which the other banks can borrow or deposit money at the central bank. It can also determine how much to buy or sell of certain assets like bonds and treasury bills, but somewhere in the system there has to be an open outlet where banks can get the cash they need. This could be a discount window, a credit line or some other arrangement. This also means that central bank borrowing and lending (B) is not under direct control either. One may object that since M is an item on the central bank's balance sheet, it should in principle be able to control M. However, the practical relevance of regimes where M or B are exogenous can still be questioned.

3.4 Currency boards, target zones and the role of foreign exchange reserves

This section discusses three issues related to fixed exchange rates. The first is how large foreign exchange reserves are needed to protect a fixed exchange rate. Next we describe the workings of a *currency board*, which is a particular institutional arrangement for ensuring that reserves are adequate and exchange rates stay fixed. Finally we describe the workings of *target zones* where the exchange rate is allowed to float within some limits.

The role of foreign exchange reserves

If capital mobility is high, foreign exchange reserves may seem to be of little use. This need not be true. We have earlier mentioned the possibility that a central bank may run out of reserves if the exchange rate is exposed to a speculative attack, or if the central bank attempts to lower the domestic interest rate. Why can the central banks not amass sufficient reserves? How can it be possible for the public to sell an unlimited amount of kroner? The answer to the last question is that if the central bank fixes the kroner interest rate, it must be ready to lend kroner in unlimited amounts. The central bank provides the speculators with money to speculate against the central bank. This happens as long as the central bank does not raise interest rates to a level where speculation is deemed unprofitable.

The central bank is obliged to sell foreign currency only against payment in domestic money – i.e. in central bank money. If initially the foreign exchange reserve is greater than the money supply, the central bank can always fend off a speculative attack by stopping all new lending of kroner and buy all central bank money which is presented to it. However, such a policy may put the country's banking system under severe strain. Speculators will want to withdraw kroner from their bank accounts to buy foreign currency. Banks will run down their cash reserves, and will be unable to borrow more from the central bank. They will then either have to raise interest rates to a level which makes kroner deposits compete with foreign currency, or they will have to borrow foreign currency and change it to kroner at the central bank. In the former case the banks will most likely lose money, in the latter case they assume a huge exchange rate risk. If the central bank wants to avoid this strain on the banking system, it must be ready to buy not just the outstanding stock of central bank money, but instead the whole of $M2$. (Actually something less might do as the public will always want some liquidity in kroner.)

Even if the central bank is prepared to buy all bank deposits, there is a problem with the interest rate. Speculators will also want to borrow from the banks. This gives banks the opportunity to raise their lending rates. If speculation continues, high lending rates may create severe problems for many of the banks' customers. The size of this problem depends on how often interest rates are adjusted on existing loans. If interest rates are fixed for long terms, the damage from a short period of high interest rates may be low. If most loans have floating rates, the problem is greater. In return for its liquidity support during a currency crisis the central bank may demand that banks do not raise interest rates on running loans, even if they have a right to. As long as the liquidity support is given on sufficiently generous terms, it need not harm the banks. At the same time it is to the benefit of their customers. The economy could probably function for a while with interest rates on new kroner loans which for most purposes would seem prohibitive.

A central bank with sufficiently large foreign exchange reserves and sufficiently low concern for interest rates may thus have a credible strategy for fending off speculative attacks. The size of the reserves should be compared to a broad measure of the money stock. However, it is not necessary to have full coverage, since people will hardly try to change all domestic money into foreign currency.

The cost of keeping sufficient reserves may be quite high, however. The reserves in question must be fairly liquid. One cannot expect to have time to arrange the necessary amount of credit when the crisis is there. For a country which has to borrow its reserves, the margin between borrowing rates and the rate of return received on liquid assets could be high. For a government with large positive net foreign currency assets, it is less expensive to keep a high degree of liquidity.

It is a paradox that if the foreign exchange reserves are large enough to create a credible defence against speculative attacks, the central bank may have less freedom in setting interest rates. If huge reserves make the fixed exchange rate fully credible, that removes all exchange rate risk. Capital mobility may then become perfect. Because of the credible commitment to the fixed exchange rate, the interest rate must be equal to the foreign interest rate.

Currency boards

Some countries with their own currency do not have a central bank in the sense of a bank which lends to the other banks.[24] Instead they have what is called a *currency board*. Examples today are Hong Kong, Argentina, Brunei and Estonia among others. A currency board in its pure form prints money and sells it at a fixed price against payment in foreign currency. The foreign exchange it acquires is kept in reserve, which means that foreign exchange reserves always cover 100 per cent of the outstanding notes. A currency board may provide a credible commitment to a fixed exchange rate, since everyone knows that the board is able to keep the exchange rate fixed. This is not by itself sufficient for credibility, however, since the ability to do something is not the same as actually doing it. The workings of a currency board depend crucially on whether the home country has actually adopted the foreign currency as its own, or whether there is still a domestic currency.

Adopting the foreign currency as one's own means that the exchange rate is eliminated. Contracts, including debt contracts, are made in the foreign currency, and the foreign currency performs all the traditional functions of money. The domestic currency effectively does not exist, and the currency board is just a way of capturing seigniorage and of organizing the local supply of bank notes efficiently. Since the domestic currency does not exist, there is of course no domestic currency interest rate. The foreign interest rate takes its place. Since there is no exchange rate in the usual sense, and since the notes have full reserve coverage, there is no room for speculation. A lack of confidence in the promise of redemption would only result in notes being redeemed and replaced in daily transactions with foreign notes, with no further consequences for the economy.

If the domestic currency continues to exist (aside from as notes) and to be used in debt contracts, there will still be a domestic currency interest rate. If the system does not have full credibility, this interest rate may deviate from the foreign interest rate. However, the currency board does not do any lending or borrowing in domestic currency, and thus it has no monetary policy proper. The interest rate is determined by the market alone. If there is a speculative run on the currency, interest rates go up, as in ordinary fixed exchange rate systems when there is no sterilization. The currency board has the ability to avoid a devaluation by buying back the notes in circulation in the necessary amounts. The problem is the same as discussed above, namely that the high interest rates can damage the economy and cause problems for the banking system. However, it is hoped that the institutional arrangement will induce the market to believe that the exchange rate target has absolute priority. As long as this is believed, there is no speculation, and the defences are not tested.

That currency boards are unable to support domestic banks with liquidity loans may put them at a disadvantage relative to foreign banks which have direct access to a central bank. The local banks must keep larger liquid reserves or have access to credit lines with foreign banks.

Target zones

Fixed exchange rates are usually not completely fixed. They are allowed to vary within a band around the official central parity. The normal width of the band, or *target zone*, was plus/minus 1 per cent in the Bretton Woods era (1945–71). Since then most countries with fixed rates have used wider bands. The purpose of having a band is twofold: first, it gives some freedom in setting interest rates even when capital mobility is high (see Svenson, 1994). Second, it creates some extra exchange rate risk which can be useful when defending the exchange rate against speculative pressure.

The workings of a target zone is illustrated in figure 3.4. Initially the supply curve for foreign currency is S_0. The equilibrium is at the official central parity, E_c, and the foreign exchange reserve is F_{g0}. The upper and lower limits of the target zone are E_{max} and E_{min}, respectively. If there is a portfolio shift away from domestic currency, the supply curve shifts to the left to S_1 or S_2. The central bank is obliged to intervene only when the exchange rate threatens to leave the target zone. Thus, when there is a

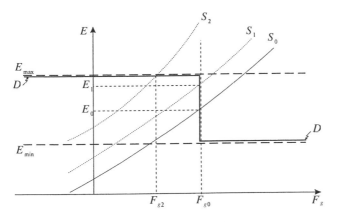

Figure 3.4 A foreign exchange market with a target zone.

small shift, as from S_0 to S_1, it does not intervene, and the exchange rate moves to E_1. However, if the shift is larger, as from S_0 to S_2, the central bank has to sell foreign currency in order to keep the exchange rate within the target zone. The new exchange rate is E_{max} and the foreign exchange reserve is reduced to F_{g2}. The behaviour of the central bank can be represented by the curve marked D. This shows how much foreign currency the central bank buys depending on what the exchange rate is. The equilibrium is where this curve intersects with the supply curve.

If an exchange rate is completely fixed, and the public perceives no risk that it will ever change, then capital mobility is perfect, expected depreciation is zero and domestic and foreign interest rates have to be equal. Matters are different in a target zone. Suppose the zone is fully credible in the sense that the probability that the exchange rate leaves the zone is zero. The exchange rate can still vary within the band. Hence, neither expected depreciation nor exchange rate risk are zero. This makes deviations in interest rates possible, although within a limited range.

When the target zone is fully credible, the best return on a foreign currency investment is obtained when the exchange rate depreciates to E_{max}. Hence, when today's exchange rate is E, the maximum return on foreign currency is $(1 + i_*)E_{max}/E$. Similarly, the minimum return is $(1 + i_*)E_{min}/E$. Thus, for any initial E the domestic interest rate is constrained to the interval defined by

$$(1 + i_*)E_{min}/E \leq 1 + i \leq (1 + i_*)E_{max}/E \tag{3.37}$$

If i is outside of this interval, one of the currencies is certain to yield the highest return, and all investments will go in that direction. The interval can be used to test whether a target zone is fully credible (see Svensson, 1991). If the observed interest rates and exchange rate violate one of the inequalities, investors must believe that there is a positive probability for a parity change.

Equation (3.37) also tells us how much i may deviate from i_* when the exchange rate is within a credible target zone. The highest conceivable return on foreign currency is then obtained when the exchange rate depreciates from E_{min} to E_{max}, the lowest when it appreciates from E_{max} to E_{min}. Even a rather narrow target zone permits large deviations in short-run interest rates. Suppose the width of the target zone is plus/minus 2 per cent. The maximum possible appreciation/depreciation within the zone is then 4 per cent. Over three months this corresponds roughly to a rate of depreciation of 16 per cent measured per annum. The domestic three-month interest rate can then deviate from the foreign interest rate by 16 percentage points in either direction. For long-term interest rates the range is smaller, plus/minus four percentage points for the one-year rate.

However, the figures just mentioned grossly exaggerate the potential for interest rate policy. The amount of exchange rate risk within a narrow target zone is necessarily small. Thus, capital mobility should be very high when the zone is credible, and interest rates cannot deviate much from uncovered interest rate parity. It is well documented that when the official parity is not changed, the exchange rate tends to return towards the centre of the target zone over time. Thus, investors will not be far off the mark if they expect the rate of depreciation to be $e_e = \alpha(E_c - E)/E$, where α is the speed of convergence towards E_c. Interest rate parity then implies that

$$1 + i = (1 + i_*)(1 + e_e) = (1 + i_*)\frac{\alpha E_c + (1 - \alpha)E}{E} \tag{3.38}$$

For a given i this determines E. The central bank can raise i to the point where E appreciates to E_{min}, lower i to the point where E depreciates to E_{max}. Hence, the range of possible interest rates is given by

$$(1 + i_*)\frac{\alpha E_c + (1 - \alpha)E_{max}}{E_{max}} \leq 1 + i \leq (1 + i_*)\frac{\alpha E_c + (1 - \alpha)E_{min}}{E_{min}} \tag{3.39}$$

Suppose α is equal to 0.2 per year, which is not unreasonable in light of empirical estimates. Suppose also that the width of the target zone is plus/minus 2 per cent. Then the expected rate of depreciation at E_{min} is 0.4 per cent per year. The expected rate of appreciation at E_{max} is also 0.4 per cent per year. Thus, the range that is available for the central bank when setting short-run interest rates is just plus/minus 0.4 per cent around the foreign interest rate. If the expected speed of convergence is higher, the range is wider (plus/minus 2 per cent when $\alpha = 1$). However, such interest rate differentials may be difficult to maintain for more than very short periods. If E is kept close to E_{min} or E_{max} for a long period, private agents will have reason to revise downwards their estimates of the speed of convergence. The scope for interest rate deviations is somewhat larger if we allow for a risk premium and the central bank is willing to undertake large-scale interventions. However, the potential for an independent interest rate policy within a credible target zone seems rather limited.

The extra uncertainty that a target zone yields is most useful when the zone is not fully credible. Suppose the public perceives that there is a certain probability for a devaluation while a revaluation is excluded. If the exchange rate is completely fixed, the risk is one-sided. If there is a target zone, the central bank can allow the exchange rate to depreciate to E_{max}. There is then some probability that the exchange rate appreciates towards, or even beyond, E_c. The risk has become two-sided. This reduces the expected rate of depreciation. It may then be easier to fend off a speculative attack. Small adjustments of the official central parity may also be carried out without jumps in the actual exchange rate from one day to the next. This can be accomplished by letting the new target zone overlap with the old. It may then be possible to carry out frequent controlled realignments without intolerable speculative pressures building up.

In practice countries with target zones often intervene even if the outer bounds have not been reached. One reason could be that allowing the exchange rate to hit one of the bounds entails the risk of attracting the attention of new groups of speculators who may take this as a sign that a parity change is imminent.

When the private investors expects the central bank to defend the bounds of the target zone, these expectations have consequences for the supply curve and the behaviour of the exchange rate within the target zone. This intricate interplay has given rise to a large literature initiated by Krugman (1991). For surveys see Svensson (1992), Krugman and Miller (1992) and Garber and Svensson (1995). One conclusion is that a credible target zone dampens the response of the exchange rate to exogenous events that would not have brought it outside the target zone even under a free float.

Exercises

1. Use the equilibrium conditions for the foreign exchange market and the money market to derive analytic expressions for the effect on the exchange rate of a domestic open market operation, a sterilized intervention and an unsterilized intervention.

2. Suppose $e_e = v(E) + \mu$ where μ can be interpreted as a shock to exchange rate expectations and $v' < 0$. What is the effect of μ on i and F_g in regime II. Compare to regime III.

3. The degree of sterilization, s, can vary between zero and one. Discuss how the effect on the foreign exchange reserves of an increase in the foreign interest rate i_* depends on the degree of sterilization when the exchange rate is fixed.

4. Suppose the exchange rate is fixed and there is no sterilization. What is the effect of a devaluation on i? What is the total effect of the devaluation on the foreign exchange reserves?

5. In section 3.1 we assumed that the domestic price level is exogenous. Instead it may be assumed that $P = P_h^\alpha (EP_*)^{1-\alpha}$ where P_h and P_* are pre-determined prices of domestically produced and foreign goods, respectively. Assume the regime with full sterilization. How does the inclusion of the exchange rate in the price index change the effect of a devaluation on the foreign exchange reserves? Does the effect of Y on i change in any of the regimes?

6. Central banks may intervene both in the spot and in the forward market for foreign currency. Explain why a sale of kroner in the forward market is equivalent to a sterilized sale of kroner in the spot market.

7. Suppose the exchange rate is fixed. We want to compare two cases. In case A capital mobility is imperfect. The central bank uses i to keep the exchange rate fixed, while F_g is constant. In case B capital mobility is perfect. (a) Explain why i_* has the same effect on i in the two cases. (b) Is the same true for other exogenous shocks? (c) Is a regression of e on $i - i_*$ suitable for testing the hypothesis that capital mobility is perfect?

8. Suppose the exchange rate is fixed. We want to compare two policy regimes, one where B and E and one where F_g and E are exogenous. What are the effects of Y and of i_* on i and F_g in the two cases? What does the degree of capital mobility mean for the comparison?

4   The monetary theory of the exchange rate

The focus in this chapter is on a floating exchange rate. In chapters 1–3 we have seen how important exchange rate expectations are in determining the exchange rate. So far, we have just postulated that expected depreciation is a function of the present exchange rate. The main purpose of the present chapter is to show how this postulated function can be replaced by the assumption of *rational expectations*. By 'rational expectations' we here mean expectations which are consistent with the model we use for determining the exchange rate.

The monetary approach to exchange rate determination is useful for introducing rational expectations because it provides a particularly simple model. It is based on five main assumptions:

- Perfect mobility of goods and services, which implies *purchasing power parity* (PPP). Measured in the same currency goods prices are the same at home and abroad.
- Perfect mobility of capital, which implies *uncovered interest rate parity*.
- Wage flexibility, which implies that domestic output is determined from the *supply side*.
- *Exogenous money supply*.
- *Model-consistent expectations*.

We still focus on a small economy, which means that the foreign price level and the foreign interest rate are exogenous.

The monetary approach to exchange rate determination has a long history (see Frenkel, 1976). Of particular importance were the writings of *Gustav Cassel* in the period 1919–30. Promoted by Robert Mundell (1968) and Harry Johnson, the monetary approach had a revival in the early and mid-1970s as documented in the collection by Frenkel and Johnson (1978). In this period rational expectations were fully integrated into the theory. Before the mid-1970s the stock-based monetary approach competed with approaches that focused on the current account. The monetary approach can be seen as a precursor to the more general portfolio approach. It is the special case we get by assuming perfect capital mobility and an exogenous money supply.[25]

Section 4.1 presents the basic monetary model and shows how a solution with rational expectations can be found. It also discusses the effect of monetary policy. In section 4.2 we contrast the effects of anticipated and unanticipated changes in the exogenous variables. Section 4.3 contains some concluding remarks about the need for a 'nominal anchor' in order to make the exchange rate determinate.

4.1 Exchange rate equilibrium with rational expectations

As we saw in section 3.1, when we have perfect capital mobility and the money supply is exogenous, the exchange rate can be determined by the interest parity condition and the equilibrium condition for the money market. That was for a given price level, P, and a given output level, Y. In the monetary approach the domestic price level is given by the purchasing power parity condition, $P = EP_*$, where E is the exchange rate and P_* the foreign price level. Owing to wage flexibility, the output level, Y, is given from the supply side and exogenous relative to the foreign exchange market.

Taking account of the fact that $P = EP_*$, the equilibrium condition for the money market can be written

$$\frac{M}{EP_*} = m(i, Y) \tag{4.1}$$

Since we have perfect capital mobility and model-consistent expectations, $i = i_* + e$. We can write this as a differential equation for E:

$$\frac{\dot{E}}{E} = i - i_* \tag{4.2}$$

Equations (4.1) and (4.2) form a closed system in two endogenous variables, E and i. The exogenous variables are P_*, i_*, Y and M. This simple system of two equations constitutes the basic version of the monetary approach.

The equilibrium condition for the money market (4.1) can be inverted to yield

$$i = i\left(\frac{M}{EP_*}, Y\right)$$

where $i_1 < 0$ and $i_2 > 0$. If we insert this in the differential equation (4.2), we get

$$\frac{\dot{E}}{E} = i\left(\frac{M}{EP_*}, Y\right) - i_* \tag{4.3}$$

E is the only endogenous variable in this equation.

In order to determine the solution of a differential equation we normally need an initial condition. Here we have none. At any moment of time, the exchange rate is free to jump to any level. It is not bound by what it has been in the past. The lack of an initial condition for E means that, unless we impose a new condition, the model has an infinity of solutions.[26]

The differential equation (4.3) is fundamentally unstable, as illustrated in the phase diagram in figure 4.1. The exchange rate E has a positive feedback on itself. The higher the level of E, the higher its rate of growth $\dot{E}/E$. The slope of the relationship between $\dot{E}/E$ and E is $-i_1 M/E^2 P_* > 0$. A higher exchange rate means a lower real quantity of money and, thus, a higher interest rate. Since interest parity holds, a higher interest rate could come about only if the rate of depreciation is higher.

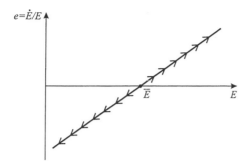

Figure 4.1 Exchange rate dynamics in the monetary model.

The background for the upward-sloping relationship may be easier to grasp if we turn the argument round and start with the rate of depreciation. We have assumed that actual and expected depreciation are equal. A higher actual rate of depreciation also means higher expected depreciation. Higher expected depreciation means a higher interest rate, since there is perfect capital mobility. A higher interest rate means lower demand for money. As the investors try to rid themselves of domestic money, they demand more foreign currency, and the price of foreign currency goes up. The upward-sloping curve thus represents the familiar result that an expected depreciation leads to an immediate actual depreciation. The only thing we have added is that the expected depreciation and the actual future depreciation are equal.

We shall discuss the solution of the model in two steps, starting first with the case where the exogenous variables, P_*, i_*, M and Y, are constant. Since no initial value for E is given, any starting point along the E axis is possible. The stationary point, $\bar{E}$, is defined as the value of E which makes $\dot{E} = 0$ – i.e. which makes E constant. If we start with $E > \bar{E}$, then $\dot{E} > 0$ and the exchange rate continues to depreciate forever. Not only does it depreciate, it does so at an accelerating speed ($\dot{E}/E$ increases). If we start with $E < \bar{E}$, then $\dot{E} < 0$ and the exchange rate continues to appreciate forever. Only if we start exactly at the stationary solution will the exchange rate ever become constant.

The monetary approach pins down the initial exchange rate by assuming that E jumps immediately to the stationary value, $\bar{E}$. Then it stays there. Since M and P_* are also constant, this implies that the real quantity of money, M/EP_*, stays constant after the initial jump. According to the differential equation (4.3) the exchange rate is stationary ($\dot{E} = 0$) if, and only if, $i = i(M/EP_*, Y) = i_*$, which is the same as

$$\frac{M}{EP_*} = m(i_*, Y) \tag{4.4}$$

In other words, the equilibrium exchange rate is the exchange rate which makes the domestic interest rate, determined in the domestic money market, equal to the foreign interest rate. The equilibrium condition for the money market with $i = i_*$ inserted determines the exchange rate.

The argument for choosing $E = \bar{E}$ is derived from the long-run consequences of following any of the alternative, explosive paths starting outside $\bar{E}$. The paths with accelerating *de*preciation imply a steadily increasing price level, and thus the real quantity of money tends to zero as time goes towards infinity. The inflation rate and the nominal interest rate are also increasing steadily. In the end currency substitution will take place (see section 3.2), as it becomes more attractive to use foreign money, or even certain commodities, as means of exchange. The end would be hyperinflation and a breakdown of the monetary system.

The paths with accelerating *ap*preciation imply a steadily decreasing price level, and thus the real quantity of money tends to increase. The interest rate is decreasing steadily as the rate of appreciation increases. As the model stands, domestic interest rates will in the end become negative. People may then hold on to their money, which gives a higher return than bonds, and instead find other means of transaction.

Either way, if the economy goes too far on one of the explosive paths, money seems to lose its function as a means of exchange. The belief in the solution $E = \bar{E}$ can thus be interpreted as a belief in the stability and continuation of the country's monetary system. This belief could be underpinned by a belief that if the economy ventures on one of the unstable paths, the authorities must sooner or later step in and somehow break the trend of ever-depreciating or ever-appreciating exchange rates.

One criticism against this explanation is that we have not actually modelled what happens when the economy goes to the extremes, or government intervenes. In particular, one can argue that in a more realistic model the money demand function changes when the interest rate becomes zero. Then bonds cease to dominate money as a store of wealth. Agents are indifferent between holding their wealth in money, domestic bonds and foreign bonds. Thus, the money demand function of the model breaks down when $\dot{E}/E = -i_*$. We can think of money demand as becoming infinitely elastic when the interest rate goes to zero. A possible solution is that the appreciation continues at a constant speed equal to $-i_*$. The price level continues to fall. The real money supply continues to increase towards infinity. Sooner or later it will exceed the net wealth of the private sector. This will not destroy the monetary system in the same way as an accelerating appreciation. However, it may create some extremely unbalanced portfolios. Investors may start to care about exchange rate risk. Even in this case one can argue that there are some unmodelled features which will prevent the economy from continuing on the predicted path forever. That people believe in the stable solution may still be a good working hypothesis.

So far we have assumed that the exogenous variables are constant. The solution method can be generalized to cases where the exogenous variables are expected to change over time. The basic differential equation (4.3) is, of course, unstable in the general case too. This means that the exchange rate explodes unless one chooses a particular initial value for it. In other words, people are assumed to believe in the only exchange rate path which is stable in the sense that it does not explode. An example is given in section 4.2.

The principle of choosing the non-explosive path for the exchange rate is not completely general. An important part of the argument for choosing $E = \bar{E}$ was that along the alternative explosive paths the real quantity of money went either towards zero or towards infinity. This argument breaks down if M or P_* are themselves growing continuously. We can imagine cases where the exchange rate continues to appreciate or depreciate forever, while all the real magnitudes in the economy are constant. Then, rather than requiring that E should not explode, it seems reasonable to require that the real quantity of money, M/EP_* should not explode.

We shall see how the solution can be generalized to a case where the nominal quantity of money, M, and foreign prices, P_*, grow at constant rates μ and p_*, respectively. Define a stationary equilibrium as one where the real quantity of money is constant. This means that

$$\frac{\dot{M}}{M} - \frac{\dot{E}}{E} - \frac{\dot{P_*}}{P_*} = 0 \text{ – i.e. } \mu - e - p_* = 0$$

or

$$e = \mu - p_*$$

The domestic interest rate is then $i = i_* + e = i_* + \mu - p_*$. Insert this in the equilibrium condition for the money market and you get

$$\frac{M}{EP_*} = m(i_* + \mu - p_*, Y) \tag{4.5}$$

or

$$E = \frac{M}{P_* m(i_* + \mu - p_*, Y)}$$

In analogy with (4.4) above, this determines the level of the exchange rate which is consistent with M/EP_* being stationary (E is the only endogenous variable in the equation). The presumption is that the exchange rate jumps immediately onto the path determined by (4.5). As can easily be shown, all other paths consistent with (4.3) makes the real quantity of money either explode or go to zero.[27] The previous solution (4.4) is a special case of (4.5).

If we combine the stationarity condition $e = \mu - p_*$ with the equation $p = e + p_*$, derived from purchasing power parity, we find that $p = \mu$, or: *domestic inflation is equal to the rate of growth of the money supply.*

Equation (4.5) can be used to discuss the effect of monetary policy on the exchange rate. It is necessary to distinguish between one-time changes and changes in the rate of growth of the money supply. If there is a one-time increase in M by, say, x per cent, the exchange rate E immediately depreciates by x per cent. After that the exchange rate continues to grow at the rate $\mu - p_*$, as before. An increase in the yearly growth rate of the money supply, μ, means an equal increase in the yearly rate of depreciation, e. The nominal interest rate increases by the same amount. This lowers the demand for money. The result is an immediate depreciation now. Thus a move to a more inflationary monetary policy not only leads to a continuous depreciation, but also to an immediate upward jump in E and P.

In the monetary model the domestic price level and the domestic interest rate are completely insulated against nominal shocks from abroad. By a 'nominal shock' is meant either a change in P_* or a change in p_* accompanied by an equal change in i_*, leaving the foreign real interest rate, $i_* - p_*$, constant. An upward jump in the foreign price level of x per cent leads to an immediate appreciation of x per cent, and the domestic price level is unaffected. Since $e = \mu - p_*$, a higher p_* leads to an equal decline in e. The domestic inflation rate, $p = e + p_* = \mu$, is unaffected. The domestic interest rate $i = i_* + e = i_* + \mu - p_*$ is also unaffected since by assumption $i_* - p_*$ is constant. There is then no effect on money demand, and no effect on the initial exchange rate or price level.

4.2 Temporary and permanent shocks, anticipations and news

Note: The notation in this section deviates from the standard notation in the rest of the book. For some level variables we use small letters to denote their natural logarithms. In particular $e = \ln E$, $m = \ln M$, $p = \ln P$, $p_* = \ln P_*$, $y = \ln Y$. Relative rates of change are denoted $\dot{e} = \dot{E}/E$, $\dot{p} = \dot{P}/P$ and $\dot{p}_* = \dot{P}_*/P_*$.

In section 4.1 we focused on particularly simple cases where the exogenous variables were either constant or grew with constant rates. In general a non-explosive solution to the differential equation (4.3) must depend on the whole future time path of all the exogenous variables. In order to get a better grip on what this means, we shall now study a log-linearized version of the model. The advantage of this simplification is that we can derive an explicit solution for the time path of the exchange rate. This enables us to say more about the effects of anticipated and unanticipated shocks. In an example we shall also see how we can think of the exchange rate between two countries as determined jointly by the monetary policies of both.[28]

The log-linear version of the money demand function (4.1) is

$$m - p = -\eta i + \kappa y \tag{4.6}$$

where η and κ are positive constants. By taking logs of $P = EP_*$, the purchasing parity condition can be written

$$p = e + p_* \tag{4.7}$$

The interest parity condition can be written

$$\dot{e} = i - i_* \tag{4.8}$$

where $\dot{e}$ is by definition the same as $\dot{E}/E$.

By inserting for i from (4.6) and for p from (4.7) in the interest parity condition (4.8), we get the differential equation

$$\dot{e} = (1/\eta)e - z \tag{4.9}$$

where

$$z = (1/\eta)(m - p_* - \kappa y) + i_*$$

summarizes the exogenous influences. Since (4.9) is just a special case of (4.3), it is no surprise to find that the equation is unstable. The equation is linear. Its general solution can be written (e is the base of the natural logarithms)

$$e(t) = \left[e(t_0) - \int_{t_0}^{t} z(\tau)e^{-(1/\eta)(\tau - t_0)}d\tau \right] e^{(1/\eta)(t - t_0)}$$

As in section 4.1, $e(t_0)$ is determined by the requirement that $e(t)$ should tend to a finite, strictly positive value when t goes to infinity. In the expression for $e(t)$ the exponential term at the end obviously goes to infinity as t goes to infinity. Thus, in order for the solution for $e(t)$ not to explode, the term in brackets must go to zero. It does so if, and only if:

$$e(t_0) = \int_{t_0}^{\infty} z(\tau)e^{-(1/\eta)(\tau - t_0)}d\tau$$

When this is inserted in the expression for $e(t)$ above, and $z(\tau)$ is spelled out, we get

$$e(t) = \int_{t}^{\infty} \left[(1/\eta)(m - p_* - \kappa y) + i_* \right] e^{-(1/\eta)(\tau - t)}d\tau \tag{4.10}$$

Naturally, this is the same as $e(t_0)$ above with t_0 replaced by t. Any t is a new starting point. Among the many possible solutions to (4.9) we choose (4.10) because it is the only one which does not explode. It says that the present exchange rate is the discounted sum of the whole future path of the exogenous variables as they enter in z. The discount rate is the inverse of the interest elasticity of the demand for money.[29]

The rational expectations solution for e in (4.10) should be compared to the solution for e in the case with perfect capital mobility and regressive expectations in section 3.1. The signs of the effects of m, p_* and i_* are the same even if the modelling of expectations is changed. However, in (4.10) changes in the exogenous variables must last for some period if they are to have a measurable effect on e. It is the integral over time which counts. In general, regressive expectations will mimic the rational expectations of the model above if the changes in the exogenous variables are expected to be temporary.

In principle, any change in the expected future path of the exogenous variables affects the present exchange rate. However, the discounting in (4.10) means that changes far into the future have little effect, especially if the interest elasticity of the demand for money is low.

There is one qualification to the solution we have found. The integral in (4.10) must converge. This means that the growth rate of z must be below $1/\eta$ in absolute value as t goes to infinity. If this is not the case, the integral does not exist and our method of solution breaks down. Presumably one must then give up the requirement that e

should tend to a finite value, as we did in section 4.1 when we investigated the effect of money growing at a constant rate forever. Instead we may, as there, require that the real money stock approach a finite, strictly positive level.

Temporary and permanent changes

When studying the effect of changes in the exogenous variables, it is convenient to write $z(t)$ as

$$z(t) = \bar{z}(t) + \Delta z(t)$$

where $\bar{z}(t)$ is the original path which we take as our starting point and $\Delta z(t)$ is the change in the path of z caused by the change in the exogenous variables. Given this decomposition the solution (4.10) can be expressed as

$$e(t) = \bar{e}(t) + \int_t^\infty \Delta z(\tau) \mathrm{e}^{-(1/\eta)(\tau-t)} d\tau \tag{4.11}$$

where

$$\bar{e}(t) = \int_t^\infty \bar{z}(\tau) \mathrm{e}^{-(1/\eta)(\tau-t)} d\tau$$

is the time path of the exchange rate that was expected before the changes in the exogenous variables.

In order to study the effect of temporary versus permanent changes in exogenous variables, assume that

$$z(t) = \begin{cases} z_0 + \Delta z & \text{if } t_0 < t < t_1 \\ z_0 & \text{if } t_1 < t \end{cases} \tag{4.12}$$

Here z_0 and Δz are constants. According to (4.11) the solution for the exchange rate for $t_0 < t < t_1$ is then

$$e(t) = \bar{e} + \eta \left[1 - \mathrm{e}^{-(1/\eta)(t_1-t)} \right] \Delta z \tag{4.13}$$

Since z_0 is constant, $\bar{e}$ too is constant. If the exogenous change is an increase in the quantity of money, $\Delta z = (1/\eta)\Delta m$ and

$$e(t) = \bar{e} + \left[1 - \mathrm{e}^{-(1/\eta)(t_1-t)} \right] \Delta m$$

We can find the effect of a permanent change in m by letting t_1 go to infinity. This gives $e(t) = \bar{e} + \Delta m$, and confirms the analysis of section 4.1, which showed that a permanent increase in the money supply by x per cent makes the exchange rate depreciate by x per cent.

In figure 4.2 the solid line illustrates the effect on e of a temporary increase in m. At t_0, when the increase in m occurs, e immediately jumps to a higher level – i.e. it depreciates, but less than it would have done if the increase had been permanent.

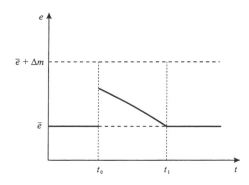

Figure 4.2 Effects of a temporary increase in the money supply.

Then e appreciates gradually towards its old level, which it reaches at the same moment as the increase in m is reversed at t_1. There is no jump in the exchange rate at this time.

The logic behind the path shown in figure 4.2 can best be seen by reasoning backwards from t_1. We know that at t_1 the exchange rate must be back at its old level and from then on it is constant. Immediately before t_1 the money supply is higher. This means that money demand must be higher. That can be the case only if the interest rate is lower, or if the exchange rate is higher, or both. This shows that the exchange rate must appreciate towards its long-run equilibrium. Along the path towards t_1 e is higher and i is lower than in the long-run equilibrium. In order for the exchange rate to get onto the path which leads to long-run equilibrium, it must first jump to a higher level at t_0.

In previous chapters we relied heavily on the assumption of regressive expectations. The expectations produced by a temporary change in the money supply in figure 4.2 are in a sense regressive. The discrete depreciation at t_0 is expected to be followed by an appreciation. This is a general feature of the solution. By taking the time derivative of (4.13) at $t = t_0$, we find that

$$\dot{e}(t_0) = -\Delta z e^{-(1/\eta)(t_1 - t_0)}$$

We can use (4.13) to substitute for Δz in this equation. This gives us

$$\dot{e}(t_0) = -\frac{1}{\eta} \frac{e^{-(1/\eta)(t_1 - t_0)}}{1 - e^{-(1/\eta)(t_1 - t_0)}} [e(t_0) - \bar{e}]$$

which shows that when there is a temporary change in an exogenous variable, the rate of depreciation is negatively related to the level of the exchange rate. In this sense it is rational to have regressive expectations if the exogenous shocks that happen are expected to be reversed later. However, the rational degree of 'regressiveness' depends on how long the change in the exogenous variable is expected to last, and on the interest elasticity of the money demand function.

Anticipated and unanticipated events

Equation (4.11) allows us to compare the effects of an immediate and an expected future change in an exogenous variable. As an example we shall look at an increase in the money supply. Suppose m has been constant, and has been expected to stay constant. At t_0 it is announced that m will increase by the amount Δm at the future date t_1. The expected path for m after t_0 is thus:

$$m(t) = \begin{cases} m_0 & \text{for } t_0 \le t < t_1 \\ m_0 + \Delta m & \text{for } t_1 \le t \end{cases}$$

where $\Delta m > 0$. By computing the integral in (4.11) we find (assuming the other exogenous variables are constant) that the expected time path of the exchange rate after the announcement at t_0 is

$$e(t) = \begin{cases} \bar{e} + \Delta m e^{-(1/\eta)(t_1-t)} & \text{if } t_0 \le t < t_1 \\ \bar{e} + \Delta m & \text{if } t_1 \le t \end{cases} \tag{4.14}$$

The result is illustrated in figure 4.3. If there had been no change in the money supply, the exchange rate would have stayed at $\bar{e}$. At t_0, when the increase in the money supply is first announced, e jumps up immediately – i.e. there is an immediate depreciation. After that, the exchange rate depreciates continually towards its new long-run equilibrium level, $\bar{e} + \Delta m$, which is reached at t_1 – i.e. at the moment the increase in the money supply actually occurs. There is no jump in the exchange rate at t_1. The final increase in e is equal to the increase in m. Reverting to levels, in the end E increases with the same percentage as M.

The mechanism at work is this: when it is announced that the money supply will increase with, say, 10 per cent, we know that the exchange rate at t_1 must be depreciated with 10 per cent relative to the old level. The expectation of a future depreciation creates an immediate depreciation. The reason we do not go all the way at once is that the depreciation raises money demand and, until the increase in the money supply has

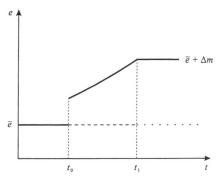

Figure 4.3 Effect of an anticipated increase in the money supply.

materialized, this produces a higher domestic interest rate. The higher interest rate compensates investors for the gradual depreciation between t_0 and t_1. As we approach t_1, the interest rate gets higher and higher, and the depreciation accelerates. At t_1 the gradual depreciation ends, and the domestic interest rate immediately drops to i_*.

The more interest elastic the demand for money is, the lower the initial increase in the interest rate, and the higher the initial jump in the exchange rate (cf. (4.14)).

If the increase in the money supply had not been announced in advance, the exchange rate would have stayed constant at the old equilibrium level until t_1 and then jumped immediately to the new equilibrium level. Domestic interest rates would not have deviated from the foreign rates.

The general lesson to be learned from this is: The exchange rate jumps when new information arrives. It does not jump when an expected event materializes. In fact, jumps in the exchange rate are never expected, since if a jump were expected, investors would rush to buy or sell the currency immediately before the jump. In that way they would move the exchange rate until it was infinitesimally close to its expected level. The expected future path of the exchange rate is always smooth.

The role of news

The above theory leads to an interesting decomposition of exchange rate changes in one part that is expected and one part that is due to 'news'. Let $z_e(t, \tau)$ be the level of z that is expected at time t to be realized at time τ. With this more elaborate notation (4.10) can be written

$$e(t) = \int_t^\infty z_e(t, \tau) e^{-(1/\eta)(\tau - t)} d\tau \tag{4.15}$$

It follows that the exchange rate expected at time t_1 to prevail at time t_2 is

$$e_e(t_1, t_2) = \int_{t_2}^\infty z_e(t_1, \tau) e^{-(1/\eta)(\tau - t_2)} d\tau \tag{4.16}$$

From (4.15) the actual change in the exchange rate from t_1 to t_2 is

$$e(t_2) - e(t_1) = \int_{t_2}^\infty z_e(t_2, \tau) e^{-(1/\eta)(\tau - t_2)} d\tau - e(t_1) \tag{4.17}$$

If we add and subtract $e_e(t_1, t_2)$ on the right-hand side and use (4.16), this can be written as

$$e(t_2) - e(t_1) = e_e(t_1, t_2) - e(t_1) + \int_{t_2}^\infty [z_e(t_2, \tau) - z_e(t_1, \tau)] e^{-(1/\eta)(\tau - t_2)} d\tau \tag{4.18}$$

The first term on the right-hand side, $e_e(t_1, t_2) - e(t_1)$, is the expected depreciation. Then comes the depreciation that is caused by the revision of expectations about the period after t_2. This is the effect of the *news* that has arrived over the period from t_1 to t_2. Since the model assumes perfect capital mobility, the expected depreciation $e_e(t_1, t_2) - e(t_1)$ can be measured by the interest rate differential observed at t_1 for loans where the interest is fixed for the period from t_1 to t_2. In other words, exchange rate movements can be explained by past interest rate differentials and by news about the fundamental exogenous variables driving the exchange rate.

One corollary is that it is futile to explain exchange rate movements by movements in the fundamental explanatory variables if one cannot distinguish between expected and unexpected changes.

A two-country model

The solution for the exchange rate depends on the future path of the foreign interest rate i_*. By extending the model with a foreign money demand function with the same elasticities as the domestic demand function, it is possible to eliminate i_* and derive a solution which treats the two countries symmetrically.

Let foreign money demand be m_* (measured in logs). The foreign money demand function is then

$$m_* - p_* = -\eta i_* + \kappa y_* \tag{4.19}$$

If we solve this for i_* and substitute in (4.10), we get

$$e(t) = \int_t^\infty (1/\eta)\big[m - m_* - \kappa(y - y_*)\big]e^{-(1/\eta)(\tau - t)}\,d\tau \tag{4.20}$$

The exchange rate is determined by relative money supplies and relative outputs.

Note, however, the restrictive nature of this result. In fact it is derived from a model with four equations, (4.6), (4.7), (4.8) and (4.19), and five endogenous variables, p, p_*, i, i_* and e. In order to determine all five variables we need to bring in a fifth equation: the demand for goods. It is only in the special case where the two money demand functions have the same elasticities that it is possible to determine the exchange rate without bringing in the demand for goods.

Empirical results

As mentioned in section 3.5, empirical tests generally tend to reject the joint hypothesis of perfect capital mobility and rational expectations. As we shall see in chapter 8, the evidence is not in favour of continuous purchasing power parity either. This would seem to indicate that the model is oversimplified. However, reduced form equations similar to (4.10) derived from the monetary approach have been able to explain a large fraction of the variations in exchange rates in many historical episodes. Two examples are Frenkel's (1976) study of the German hyperinflation and Bilson's (1978) study of the float between the major currencies in the mid-1970s. The model seems to capture some important aspects of exchange rate determination, but not all of them. It works best when inflation is high.

Several studies have attempted to single out the effect of 'news' (see the survey in section IV of MacDonald and Taylor, 1992). The main difficulty is to measure the expected changes in the exogenous variables. Both model-based and survey-based methods have been used. Several authors claim to have found significant effects of news in accord with the monetary model.

In later chapters we shall look at models which allow for imperfect capital mobility and for deviations from purchasing power parity. However, there are some lasting lessons from the simple monetary model: the method of solution (choosing a path which does not explode); the different effects of permanent and temporary and of anticipated and unanticipated shocks; the importance of 'news'; the importance of relative developments between countries. These are features which should be present also in more general models.

4.3 The nominal anchor

At the close of this chapter I want to draw attention to the important role played by the *exogeneity* of the quantity of money for the determination of the exchange rate in the above model.

An exchange rate is the relative price of two intrinsically useless pieces of paper. In a fundamental sense the exchange rate is an arbitrary number, as is also the absolute price level. If we do our accounts and pay our bills in cents instead of in dollars, that makes no difference to the real economy. The foreign exchange rate is a nominal variable. It has real effects only if the value of some other nominal variable is given in the domestic currency. That the nominal quantity of money is given exogenously makes it possible for the exchange rate to have real effects. In particular, it has an effect on the real quantity of money. Later we shall see how the exchange rate can have real effects when stocks of other assets are given in kroner or when one or more prices are given in kroner.

In earlier chapters we treated the expected future exchange rate as more or less exogenous. In this chapter we tried instead to determine the expected exchange rate in a rational way, consistent with a model of how the exchange rate is determined. We saw that this can be difficult. That M was exogenous was not enough to single out a unique rational expectation. We needed to invoke a somewhat dubious assumption about a belief in long-run stability. This should be no surprise. Indeed it must be difficult to figure out in a rational way what the future exchange rate between intrinsically worthless pieces of paper will be.

However, it is worthwhile to consider the even greater problems which would have arisen had i, not M, been exogenous. With perfect capital mobility, the differential equation for the exchange rate is in the notation from section 4.2 $\dot{e} = i - i_*$. This determines a unique rate of depreciation, but the *level* of the exchange rate is absent. There seems to be no way that agents can rationally focus their attention on a particular path for the level of the exchange rate.

The exogenous money supply functions as an *anchor for the expectations of the* levels of nominal prices (including the price of foreign currency). Other variables may perform the same function. In the monetary model an exogenous exchange rate can replace the exogenous money supply. Other solutions are presented in chapter 10.

It may seem that we took a long step forward when the postulated regressive expectations from earlier chapters were replaced by rational, model consistent expectations. However, section 4.2 revealed that we have moved the problem of expectations formation only one step. The expected exchange rate depends on the expected time paths of a large number of exogenous variables, money supply being one of them. We shall not try to answer the question of what determines monetary policy here. Rather the point is that it may be important that monetary policy is conducted in such a way that it provides an anchor for expectations about nominal *levels*. Furthermore, if monetary policy is unpredictable, the exchange rate could be highly volatile, and it could be difficult to form rational expectations.

Exercises

1. In the model of section 4.1, what is the effect of a permanent increase in the foreign interest rate on the exchange rate today and in the future?
2. In the model of section 4.1, what is the effect on the time paths of the exchange rate, the price level and the domestic interest rate of an increase in the foreign inflation rate? Draw graphs that show the time paths. You may assume that the foreign interest rate is constant.
3. Let $N = M/P$ be the real money supply. Derive the differential equation which governs the behaviour of N over time. Assume that M and P grow at the constant rates μ and p_*. Show that the differential equation is unstable, and that the path for N will be explosive unless the initial exchange rate jumps to the level determined by (4.5).
4. Suppose that it is announced today that a new resource has been discovered. Owing to this output, Y, is expected to increase by 10 per cent two years from now. Sketch the effect this will have on the time paths of the exchange rate and the interest rate.
5. Suppose that on a certain day the foreign central bank raises its interest rate but the exchange rate hardly depreciates at all. What could be the explanation(s)?
6. Suppose output grows by 2 per cent per year. What does this imply for the path of the money supply if the price level is going to be constant? Will a constant money growth rate always imply a constant inflation rate?

Part 2

The open economy

5   The extremely open economy

After four chapters on the financial markets, it is time to shift focus to the markets for goods and for labour. In chapters 5–8 we shall explore the determination of output, employment, the current account, the foreign debt and the rate of inflation. However, the financial markets will not be left out. One main purpose of chapters 5–7 is to describe the links between the foreign exchange market and the goods market. These go both ways. In section 1.6 we saw that a current account deficit may lead to a gradual depreciation of the exchange rate. In the present chapter we shall see that a depreciation may affect the current account through at least three channels: real wealth, real interest rates and real wage rates. Since wealth accumulation and current account deficits change financial balances only gradually, it is essential to study both the short and the long run.

As explained in the introduction (p. 3) the main difference between this and chapters 6–8 is the assumptions on the structure of the goods market. In the present chapter the home country can buy or sell as much as it wishes of all goods on an international market where all prices are exogenously given in foreign currency. For every good that is produced domestically there exists a perfect substitute produced abroad. This is the basis for the chapter title 'The extremely open economy'.

Since we disregard transport costs, customs and other impediments to trade, we have *perfect mobility of goods*, and for each good the law of one price must hold. An immediate implication is that, as in chapter 4, we always have absolute *purchasing power parity* (PPP) in the sense that, measured in the same currency, the same basket of goods costs the same at home and abroad. Thus,

$$P = EP_* \tag{5.1}$$

where P_* is the foreign price level measured in foreign currency, E the exchange rate (domestic currency per unit of foreign currency) and P the domestic price level.[30] One immediate implication is that the inflation rates at home and abroad, $p = \dot{P}/P$ and $p_* = \dot{P}_*/P_*$ are related by

$$p = e + p_* \tag{5.2}$$

where $e = \dot{E}/E$ is the rate of depreciation of the domestic currency. In words: the domestic rate of inflation is equal to the rate of depreciation of the domestic currency plus the foreign rate of inflation. There are many reasons for deviations from purchasing power parity. We shall come to some of them in chapters 6–8.

Obviously we must be looking at a 'small' country, since foreign prices are given independently of what happens in this country. The country must be so small that its supply and demand has a negligible influence on international goods prices. Together with purchasing power parity this means that the domestic price level is determined by the foreign price level and the exchange rate. Domestic demand for goods can affect the price level only through the exchange rate.

Since all relative prices are given exogenously from the world market, there is no aggregation problem. There may be many goods, but we can conduct our analysis as if there is a single commodity without any loss of generality.

One recurrent topic in the present chapter is: what causes current account imbalances? Are there self-correcting mechanisms which tend to bring the current account into balance? In fact we are going to identify five causes and five self-correcting mechanisms:

- A high private wealth implies low savings and a current account deficit. As private wealth declines, savings rebound and the current account is balanced (section 5.3).
- If output varies over time, while consumers smooth consumption, a level of output below average causes a current account deficit. The counterpart of this deficit is a surplus when output is above average (section 5.3).
- If capital mobility is imperfect, a current account deficit causes a gradual increase in real interest rates (unless monetary policy is set to prevent it). This tends to depress domestic demand and improve the current account (sections 5.4 and 5.5).
- If there is wage rigidity and wages are too high, output and incomes will be low. This implies low savings and a current account deficit. Equilibrating mechanisms in the labour market may then lower wages, raise output and bring the current account towards equilibrium (section 5.7).
- High wages also mean low returns on capital and low real investments. Contrary to the effect just mentioned, this means that high wages may be associated with a current account surplus. Equilibrating mechanisms in the labour market may also in this case lower wages. Real investment will then increase and current account balance will be restored (section 5.8).

However, current account deficits may also be caused by government deficits (section 5.6), and then a change in policy is required for the current account to get balanced.

The present chapter has two main parts. In sections 5.3–5.6, wages are assumed to be fully flexible, which implies that the level of output is constant, determined by the available amounts of labour and capital. In sections 5.7–5.9 wage rigidities affect the level of output and lead to varying degrees of unemployment. The basic model of the chapter, a dynamic model for the determination of the foreign debt and the current account, is presented in section 5.3. In sections 5.4 and 5.5 it is extended to cover imperfect capital mobility, in section 5.6 to cover government deficits. In section 5.7

wage rigidity is introduced, in section 5.8 real investments are added and in section 5.9 another form of wage rigidity caused by trade union behaviour. Some considerations about the effects of economic growth are introduced in section 5.10. Before the basic model is presented we need some preliminaries on real interest rates (section 5.1) and national accounting (section 5.2). At the end of the chapter (section 5.11) we discuss some objections and possible extensions.

5.1 Real interest rates

In chapters 1–4 we have discussed the relationship between nominal interest rates in different currencies. It is now time to look at the relationship between real rates. The domestic and foreign expected real interest rates are by definition

$$\rho = i - p_e \quad \text{and} \quad \rho_* = i_* - p_{*e}$$

When purchasing power parity holds, inflation at home and abroad are related by $p = e + p_*$. Rational expectations of inflation in the two countries should obey the same equation: $p_e = e_e + p_{*e}$. From chapter 1 we know that by definition $i = i_* + e_e + r$. By exploiting these equations we find that

$$\rho = i - p_e = i_* + e_e + r - (e_e + p_{*e}) = i_* - p_{*e} + r = \rho_* + r$$

Thus, the domestic real interest rate is equal to the foreign real interest rate plus the risk premium. It is only by varying the risk premium that the central bank can influence the expected real interest rate in the extremely open economy. This holds irrespective of whether the exchange rate is fixed or floating, and irrespective of how expectations are formed as long as purchasing power parity is expected to hold.

If capital mobility is perfect, the risk premium is always zero, and the central bank is unable to change the expected real interest rate. We then have *real interest rate parity*. The central bank is able to influence the real interest rate only if there are deviations from purchasing power parity or from uncovered interest rate parity.

Since uncovered interest rate parity is so often rejected in empirical tests (section 2.5), it is not surprising that real interest rate parity also tends to be rejected (see Mishkin, 1984, for an example). Still models with perfect capital mobility and perfect mobility of goods are important reference points. Marston (1993) contains a more extensive discussion of the relationship between the different parity conditions.

5.2 Income accounting

We are going to use Hicks' (1939) concept of income. He defined the income of an economic agent as the maximum amount she can consume without reducing her real wealth. The difference between Hicks' income concept and standard national accounting is the use of real instead of nominal rates of return.

Throughout this chapter we assume for simplicity that the balance sheet is the same as in section 3.1. We remember that there were three assets: money, domestic bonds and foreign currency assets. Foreigners did not hold assets denominated in domestic currency. The financial portfolio of the private sector could be written

$$W_p = \frac{M + B + EF_p}{P}$$

According to standard national accounting the real income that the private sector receives from its financial portfolio is

$$i\frac{B}{P} + i_*\frac{EF_p}{P}$$

According to Hicks' definition the real income is instead

$$-p\frac{M}{P} + (i - p)\frac{B}{P} + (i_* + e - p)\frac{EF_p}{P} \tag{5.3}$$

The stock of each asset is multiplied with its real instead of its nominal rate of return. The real return on money is the negative of the inflation rate, since money receives no interest. The real return on foreign currency assets includes the gain from exchange rate changes.

The real income from the financial portfolio can also be written

$$\rho_* W_p + r\frac{M + B}{P} - i\frac{M}{P}$$

If we insert in this from the definitions $\rho_* = i_* + e - p$, $r = i - i_* - e$ and $W_p = (M + B + EF_p)/P$, we get the same expression as (5.3). One way of interpreting the last expression is that we use the real return on foreign assets as a benchmark to calculate a first estimate of the real return on the whole portfolio, $\rho_* W_p$. To this we add the risk premium in favour of the domestic currency times the volume of domestic currency assets, $r(M + B)/P$. Finally, we subtract the nominal interest rate times the quantity of money since the public gets no interest on that part of financial wealth. As mentioned in section 3.2, iM/P is called the amount of *seigniorage*. M is an interest-free loan from the public to the central bank. Seigniorage is the gain that the central bank has from this.[31]

We looked above at the private sector's income from financial assets. We can obviously do the same calculations for the other sectors. Suppose the private sector gets the whole output, Y, from domestic production. Denote taxes in real value with T. Then the real disposable incomes of the private and the government sectors are, respectively,

$$Y_p = Y + \rho_* W_p + r\frac{M + B}{P} - i\frac{M}{P} - T \tag{5.4}$$

$$Y_g = \rho_* W_g - r\frac{M + B}{P} + i\frac{M}{P} + T \tag{5.5}$$

Their sum, $Y - \rho_* W_*$, is *national income* (also called the national product).

Savings are defined as income minus consumption. We use C for private and G for government consumption. Then private savings are $Y_p - C$ and government savings are $Y_g - G$. In line with that the private sector receives the whole output, we assume that all real investment, I, is undertaken by the private sector. The growth over time in the financial wealth of the three sectors is then by definition

$$\dot{W}_p = Y_p - C - I$$
$$\dot{W}_g = Y_g - G \tag{5.6}$$
$$\dot{W}_* = \rho_* W_* + C + G + I - Y$$

In other words, the growth in financial wealth is equal to the difference between savings and real investment, with an obvious sign reversal for $\dot{W}_*$. The latter is equal to investment minus national savings. $\dot{W}_*$ is also equal to the deficit on the current account of the balance of payments. This is the sum of the deficit on the interest account, $\rho_* W_*$, and on the trade account, $C + G + I - Y$. The latter is the difference between domestic use of goods and services, $C + G + I$, often called *absorption*, and domestic production. Note that the definition of the current account differs from standard national accounting, since we use the real instead of the nominal interest rate. Similarly, we define the government surplus as $Y_g - G$.

One advantage of Hicks' definition of income and the corresponding definitions of savings and sectoral surpluses is clear from (5.6). We can write the change in financial wealth as equal to savings minus real investment. If we did not use Hicks' definition, this would no longer be true, since we would have to take account of the capital gains at this point instead. Equation (5.6) should be compared to the corresponding equations based on standard national accounting in section 1.6.

Except in sections 5.6 and 5.10 we assume in the sequel that the government budget is balanced in the sense that $\dot{W}_g = 0$. Then from (5.6) and (5.5)

$$T = G - \rho_* W_g + r(M + B)/P - iM/P.$$

If we insert this in (5.4), we find that

$$Y_p = Y + \rho_*(W_p + W_g) - G = Y - \rho_* W_* - G \tag{5.7}$$

In other words: if the government balances its budget, private disposable income is equal to national income minus government consumption.

5.3 The specie–flow mechanism

This section describes an automatic adjustment mechanism which tends to bring the current account of the balance of payments into equilibrium in the long run. The most famous description of this mechanism was given by the philosopher David Hume in the eighteenth century. Hume assumed a world in which the international means of payment was specie (i.e. gold or silver). Suppose a country had a surplus in its trade with foreign countries. Then specie would flow into that country. As the stock of specie accumulated, the wealth of the citizens of the surplus country increased. The citizens would then raise their expenditures and thus import more. This meant that the trade surplus declined. Eventually expenditures would increase enough to make foreign trade balanced. Naturally, this process would be reinforced by a similar process with opposite sign going on in deficit countries.[32]

In the modern world current account deficits are normally settled by interest bearing debt. This introduces an extra destabilizing force which Hume did not have to reckon with. A deficit country accumulates debt. This means that increasing interest payments contribute to widening the deficit over time. The stabilizing force, the wealth effect, needs to overcome this destabilizing force if the self-correcting mechanism is going to work.

The main assumptions behind the model are:

1. Perfect mobility of goods, which means continuous purchasing power parity $P = EP_*$.
2. Perfect capital mobility, which means continuous interest rate parity $i = i_* + e_e$.
3. Expectations are model-consistent (rational), which means that $e_e = e$.
4. Factor prices are flexible, which means that the level of output, Y, is determined by the available supply of labour and capital.
5. Government budgets are balanced and there is no government consumption. This means that the private sector receives the whole national income.
6. There is no real investment.

The assumptions about purchasing power parity and rational expectations are maintained throughout this chapter. The other assumptions are relaxed in the ensuing sections. In particular sections 5.4 and 5.5 are devoted to the case of imperfect capital mobility.

The assumption of a balanced budget needs an explanation. As mentioned in section 1.2, the sum of financial wealth added over all sectors is zero. Since we have purchasing power parity, we can write this simply as $W_g + W_p + W_* = 0$. By implication, the foreign debt is the negative of the financial wealth of the two domestic sectors: $W_* = -W_p - W_g$. The mechanism we are describing works through stabilizing private wealth. If the foreign debt is going to be stabilized, the government must also stabilize its debts – i.e. stabilize W_g. In order to focus on the possible self-correcting mechanism in the private sector, we have assumed that the government balances its budget.

The equations of our model, which we, with a reference to Hume's original discussion, called the specie–flow model, are:

$$\dot{W}_* = \rho_* W_* + C - Y \tag{5.8}$$

$$C = C(Y_p, W_p, \rho_*) \tag{5.9}$$

$$Y_p = Y - \rho_* W_* \tag{5.10}$$

$$W_p = -W_* - W_g \tag{5.11}$$

Equation (5.8) is the definitional equation (5.6) for the time rate of increase of foreign debt, where we have set $G = I = 0$. Equation (5.9) is the consumption function. We make the standard assumptions that $0 < C_Y < 1$, $C_W > 0$ and $C_\rho < 0$. A rise in the interest rate lowers present consumption because of sufficiently strong intertemporal substitution effects. After the consumption function two definitional equations follow. Since the government budget is balanced and $G = 0$, private disposable income is equal to national income. Private wealth is the opposite of the foreign debt and government wealth.

The model has four equations. They determine the time paths of the four endogenous variables: W_*, W_p, Y_p and C. The time paths of ρ_*, Y and W_g are exogenous. The first is determined from abroad, the second by the productive capacity of the economy and the third by past history. The whole time path of the exogenous variables needs to be given before we can determine the endogenous variables. In addition, since the model is dynamic (it includes both W_* and its rate of change $\dot{W}_*$), we need an initial value for the state variable W_*. We can as well write down the initial wealth for all three sectors, which are (cf. (3.1)–(3.3))

$$W_p(0) = \frac{F_{p0}}{P_{*0}} + \frac{B_0 + M_0}{E(0)P_{*0}}$$

$$W_g(0) = \frac{F_{g0}}{P_{*0}} - \frac{B_0 + M_0}{E(0)P_{*0}} \tag{5.12}$$

$$W_*(0) = \frac{F_{*0}}{P_{*0}}$$

As in section 3.1, we assume that foreigners do not hold domestic currency.

Note that the exchange rate does not appear explicitly in any of the equations (5.8)–(5.11). However, it enters in the initial condition (5.12). If the exchange rate is fixed, $E(0)$ is given exogenously. If the exchange rate is floating, we need to determine the initial exchange rate somehow. The environment we have assumed is the same as the environment for the monetary model of exchange rate determination in chapter 4. Thus, if the money supply is exogenous, the exchange rate E must be determined in the same way as there – i.e.:

$$E(0) = \frac{M(0)}{P_{*0} m(\rho_* + \mu, Y)} \tag{5.13}$$

where $\mu = \dot{M}/M$ (cf. (4.5)). Here it is presumed that ρ_*, μ and Y are constant.

Given the initial exchange rate, the dynamics described by the equation system (5.8)–(5.11) is the same irrespective of whether the exchange rate is fixed or floating. The model can be compressed into one differential equation. Substitute from (5.10) and (5.11) in (5.9) and then from this again in (5.8) and you get

$$\dot{W}_* = \rho_* W_* + C(Y - \rho_* W_*, -W_* - W_g, \rho_*) - Y \tag{5.14}$$

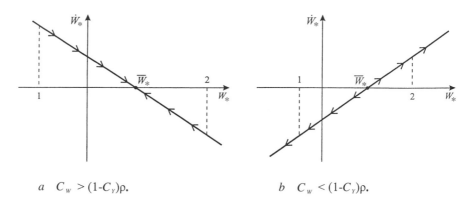

a $C_W > (1-C_Y)\rho.$ b $C_W < (1-C_Y)\rho.$

Figure 5.1 Foreign debt dynamics.

where W_* is the only unknown. Alternative phase diagrams for this equation are drawn in figures 5.1a and 5.1b. The slope of the relation between W_* and $\dot{W}_*$ is

$$\frac{d\dot{W}_*}{dW_*} = (1 - C_Y)\rho_* - C_W \tag{5.15}$$

The first term is always positive, the second negative. The first term is the destabilizing effect of higher interest payments when foreign debt is higher. This effect is dampened because higher interest payments reduce disposable income and thus consumption. The second term is the stabilizing wealth effect.

When the wealth effect dominates ($C_W > (1 - C_Y)\rho_*$), panel a of figure 5.1 shows the relevant case. If we start with a high foreign debt (as in 2), private wealth and private consumption demand is low. In spite of high interest payments the current account is in surplus and the foreign debt declines gradually. As the decline continues, consumption rises until we reach the point where the current account balances – i.e. where $\dot{W}_* = 0$. If we start with a low foreign debt (as in 1), consumption demand is high and the foreign debt increases until the current account is again balanced. Where the curve cuts the horizontal axis, there is a stationary equilibrium. If we start with a foreign debt at this level, the debt just stays constant.

The stationary equilibrium is defined by

$$\dot{W}_* = 0 \Leftrightarrow C(Y - \rho_* W_*, -W_* - W_g, \rho_*) = Y - \rho_* W_* \tag{5.16}$$

where the equivalence follows from (5.14). Hence, the stationarity condition is that consumption should equal national income. Equation (5.16) can be solved for the long-run equilibrium value of W_*, which is marked $\bar{W}_*$ in figure 5.1.

Panel b of figure 5.1 shows the unstable case ($C_W < (1 - C_Y)\rho_*$). If the country starts with a foreign debt which is higher than the stationary level (as in point 2), the debt will grow over time without limit. Conversely, if the country starts with a low foreign debt (as in point 1), it ends up accumulating infinitely large claims on foreign countries. The common presumption is that the wealth effect in the consumption function and the effect of net interest income on consumption together are strong enough to prevent this. Thus we assume that the relevant case is the stable one.

A one-time devaluation

We shall now look at the effect of a one-time devaluation at time 0. After that the exchange rate remains constant ($e = 0$), and this is also expected by the market participants. Note that if the exchange rate is floating and determined according to (5.13), a one-time increase in the money supply (brought about by a purchase of domestic bonds) at time 0 leads to an immediate one-time depreciation. The effects of a one-time devaluation and a one-time increase in the money supply are thus equivalent.

The exchange rate is not an argument in the differential equation (5.14). As already mentioned, it affects the dynamics of the foreign debt only through the initial condition (5.12), where it determines W_g. If the government is a net debtor in the domestic currency – i.e. if $M_0 + B_0 > 0$, a devaluation causes an initial transfer of wealth from the private sector to the government. Let us assume that this is the case.

Suppose we start from a point of stationary equilibrium, as point A in figure 5.2. The initial transfer of wealth from the private sector to the government means that consumption demand falls. The relationship between the level of foreign debt and its rate of growth shifts downwards. At the initial level of foreign debt there is now a surplus on the current account ($\dot{W}_* < 0$). This surplus leads to a gradual decline in the foreign debt towards a new and lower stationary equilibrium (point B in figure 5.2).

By implicit differentiation of (5.16) we find that the final effect on the foreign debt is

$$\frac{dW_*}{dW_g} = -\frac{C_W}{C_W - \rho_*(1 - C_Y)} < -1 \tag{5.17}$$

Note that we use the stability condition $C_W > \rho_*(1 - C_Y)$ to sign the denominator. That $dW_*/dW_g < -1$ means that the final reduction in foreign debt is somewhat larger than

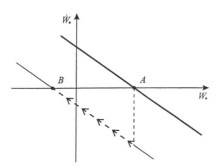

Figure 5.2 The effect of a devaluation.

the initial increase in government financial wealth (unless $C_Y = 1$). This means that the final effect on private wealth is positive.

One way of describing what happens is this: by devaluing the government effectively confiscates part of private wealth. The private sector wishes to keep wealth in a certain relation to current income, and sets out to save in order to rebuild its wealth. This is done by accumulating claims on foreigners and, thus, requires a (temporary) current account surplus. The reason why private wealth ends up *higher* than before is that disposable income has increased because the increased interest income of the government is transferred to the private sector. This part of the result may be sensitive to the way interest income is included in the consumption function.

A numerical example may illustrate the possible magnitude of the effects we are talking about. Estimated marginal propensities to consume out of wealth are almost always well below 0.1 per year. Let us assume that $C_W = 0.05$. Let us also assume that government net debt denominated in domestic currency ($M + B$) is equal to one year's GDP. Few OECD countries have higher debt ratios today. The initial reduction in private wealth following a 10 per cent devaluation is then equal to 10 per cent of one year's GDP. The immediate effect on consumption is 0.5 per cent of GDP ($0.05 \cdot 0.1 = 0.005$). This means that the initial effect of the devaluation is an improvement in the current account equal to half a percentage point of GDP. Suppose the marginal propensity to consume out of income is 0.8 and the real interest rate is 0.05. If we treat the marginal propensities as constants, the final effect on the foreign debt, calculated from (5.17), is equal to 12.5 per cent of GDP. This is 25 times the first-year effect on the current account. We know that the effect on the current account declines over time. Obviously the adjustment is quite slow. This must also mean that there is a perceptible current account effect for many years after the devaluation. If the domestic currency debt of the government is smaller, all effects are of course smaller.

Naturally, if the private sector initially had negative net assets in domestic currency, the conclusions are reversed. A devaluation transfers wealth from the government to the private sector and produces a temporary current account deficit.

However, a devaluation may seem less likely if the private sector is a net debtor and the government a net creditor in domestic currency. Historically the cause of many devaluations has been that the government has accumulated a large debt (for example, because of war) and needs to reduce the debt burden. In this perspective a devaluation is an alternative to a default on a part of the government debt. Both make it possible to reduce taxes without reducing government expenditure. Remember that the taxes needed to balance the budget are (when $r = 0$)

$$T = G - \rho_* W_g - i\frac{M}{P}$$

When $M + B > 0$, a one-time devaluation means a one-time increase in W_g. This reduces taxes. Seigniorage income is unchanged, since the interest rate and the demand for real balances are unchanged. (Remember that people get as much money as they demand, since we have perfect capital mobility.)

Continuous devaluation

A country can choose to have a different inflation rate from abroad by devaluing or revaluing its exchange rate continuously – i.e. by having $e \neq 0$. We know from section 5.1 that e has no effect on the real interest rate in domestic currency, as long as purchasing power parity holds. As we can see from the differential equation (5.14), and the initial conditions (5.12), e has no effect on the time path of the foreign debt and the current account either.

However, a continuous devaluation is not completely without real effects. Since $i = i_* + e$, it raises the nominal interest rate. This in turn has an effect on seigniorage income, which is iM/P. Suppose the money demand function is the standard one:

$$\frac{M}{P} = m(i, Y)$$

Perfect capital mobility together with a fixed exchange rate implies that the money supply is endogenous. Seigniorage revenue is then

$$i\frac{M}{P} = (i_* + e)\, m(i_* + e, Y)$$

A higher rate of devaluation, and thus of inflation, has two effects on seigniorage income. It raises the 'tax rate' $i_* + e$ and lowers the 'tax base' M/P. The net result is an increase in seigniorage if $|El_i m| < 1$, a reduction if $|El_i m| > 1$. Presumably, if we start with a sufficiently low e, and thus a low level of inflation, an increase in e increases seigniorage. This means that ordinary taxes can be lowered. Increased inflation has a real cost, because people save on cash balances (which can be produced at virtually no cost) and incur real transaction costs instead. However, if we venture outside our model, taxes create distortions. This means that the costs of a higher inflation tax should be balanced against the costs of collecting ordinary taxes.

In advanced economies seigniorage is usually a relatively unimportant source of income for the government even at fairly high interest rates.

Above we mentioned that a one-time devaluation was equivalent to a one-time increase in the money supply in the case of floating. The relationship between the effects of increases in the two growth rates, e and μ are not quite so simple. The reason is that, as we saw in section 4.1, an increase in μ not only leads to a gradual depreciation, but also to an immediate jump in E. The effects of an increase in μ are thus a combination of the effects of an increase in e and in $E(0)$.

Consumption smoothing

So far, we have assumed constant output. However, even in an essentially stationary economy there are several reasons why output may vary over time. One example is stochastic variations in productivity – for example, due to weather conditions. Standard economic theory tells us that consumers try to smooth their consumption relative to such income variations. If there are no credit constraints, consumption should depend on expected life-time income, and not on income in a single year. Consumption smoothing means that when income is temporarily high, consumption tends to fall short of income. *Ceteris paribus* this creates a temporary current account surplus. When income is temporarily low, consumption exceeds income and the current account tends to be in deficit.

Assume that Y varies stochastically around a stationary expected value $\bar{Y}$. Suppose there is complete consumption smoothing, meaning that consumption depends on $\bar{Y}$ only, not on Y. Then the equation for the accumulation of foreign debt may be written

$$\dot{W}_* = \rho_* W_* + C(\bar{Y} - \rho_* W_*, -W_* - W_g, \rho_*) - Y$$

Note the way both Y and $\bar{Y}$ enter: actual output determines what can be sold, average or normal output determines consumption. $\bar{W}_*$, the long-run equilibrium value of W_*, is now defined by

$$C(\bar{Y} - \rho_* \bar{W}_*, -\bar{W}_* - W_g, \rho_*) = \bar{Y} - \rho_* \bar{W}_*$$

Thus, $\bar{W}_*$ is now defined as the value of W_* which makes $\dot{W}_*$ equal to zero when $Y = \bar{Y}$. By comparing the two equations above, we find that if $W_* = \bar{W}_*$, the current account deficit is

$$\dot{W}_* = \bar{Y} - Y$$

In other words, the deficit is equal to the difference between permanent and actual income. Thus, if permanent income exceeds actual income, this causes a current account deficit. The deficit is self-correcting in the sense that if expectations are fulfilled, it will be matched by surpluses at other points in time.

The theories expounded in the present section are developed further in the intertemporal theory of the current account, where the consumption decisions of optimizing agents are modelled more explicitly. An excellent exposition is given in Obstfeld and Rogoff (1996); for a brief survey see Obstfeld and Rogoff (1995a).[33] An important consideration is whether the variations in output are specific to the country we look at or common to the world economy. In the latter case, the world real interest rate will be affected. Since world consumption cannot exceed world output (unless there are inventories), temporarily low world output must be accompanied by low world consumption. It is only when the temporarily low output is a local phenomenon that we can expect a current account deficit. Even then certain insurance contracts may wipe out the current account effect.

5.4 Imperfect capital mobility: fixed exchange rate

The new questions that are raised by imperfect capital mobility are of two kinds. First, how does monetary policy interact with the self-correcting mechanism for foreign debt: is stability promoted or not? Second, what is the influence of the current account on the foreign exchange reserves?

When capital mobility is perfect, the private sector's demand for foreign bonds is infinitely elastic. In this case the government's foreign exchange reserves are not determined by the supply of foreign exchange from the private sector. Instead the government can choose the currency composition of its debt freely, since the private sector accepts whatever mix of domestic and foreign currency bonds it is offered. If the government keeps its net foreign currency assets constant, the private sector is ready to finance a current account deficit 100 per cent by reducing its foreign currency assets or borrowing foreign currency. This does not require any change in interest rates. When capital mobility is imperfect, this is no longer true. A current account deficit then forces the central bank to change interest rates or to intervene in the foreign exchange market.

The alternative to consumption now is to invest in a portfolio consisting of an optimal combination of assets denominated in foreign and domestic currency. This means that the relevant interest rate for savings decisions is some average of the rates of return on investments in domestic and foreign currency, $\rho = \rho_* + r$ and ρ_*, respectively. Presumably the two interest rates should be weighted according to their shares in the portfolio. The consumption function (5.9) should thus be rewritten to give room for two real interest rates:

$$C = C(Y_d, W_p, \rho_* + r, \rho_*) \tag{5.18}$$

We assume the partial derivatives with respect to both interest rates (C_ρ and C_{ρ_*}) to be negative.

The differential equation for foreign debt is now

$$\dot{W}_* = \rho_* W_* + C(Y - \rho_* W_*, -W_* - W_g, \rho_* + r, \rho_*) - Y \tag{5.19}$$

where the only change from (5.14) is that we have two interest rates in the consumption function. As long as the risk premium is constant, the dynamics of foreign debt are the same as with perfect capital mobility.

In general, r is not constant. When we can no longer use the interest parity condition, we have to supplement (5.19) for the real side with the portfolio model from section 3.1 to describe the financial side. This means that the model is extended with four new equations:

$$r = i - i_* - e \tag{5.20}$$

$$\frac{M}{EP_*} = m(i, Y) \quad m_i < 0, m_Y > 0 \tag{5.21}$$

$$\frac{B}{EP_*} = -W_* - W_g - f(r, -W_g - W_*) - m(i, Y) \tag{5.22}$$

$$\frac{F_g}{P_*} + f(r, -W_* - W_g) + W_* = 0 \quad f_r < 0, 0 < f_W < 1 \tag{5.23}$$

These are, respectively, the definition of the risk premium and the equilibrium conditions for the money, bond and foreign exchange markets from section 3.1. We have used that $P = EP_*$, $W_p = -W_g - W_*$ and $F_* = P_* W_*$.

In addition to P_* and i_* which are exogenous, there are now six new variables M, B, F_g, i, r and E. Depending on the policy regime two of them are exogenous, the other four endogenous. In the present section the exchange rate is fixed, which means that E is exogenous. We look at three different possibilities for monetary policy: full sterilization (M exogenous), no sterilization (B exogenous) and a regime where the interest rate is used instead of interventions in order to keep the exchange rate constant (F_g exogenous). The initial conditions are still given by (5.12).

The first question is what the different monetary regimes mean for the self-correcting mechanism. The new argument in the differential equation (5.19) is the risk premium, r. From the financial side of the model this may depend on W_*. Hence the stability condition which we get by differentiating (5.19) is

$$\frac{d\dot{W}_*}{dW_*} = (1 - C_Y)\rho_* - C_W + C_\rho \frac{dr}{dW_*} < 0 \tag{5.24}$$

The last term is new and depends on the monetary policy that is in place.

Since we have a fixed exchange rate, the effect of W_* on r and on i is the same. With M exogenous the interest rate is determined by the equilibrium condition for the money market (5.21). Hence,

$$\frac{dr}{dW_*} = 0 \quad \text{with } M \text{ exogenous} \tag{5.25}$$

With B exogenous the interest rate is determined by the equilibrium condition for the bond market (5.22). Differentiation of this with respect to r and W_* (taking account of the fact that $i = i_* + e + r$), yields

$$\frac{dr}{dW_*} = \frac{1 - f_W}{-f_r - m_i} > 0 \quad \text{with } B \text{ exogenous} \tag{5.26}$$

An increase in the foreign debt increases the interest rate and therefore the risk premium. The reason is that a transfer of wealth from local residents to foreigners reduces the demand for domestic bonds.

With F_g exogenous the interest rate is determined by the equilibrium condition for the foreign exchange market (5.23). By differentiating this we find

$$\frac{dr}{dW_*} = \frac{1-f_W}{-f_r} > 0 \quad \text{with } F_g \text{ exogenous} \tag{5.27}$$

An increase in the foreign debt reduces the total supply of foreign currency. The demand for foreign currency from the domestic private sector is also reduced, but with a smaller amount since $0 < f_W < 1$. Since the central bank keeps its reserves constant, it is forced to raise the interest rate to prevent the exchange rate depreciating. The interest rate increases more when F_g is exogenous than when B is exogenous.

Thus, the effect of the current account deficit on interest rates depends on the way monetary policy is conducted. If the interest rate rises, this reduces domestic demand and, hence, improves the current account. The negative feedback from the level of foreign debt to its growth in (5.24) is reinforced, and the self-correcting mechanism is speeded up.

The different effects on the interest rate has its parallel in different effects on the foreign exchange reserve. For simplicity, assume that all exogenous variables are constant over time. Differentiation of (5.23) with respect to time yields

$$\frac{\dot{F}_g}{P_*} = -(1-f_W)\dot{W}_* - f_r \dot{r}$$

Because all exogenous variables are constant, the only variable which can cause r to change over time is W_*. Hence, $\dot{r} = (dr/dW_*)\dot{W}_*$ Thus,

$$\frac{\dot{F}_g}{P_*} = -(1-f_W)\dot{W}_* - f_r \frac{dr}{dW_*} \dot{W}_* \tag{5.28}$$

Since foreigners do not hold domestic currency in the present model, the whole current account deficit must in the end be financed by borrowing foreign currency or drawing on foreign currency assets. When the central bank sterilizes, $dr/dW_* = 0$ and the last term in (5.28) drops out. A fraction $1 - f_W$ of the deficit is then financed by the government by drawing on the foreign exchange reserve or borrowing foreign currency abroad. If the central bank does not sterilize (B exogenous), the interest rate increases when there is a deficit and the reduction in the foreign exchange reserve is smaller. When F_g is exogenous, the domestic interest rate is raised enough that the second term in (5.28) cancels the first. Then the whole deficit is financed by the private sector by borrowing foreign currency. Thus, the more the interest rate increases, the less of the deficit is financed in foreign currency by the government and the more the self-correcting mechanism is speeded up.

Put differently, the conclusion is that a current account surplus gives room for either an increase in foreign exchange reserves or a reduction in the interest rate. Alternative monetary policies distribute the result differently between these two variables. The policy which yields the largest reduction in interest rates also sets the highest speed for the convergence towards current account equilibrium.

In section 5.3 a one-time devaluation had real effects only through the initial wealth distribution and the wealth effect in the consumption function. With imperfect capital mobility the exchange rate may also affect the risk premium, and through that consumption demand. Again, the result depends on the monetary policy with which the devaluation is combined.

The simplest case is when F_g is exogenous. Then the interest rate is determined by the equilibrium condition for the foreign exchange market (5.23). When $M_0 + B_0 > 0$, a devaluation reduces private wealth, and hence reduces the private demand for foreign currency. This allows the central bank to reduce i and r without losing reserves. This raises consumption demand and increases the current account deficit. Thus the interest rate channel works in the opposite direction to the wealth channel that was analysed in section 5.3, and the net result is ambiguous.

This can be contrasted with the case where M is exogenous. From the money market equilibrium condition (5.21) it then follows that i increases, because of the reduction in the real money supply. This means that the current account should improve also through the interest rate channel. However, the government could choose to keep the interest rate constant. When M is exogenous, this can be done with an open market operation in the domestic bond market that raises M in the same proportion as E. Monetary policy is then said to *accommodate* the devaluation.

When F_g is exogenous, money supply is determined by money demand. This means that the devaluation is accommodated 'automatically'. Because the interest rate is lowered, the money supply is increased even more than full accommodation requires. Thus, the key to eventual interest rate effects of a devaluation is the extent to which the devaluation is accommodated by increases in the money supply.

5.5 Imperfect capital mobility: floating exchange rate

With imperfect capital mobility, exogenous money supply and a fixed exchange rate we saw that a surplus on the current account leads to a gradual increase in the foreign exchange reserves. Usually events which lead to increased reserves under fixed rates lead to appreciation under floating rates. Intuition therefore tells us to expect that a surplus on the current account is accompanied by a gradual appreciation under floating rates. One main point of the present section is to prove this intuition. We shall also see that once we have determined the initial exchange rate and wealth distribution, the self-correcting mechanism works in much the same way as with a fixed exchange rate.

The model is the same as in section 5.4 except that now E is endogenous while F_g is exogenous. The money supply, M, is exogenous. Hence, the full list of endogenous variables is W_*, E, i, r and B.

In order to solve the model, first note that for given values of W_*, W_g and F_g/P_* the equilibrium condition of the foreign exchange market (5.23) uniquely determines, r. Thus (5.23) can be solved for r, and the solution can be written

$$r = r(W_*, W_g, F_g/P_*) \quad r_1 > 0, r_2 < 0, r_3 > 0 \tag{5.29}$$

Equation (5.29) also describes how the risk premium is determined under fixed exchange rates when F_g is exogenous. r_1 is actually given by (5.27).

The dynamics of the foreign debt is still described by (5.19), which when (5.29) is inserted reads:

$$\dot{W}_* = \rho_* W_* + C(Y - \rho_* W_*, -W_* - W_g, \rho_* + r(W_*, W_g, F_g/P_*), \rho_*) - Y \qquad (5.30)$$

As before, the initial value of W_* is given. Once an initial value for the exchange rate, and thus for W_g, has been determined, this differential equation can be solved for the whole future path of the foreign debt. The differential equation is actually the same as when the exchange rate is fixed and F_g is exogenous. Once the initial E has been determined, the dynamics of the foreign debt is the same irrespective of whether the central bank has an exogenous money supply target or an exogenous exchange rate target as long as it does not buy or sell foreign currency. Refraining from foreign exchange market interventions speeds up the convergence towards current account balance, because a high debt then means a high real interest rate.

Exchange rate determination in the present model resembles exchange rate determination in the monetary model of chapter 4. As there, we can invert the money market equilibrium condition (5.21) and get

$$i = i\left(\frac{M}{EP_*}, Y\right) \quad i_1 < 0, i_2 > 0 \qquad (5.31)$$

By rearranging the definition of the risk premium, $r = i - i_* - e$, we get the differential equation for the exchange rate:

$$\dot{E}/E = i - i_* - r$$

or, when we insert from (5.29) and (5.31)

$$\frac{\dot{E}}{E} = i\left(\frac{M}{EP_*}, Y\right) - i_* - r(W_*, W_g, F_g/P_*) \qquad (5.32)$$

This resembles the differential equation which chapter 4 centred on, but it has got an extra term which relates depreciation and foreign debt. As in chapter 4, we lack an initial condition for E. We also have a positive feedback from E to $\dot{E}$ in (5.32), which means that we have the same type of instability. As in chapter 4, we can solve the problem of the missing initial condition by imposing that, in spite of the general instability, the economy approaches a stationary equilibrium in the long run.

There is an additional problem, however. Imperfect capital mobility means that the two differential equations, (5.32) and (5.30), are interrelated. We cannot solve (5.32) for E before we know W_*. Nor can we solve (5.30) for W_* before we know $E(0)$, since W_g depends on the initial exchange rate (5.12). Thus, we need to treat the two differential equations as a system.

For simplicity we assume that both M and P_* are constant over time. Little is lost by this, and generalizations are quite obvious.

We can then define a stationary equilibrium as a combination of E and W_* which yields a constant foreign debt and a constant exchange rate – i.e. $\dot{W}_* = 0$ and $\dot{E}/E = 0$. If we impose these conditions on (5.32) and (5.30), we get

$$\dot{W}_* = 0 \Leftrightarrow C(Y - \rho_* W_*, -W_* - W_g, \rho_* + r(W_*, W_g, F_g/P_*), \rho_*)$$

$$= Y - \rho_* W_* \tag{5.33}$$

$$\frac{\dot{E}}{E} = 0 \Leftrightarrow i\left(\frac{M}{EP_*}, Y\right) = i_* + r(W_*, W_g, F_g/P_*) \tag{5.34}$$

These two equations determine the stationary values of W_* and E for a given W_g. However, since W_g depends on $E(0)$ and $E(0)$ depends on where the stationary state is, we have to determine $E(0)$ and the stationary state simultaneously. Technically this is a rather difficult and unusual problem. We shall first avoid it by looking at the special case where $M_0 + B_0 = 0$. This means that W_g is given independently of the initial exchange rate.

With W_g given we can in principle solve (5.30) for W_* first, and then (5.32) for E. However, the results are easier to generalize if we treat the two equations jointly. In figure 5.3 we have drawn a phase diagram for this system. Equation (5.33) defines one value of W_* which is compatible with external balance – i.e. with a constant W_*. This is shown in figure 5.3 as the $\dot{W}_* = 0$ line. To the left of this line the foreign debt is increasing, to the right it is falling, as the horizontal arrows indicate. This follows from the assumption (5.24) that the equation is stable.

Equation (5.34) defines the combinations of E and W_* which make the exchange rate constant. It is shown in figure 5.3 as the $\dot{E} = 0$ locus. It slopes upwards. The reason is that a higher foreign debt means a higher risk premium. If the exchange rate is expected to be constant, a higher risk premium can be brought about only by a higher nominal interest rate. A higher interest rate in turn can be brought about only by a tighter money market. Since the nominal quantity of money is constant, this requires

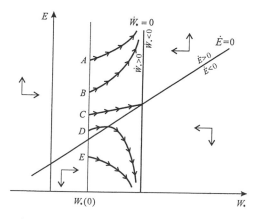

Figure 5.3 Exchange rate and foreign debt dynamics.

higher prices, which because of purchasing power parity is the same as a higher exchange rate. As the vertical arrows indicate, above the $\dot{E} = 0$ locus the exchange rate depreciates, below it it appreciates. This is a consequence of the basic instability of the exchange rate equation. More formally in (5.32) the right-hand side increases monotonically in E, and this proves that $\dot{E}$ is positive when we are above, negative when we are below, the equilibrium locus.

The two equilibrium loci ($\dot{W}_* = 0$ and $\dot{E} = 0$) divide the plane in four regions, and the arrows in each region indicate the direction of movement of W_* and E from any starting point within that region.

The initial foreign debt, $W_*(0)$ is given by past history. Thus, the economy starts off from a point along the vertical line at $W_*(0)$. Since the initial exchange rate is free to jump, any point along this line is a potential starting point. In figure 5.3 $W_*(0)$ is below its stationary value, which means that irrespective of what $E(0)$ is, the foreign debt will be increasing. The self-correcting mechanism for the current account works in the same way as before.

In figure 5.3 we have drawn five paths from five alternative starting points (five alternative values of $E(0)$). Paths A and B start with fairly high exchange rates, well above the $\dot{E} = 0$ locus. The arrows in this region indicate that the direction of the paths from A and B should be towards the north-east, with depreciation and an increasing foreign debt. The exchange rate depreciates for the same reason that an initial exchange rate above the equilibrium in the monetary model of section 4.1 would depreciate. The depreciated exchange rate is consistent with simultaneous equilibrium in the money and foreign exchange market only if a further depreciation is expected, and since expectations are model-consistent this is also what happens. Thus, if we start with a high exchange rate, (5.32) and (5.30) mean that we go on a path with a steadily depreciating exchange rate. In the long run the foreign debt approaches its stationary value, while the exchange rate continues to depreciate at an accelerating speed.

Path D also starts from a point above the $\dot{E} = 0$ locus, but a bit further down than A and B. Relative to the two curves that define the stationary equilibrium, path D starts in the same region as A and B. Hence, the movement is in the same direction to begin with. But after a while the path hits the $\dot{E} = 0$ locus. After that the currency starts to appreciate while the foreign debt continues to increase.

Path E is typical of those paths which start below the $\dot{E} = 0$ locus. As the arrows in this region indicate, the exchange rate appreciates at the same time as there is a current account deficit. The foreign debt increases. In the long run the foreign debt approaches its stationary level, while the appreciation goes on forever.

Between paths B and D there must be one path which hits the intersection between the two loci. In figure 5.3, this is drawn as path C. Such a path is called a *saddle path*.

All the paths depicted in figure 5.3 are potential solutions of the model. The common presumption among exchange rate theorists is that the economy will follow the only path which leads to the stationary equilibrium – i.e. path C, the saddle path. The reason is the same as when we chose the non-explosive solution in chapter 4. All

the other paths lead either to hyperinflation or hyperdeflation. A belief in the saddle
path is a belief in the stability of the monetary system itself.

Note that the saddle path slopes upwards. This means that if we start with a low
foreign debt, the currency depreciates as the country accumulates more foreign debt.
The depreciation means a gradual increase in the nominal demand for money. This
results in a higher nominal interest rate. At the same time the risk premium goes up
because of the increase in foreign debt. In the end the exchange rate is stabilized at a
higher level than before, and there is an increase in the risk premium.

If we start with a foreign debt higher than in the stationary equilibrium, there is
another saddle path which leads to the stationary equilibrium from the other side. This
is illustrated in figure 5.4 with the path approaching A from the right. Along this path a
falling foreign debt is accompanied by an appreciating currency, a declining kroner
interest rate and a falling risk premium. The slope of the saddle path means that a
current account deficit is accompanied by a depreciation, a current account surplus by
an appreciation.

Intuitively we may describe the solution like this: the exchange rate today depends
on the exchange rate that is expected for tomorrow. The investors have rational expectations. When they form expectations about tomorrow's exchange rate, they must take
into account the fact that tomorrow's exchange rate depends on what exchange rate
will then be expected to prevail on the day after tomorrow. In this way the exchange
rate today depends on the whole time path of expected exchange rates to infinity.
However, the investors expect that as time tends towards infinity the economy will
tend towards the stationary equilibrium. When forming their expectations they can
then start with the stationary equilibrium and reason backwards. To get to the stationary equilibrium the exchange rate must follow the saddle path, which is the only
path leading there. By following the saddle path backwards in time from the stationary
equilibrium the investors will in their reasoning sooner or later come to the point
where the saddle path meets the line $W_*(0)$. This point tells what rate of depreciation

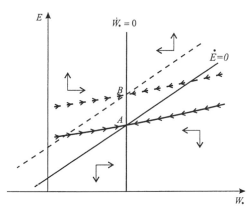

Figure 5.4 The effect of increased money supply.

to expect today, and this determines the initial equilibrium. From that the economy follows the saddle path. The investors' expectation becomes a self-fulfilling prophecy. Other self-fulfilling prophecies are possible, but the belief in long-run equilibrium determines that the saddle path is chosen.

In figure 5.4 we have illustrated the effect of a once and for all increase in the supply of money. We assume that initially we are in the stationary equilibrium A. The $\dot{E} = 0$ locus shifts upwards in the same proportion as M. The $\dot{W}_* = 0$ locus is independent of the quantity of money. We see from figure 5.4 that the new stationary equilibrium B is right above the old one. The exchange rate immediately jumps to the saddle path which leads into the new stationary equilibrium and stays there. In our case, this means that the economy jumps to the new stationary equilibrium. In other words, we get an immediate depreciation with the same percentage as the increase in the money stock. The current account, the foreign debt and the domestic interest rate are unaffected.

Note that the effects of an increase in the money supply with floating rates are the same as the effects of a devaluation under fixed rates when $M + B = 0$. Then the devaluation leads to no initial redistribution of wealth and, thus, has no effect on real variables. The short-run neutrality of money that we just discovered obviously depends on the fact that $M + B = 0$.

The solution to the more general case, where $M + B$ may differ from 0, has many traits in common with the above. When the initial exchange rate has been chosen, the foreign debt W_* evolves independently of further changes in the exchange rate, as we can see from (5.32). This means that once started the self-correcting process works as under fixed exchange rates.

In a way figure 5.3 describes the solution also in the general case. We still have to choose a saddle path in order to get a solution which leads to the stationary equilibrium. However, the two equilibrium schedules depend on W_g, which again depends on the initial exchange rate. Thus, the stationary equilibrium depends on the initial exchange rate. The method we used to determine the initial exchange rate was to start from the stationary equilibrium and move backwards along the saddle path. In the general case the initial and stationary equilibria must be determined simultaneously.

We can imagine that the solution is found in the following way: we start with a guess at the initial exchange rate. We then find the stationary solution corresponding to this initial exchange rate. Next we move backwards along the saddle path until we get to the initial foreign debt. If the exchange rate is then equal to our initial guess, we have the right solution. If not, we try with a new guess (perhaps in the range between our first guess and the initial exchange rate it led to) and repeat the procedure. The final solution must in any case look like figure 5.4. If we start with a low foreign debt, we go through a phase with current account deficits and depreciation before we reach the stationary equilibrium. If we start with a high foreign debt, we go through a phase with current account surpluses and appreciation before we reach the stationary equilibrium. In the general case an increase in the money supply has real effects, just as a devaluation has real effects when $M_0 + B_0 \neq 0$.

The quantitative importance of many of the effects we have discussed in this section depends on the degree of capital mobility. The higher capital mobility is, the closer r is to being independent of W_g and W_*, and the more will the results resemble those we got with perfect capital mobility in section 5.3.

5.6 Government deficits

In section 5.2 ((5.5) and (5.6)) we defined the government surplus as

$$\dot{W}_g = \rho_* W_g - r\frac{M+B}{P} + i\frac{M}{P} + T - G \tag{5.35}$$

If we insert in this from the definition of W_g and from the money demand function, and rearrange, we get the alternative expression

$$\dot{W}_g = \rho_* \frac{EF_g}{P} - (\rho_* + r)\frac{M+B}{P} + im(i, Y) + T - G \tag{5.36}$$

which makes clear how the surplus depends on the price level. Above we assumed that the government budget was balanced in the sense that $\dot{W}_g = 0$. This was done by adjusting T. In this section we sketch some consequences of government deficits ($\dot{W}_g < 0$). T and G are treated as exogenous.

There is no automatic self-correction of government deficits. On the contrary, there is an obvious tendency to instability in (5.35) owing to the interest payments on the debt. Presumably, in a stationary environment governments cannot go on having deficits forever. (The limits on deficits are discussed in section 5.10.) Sooner or later some political action must be taken to stop the deficit. If $M + B > 0$, there are four main alternatives: (1) increase T; (2) reduce G; (3) reduce the real value of government debt by raising the price level (which means a one-time depreciation); (4) increase seigniorage revenue by increasing inflation (which implies a continuous depreciation).

The self-correcting mechanism for the current account that we studied in sections 5.3–5.5 is really a self-correcting mechanism for the financial surplus of the private sector, $\dot{W}_p$. By definition $W_p + W_g + W_* = 0$, and when W_g is constant, the dynamics of W_p and W_* are mirror images of each other. Even if the government runs a deficit, the main lessons of section 5.5 hold for W_p, and thus for that part of the current account and the foreign debt that is related to the private sector. In the long run we expect $\dot{W}_p$ to go towards zero, which means that the current account deficit equals the government deficit.

In the general case the full dynamics are cumbersome to work out because of the many interest flows one has to take account of. However, a simple example illustrates the main point. Assume perfect capital mobility ($r = 0$) and disregard seigniorage. Then the disposable income of the government is $Y_g = \rho_* W_g + T$, and of the private sector $Y_p = Y + \rho_* W_p - T$. The growth in the financial wealth of the two domestic sectors is then

$$\dot{W}_p = Y + \rho_* W_p - T - C(Y + \rho_* W_p - T, W_p, \rho_*) \tag{5.37}$$

$$\dot{W}_g = \rho_* W_g + T - G \tag{5.38}$$

The two differential equations are completely separate. For given initial values of W_p and W_g, (5.37) determines the time path of W_p and (5.38) that of W_g. The time path of W_* follows from $W_p + W_g + W_* = 0$. Equation (5.37) is the mirror image of the one we studied in section 5.3, and the stability condition is the same. Equation (5.38) is inherently unstable when $\rho_* > 0$. As long as no corrective measures are taken, the deficit grows over time because of the interest payments on the accumulated debt.

The picture given above neglects one important point. There is always some probability that the government resorts to inflation, either one-time or continued, in order to restore the budget balance. When the price level abroad is constant, this possibility makes e_e positive (unless there is also a chance that the foreign government uses inflation in order to reduce its budget deficit). The larger the deficit, the more likely it is that the government eventually resorts to inflation, and the higher e_e is likely to be. Since the deficit grows over time, there is a tendency for e_e to grow over time.

Assume a *fixed exchange rate*. With perfect capital mobility, an increase in e_e is reflected one for one in i. This means that countries with government deficits tend to have high and rising nominal interest rates. If expectations are consistent with purchasing power parity, we still have real interest rate parity, meaning that $\rho = \rho_*$. However, this holds only *ex ante*, based on expected inflation and expected depreciation. As long as no devaluation takes place, $e = 0$ while $e_e > 0$. The *ex post* real interest rate is then

$$i - p = i_* + e_e - p_* = \rho_* + e_e \tag{5.39}$$

While the *ex ante* rate is relevant for the consumption decision, the *ex post* rate is the one which matters for the actual growth of government debt over time. Thus the accounting in (5.35) and (5.36) should be adjusted to take account of the *ex post* real interest rates. In general an extra term $(e - e_e)(M + B)/P$ should be added. As long as $e < e_e$ and $M + B > 0$, this means a further increase in the deficit.

The upshot is that a government which is fixing the exchange rate should take care not to have a persistent (or unsustainable) deficit. If corrective action is not taken in the form of a reduction in G or an increase in T, the increase in e_e could after a while accelerate rapidly and a currency crisis could arise. With extremely high interest rates and rapidly increasing debts, the government may find no better way out than to devalue. The literature on government deficits as a source of currency crisis is surveyed in Obstfeld (1994) and in Garber and Svensson (1995). An influential paper which started much of the literature was Krugman (1979).

The likelihood that the government resorts to a devaluation must depend on the currency composition of the government debt. In principle the government can decide this freely when there is perfect capital mobility. It is the interest rate which keeps the exchange rate fixed. The government may remove the fear of a one-time devaluation by keeping $M + B = 0$, which means that it finances the whole deficit by borrowing foreign currency. With $M + B = 0$ there is nothing to gain by devaluing. Persson, Persson and Svensson (1987) show how this can be the optimal behaviour for the government when the private agents have expectations that are model-consistent. Starting from zero, an increase in $M + B$ must raise e_e. However, it is not obvious that the expected rate of depreciation increases monotonically in the share of the debt that is denominated in domestic currency. If a large share of the debt is in domestic currency, a small devaluation is enough to reduce the debt burden substantially.

When capital mobility is imperfect, the financing of the deficit may also affect the risk premium. However, the financing has to be consistent with the exchange rate target. As we saw in section 3.1, when there is an exchange rate target, only one of the items on the government balance sheet can be chosen freely. The others are then tied up by the exchange rate target. Thus, we may ask about the consequences of the deficit when either M, B or F_g is kept constant.

Let us now disregard the eventual effects on e_e that were discussed above. For the sake of the argument, let us also keep W_p constant. The current account deficit is then equal to the government deficit. A constant M implies a constant i and, thus, a constant r. As can be seen from (5.22), the demand for domestic bonds is then unaffected by W_*. This means that B must be constant, too. The only way the deficit can be financed with both a fixed exchange rate and a fixed money supply is if it is 100 per cent financed by borrowing foreign currency or drawing on the foreign exchange reserves. Obviously, the same can be said if B is kept constant. Note the similarity with the result from section 1.6 (p. 33). If foreigners do not hold domestic currency, if the interest rate is constant and if the government and current account deficits are equal, the result there too says that a government deficit leads to a reduction of the same size in the foreign exchange reserves.

A constant F_g means that the interest rate is used to keep the exchange rate fixed. The current account deficit means that F_* declines over time. There is then less room for private holdings of foreign currency, and the interest rate has to be increased in order to induce the private sector to shift to domestic currency. But the increased interest rate means a reduced demand for money. The upshot is that not only is the deficit financed 100 per cent by domestic bonds, the central bank in addition has to sell bonds to retract some of the money supply in order to keep the interest rate high enough.

Thus the conclusion is: the government can either borrow foreign currency, and let the interest rate stay constant, or it can induce the private sector to borrow foreign currency by raising the domestic interest rate. How much foreign currency the government borrows decides how strong the increase in the interest rate is going to be.

To this, two modifications should be added. A higher interest rate due to a higher risk premium may induce the public to save more, and in the short run this reduces the current account deficit. Over time W_p increases, and W_* increases less than if there was only the government deficit. This dampens the increase in i that is needed to keep the foreign exchange market balanced. Another way to put it is that the growth in W_p increases the demand for domestic currency bonds, and allows the government to borrow more in domestic currency for a given increase in i.

The other modification is that if foreigners invest a share of the increase in W_* in domestic currency bonds, then this share can be financed in domestic currency without an increase in interest rates. This can be seen from section 1.6. However, the more of the deficit that is financed by foreigners lending domestic currency, the more tempting it may be for the government to devalue, and solve the budget problem at the expense of the foreigners. This strategy may thus result in a high e_e and require high interest rates because of that.

If there is a *floating exchange rate* and M is exogenous, the story has many similarities to the one just told for fixed rates, but there is also a crucial difference. The risk that the government will solve the budget problem by resorting to inflationary finance is the same. However, with a floating exchange rate, an expected depreciation must lead to an immediate actual depreciation even if the money supply is constant. When $M + B > 0$ this jump in the exchange rate reduces the real deficit immediately, but not by enough to eliminate it. The depreciation also raises the price level and, hence, the interest rate that is required to keep the money market in equilibrium.

In the same way as above, we can argue that there will be a tendency for e_e to increase gradually over time as long as the budget problem is not solved. However, this now leads to a gradual depreciation and an accompanying inflation. As long as M is constant while P increases, the interest rate also tends to increase. This yields some extra seigniorage revenue, but not enough to remove the deficit, since if the deficit were removed, inflation would cease too. Thus, in order to keep the price level constant, it is not enough to have a constant money supply. A budget which is balanced over the long run (or a sustainable deficit) is required. Sargent (1986) makes this point forcefully with a number of examples.

When the exchange rate is floating and M is fixed, the government can choose to finance the deficit by selling either foreign or domestic bonds. Assume that capital mobility is imperfect and abstract from the expectations effect discussed above, and from eventual movements in W_p. Then 100 per cent financing in foreign currency keeps the foreign exchange market in equilibrium without any movement in the exchange rate, since a constant amount of foreign currency is then available for the private investors. If the government instead finances some of the deficit in domestic currency, private investors must take over a similar share of the foreign currency financing, since the government deficit is paralleled by an equally large current account deficit. What happens is that as the current account deficit gradually reduces the supply of foreign currency, this leads to a gradual depreciation and inflation, which by itself may raise the *nominal* demand for domestic bonds. In addition the interest rate increases, because the nominal demand for money goes up, while the supply is constant. Thus, with imperfect capital mobility, a constant money supply leads to price stability only if government deficits are financed in foreign currency.

5.7 Wage rigidity

So far in this chapter we have assumed that wages are flexible, and that employment always is at its equilibrium level. Combined with a given capital stock this labour input has produced a constant level of output. We now allow for wage rigidity. This means that in the short run output and employment are determined by how much labour producers demand at the given wage rate. Over time wages change according to a Phillips curve relation. Our task is to look more closely at the time path of output and employment, and at the interaction between the dynamics of the wage rate, the exchange rate and the foreign debt.

One conclusion is that a higher real wage produces a higher current account deficit. Another conclusion is that the short-run effect of a devaluation depends crucially on whether it is real or nominal wages which are sticky. A third conclusion is that if the economy starts with a wage rate above equilibrium, and the exchange rate is floating, the path towards equilibrium will involve a gradual appreciation. The appreciation accompanies the gradual reduction of the real wage which is produced by an excess supply of labour.

Our starting point is the model of section 5.3, where we are going to endogenize Y. We return to the case of perfect capital mobility to avoid too many complexities at one time. First we shall write down the new relations which we need in order to discuss wage rigidity, and then we shall look at the cases of fixed and flexible exchange rates in turn.

Aggregate output Y is a function of the input of labour, N, and capital, K:

$$Y = \Phi(N, K) \tag{5.40}$$

The production function Φ is homogeneous of degree one in N and K and has all standard neo-classical properties. For the moment we shall treat K as a factor which is fixed both in the short and the long run. Profit maximization for a given output price P and a given nominal wage rate W gives the usual first-order condition

$$P\Phi_N(N, K) = W \tag{5.41}$$

from which it follows that the demand for labour in the economy is[34]

$$N = N(W/P, K) = N(\omega, K), \quad N_\omega < 0, \quad N_K > 0 \tag{5.42}$$

where $\omega = W/P$ is the *real wage*. Similarly the supply of output, which we need later, is

$$Y = Y(\omega, K), \quad Y_\omega < 0, \quad Y_K > 0 \tag{5.43}$$

Over time wages grow according to the expectations augmented Phillips curve

$$\frac{\dot{W}}{W} = \frac{\dot{P}}{P} + \gamma(N - \bar{N})$$

where we continue to assume model-consistent expectations, and where $\gamma > 0$. $\bar{N}$ can be interpreted as the equilibrium level of employment corresponding to an equilibrium rate of unemployment. If we recall the definition of the real wage, we can rewrite the Phillips relation as

$$\frac{\dot{\omega}}{\omega} = \gamma(N - \bar{N}) \tag{5.44}$$

We shall focus on two main types of wage rigidity. When there is *nominal wage rigidity,* the initial level of the nominal wage w is given by past history. The real wage is free to jump at any time, if there is a jump in the price level P. When there is *real wage rigidity,* the initial real wage ω is given by past history. If there is a jump in the price level, the nominal wage immediately jumps with the same proportion. This could be the case when wages are automatically indexed to the price level. Equation (5.44) describes the development over time of the real wage in both cases. The difference between the two types of wage rigidity manifests itself only when there is a jump in the price level.

If we insert (5.42) in (5.44) we get a differential equation

$$\frac{\dot{\omega}}{\omega} = \gamma(N(\omega, K) - \bar{N}) \tag{5.45}$$

in one unknown, ω. For a given initial level of ω this determines the whole time path of ω.

When there is real wage rigidity, the solution of the model is simple. The initial value of ω is given by past history. We can solve (5.45) for ω first. Y and N then follows from (5.43) and (5.42). Thus, the time paths of the real wage, output and employment are independent of the exchange rate and of domestic demand. Afterwards we can use the monetary model from section 4.1 to find the path of the exchange rate – or, if the exchange rate is fixed, to find the money supply. Finally we can solve (5.14) for the foreign debt.

When there is nominal wage rigidity, things get more complicated, since the initial real wage may have to be determined together with the initial exchange rate. In order to look more closely at how this works, we need to distinguish between fixed and flexible exchange rates.

Fixed exchange rate

We can draw the differential equation for the real wage (5.45) in a phase diagram, as in figure 5.5. It slopes downwards since

$$\frac{d\dot{\omega}/\omega}{d\omega} = \gamma N_\omega < 0 \tag{5.46}$$

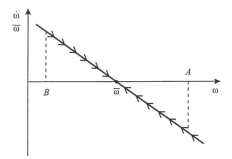

Figure 5.5 Real wage dynamics with a
fixed exchange rate.

A higher real wage means lower employment, which again means less real wage
growth.

The stationary equilibrium, $\bar{\omega}$, is where the curve hits the ω axis. It is defined by

$$\dot{\omega} = 0 \quad \Leftrightarrow \quad N(\bar{\omega}, K) = \bar{N} \tag{5.47}$$

Since, as (5.46) tells us, there is a negative feedback from the real wage to its own rate
of growth, the stationary equilibrium is stable. If we start with a high real wage, as in
point A in figure 5.5, employment will be low and the real wage tends to decline. This
means that the nominal wage increases less than the price level. As the real wage
gradually declines, the demand for labour increases accordingly. This continues
until the real wage has reached its stationary level, at which point employment is
also in equilibrium. If we start with a low real wage, as in point B, the movement is
the opposite.

The difference between real and nominal wage rigidity appears if we look at the
effect of a one-time devaluation. The exchange rate is not an argument in the differential equation (5.45). Thus, a devaluation does not affect the curve depicted in figure
5.5. If there is real wage rigidity, the initial real wage is unchanged, too. The nominal
wage W immediately goes up in the same proportion as the price level. Thus, in figure
5.5 nothing happens. If the economy is initially in the stationary equilibrium, it stays
there.

If there is nominal wage rigidity, a devaluation immediately reduces the real wage,
since $\omega = W/EP_*$. If the economy is initially in the stationary equilibrium, the devaluation moves it to a point like B in figure 5.5. At the lower real wage employment is
higher. There is upward pressure on wages, and the real wage starts to increase gradually. As the real wage increases, employment declines until the stationary equilibrium is reached again. As far as output, employment and the real wage are concerned,
the long-run effect of a devaluation is zero irrespective of whether there is real or
nominal wage rigidity. The short-run effect on output and employment is positive
with nominal wage rigidity, zero with real wage rigidity.

Suppose the initial equilibrium were at A. Then, if there is no devaluation, the economy has to go through a period of high unemployment before the stationary equilibrium is reached. International competitiveness (measured by ω) has to be improved before one can get to the equilibrium level of employment. If there is nominal wage rigidity, a suitable devaluation can produce the required improvement in international competitiveness and bring the economy to the full equilibrium.

Note that continuous devaluations have no effect on employment or the real wage. $\dot{E}/E$ is not in the differential equation (5.45), nor does it make the initial real wage jump. A continuous devaluation, which is anticipated, produces only higher inflation.

The time path of Y will of course affect the time path of W_* in (5.14). However, as long as employment tends towards its equilibrium level $\bar{N}$ in the long run, output will also tend towards a long-run equilibrium $\bar{Y} = \Phi(\bar{N}, K)$. This means that the stationary equilibrium and the stability condition for the foreign debt are the same as before. Periods where the real wage is below equilibrium will be characterized by a high output level Y. Since the marginal propensity to consume out of income is less than one, a low real wage thus contributes to a high current account surplus. A high real wage – i.e. poor international competitiveness – will similarly contribute to a high current account deficit.

If we assume nominal wage rigidity and take a devaluation starting from a stationary equilibrium as an example, the dynamics of the foreign debt will be as follows: there is an immediate improvement in the current account both because of the increased output and because of the transfer of wealth from the public to the government. This means a more rapid accumulation of domestic private wealth than when there was only the latter effect. Thus the move towards the new stationary level of the foreign debt is speeded up. The final result, however, is the same as if wages were flexible and employment always equal to $\bar{N}$.

Floating exchange rate

In chapter 4 the exchange rate was determined by the differential equation (4.3), which was derived from the interest parity condition $\dot{E}/E = i - i_*$ and the equilibrium condition for the money market written in the form $i = i(M/EP_*, Y)$. The only thing we have to add is that Y now depends on the real wage. Hence, the exchange rate equation is now

$$\frac{\dot{E}}{E} = i\left(\frac{M}{EP_*}, Y(\omega, K)\right) - i_* \tag{5.48}$$

Together with (5.45) this forms a system of two differential equations in two unknown endogenous variables, E and ω. This can be used to solve for the time paths of the two variables when the initial values of ω and E are given. However, we have only one initial condition. Either W or ω is given. The initial E is free to jump to any level. We can still find a unique solution if we apply the same principle as in chapter 4 – namely, that we exclude explosive paths for E. Because of the need to choose the initial E, it is necessary to treat the equations jointly even though (5.45) appears to be independent of E.

The stationary equilibrium is defined by

$$\dot{\omega} = 0 \Leftrightarrow N(\omega, K) = \bar{N} \tag{5.49}$$

$$\dot{E} = 0 \Leftrightarrow i\left(\frac{M}{EP_*}, Y(\omega, K)\right) = i_* \tag{5.50}$$

These two equilibrium relations are shown in figure 5.6. As above, there is a unique equilibrium real wage, $\bar{\omega}$, defined by (5.49). At this wage rate there is equilibrium in the labour market. As the vertical arrows indicate, if the real wage is higher, it tends to decline. If the real wage is lower, it tends to increase. This is the same Phillips curve mechanism we just saw operating under fixed exchange rates.

The combinations of ω and E which yield equilibrium in the foreign exchange market according to (5.50) form an upward-sloping curve in the E-ω diagram. A high real wage means a low output level. This means a low money demand. However, M is given exogenously. When $e = 0$ and, hence, $i = i_*$, the only thing which can then keep the money market in equilibrium is a depreciated exchange rate. The counterpart to the low demand for money is a high demand for foreign assets (and domestic bonds), and this causes the depreciated exchange rate. Formally we find the slope of the $\dot{E} = 0$ curve by differentiating (5.50) with respect to ω and E. This yields

$$\frac{d\omega}{dE} = \frac{i_1(M/E^2 P_*)}{i_2 Y_\omega} > 0$$

As usual, there is a tendency to instability around the equilibrium locus for the foreign exchange market. As in section 4.1 a depreciated exchange rate leads to further depreciation according to (5.48) ($\partial \dot{E}/\partial E$ is positive). Hence, the horizontal arrows indicate that the exchange rate tends to move away from equilibrium. If the exchange rate is low, that means a high real money supply. The domestic interest rate will then be low.

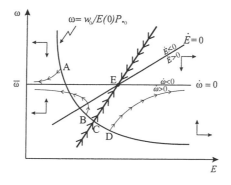

Figure 5.6 Real wage dynamics with a floating exchange rate.

That can be reconciled with interest rate parity only if the domestic currency is appreciating.

The two equilibrium loci $\dot{E} = 0$ and $\dot{\omega} = 0$ divide the plane in figure 5.6 in four sections. In each section the arrows indicate the direction of movement of ω and E from any starting point within the same region.

The problem now is to find the right starting point in figure 5.6. Suppose there is nominal wage rigidity. This means that the initial real wage is $\omega(0) = W_0/E(0)P_{*0}$. Since W_0 is predetermined and P_{*0} is exogenous, this defines a curved relation between the initial exchange rate and the initial real wage. Any starting point has to be on this curve. Since the initial exchange rate $E(0)$ is free to jump, any point along the curve is a potential starting point. Four alternatives, A, B, C and D are shown in figure 5.6. Once started, the dynamics of the real wage is independent of the exchange rate and leads towards $\bar{\omega}$. Hence, all paths converge towards $\bar{\omega}$ in the long run. However, if we start with an appreciated exchange rate, as in A, there is a never-ending tendency to further appreciation. This is just as when we started with an appreciated exchange rate in chapter 4, and the reasons are the same. Starting from B there is first a depreciation, but then the equilibrium curve for the foreign exchange market is crossed, and after that the exchange rate appreciates in infinity. Starting from D there is a depreciation which continues forever. However, somewhere between B and D there must be a starting point with a path that leads right to the stationary equilibrium E. In figure 5.6 this is the path starting from C. As mentioned in section 5.5, such a path is called a saddle path. For the same reason as the stationary solution was chosen in section 4.1, we here choose the only starting point which leads us to the stationary solution. Thus, with nominal wage rigidity, the solution of the model is the saddle path that starts at C and leads to E.

Once we know that the solution must be on a saddle path which leads to E, we could proceed differently. From each side there is only one saddle path which leads to E. Both are shown in figure 5.6. The saddle paths are located in the part of the diagram where the arrows consistently point towards E. Draw the saddle path first; the starting point is where it hits the curve that the initial values of ω and E must be on.

If there is real instead of nominal wage rigidity, the initial exchange rate is at the point where a horizontal line at the given ω_0 hits the saddle path. The starting point may differ, but the further dynamics are the same as with nominal rigidity.

Note that the saddle path slopes upwards. This means that if the economy starts with a real wage above equilibrium, it goes through a period where a *nominal appreciation* is combined with a *real depreciation* (the latter meaning that the economy gets more competitive because the real wage declines). If we start with a low real wage, it is the other way around. These results can be explained as follows: the dynamics of the labour market moves the real wage and the level of output towards equilibrium irrespective of what happens in the foreign exchange market. If we start with a high real wage, this means that output is increasing continuously. The increase in output raises the demand for money – i.e. for the domestic currency – and, hence, the domestic currency appreciates.

When $\omega > \bar{\omega}$, output Y is below its equilibrium level. As under fixed rates, this tends to produce a current account deficit. Since the currency appreciates when $\omega > \bar{\omega}$, we have here a case where an appreciation takes place simultaneously with a current account deficit. Conversely, if $\omega < \bar{\omega}$ there is a depreciation together with a current account surplus. This result may surprise. However, we have assumed perfect capital mobility which removes the portfolio shift effects of current accounts discussed in sections 1.6 and 5.5. The driving force behind the present result is that current account deficits are accompanied by wage deflation, while current account surpluses are accompanied by wage inflation.

The effect of an exogenous one-time increase in the money supply is shown in figure 5.7. The equilibrium locus for the foreign exchange market shifts to the right in the same proportion as the increase in the money supply. The reason is that for a given ω, Y is constant. The equilibrium exchange rate is then proportional to the money supply (cf. (5.50)). The equilibrium real wage is unaffected by the increased money supply. Figure 5.7 illustrates what happens when there is nominal wage rigidity and the economy is initially in the stationary equilibrium A. It jumps immediately to B where the curve for possible initial equilibria intersects the saddle path to the new stationary equilibrium E. This means that initially the currency is depreciated and the real wage reduced. Then, since the saddle path slopes upwards, we go through a period where the currency depreciates further while the real wage increases towards its old level. During this period there is 'overfull' employment ($N > \bar{N}$). It is this overfull employment which makes wages rise faster than prices. In the end the real wage as well as the real quantity of money return to their initial levels.

Note that during the transition period the domestic interest rate must be higher than the foreign interest rate. This follows since the interest rate differential is equal to the rate of depreciation. We have the rather unusual result that *an increase in the money supply increases the rate of interest*. The reason is that the increase in the money supply

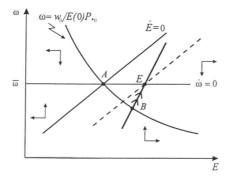

Figure 5.7 The effect of an increased money supply.

is expected to be permanent, and that the effect on the price level is delayed because of the nominal wage rigidity.

A monetary expansion has a similar effect on the foreign debt as a devaluation. The immediate jump in the exchange rate redistributes wealth between the government and the private sector. However, the redistribution which follows a 10 per cent increase in the money supply is less than the redistribution which follows a 10 per cent devaluation. The reason is that the immediate jump in the exchange rate is smaller. As with a devaluation, the adjustment of the foreign debt is speeded up by the increased output during the transition period.

5.8 Real capital and investment

In this section we include real investment in the model. As a preparation we already included real capital in the production function (5.40) of section 5.7. Now it is time to make real capital endogenous.[35]

We have assumed perfect mobility of financial capital. If physical capital could also be moved across borders without costs, the domestic capital stock would be free to jump at any time. Profit-maximizing producers would buy enough real capital to equate the marginal product of capital to the international real interest rate. This kind of model may be relevant for international shipping, since the cost of changing the home registration of a ship can be negligible. However, the aggregate capital stock usually develops more continuously, not in big jumps. If we are to analyse such a gradual build-up, we have to assume that there are some kind of adjustment costs (or assume that capital goods are non-traded, see chapter 7).

Since the production function is homogeneous of degree one, the rate of return on capital, π, can be written as a function of the real wage only – i.e. $\pi = \pi(\omega)$. A higher real wage means lower return to capital – i.e. $\pi' < 0$ (see appendix B, p. 359). The investment function we assume is

$$\frac{\dot{K}}{K} = I(\pi(\omega) - \rho_*) \tag{5.51}$$

where $I(0) = 0$ and $I' > 0$. This means that investment is positively related to the rate of return differential between real and financial investments. The return on the latter is represented by ρ_* since there is perfect mobility of financial capital. If the two rates of return are equal, real investment is zero. In spite of that the capital goods are traded, the capital stock changes only gradually through a continuous investments process. Presumably this is because there are adjustment costs, but these are not modelled explicitly.[36]

In addition to the investment function (5.51) our model consists of the Phillips relation

$$\frac{\dot{\omega}}{\omega} = \gamma(N(\omega, K) - \bar{N}) \tag{5.52}$$

and the differential equation for the foreign debt which should be modified to

$$\dot{W}_* = \rho_* W_* + C(Y(\omega, K) - \rho_* W_*, K - W_* - W_g, \rho_*)$$
$$+ I(\pi(\omega) - \rho_*)K - Y(\omega, K)$$

(5.53)

In this, we have taken account of the fact that real investment adds to the current account deficit in the same way as consumption, and that real capital is a part of wealth.

Equations (5.51), (5.52) and (5.53) are three differential equations in three unknowns: ω, K and W_*. The initial values of K and W_* are given by past history. With a fixed exchange rate the initial value of ω is also given; either directly, with real wage rigidity, or indirectly through $\omega = W/EP_*$, with nominal wage rigidity. With a floating exchange rate and nominal wage rigidity we also need to include the exchange rate equation (5.48), and the determination of the initial value is more complicated, as we saw in section 5.7.

Fortunately the two equations (5.51) and (5.52) do not include W_*. This means that we can solve them first to yield the time paths of ω and K. At least this is true when somehow the initial value of ω is given to us, as with real wage rigidity or in general with a fixed exchange rate. The phase diagram for this subsystem is drawn in figure 5.8. The stationary solution is defined by

$$\dot{K} = 0 \Leftrightarrow \pi(\omega) = \rho_*$$

(5.54)

$$\dot{\omega} = 0 \Leftrightarrow N(\omega, K) = \bar{N}$$

(5.55)

Equation (5.54) tells us that there is just one real wage, $\bar{\omega}$, which yields the right return on capital. $\bar{\omega}$ is defined by $\pi(\bar{\omega}) = \rho_*$. If the real wage is above $\bar{\omega}$, the domestic industry is not competitive. It will shrink gradually and in the end vanish. If the real wage is below $\bar{\omega}$, investing in the country is so profitable that the capital stock will expand without limit. Thus, the $\dot{K} = 0$ locus in figure 5.8 is a straight horizontal line. Above the line the capital stock declines, below the line it increases.

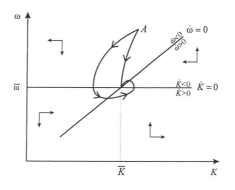

Figure 5.8 Supply-side dynamics with endogenous capital.

Equation (5.55) is the equilibrium condition for the labour market. It slopes upwards in figure 5.8, since a higher capital stock means more demand for labour and this gives room for a higher real wage. As in section 5.7, a real wage above the equilibrium level means high unemployment and a tendency to decline in the real wage. A real wage below the equilibrium level means low unemployment and the real wage will then be increasing over time.

The stationary equilibrium is where the $\dot{K}=0$ and the $\dot{\omega}=0$ loci intersect. The stationary equilibrium is stable. Two possible paths from the initial point A are shown in figure 5.8. The approach to the stationary equilibrium can be either direct or cyclic. Which it is depends on the parameters of the model. Stability cannot be proved by looking at figure 5.8 alone; we have to check the mathematical conditions for stability. In order to do that, we form the Jacobian matrix

$$A = \begin{bmatrix} \frac{\partial \dot{\omega}}{\partial \omega} & \frac{\partial \dot{\omega}}{\partial K} \\ \frac{\partial \dot{K}}{\partial \omega} & \frac{\partial \dot{K}}{\partial K} \end{bmatrix} = \begin{bmatrix} \omega \gamma N_\omega & \omega \gamma N_K \\ K I'\pi' & 0 \end{bmatrix}$$

where the derivatives are evaluated at the stationary equilibrium. Stability is ensured if $\text{tr}(A) < 0$ and $|A| > 0$ (see appendix A). We find

$$\text{tr}(A) = \omega \gamma N_\omega < 0$$

$$|A| = -\omega K \gamma N_K I'\pi' > 0$$

These conditions are always satisfied, and thus the equilibrium is stable.

Because of the homogeneity of the production function, the labour demand function can be written $N = n(\omega)K$ where $n(\omega) = -\pi'(\omega)$ (see appendix B). The trace and determinant can thus alternatively be written as $\text{tr}(A) = \omega \gamma n' K$ and $|A| = \omega \gamma n(\omega)^2 K I'$.

The condition for the adjustment path to be direct, not cyclic, is that $|A| < \frac{1}{4}(\text{tr}(A))^2$ or, after some algebra and use of the alternative expression above,

$$\frac{I'}{K} < \frac{1}{4}\frac{\gamma}{\omega}(\check{n})^2$$

where $\check{n} = n'\omega/n$ is the labour demand elasticity. The main point to note is that a direct approach is likely if the adjustment of the capital stock is slow relative to the adjustment of real wages (I'/K low relative to γ). If this is the case, the economy moves quickly towards the curve where $\dot{\omega} = 0$, and follows this towards the stationary state. If instead the adjustment of the capital stock is fast, the level of the capital stock may easily overshoot its equilibrium value, and the stationary state may then be approached in cycles.

In the long run the real wage of the extremely open economy is determined by the requirement that capital must get the international rate of return. There is just one real wage which ensures that. Given this wage, the supply of labour determines the capital stock in the long-run equilibrium. Formally, the long-run equilibrium level of the capital stock, $\bar{K}$, is determined by the equation $N(\bar{\omega}, \bar{K}) = n(\bar{\omega})\bar{K} = \bar{N}$ (cf. (5.55)). The capital stock is not in any way affected by the level of domestic savings. The level of output in the long-run equilibrium, $\bar{Y}$, is determined from the supply side alone – i.e. by the given supply of labour, $\bar{N}$, and the corresponding capital stock, $\bar{K}$ as $\bar{Y} = \Phi(\bar{N}, \bar{K})$.

The long-run equilibrium for the foreign debt is determined by (cf. (5.53))

$$\dot{W}_* = 0 \Leftrightarrow C(\bar{Y} - \rho_* W_*, K - W_* - W_g, \rho_*) = \bar{Y} - \rho_* W_* \tag{5.56}$$

As before, consumption is equal to national income in equilibrium. Investment drops out of the equation because it is equal to zero in equilibrium. The capital stock enters as a part of private wealth. It also takes part in determining $\bar{Y}$. The equilibrium condition is easier to interpret if we decompose $\bar{Y}$ into factor incomes. Since the production function is homogeneous of degree one, $Y = \omega N + \pi K$. Thus $\bar{Y} = \bar{\omega}\bar{N} + \rho_*\bar{K}$. This means that (5.56) can also be written

$$C(\bar{\omega}\bar{N} + \rho_*(\bar{K} - W_*), \bar{K} - W_* - W_g, \rho_*) = \bar{\omega}\bar{N} + \rho_*(\bar{K} - W_*) \tag{5.57}$$

In (5.57) $\bar{K}$ and W_* always appear together in $\bar{K} - W_*$ which is national wealth. Thus, in (5.57) domestic savings behaviour determines national wealth. Above we described how technology, labour supply and the international real interest rate determines $\bar{K}$. W_* is then determined residually. This means that an increase in the capital stock will, *ceteris paribus*, lead to an equal increase in the equilibrium foreign debt, national wealth being unchanged. However, we should remember that the capital stock is an endogenous variable. If it changes, it will be because something else has changed, and that something else may affect national wealth.

Including real investment does not change the stability condition for the foreign debt. Real investment still has an effect on the path towards equilibrium, as is evident from (5.53). In section 5.7 we explained how a low real wage meant a high output level and, thus, a high surplus on the current account. When we include investment, this need not be so. The reason is that a low real wage also means a high level of investment, and that detracts from the current account surplus. Which effect is the stronger is in general not possible to tell.

5.9 Unions and wage bargaining

Trade unions and wage bargaining can be incorporated into the model of section 5.8. We shall then have to revise the wage equation and the long-run equilibrium condition for the labour market. However, the equilibrium condition for real capital is unchanged. This means that in the long run unions are unable to influence the real wage, while they have a lasting influence on employment.

In order to see the effects of incorporating unions, we shall give a simple example.[37] Think of the economy as consisting of a large number of identical firms. At each firm the wage rate is first set through a bargain between the firm and the local union. The firm then decides how much labour to employ. (The firm has the 'right to manage'.)

The firms maximize profits. Production functions in each firm are homogeneous of degree one in labour and capital. In the short run the capital stock is given, and the profit function of a typical firm can be written (see appendix B)

$$\Pi = \pi(\omega)K \tag{5.58}$$

where Π is total real profits at the firm, π profits per unit of capital, K the capital stock in the firm (being equal to the aggregate capital stock divided by the number of firms) and ω the producer real wage at the firm. The latter is the nominal wage the firm pays divided by the price of its output which is here taken to be exogenous. From standard theory it follows that the firm's demand for labour is $-\pi'(\omega)K$ (see appendix B).

The union wants to maximize the utility of a worker employed at the firm, $v(\omega)$. The utility function is increasing and concave – i.e. $v' > 0$ and $v'' < 0$. We assume that the outcome of the bargaining can be described by an asymmetric Nash bargaining solution. This means that the outcome is the real wage which maximizes the Nash product

$$[v(\omega) - v_0(\Omega, U)]^\beta [\pi(\omega)K]^{1-\beta}$$

β is a parameter between zero and one which measures the relative bargaining strength of the unions. v_0 is a fall-back or reference utility. The reference utility should be interpreted as in Nash's original version as the utility that the workers can obtain outside the firm. This should obviously depend positively on the average real wage in the economy, Ω, and negatively on the economy-wide unemployment rate, U. The reference utility could also depend on the level of unemployment benefits.[38] We can think of the reference utility as a sum of the utilities which can be achieved in different states outside the firm weighted by the probabilities of ending up in each state. Employment in a new firm may be one state and unemployment another. The overall unemployment rate affects the probability of ending up in the different states.

Since it simplifies computation, it is convenient to transform the Nash product by taking logs before we carry out the maximization. This gives us

$$\Gamma(\omega, \Omega, U) = \beta \ln[v(\omega) - v_0(\Omega, U)] + (1-\beta)\ln\pi(\omega) + (1-\beta)\ln K \tag{5.59}$$

The first-order condition for a maximum of Γ is

$$\Gamma_\omega(\omega, \Omega, U) = \beta \frac{v'(\omega)}{v(\omega) - v_0(\Omega, U)} + (1-\beta)\frac{\pi'(\omega)}{\pi(\omega)} = 0 \tag{5.60}$$

which can also be written

$$\frac{v'(\omega)}{v(\omega) - v_0(\Omega, U)} = -\frac{1-\beta}{\beta}\frac{\pi'(\omega)}{\pi(\omega)}$$

At the chosen real wage the relative gain to the union of a wage increase should be proportional to the relative loss to the firm, the factor of proportionality being determined by relative bargaining strength.

The first-order condition (5.60) can be solved for the real wage in a typical firm, ω, as a function of the aggregate real wage, Ω, and the aggregate unemployment rate, U.

However, we are more interested in the aggregate wage level. Since all firms are identical, we can solve for the aggregate wage level by setting $\Omega = \omega$ in (5.60). This yields ω as a function of U. By definition $U = (L - N)/L$, where N is total employment and L the exogenous labour supply. Thus, we can write ω as a function of N as well:

$$\omega = g(N) \quad g' > 0 \tag{5.61}$$

This relationship, which represents the first-order condition for maximization of the Nash product, is usually called the *wage-setting curve*. It has a positive slope, as in figure 5.9, provided that a mild regularity condition is satisfied. An increase in aggregate employment raises the reference utility, v_0. The relative gain to the union from increased wages, $v'/(v - v_0)$, is then increased, and as long as the union has some bargaining power, this results in higher wages. (This can be shown by differentiating the first-order condition and exploiting the second-order condition.) There is a secondary effect as the increase in the wage at each firm means an increased average wage which leads to further wage increases in each firm. However, if the effect of Ω on ω is less than one to one, the process will converge, and the final effect will be an increase in the real wage. The regularity condition will be satisfied if $\partial v_0/\partial \Omega$ is not too large compared to $\partial v/\partial \omega$.

As illustrated in figure 5.9 in equilibrium total employment is determined by the intersection of the wage curve and the aggregate labour demand curve

$$N = n(\omega)K \quad \text{where} \quad n' < 0 \tag{5.62}$$

This is really the same as (5.42), but we have exploited the fact that since the production function is homogeneous of degree one, the labour demand function takes this simple form.

In practice, the union will not reach its desired wage level at every moment of time. One way of modelling this is to assume that wages are adjusted gradually according to:

$$\frac{\dot{\omega}}{\omega} = -\gamma\left[\omega - g(N)\right] = \gamma\left[g(n(\omega)K) - \omega\right] \tag{5.63}$$

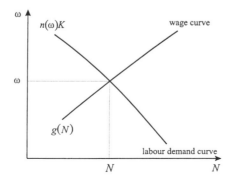

Figure 5.9 Union wage determination.

Here $\gamma > 0$ is a constant parameter. The equation says that the higher the actual real wage, ω, is relative to the equilibrium real wage, $g(N)$, the lower is the rate of increase in the real wage. If the economy is outside the wage curve, the real wage moves towards it. The further away, the faster the real wage moves.

Of course it would be more satisfying to have an explicit theory of why adjustments are not instantaneous. However, empirical researchers in this area generally find it necessary to include adjustment lags in order to get a reasonable fit. Equation (5.63) is more general than the particular union model used here. A number of efficiency wage models lead to wage equations which closely resemble the wage curves from union models (see Layard, Nickell and Jackman, 1991). Thus, our wage equation could also represent gradual adjustment within an efficiency wage model.

The modified wage equation (5.63) together with the old investment equation (5.51) form a dynamic system in two unknowns, ω and K. As before, the stationary solution is defined by $\dot\omega = 0$ and $\dot K = 0$. It is stable. This can be shown by calculating the Jacobi matrix as in section 5.8. Only the derivatives in the wage equation are changed, and they are now

$$\frac{\partial\dot\omega}{\partial\omega} = \omega\gamma(g'n'K - 1) < 0$$

$$\frac{\partial\dot\omega}{\partial K} = \omega\gamma g'n(\omega) > 0$$

at the stationary equilibrium. As before, a higher wage level implies reduced wage growth because it lowers employment (the first term inside the parentheses in $\partial\dot\omega/\partial\omega$). In addition there is now a direct negative effect on wage increases (the last term). As before, a higher capital stock leads to higher employment and, hence, increased wage growth. The pattern of signs in the Jacobi matrix is thus the same as in section 5.8, and the trace and determinant conditions are satisfied. We can draw phase diagrams that look qualitatively the same. However, the curve $\dot\omega = 0$ is now defined by the wage curve ($g(n(\omega)K) = \omega$) instead of by the standard labour market equilibrium condition ($n(\omega)K = \bar N$). The speed of adjustment towards the $\dot\omega = 0$ curve is also altered. The new direct effect of the wage level on wage growth tends to increase the speed. However, the speed of adjustment also depends on γ and g'.

As in section 5.8, the real wage in the stationary state, $\bar\omega$, is determined solely by the requirement that $\pi(\bar\omega) = \rho_*$, or that capital should get the international rate of return. Thus, in the long run the unions have no influence on the real wage. The long-run equilibrium employment level, $\tilde N$, is then determined by the requirement that $\dot\omega = 0$ or $g(\tilde N) = \bar\omega$. In section 5.8 equilibrium employment was determined by an exogenous labour supply. Now it is determined by the wage curve, which means that it is also influenced by union preferences, union power and the shape of the profit function. The equilibrium capital intensity is determined by $\bar\omega$. The capital stock then has to be large enough to create a demand for labour equal to $\tilde N$ – i.e. it has to be $\tilde K = \tilde N/n(\bar\omega)$. It is determined in the same way as before, but its level is different.

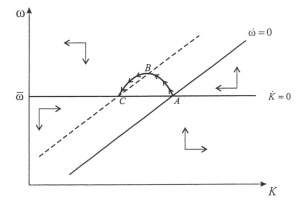

Figure 5.10 Dynamic effects of increased union bargaining power.

The effect of an increase in union bargaining power, β, is illustrated in figure 5.10. More wage pressure means that $g(\omega)$ shifts upwards. The $\dot{\omega} = 0$ locus then shifts upwards, too. At the original equilibrium A there is upward pressure on wages. They start to increase gradually. Higher wages induce a reduction of the capital stock. Both the wage increase and the decline of the capital stock leads to reduced employment. Unemployment is higher than before, but because of the increased union bargaining power, there still is upward pressure on wages. After a while the economy is on the new $\dot{\omega} = 0$ locus (point B). Then the real wage begins to decline. Since the level of the real wage is still high, however, the capital stock continues to decline. In this way the new equilibrium is reached at C (or through a loop around C). At this point the increased bargaining power has resulted only in lower employment and output. The real wage is the same as before.

Another interesting application is to an increase in the international real interest rate, ρ_*. Obviously, this reduces the equilibrium real wage as well as the equilibrium capital intensity.

Unions are sometimes assumed to also have preferences for a high level of employment at the firm. This does not change the basic picture given here. As an example, the union objective may be to maximize

$$N[v(\omega) - v_0(\Omega, U)]$$

i.e. to maximize the total utility gain of those employed at the firm relative to their outside opportunities. The Nash product is then

$$N^{\beta}[v(\omega) - v_0(\Omega, U)]^{\beta}[\pi(\omega)K]^{1-\beta}$$

and we can derive a wage curve in the same way as before. Qualitatively it has the same properties, but the concern for employment obviously shifts the wage curve downwards.

5.10 Wealth dynamics in a growing economy

Throughout this chapter we have assumed a stationary environment. The mechanisms we have studied work in the same way also against a background of economic growth. However, the definition of long-run equilibrium has to be modified. Along a balanced growth path debts should grow at the same pace as output. This may require deficits. When the economy is growing, a country may thus have continuing current account and government deficits. In order to study this more thoroughly, we shall look at the dynamics of financial wealth in a growing economy. The background is the same as in section 5.3: perfect capital mobility $(r = 0)$, output determined by supply, no real investment. Towards the end of the section we also discuss briefly what constraints there may be on government borrowing.

Requirements for balanced growth

Define

$$w_i = \frac{W_i}{Y} \quad i = g, p, * \tag{5.64}$$

For each sector w_i is the ratio of wealth to GDP, or the *wealth ratio*, for short. We define a balanced growth path as a path where the three wealth ratios are constant. By differentiation of (5.64)

$$\dot{w}_i = \frac{\dot{W}_i}{Y} - \frac{\dot{Y}}{Y}\frac{W_i}{Y} = \frac{\dot{W}_i - \gamma W_i}{Y} \tag{5.65}$$

where γ is now the growth rate of output $(\gamma = \dot{Y}/Y)$. The condition for balanced growth, $\dot{w}_i = 0$, is then equivalent to

$$\dot{W}_i = \gamma W_i \quad i = g, p, *$$

If we apply this to the current account deficit, $\dot{W}_*$, we see that balanced growth is compatible with a current account deficit equal to the growth rate times the existing foreign debt. In the same way, balanced growth is compatible with a government deficit equal to the growth rate times the initial government debt. This shows how long-run equilibrium may permit continuing deficits when there is growth. If, for example, the initial foreign debt is 50 per cent of GDP and the growth rate is 4 per cent, balanced growth requires a current account deficit of 2 per cent of GDP each year.

Recall that the deficits here are corrected for inflation – i.e. calculated on the basis of real rather than nominal interest rates. If the initial foreign debt is 50 per cent of GDP and the inflation rate is 2 per cent per year, the difference between our measure of the current account deficit and the national account measure is 1 per cent of GDP. With 4 per cent real growth as above, the conventionally measured deficit compatible with balanced growth is 3 instead of 2 per cent of GDP.

The next question is whether the economy converges towards a balanced growth path, and what different rates of growth imply for the equilibrium levels of wealth. It is convenient to approach this question by first looking at private and then government wealth ratios, remembering that if they are stable, the foreign debt is also stable. The presumption from the previous analysis is that the private sector wealth ratio should be stable if the wealth effect on consumption is sufficiently strong. This will be confirmed below. More surprisingly, stability of the government wealth ratio does not necessarily constrain fiscal policy in the same way as before.

Stability of the private wealth ratio

From (5.65) and the fact that by definition $\dot{W}_p = Y_p - C = \rho_* W_p + Y - T - C$ the growth rate of the private wealth ratio can be written

$$\dot{w}_p = 1 - T/Y + (\rho_* - \gamma)w_p - C(Y - T + \rho_* W_p, W_p, \rho_*)/Y$$

if the consumption function is the same as before. Suppose the tax rate $\tau = T/Y$ is constant. For a balanced growth path to exist, a constant consumption ratio C/Y must be compatible with a constant wealth ratio w_p. The consumption ratio can be written

$$C/Y = C(Y(1 - \tau) + \rho_* Y w_p, Y w_p, \rho_*)/Y$$

Constancy of this ratio while Y grows and w_p is constant obviously requires that the consumption function is homogeneous of degree one in income and wealth. Only then does a balanced growth path exist. If we assume homogeneity, we can rewrite the equation for the growth in the private wealth ratio as

$$\dot{w}_p = 1 - \tau + (\rho_* - \gamma)w_p - C(1 - \tau + \rho_* w_p, w_p, \rho_*) \tag{5.66}$$

The long-run equilibrium, w_p, is found by setting this equal to zero. The stability condition is

$$\frac{d\dot{w}_p}{dw_p} = \rho_*(1 - C_Y) - \gamma - C_W < 0 \tag{5.67}$$

The only new element in it is the term $-\gamma$, which promotes stability. The continuous growth in Y tends to keep the ratio W_p/Y from exploding. Thus, if a balanced growth path exists, the self-correcting mechanism works for w_p under conditions that are less stringent than if there was no growth.

Formally the long-run effect of an increased γ on w_p can be found by differentiating the stationarity condition. One should be careful in using the apparatus in this way, though, because γ may affect the consumption function directly through the expected permanent income.

Stability of the government wealth ratio[39]

The rate of growth of government financial wealth over time is by definition (see section 5.2):

$$\dot{W}_g = \rho_* W_g + (\rho_* + p)\frac{M}{P} + T - G \tag{5.68}$$

The terms on the right-hand side are first real interest income, then seigniorage ($i = \rho_* + p$ is the nominal interest rate) and last the difference between current tax income and government expenditure on goods and services. The excess of seigniorage and taxes over government expenditure on goods and services

$$(\rho_* + p)\frac{M}{P} + T - G$$

is called the government's *primary surplus*. The actual surplus is equal to the primary surplus plus net interest income from the accumulated wealth.

The time rate of change of the wealth ratio is

$$\dot{w}_g = \frac{1}{Y}\dot{W}_g - \frac{W_g}{Y}\cdot\frac{\dot{Y}}{Y}$$

$$= \rho_* w_g + (\rho_* + p)m + \tau - g - \gamma w_g$$

where we have inserted from (5.68) in (5.65) and introduced new symbols $m = M/YP$ and $g = G/Y$. Measured relative to output the primary surplus is

$$s = (\rho_* + p)m + \tau - g \tag{5.69}$$

In a growing economy, keeping s constant can be seen as a form of constant fiscal policy. The tax rate, the share of government consumption in GDP and the inflation rate can then be constant.[40]

Given the definition of s, we can simplify the equation for $\dot{w}_g$ to

$$\dot{w}_g = (\rho_* - \gamma)w_g + s \tag{5.70}$$

This equation has a stationary state, $\bar{w}_g$ defined by $\dot{w}_g = 0$, or

$$(\rho_* - \gamma)\bar{w}_g + s = 0$$

This yields the stationary level of the wealth ratio (the negative of the debt ratio)

$$\bar{w}_g = -\frac{s}{\rho_* - \gamma} \tag{5.71}$$

The stability condition for (5.70) is

$$\frac{d\dot{w}_g}{dw_g} = \rho_* - \gamma < 0$$

Thus the stationary solution is stable if $\rho_* < \gamma$, unstable if $\rho_* \geq \gamma$. In other words: stability requires that the real interest rate is lower than the growth rate.

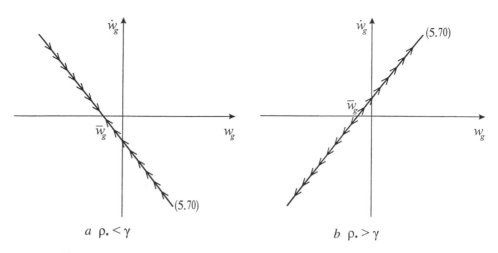

Figure 5.11 Dynamics of the government wealth ratio.

What this means for the time path of the wealth ratio, w_g, is illustrated in figure 5.11. The stable case ($\rho_* < \gamma$) is shown in panel a. The higher the wealth ratio, the lower its rate of growth. Irrespective of which w_g we start from, in the long run we end up at the stationary level $\bar{w}_g$ defined by (5.71). The unstable case ($\rho_* > \gamma$) is shown in panel b. The higher w_g is, the greater its growth rate. If we start with w_g greater than the stationary level $\bar{w}_g$, the growth rate of w_g is positive. The wealth ratio grows forever, and even its growth rate is increasing over time. In the long run the wealth ratio explodes. If the initial w_g is below $\bar{w}_g$, then the wealth ratio declines forever, and in the end approaches minus infinity. In other words, the debt ratio increases forever and grows beyond all limits. The debt ratio stays constant only if the initial wealth is equal to $\bar{w}_g$.

One way of describing the dynamics is this: when the primary surplus is constant as a share of GDP, there are two opposing forces which determine the growth of the wealth ratio. On the one hand, the accumulation of interest, over time, tends to raise the effect of past surpluses and deficits on the present level of debt. On the other hand, the growth of GDP makes past deficits smaller and smaller relative to the present size of the economy. If $\rho_* > \gamma$, the interest effect dominates, and the effects of past surpluses or deficits on the present wealth ratio are magnified with time. If $\rho_* < \gamma$, the growth effect dominates and past surpluses become less significant the more time has passed since they were incurred.

The case where the real interest rate exceeds the growth rate is not fundamentally different from the case without growth analysed earlier. As there, if a debt is first accumulated one has to run a primary surplus later (or reduce the debt by surprise inflation). Spending more now entails an obvious cost later. Balanced growth requires that the government surplus is adjusted to the level of the debt. If this is not done, and the budget deficit is excessive, the ratio of foreign debt to GDP explodes.

The case where $\rho_* < \gamma$ is radically different. In this case balanced growth is apparently possible with any level of the primary surplus without the government debt ratio exploding. There is nothing which corresponds to the balanced budget requirement in the zero growth case. The rapid growth means that we have self-correction also for the part of foreign debt which is created by government debt.

Along a balanced growth path the relation between the primary surplus and the wealth ratio is given by (5.71). This implies similiar relations between the wealth ratios and other surplus concepts along a balanced growth path. These requirements for balanced growth can be summarized as

- Primary surplus = $s = -(\rho_* - \gamma)w_g$
- Inflation-corrected surplus = $s + \rho_* w_g = \gamma w_g$
- Ordinary surplus = $s + (\rho_* + p)w_g = (\gamma + p)w_g$.

First look at the case where $\rho_* > \gamma$. If the government has net debts (i.e. if $w_g < 0$), the required primary surplus is positive. An inflation-corrected deficit is permitted, though, and if there is inflation ($p > 0$) an even greater ordinary deficit is permitted. If $w_g > 0$ this is reversed. There must be a budget surplus as conventionally measured. However, the advantage of good government finances is that a primary deficit is permitted, which means that one can spend more on goods and services than is collected in taxes.

Note that when $w_g < 0$, the required primary surplus is just enough to pay the part of real interest which exceeds the growth rate. The remaining interest payments are financed by new loans. Still the debt does not grow relative to income.

In the case where $\rho_* < \gamma$, it is the wealth ratio which adjusts to the surplus. Along a balanced growth path with debt ($w_g < 0$), there must also be a primary deficit ($s < 0$). The inflation-corrected and the ordinary deficits will then be even greater. This means that all interest payments are financed by new loans, and in addition new loans are used to finance the primary deficit – i.e. to finance expenditures on consumption that exceed tax and seigniorage revenue. A natural question to ask is whether creditors will be content with such a state of affairs going on indefinitely. This brings us to the next subject.

Government borrowing constraints

So far we have looked at balanced growth paths without explicitly considering constraints on government borrowing set by creditors. This is a difficult subject which we cannot go deeply into. However, there is fairly general agreement that creditors will not accept that a country remains on a path which makes the debt ratio explode. All the balanced growth paths studied above by definition conform to this requirement. However, creditors may set tighter limits.

If the only requirement is that the debt ratio should not explode, the analysis of balanced growth paths above gives a simple theory of the sustainability of fiscal policy:

if $\rho_* < \gamma$, any primary deficit s is sustainable, if $\rho_* \geq \gamma$, sustainability requires that $s \geq -(\rho_* - \gamma)w_g$.

It may seem strange that in the case where $\rho_* < \gamma$ creditors allow governments to borrow without ever actually paying interest. However, governments differ from individuals in that they do not have a definite finite life, and from corporations by not being able to go legally bankrupt. Along the balanced growth path each individual creditor gets his interest and principal paid. That they are paid with new loans need not be a matter of concern as the process can continue forever.

However, one concern of creditors must be that conditions can change. Suppose ρ_* were to increase at some future date. If it is not higher than γ already, it may become higher then. The higher the initial debt ratio is, the higher the required primary surplus will be. From the point of view of the creditors this raises two worrying prospects. First, it may be infeasible for the government in question to raise the necessary primary surplus to prevent a debt explosion. Second, the government may prefer to default on the debt even if it is in principle possible to avoid default.

For the discussion of the first problem it is useful to recall that the primary surplus is defined as $s = (\rho_* + p)m + \tau - g$. There must be an upper limit on the average tax rate, τ. There must also be a lower limit on g. No state can exist without some government expenditure. Up to a point seigniorage income can be increased by increasing inflation, p. However, this means a higher nominal interest rate and, thus, lower money demand m. There is thus a limit also to $(\rho_* + p)m$. Moreover, taxes create distortions which reduce efficiency. Too low government expenditures and too high inflation can also hurt efficiency. Attempts to increase s can thus lead to a fall in the *level* of Y. Since the level of W_g is given historically, w_g will increase in absolute value when Y falls. This makes the required primary s even greater, and increases the likelihood that the government will not be able to prevent a debt explosion.

If a government is not able to create a sufficient primary surplus, and it cannot get more credit, it has two options: (1) it can default on some of its debt by not paying interest and/or principal; (2) if a sufficiently large part of the debt is denominated in domestic currency, it can reduce the real value of the debt by a one-time devaluation.[41]

If private investors – be they foreign or domestic – perceive that there is some possibility for one of these outcomes, they will take account of that in their assessment of expectations and risk. The government may then have to pay a default premium in the interest rate on its debt. On the debt denominated in domestic currency it may – in addition – have to pay a premium to compensate for the expected devaluation. There may also be risk premia. As long as no devaluation or default takes place, the real interest rates on government debt exceed ρ_*, which increases the required primary surplus even further. Thus, doubts about the government's ability to prevent a debt explosion may quickly precipitate a debt crisis.

The other question is whether the government may choose to default or devalue even if it can be avoided. After the debt crisis in developing countries in the early 1980s a large literature on 'sovereign debt' has emerged. It is surveyed by Eaton and

Fernandez (1995) who were among the first contributors. It deals with the problem of whether sovereign governments or sovereign countries have an incentive to honour debt obligations to foreigners. An implicit assumption is that the debt is not denominated in domestic currency. A crucial and reasonable assumption is that it is not possible to roll over the debt and pay interest with new loans forever. We are in the case where $\rho_* \geq \gamma$.

Some relevant considerations which the literature on sovereign debt has brought forward are:

- Default means that one avoids a future net transfer of resources abroad (the trade surplus to make the necessary payments to avoid default). This is an incentive to default.
- The creditors cannot seize the assets of the government through bankruptcy proceedings as they can when the debtor is private.[42] Government assets abroad may be seized, though.
- However, foreigners may react by denying future credits. This may prevent future consumption smoothing and make it difficult to exploit some future investment opportunities. In short, it becomes more difficult to run deficits in the future.
- The country's reputation for honouring agreements and contracts may be hurt. This may complicate trade relations and damage international cooperation in other areas.

There is an incentive to default, but also some checks against default. However, seizure of assets, which is an important check on private borrowers contemplating default, is a less effective check on the government. A main conclusion from the literature is that if the foreign debt is above a certain critical level, it is in the government's best interest to default. Below the critical level it is better to honour the debt. If creditors are well informed, the critical level constitutes an upper bound on how much the government (or the country) can borrow abroad. When uncertainty is involved, in addition to an upper bound on borrowing, there may also be a range of debt levels where borrowing is possible, but a default premium is added to the foreign currency interest rate when the government borrows.

When $\rho_* > \gamma$, we now have two constraints on government debt, one determined by how much debt it is feasible for the government to serve, and one incentive constraint. Presumably the latter is stricter than the former. Default is the best choice before it is the only choice.

The literature on sovereign debt usually treats the government and the country as one and the same. In one sense, there is a reality to this. If the government acts in the interest of the citizens it may have an incentive to let the citizens default and deny foreign creditors access to their assets. The checks against such policies are the same as against government default, but one should remember that the private sector often has more assets abroad than the government. These can be seized.

If the government debt is denominated in domestic currency, a devaluation is an alternative to default. For foreign creditors the consequences are more or less the same. However, a devaluation is not a formal breach of contract. In practice it is not likely to harm cooperation in other areas to the same extent as a default, and eventual government assets abroad cannot be seized. If there is a large foreign debt denominated in domestic currency, the incentive to devalue could be strong. This means a high expected rate of depreciation and a high domestic interest rate. It may also mean a high risk premium and thus an even higher interest rate. A government which does not intend to devalue will naturally want to avoid these interest costs, and thus prefer to borrow foreign currency when it borrows abroad. This makes borrowing of domestic currency abroad all the more suspect. The upshot is that it will not be possible for governments to borrow large amounts of domestic currency abroad.

Borrowing domestic currency from domestic residents is another matter. Then the government does not gain at the expense of foreigners and the political calculation about devaluation becomes more difficult.

The capacity of the rest of the world for absorbing debt is also relevant. If the growth rate of the home country is above the world average, then the world capacity for absorbing debt grows more slowly than the domestic economy. Obviously, if this goes on for long enough, the country we look at ceases to be small as far as financial markets are concerned, and financing the deficit may become difficult.

5.11 Some further questions

In this chapter we have presented a family of models which together should give a fairly comprehensive review of the macroeconomics of a small open economy. Before we conclude the chapter we should go through some critical questions which can be asked about the relevance of the analysis. Many of the questions will be fairly obvious to students who are familiar with modern macroeconomic theory. This only makes it more necessary to comment on them.

The relation to utility maximization

Our analysis in the present chapter started with the consumption function. We could have gone one step behind it and started with individual consumers maximizing intertemporal utility subject to budget constraints. Our consumption function is broadly consistent with a wide range of theories about individual consumer behaviour, as well as with empirical studies of consumption functions. In particular the consumption function is broadly consistent with standard life-cycle models of consumption demand. In such models, if labour income and interest rates stay constant, and the population is stationary, consumers go on saving until private wealth stands in a certain relation to labour income.

One exception is the so-called Ramsey model for a small open economy (see Blanchard and Fischer, 1989, ch. 2.4). In this model consumers live forever and their preferences are additive over time with exponential discounting of period utility at a constant rate. (However, Barro, 1974, has shown that specific assumptions about bequests can replace the assumption that consumers live forever.) In the Ramsey model there is no stationary level for the foreign debt of a small open economy. Consumers go on accumulating foreign assets forever if their subjective discount rates are below the real interest rate. In the opposite case they go on accumulating debts forever. This result depends crucially on the constancy of the subjective discount rates and, since people do not live forever, on the ability of debtors to pass on debts to their descendants. Children must also inherit their parents' subjective discount rates. Ramsey-type models are sometimes useful, but too removed from reality to be a realistic alternative to the consumption functions assumed here.

Are government bonds net wealth?

When the interest rate exceeds the growth rate, a necessary condition for the debt ratio not to explode is that the present value of future taxes is equal to the initial government debt plus the present value of future government expenditures. This means that the government debt is offset by future tax liabilities, and is not part of net wealth. Hence, as Barro (1974) pointed out, private consumption should not depend on whether government expenditures are financed by taxes or by issuing debt. This proposition is called 'Ricardian equivalence'. If true, it has strong consequences for some of the questions discussed in this chapter. The redistribution between the government and the private sector caused by a devaluation is irrelevant for consumption demand, and, hence, has no effect on the current account. A government deficit does not lead to a current account deficit either, since the dissaving of the government will be matched by increased private savings in order to meet future tax obligations. Furthermore, the citizens will regard the foreign exchange reserve as part of their portfolio. Thus, sterilized interventions have no effect on the exchange rate even if investors are risk averse. Whether a government deficit is financed in domestic or foreign currency is immaterial.

Ricardian equivalence requires some strong assumptions. Bernheim and Bagwell (1988) showed that these lead to drastic and often bizarre conclusions in many areas of economics. Hence, the proposition is controversial. However, even if one rejects full equivalence, one has to concede that there may be partial equivalence.

Redistribution within the private sector

In addition to the redistribution between the government and the private sector, a devaluation may cause redistribution within the private sector from those who are creditors to those who are debtors in domestic currency. Irving Fisher argued that creditors have lower propensities to spend than debtors. If that is the case, the redistribution within the private sector following a devaluation tends to increase private demand and reduce the current account surplus. If the government debt is low, the redistribution within the private sector may dominate the aggregate effect. (For a discussion of the Fisher effect, see Tobin 1980, ch. I.)

How can there continue to be a risk premium when the exchange rate stays constant?

The basis for the risk premium is exchange rate uncertainty. In our model this uncertainty is not explicit. There is perfect foresight in the sense that actual and expected depreciation are equal. At the same time our demand functions for foreign currency have been based on the fact that there is uncertainty and that nobody has perfect foresight. We have even assumed that the asset demand functions are stable over time. This requires that perceptions of risk are stable over time, in spite of the fact that the exchange rate is sometimes kept constant for an indefinite period. There is a clear inconsistency here, and some will argue that the assumption of perfect foresight should be combined with an assumption about perfect capital mobility owing to the absence of risk. In that case, the risk premium should be identically equal to zero, and we should have dropped sections 5.4 and 5.5.

However, models, like maps, are simplified pictures which should help us find our way in the actual complexities of the economy. Uncertainty about the future exchange rate is an inherent and important feature of the foreign exchange market. It is not obvious that a deterministic model with perfect capital mobility combined with perfect foresight is a better guide to the foreign exchange markets. It is quite possible that our model with imperfect capital mobility simulates more accurately the average behaviour of an economy where there is exchange rate uncertainty than does a model which is made more consistent by assuming away uncertainty.

One possible interpretation of our models is that they describe what happens *today* and the *expected future path* of the economy. The actual future depends on exogenous disturbances which happen then, and which cannot be predicted now. Still, by looking at the effect on the expected path we may get an impression of how events now (for example, a devaluation) *changes the actual future path*. We are dealing in deterministic models of a 'stochastic world' (Haliassos, 1994), and 'perfect foresight' is not really what it says, only expectations that are consistent with the model we use.

Are one-time devaluations and monetary expansions credible?

Several times we have looked at the effect of a 'once and for all' devaluation or monetary expansion. Both before and after the event people have expected the exchange rate or the money supply to stay constant forever. If the government has inflated the economy once, however, people may expect that the government will

some day do it again. This requires a consideration of the motives the government
have to inflate. Suppose the reason was to reduce the real government debt. The
devaluation achieves this immediately. It also makes it easier to balance the budget,
and if the government keeps the budget balanced after the devaluation, the reduction
in the government debt becomes permanent. If, in addition, the cause which in the
past led to the accumulation of the government debt is no longer present (for example,
after the ending of a war), it is not unreasonable for the public to believe that the
inflation is a one-time affair. On the contrary, if the public has reason to believe that
the government will recreate the debt problem, it may also have reason to expect
another devaluation in the future.

If there is nominal wage rigidity, a one-time inflation may also be used to produce a
temporary boost of employment. If the inflation raises employment above the equilibrium level, there is good reason to ask whether a devaluation will happen again. The
positive employment effect is temporary, and when it vanishes, the government may
have the same reason as before to inflate. If, on the other hand, some unique event has
led to employment well below the equilibrium level, the public perhaps need not
expect a new round of inflation in the near future.

Are savings and investment independent? The Feldstein–Horioka puzzle

Suppose capital mobility is perfect in the sense that both firms and consumers adapt to a given international real rate of interest, as we have assumed in much of
this chapter. Investment decisions and consumption decisions are then independent.
Real investment does not depend on how much domestic saving is available. The
consumption decision does not depend on domestic investment opportunities. This
kind of separation was a feature of the model of section 5.8, and is also present in
similar models with explicit intertemporal optimization. An analogy from microeconomic theory is revealing. If the utility maximizing owner of a firm is a price taker in all
markets, we can separate his optimization problem in two parts: (1) maximize profits
in the firm; (2) choose the optimal consumption bundle for a given income. The
decisions at the two levels are independent of each other except that the consumption
decision depends on profit income. In the extremely open economy with perfect capital mobility this carries over to the aggregate of all consumption and investment
decisions as well.

If capital mobility is imperfect, the domestic interest rate depends on domestic
savings. Since real investments in turn depend on the domestic interest rate, there is
a link from savings to investment.

In a study which has attracted much attention, Feldstein and Horioka (1980) showed
that in a cross-section of countries savings and real investment were highly correlated.
Countries with a high savings rate also tend to have a high investment rate. According
to the authors, this shows that capital mobility is imperfect. Later studies have confirmed the tendency to high correlation between savings and investment over long

time periods, but also shown that the correlation can be quite low over shorter periods. The 'Feldstein–Horioka puzzle' is that savings and investment are highly correlated in spite of the fact that there are relatively few restrictions on capital mobility and a high volume of international transactions in the capital markets.

There have been different responses. The simplest is to say that the results of Feldstein and Horioka and their followers confirm that the many rejections of covered interest rate parity referred to in section 2.5 should be interpreted as rejections of perfect capital mobility. A more subtle response is that saving and investment could very well be highly correlated even if capital mobility is perfect. Even if savings and investment *decisions* are separable, saving and investment can respond in the same direction to shocks. This claim is best discussed in full intertemporal equilibrium models, but we can use the model of section 5.8 as a good substitute. Suppose a country is hit by a positive permanent productivity shock. This immediately raises profitability, output and employment. Higher profitability induces higher investment. Higher output means higher incomes which raise both consumption and savings. For a period the country then has both high real investment and high savings. Generally, high capital mobility is not inconsistent with countries with high productivity growth having both high investment and high savings.[43]

Other shocks may affect savings without affecting investment. One example is a change in consumers' time preferences in the direction of less patience. This raises consumption now without affecting investment. In this case the correlation is zero.

Some claim that the owners of firms have a higher propensity to save than wage earners. A low real wage means that a high share of national income goes to owners, and this would then imply a high savings rate. At the same time real investment will be high, owing to high profitability and ample supply of internal financing. Again there is a reason for high correlation between savings and investment.

The lesson from all this is that the correlation between savings and investment depends on the kinds of shocks that hit the economy. The fact that savings and investment are correlated is not enough to prove that capital mobility is imperfect.

However, one should be aware that there is a long step from the eventual prevalence of uncovered interest rate parity in markets for standard interest bearing assets to perfect capital mobility in the sense that the real returns on investment are equated in different countries. As we saw in section 5.1, real interest rate parity requires purchasing power parity. Asymmetric information and moral hazard problems are obstacles to perfect capital mobility even between firms in the same country. For these reasons investment in firms tend to depend positively on the availability of internal financing. The savings decisions and investment decisions of the owners then get intertwined. A country where the owners of the firms have a high savings rate may also have a high rate of investment because internal financing is readily available. (For an assessment of the literature on the Feldstein–Horioka puzzle, see Frankel, 1993, ch. 2, or Obstfeld, 1995a.)

Exercises

1. Assume a fixed exchange rate. At time 0 there is a permanent increase in Y, e.g. because of some discovery. What impact does this have on the time path of the foreign debt and the foreign exchange reserves?

2. Assume a fixed exchange rate. Describe the effect of a permanent increase in the foreign interest rate, i_*, on the time path of the foreign debt and on the foreign exchange reserves of the government. Which assumption on the determination of the domestic interest rate do you consider to be most relevant?

3. We look at a case where the exchange rate is fixed, and where there is perfect capital mobility. $W_g = 0$ and is kept constant. Suppose consumption is proportional to total private wealth, which is the sum of financial wealth W_p and the discounted value of the constant income stream Y from here to infinity. What is the condition for stability of the foreign debt? Is it likely to be satisfied?

4. Assume floating exchange rates, perfect capital mobility and perfect foresight. What is the effect of a permanent increase in the foreign interest rate on the exchange rate today and in the future? What is the consequent effect on the future path of the foreign debt?

5. Consider a temporary government deficit. Taxes, T, are reduced at t_0 and raised again at t_1. Assume a fixed exchange rate and perfect capital mobility. Characterize the long-run equilibrium after budgets again have been balanced and the economy has come to rest. Does the long-run equilibrium differ if there is imperfect capital mobility?

6. Assume that there is nominal wage rigidity. The capital stock is constant. What is the effect of a permanent improvement in productivity on the time paths of (a) real wages, (b) employment, (c) the foreign debt?

7. The exchange rate is fixed and the capital mobility is imperfect. Initially the foreign debt is above its long-run equilibrium value. Draw a graph which shows the ensuing time path of the current account for three different monetary policies: full sterilization, no sterilization and no intervention (the interest rate is used to keep the exchange rate fixed).

8. The exchange rate is fixed and the capital mobility is imperfect. Initially the economy is in stationary equilibrium. Then the currency is devalued. You are asked to consider three different monetary policies after the devaluation: (1) full sterilization, full accommodation, (2) full sterilization, no accommodation, (3) no sterilization, no accommodation.
   (a) Find the effects on the new stationary level of the foreign debt.
   (b) Draw a graph showing the time paths of the current account after the devaluation.

6   Home and foreign goods

In this chapter we assume that the home country and the foreign country produce goods which are imperfect substitutes. We label them 'home' and 'foreign' goods, respectively. We still look at a small country, but its products are different from those of the rest of the world, and their price can be influenced by conditions in the small country. This gives domestic demand a role in determining output and relative prices, and that is the main difference from chapter 5. However, the law of one price still holds, and we still have absolute purchasing power parity (PPP) in the sense that the same basket of commodities costs the same at home and abroad.

In section 6.1 we formulate an equation for the trade balance under these circumstances, and discuss the partial effects of a change in the exchange rate on the trade balance. In section 6.2 we formulate a model which integrates portfolio equilibrium with equations determining the trade balance and the level of activity. It is a short-run model with nominal price rigidity. Output is determined by demand. In sections 6.3 and 6.4 the model is used to discuss fiscal and monetary policy under fixed and floating exchange rates. Section 6.5 takes a critical look at some of the assumptions behind the model. In section 6.6 it is extended with dynamic equations relating inflation to the level of activity and the growth of the foreign debt to the current account deficit. The model helps to clarify the role of savings and of relative prices in the determination of the current account and in the movement from short- to long-run equilibrium. It is also used to discuss the dynamic and long-run effects of different demand shocks under fixed exchange rates. Sections 6.7 and 6.8 do the same for floating rates. In section 6.7 a simplified model is used to show how nominal price rigidity combined with exchange rate flexibility can cause the exchange rate to 'overshoot' in response to shocks.

6.1 The trade balance and the Marshall–Lerner condition

Since exports and imports are different goods with different prices, we must choose some convention for measuring the trade balance in real terms. The standard choice is to measure the trade balance in terms of the home good. We then define the export surplus in volume terms as

$$X = Z_* - RZ = Z_* - \frac{EP_*}{P} Z \tag{6.1}$$

where

P price of home goods in domestic currency
P_* price of foreign goods in foreign currency
Z volume of our imports of foreign goods
Z_* volume of foreign imports of home goods – i.e. our export volume
X export surplus (trade surplus)
R the relative price of foreign compared to home goods, $R = EP_*/P$

A *real exchange rate* is an index for the ratio between the price levels in two countries. This means that if P_a and P_b are two broad price indices from country a and b, respectively, and E is the price of b's currency in terms of a's currency, EP_b/P_a is a real exchange rate. Since P and P_* measure producer prices, R is the real exchange rate in terms of producer prices – or, in the remainder of this chapter, 'the real exchange rate', for short.

Our demand for imports is assumed to be a function of the real exchange rate and of the level of activity:

$$Z = Z(R, Y) \quad Z_R < 0; \quad Z_Y > 0 \tag{6.2}$$

Similarly, the foreign demand for our exports is

$$Z_* = Z_*(R, Y_*) \quad Z_{*R} > 0; \quad Z_{*Y} > 0 \tag{6.3}$$

The effect on the trade surplus of a real depreciation (an increase in R) is

$$\frac{dX}{dR} = Z_{*R} - RZ_R - Z \tag{6.4}$$

The total effect is the sum of three terms: first there are the two quantity effects. An increase in the relative price of foreign goods shifts demand in both countries towards home goods. Thus, exports go up and imports go down. Both quantity effects work in the direction of an improved trade balance. Next, there is the direct effect of the increased relative price of imports. Imports become more expensive in terms of exports, and this leads to a deterioration of the trade balance. In general, we cannot tell which is the stronger: the direct price effect or the two quantity effects. Thus, in general we cannot tell whether a real depreciation improves the current account.

However, we can give conditions that allow us to sign the total effect. Assume that trade is initially balanced ($X = 0$), or that $Z_* = RZ$. The derivative (6.4) can then be rewritten

$$\frac{dX}{dR} = Z\left[\frac{Z_{*R}}{Z} - \frac{RZ_R}{Z} - 1\right]$$

$$= Z\left[\frac{RZ_{*R}}{Z_*} - \frac{RZ_R}{Z} - 1\right] \tag{6.5}$$

$$= Z\left[\check{Z}_{*R} + \check{Z}_R - 1\right]$$

where $\check{Z}_{*R} = RZ_{*R}/Z_*$ and $\check{Z}_R = -RZ_R/Z$ are the absolute values of the price elasticities of demand for exports and imports respectively. Clearly, the total effect of an increase in R on the trade balance is positive if, and only if,

$$\check{Z}_R + \check{Z}_{*R} > 1$$

or *the sum of the absolute values of the elasticities of demand for exports and imports is greater than one*. This is the *Marshall–Lerner condition*, which is necessary and sufficient for a real depreciation to have a positive effect on the trade surplus when trade is balanced initially.[44]

One obvious question is: what happens when trade is not balanced initially? It is easily seen that a sufficient condition for an increase in R to always improve the current account is that $\check{Z}_R > 1$. If this is the case, the value of imports always declines when R increases. A negative effect on the trade balance can only occur when import demand is inelastic. A high price elasticity for exports can compensate for a low elasticity for imports. If trade is balanced initially, the Marshall–Lerner condition says that it is the sum of the two elasticities which count. If initially exports are lower than imports, the price elasticity of exports work on a smaller basis than the price elasticity of imports, and thus the sum of the two elasticities must be somewhat higher than one. The Marshall–Lerner condition is no longer sufficient. If, on the other hand, there is an initial trade surplus, the Marshall–Lerner condition is always sufficient for an increase in the real exchange rate to improve the trade balance measured in home goods.

The importance of the Marshall–Lerner condition has led to a large number of econometric studies of demand elasticities. Goldstein and Kahn (1985) gives a survey. According to them the sum of the long-run (greater or equal to two years) price elasticities of imports and exports invariably exceed one for industrial countries. However, short-run elasticities (for periods shorter than six months) are often quite small. This leads to what is called the *J-curve effect*: after a depreciation the trade balance first deteriorates, because the quantity effects are small and the increase in import prices dominates the outcome. Then the trade balance gradually improves as the quantity effects become larger, and after a while the trade balance is improved also relative to before the depreciation.

Goldstein and Kahn's (1985) results for industrialized countries are confirmed by more recent studies (mainly) for the United States, Japan and Germany, surveyed in Hooper and Marquez (1995). The average of the estimated sum of the two price elasticities is -1.56 for Germany and -2.66 for the United States and -3.65 for Japan. However, Reinhart's (1995) estimates for developing countries show considerably lower elasticities, and imply that one cannot take for granted that the Marshall–Lerner condition is satisfied.

Below, the standard assumption is that the quantity effects of a depreciation are also strong enough to dominate the effect on the trade balance in the short run. The issue of the exact timing of effects is quite subtle as there are both shipping and production

lags involved. Production decisions in the export industry may be affected by a depreciation with greater speed than the actual shipment of exports. In applied modelling
one should probably account carefully for shipping and production lags.

Two other results from the survey by Goldstein and Kahn (1985) are worth mention-
ing here. For industrial countries the elasticities of imports with respect to income (Y
and Y_* in our model) fall in the range of 1 to 2. For a small country where exports
constitute a large share of aggregate demand, this means that the level of activity
abroad has a strong influence on domestic demand. Another result is that the price
elasticities of the demand for manufactures are larger than for non-manufactures.

6.2 The Mundell–Fleming–Tobin model

This section presents a model which is often used to discuss the short-run
effects of monetary and fiscal policy and of various external and internal disturbances.
By 'short run' is meant a time span which is so short that the flows of savings, real
investment and current account surpluses do not add up to significant changes in the
corresponding stocks.

The model is a marriage of the portfolio model from section 3.1 (which owes much
to Tobin) and the older Mundell–Fleming models (Fleming, 1962; Mundell, 1963). The
traditional Mundell–Fleming models improved on the earlier elasticities approach to
the foreign exchange market by combining it with Keynesian output determination
and adding capital movements[45]. From the Mundell–Fleming models we have the
assumptions that home and foreign goods are imperfect substitutes, that the prices
of home goods are predetermined and that production is determined by demand. The
latter are traditional Keynesian assumptions, and they require that there is some spare
capacity in the economy.

In the traditional Mundell–Fleming models capital movements were usually treated
as a gradual flow.[46] The foreign exchange market was primarily seen as a flow market
where the current account was a significant component of net supply also in the short
run. Except in the case of perfect capital mobility, stocks were not allowed to jump
momentarily. Around 1980 several authors extended Mundell–Fleming models with
portfolio equations and, thus, adopted a stock approach to the foreign exchange market (see e.g. Tobin and de Macedo, 1980; Frenkel, Gylfason and Helliwell, 1980; and
Gylfason and Helliwell, 1983). This, and the inclusion of more forward-looking expectations, led to a revision of many of the original conclusions.

The equations of the model are:

$$Y = C(Y_p, W_p, \rho, \rho_*) + I(\rho, \rho_*) + G + X(R, Y, Y_*) \tag{6.6}$$

$$Y_p = Y - \rho_* \frac{EF_*}{P} - T \tag{6.7}$$

$$W_p = \frac{M_0 + B_0 + EF_{p0}}{P} \tag{6.8}$$

$$\rho = i - p_e \tag{6.9}$$

$$R = \frac{EP_*}{P} \tag{6.10}$$

$$r = i - i_* - e_e(E) \tag{6.11}$$

$$\frac{M}{P} = m(i, Y) \tag{6.12}$$

$$\frac{B}{P} = W_p - f(r, W_p) - m(i, Y) \tag{6.13}$$

$$\frac{EF_p}{P} = f(r, W_p) \tag{6.14}$$

$$F_g + F_p = -F_* \tag{6.15}$$

Equation (6.6) is the *IS* curve. On the left-hand side is production (Y), and on the right-hand side are the different components of aggregate demand: private consumption (C), private investment (I), government consumption and investment (G) and net exports (X).

The consumption function is the same as in chapter 5. Equations (6.7)–(6.10) define four of its arguments. Disposable income (Y_p) is defined in (6.7) as national income ($Y - \rho_* EF_*/P$) minus net transfers to the government (T) from the other sectors. We define net transfers to include both the net taxes collected by the government and the net real interest payments received by the government.[47] In this way, we avoid keeping account of the different flows of interest payments within the country. Note that we now deflate with the price of home goods, P, when we define a real variable (e.g. Y_p, W_p). We return to the choice of deflator in section 6.5. The partial derivatives of the consumption function obey the usual conditions: $0 < C_Y < 1$, $C_W > 0$, $C_\rho < 0$, $C_{\rho_*} < 0$.

The investment function is traditional in the sense that investment depends negatively on the real interest rates – i.e. $I_\rho < 0$ and $I_{\rho_*} < 0$. Both real interest rates are included, because the alternative to investing in real capital is to invest in a portfolio containing both currencies. It is the return on this portfolio which determines the cost of capital. If the share of foreign currency is small, the effect of ρ_* may be negligible. However, for multinationals the foreign interest rate is likely to be important, and sometimes foreign currency loans are an important source of finance also for domestic investors.

The last term in the *IS* equation (6.6), the trade balance function, X, is defined by (6.1) in section 6.1. The real exchange rate, R, is defined by (6.10). We assume $X_R > 0$, $X_Y < 0$, and $X_{Y_*} > 0$. That $X_R > 0$, means that the quantity effects dominate over the direct price effect of a change in the real exchange rate. If trade is balanced initially, this requires that the Marshall–Lerner condition holds.

Equations (6.11)–(6.15) are taken from section 3.1 and should be well known by now. As usual we assume $m_i < 0$, $m_Y > 0$, $f_r < 0$, $0 < f_W < 1$ and $e'_e < 0$. We also assume that $F_{p0} > 0$. (It is a useful exercise to work out how conclusions change if $F_{p0} < 0$.) Since we assume regressive expectations, the model is best suited for analysing the effects of temporary shocks (see chapter 4). If shocks are permanent, they may also shift the e_e function.

The model has ten equations, and ten endogenous variables. Which variables are endogenous depends on which policy regime we look at. The variables which can be instruments of government policy are G, T, E, F_g, i, M, and B. Of these G and T will always be treated as exogenous, while the status of the remaining variables depends on the regime. That T is exogenous means that every change in real interest flows to or from the government is compensated by corresponding changes in taxes. In many applications it would be more relevant to assume that tax rates are given. However, that would have forced us into a discussion of a large number of different effects which are often minor, and which would draw attention away from more important relations.

Some variables are exogenous because they are given from abroad. These are P_*, i_* and Y_*. In the same spirit we also treat ρ_* as exogenous, although this is questionable, as we shall see in section 6.5. Other variables are predetermined: P, F_*, M_0, B_0, F_{p0}. The reason that P is predetermined may be that we have nominal wage rigidity, that productivity is constant and that prices are set by adding a constant mark-up to variable cost (see section 8.2). For the moment we also assume that expected inflation p_e is exogenous, but this is also something we return to in section 6.5.

A primary purpose of the model is to discuss how Y is determined, and hence Y is of course always endogenous. The 'auxiliary' variables Y_p, R, r and ρ are endogenously determined by their respective definitional equations, as is W_p. F_p is also endogenous. There are thus seven variables which are endogenous irrespective of policy regime. This leaves room for choosing three endogenous and two exogenous variables among the five remaining variables which are potential candidates for policy: E, F_g, i, M and B. This means that we can distinguish between the same six regimes, as in section 3.1. If the exchange rate is fixed, E is exogenous and F_g is endogenous. If the exchange rate is floating, it is the other way around. The monetary instrument could be either one of i, M or B. The other two variables must be endogenous.

In sections 6.3 and 6.4 we examine how the model works first under fixed and then under floating exchange rates.

6.3 Fixed exchange rate

The solution of the model can be illustrated by the familiar *IS-LM*-type diagram. The *IS* curve is defined by (6.6). In order to make this a relationship between i and Y, we must imagine that we substitute in (6.6) from the definitional equations (6.7)–(6.10). If we do this and differentiate with respect to i, we find that the slope of the *IS* curve is

$$\left. \frac{dY}{di} \right|_{IS} = \frac{C_\rho + I_\rho}{1 - C_Y - X_Y} < 0 \tag{6.16}$$

We recognize the familiar open economy multiplier. The *IS* curve slopes downwards as usual.

In addition to the *IS* curve we need a curve describing the combinations of i and Y consistent with equilibrium in the asset markets, as the *LM*-curve does in the standard closed economy model. In our case we need a different curve for each of the three monetary regimes discussed in section 3.1. We need the *LM* curve (*M* exogenous), the *BB* curve (*B* exogenous) and the *ii* curve (*i* exogenous). In figure 6.1 these are drawn together with the *IS* curve. The *LM* curve represents (6.12). It shows the combinations of i and Y which are compatible with equilibrium in the money market for a given money supply. The *BB* curve represents (6.13). It shows the combinations of i and Y which are compatible with equilibrium in the bond market for a given supply of bonds. The *ii* curve just shows the level of an exogenously given interest rate.

By implicit differentiation of (6.12) we find that the slope the *LM* curve is

$$\left.\frac{di}{dY}\right|_{LM} = -\frac{m_Y}{m_i} > 0 \tag{6.17}$$

The *LM* curve has the usual positive slope. Similarly, by implicit differentiation of (6.13) we find that the slope of the *BB* curve is

$$\left.\frac{di}{dY}\right|_{BB} = -\frac{m_Y}{f_r + m_i} > 0 \tag{6.18}$$

The *BB* curve is increasing because a higher volume of transactions reduces the demand for bonds, and a higher interest rate is then required to keep the market in equilibrium when *B* is given. The *BB* curve is less steep than the *LM* curve, because an increase in the interest rate increases the demand for bonds more than it reduces the demand for money.

The solution of the model is where the *IS* curve intersects with the three others. It is no accident that all four curves meet at the same point. Suppose the interest rate is

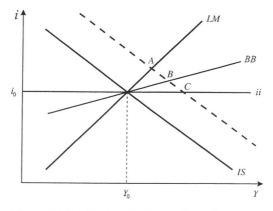

Figure 6.1 Equilibrium in the goods market and the financial markets.

exogenous. Then the equilibrium values of Y and i, Y_0 and i_0, are determined by the intersection of the IS curve and the ii curve. The central bank must adjust the level of the money supply to accommodate the ensuing demand for money. Thus, the LM curve which shows money market equilibrium given the actual quantity of money, runs through the point (Y_0, i_0). Since the money market is in equilibrium, and the foreign exchange market is kept in equilibrium by interventions, the bond market too must be in equilibrium at (Y_0, i_0). This follows from Walras' law. Thus, even the BB curve must run through (Y_0, i_0). Similar arguments can be made if M or B are exogenous.

The workings of the model is illustrated by a shift of the IS curve to the right in figure 6.1. Such a shift could be caused, for example, by an increase in G. If M is kept constant, the new equilibrium is along the original LM curve at A. If B is kept constant, the new equilibrium is along the original BB curve at B. If i is kept constant, the new equilibrium is along the original ii curve at C.

Suppose i is actually kept constant. Then the ii curve is not affected by the increase in G. The LM and BB curves have to shift so that they too run through the new equilibrium at C. The shift is brought about as the central bank increases the money supply to accommodate the increased demand for money. Similarly, if M is kept constant, the BB and ii curves will have to shift so that they too intersect the IS curve at the new equilibrium A.

Fiscal policy

Figure 6.1 shows that fiscal policy has the strongest effect on Y when the interest rate is constant. The impact is smaller when the central bank keeps the stock of outstanding government bonds, B, constant, and even smaller when the central bank is sterilizing – i.e. keeping the money supply constant. The ranking of the effects on the interest rate is the opposite. The effect on the foreign exchange reserves is determined by the effect on the interest rate (cf. (6.14) and (6.15)). Y has no direct impact on the demand for foreign exchange. An increase in the interest rate raises the foreign exchange reserves. Thus the highest increase in the foreign exchange reserves is when the central bank sterilizes. If the interest rate is kept constant, there is no effect on F_g.

One way of describing the difference between the regimes is this: an expansion of Y raises the demand for money. If the interest rate is kept constant, the central bank accommodates the new demand for money by buying kroner bonds from the public. If, on the other hand, the central bank keeps the stock of money constant, the increased money demand has the usual effect of raising interest rates, and this dampens the original increase in the demand for goods. In the intermediate case, where the central bank keeps B constant, the increased demand for money is partly accommodated as the public sells foreign currency. The addition which this makes to the money supply is not sterilized by the central bank.

An expansionary fiscal policy leads in all regimes to increased demand for imports and, hence, to a deterioration of the trade balance and the current account. Over time this means a loss of foreign exchange reserves, as in section 1.6 (p. 32). Within the short period for which the present model is designed, this effect is assumed to be negligible. After some time has passed, however, the accumulated current account effect may dominate over the interest rate effect, and the net result may be a loss of reserves.

In traditional Mundell–Fleming models with imperfect capital mobility, where capital movements are treated as a flow, the short-run effect of an expansionary fiscal policy on the foreign exchange reserve is ambiguous (see, for example, Gärtner, 1993). The reason is that the increased interest rate leads only to a gradual inflow of foreign exchange. Thus, the outflow caused by the current account may dominate the result even in the short run.[48]

Monetary policy

The effects of an exogenous increase in i are obvious and need no further comment.

An open market purchase of domestic bonds shifts the *LM* and *BB* curves downwards, as in figure 6.2. We know from section 3.1 that for a given Y an expansionary open market operation lowers interest rates irrespective of whether or not the ensuing capital flows are sterilized. The size of the shifts are easiest to compare if we measure them horizontally. Irrespective of whether the central bank sterilizes or not, the increase in Y which is required to restore equilibrium in the two markets when i is constant is the same. The reason is that the effect of Y on the demand for money and for kroner bonds are opposite and of exactly the same magnitude (cf. (6.12) and (6.13)).

However, the final result of an expansionary open market operation depends on which regime is in place. Without sterilization the new equilibrium is at A, with sterilization at B. We can see that an expansionary open market operation by, for

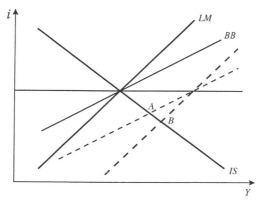

Figure 6.2 Effects of a monetary expansion.

example 1 billion kroner, has the strongest effect on both i and Y if the central bank sterilizes. The reason is this: the initial effect of a purchase of 1 billion kroner of bonds is to lower the interest rate. The reduced interest rate leads to an outflow of foreign currency, which reduces the money supply. If this is not sterilized, the interest rate increases somewhat again. If it is sterilized, there is no such countervailing effect.

Since sterilization means the greatest decline in i, it also means the greatest decline in the foreign exchange reserves.

Shock absorption and stabilization

The economy is hit from time to time by various exogenous shocks. These can be thought of both as changes in the exogenous variables of our model and as shifts in the functions that form the equations of the model. Three main types of shocks are *real demand shocks, monetary shocks and foreign exchange shocks*. A pure real demand shock can be a shift in one of the component demand functions (C, I and X) or a shift in variables such as P_* or Y_* which determine the IS curve, but has no direct impact on the financial markets. A pure monetary shock can be a shift in the demand function for money. A pure foreign exchange shock can be a shift in the f function or in exchange rate expectations (e_e). Some exogenous variables may cause 'composite' shocks. For example, i_* affects both the foreign exchange market and the goods market directly.

Pure real demand shocks shift the IS curve in the same way as fiscal policy does. Pure monetary shocks shift the equilibrium conditions in the money and bond markets in the same way as monetary policy does when carried out through open market operations. Pure foreign exchange shocks shift the equilibrium condition in the foreign exchange market and, when there is no sterilization, also the equilibrium condition in the bond market. Activist economic policies can in principle be used to neutralize the effects of each type of shock.

Activist fiscal policy can be used to neutralize the output effects of demand shocks. One example is that a fall in private investment demand can be met by an equal increase in government investment demand. This will keep the IS curve from shifting. Another example is that an increase in consumer demand may be met by a tax increase which reduces consumer demand back to its old level. The amount of fiscal intervention which is needed in order to neutralize a given demand shock is the same irrespective of the monetary policy regime. If private investment falls by, for example, 50 billion kroner, it takes 50 billion kroner of government investment to neutralize the effect and keep the IS curve in place irrespective of whether the central bank sterilizes or not.

Similarly open market operations can neutralize the effects of a money demand shock on interest rates and on aggregate demand. Sterilized foreign exchange interventions can neutralize the effects of foreign exchange shocks on interest rates and output. These policies can be carried out irrespective of which monetary policy regime we are in. As we learned in section 3.1, though, sterilization may be difficult or impossible if capital mobility is high.

However, there are many well known problems with activist policies. The lags and uncertainties which in practice are involved makes it difficult to get the dose and timing right. Instability in government consumption and investment or in tax rates may have high costs of their own. Thus, it is interesting to compare to what extent the different monetary regimes contribute to automatic stabilization of output. If we compare complete sterilization with no sterilization, the results are that sterilization

- reduces the impact of real demand shocks (shifts in *IS*)
- increases the impact of money demand shocks (shifts in *LM* or *BB* of equal size)
- removes the impact of foreign exchange shocks (which shifts only *BB*)

The third alternative, a fixed interest rate, removes the impact of both money demand and foreign exchange shocks, but it maximizes the impact of real demand shocks. Thus, which regime gives the greater output stability depends on what shocks the economy is exposed to. If real demand shocks are the main driving force behind output variations, there is much to say in favour of sterilization. Note, however, as we learned from the analysis of fiscal policy, that shifts in the *IS* curve produce larger changes in interest rates and foreign exchange reserves when the central bank sterilizes. Thus, a price is paid for greater output stability.

The impact of the degree of capital mobility

A higher degree of capital mobility means a less steep *BB* curve, as can be seen from (6.18). The reason is that a small increase in i attracts a large inflow of foreign exchange when capital mobility is high. This means a large increase in the money supply. When Y increases a large share of the increased transaction demands are satisfied in this way. If capital mobility is perfect, the *BB* curve becomes a horizontal line (like the *ii* curve) at $i = i_* + e_e(E)$. Sterilization becomes impossible, which means that the *LM* curve ceases to be relevant. It is no longer possible to fix the interest rate at an arbitrary level, and thus the original *ii* curve also ceases to be relevant. Even if capital mobility is not perfect, it may be so high that sterilization is in practice not a possible strategy. In the further discussion of the consequences of a high degree of capital mobility we shall thus focus on the case where B is exogenous.

As can be seen from figure 6.1, a flatter *BB* curve means that a fiscal expansion has a stronger effect on Y and less effect effect on i. In other words: high capital mobility increases the impact of fiscal policy on aggregate demand.

On the other hand, we can see from figure 6.2 that a flatter *BB* curve means that a market operation of a given size has a smaller effect on both Y and i. In other words: high capital mobility means that monetary policy has less effect on aggregate demand.

These are traditional conclusions from Mundell–Fleming-type models. However, they may be somewhat misleading. It is not only fiscal policy which has more effect on aggregate demand when capital mobility is greater, so has every real demand shock. If fiscal policy is going to be used to neutralize real demand shocks, the required amount of fiscal action is independent of the degree of capital mobility. If private investment falls by 50 billion kroner, it still takes 50 billion kroner of government investment to compensate for that. Thus, if we see fiscal policy as a tool for neutralizing the short-run effects of real demand shocks, a higher capital mobility does not mean that we can do with a less active fiscal policy. It means, however, that errors in demand management have a stronger impact on output.

The statement that monetary policy becomes less effective when capital mobility is higher is more accurate. However, by itself it is not particularly important that a market operation of a given size has a smaller effect on i and Y. It is easy to increase the size of a market operation (much easier than to increase the size of a change in government consumption). The real problem lies in an effect which is not visible in figure 6.2 – namely, that a given reduction in the interest rate leads to a larger reduction in the foreign exchange reserves when capital mobility is high. It is this fact which limits the potential of monetary policy when capital mobility is high.

Perfect capital mobility means that the interest rate is determined by the parity condition $i = i_* + e_e(E)$. Real demand shocks have their maximum effect. Foreign exchange shocks, which in this case must be exogenous changes in the perceived risk of parity changes, are reflected directly in interest rates. Money demand shocks have no effect as money supply adjusts passively to money demand. If real demand shocks or shocks to exchange rate expectations are important relative to money demand shocks, it would thus seem that we lose a useful opportunity for automatic stabilization when capital mobility becomes so high that the central bank cannot sterilize.

Devaluation

A devaluation is usually assumed to shift the IS curve to the right, as in figure 6.3. In order to check whether a devaluation has such an expansionary effect on the IS curve, it is useful to differentiate (6.6) with respect to E and Y, keeping i constant. We then find that the size of the shift measured horizontally is

$$\frac{dY}{dE} = \frac{(-C_Y \rho_* F_* + C_W F_{p0} + X_R P_*)/P}{1 - C_Y - X_Y} = \frac{\Delta_E}{1 - C_Y - X_Y} \tag{6.19}$$

The denominator is positive as usual. The numerator has three terms:

1. The competitiveness effect ($X_R P_*$): an increase in E raises the real exchange rate R and thus has a positive impact on net exports.

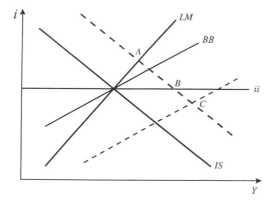

Figure 6.3 Effects of a devaluation.

2. The wealth effect ($C_W F_{p0}$): when $F_p > 0$, an increase in E increases the wealth of the private sector and thus consumption.
3. The income effect ($-C_Y \rho_* F_*$): if $F_* > 0$, a devaluation lowers real disposable income (cf. (6.7)), if $F_* < 0$ it is the other way around.

In other words, when $F_p > 0$ a devaluation raises demand for home goods both because people get wealthier and because the change in relative prices directs more demand towards home goods. An increased real interest burden may work in the opposite direction, but in that case we may assume that this effect is dominated by the other two.[49] Thus, the assertion that a devaluation shifts the IS curve to the right. For later use we denote the direct impact of E on the demand for home goods by Δ_E and assume $\Delta_E > 0$.

If the private sector has large debts in foreign currency, the possibility that $\Delta_E < 0$ cannot be excluded. A devaluation then has a contractionary effect on the IS curve. This may have played a role in the 1997–8 Asian crisis (see Furman and Stiglitz, 1998). Another possible source of contractionary effects of devaluations is low price elasticities of exports and imports which make $X_R < 0$. Edwards (1989) claims that devaluations are usually contractionary in developing countries. Lizondo and Montiel (1989) give an overview of mechanisms that can cause contractionary effects of devaluations.

The LM and ii curves do not depend on the exchange rate. The BB curve, however, shifts downwards after a devaluation. One reason is that when the public has more wealth, it wants to invest more in kroner bonds for any given level of Y. However no more kroner bonds are available, and this means that the sellers of kroner bonds can lower the interest rates they offer. Another reason is that an increase in E reduces e_e since we have assumed regressive expectations.

The various shifts following a devaluation are shown in figure 6.3. With full sterilization the economy ends up in A, with a fixed interest rate in B, and with no sterilization in C. As figure 6.3 is drawn, C is to the right of B, which means that the regime of no sterilization leads to a reduction in the interest rate and thus has the strongest positive impact on Y. However, in general we do not know the relative magnitudes of the shifts in the IS and BB curves. Thus we cannot tell whether the intersection point between the new BB and IS curves is above or below the ii curve. If capital mobility is perfect, the conclusion is simple. The BB curve is then horizontal. The domestic interest rate is given by $i = i + e_e(E)$. Hence, i is reduced to the same extent that $e_e(E)$ is reduced. If capital mobility is high, the result will be close to this.

However, the above analysis neglects the fact that the devaluation may cause a shift in the e_e function. This is likely if the devaluation is unexpected, since then the expected long-run value of the exchange rate may be revised upwards. The e_e function then shifts upwards. Governments are sometimes warned against a devaluation with the argument that it may shift the e_e function upward to such an extent that $e_e(E)$ actually increases. If capital mobility is close to perfect, this means that the BB curve shifts upwards and the interest rate increases. If this effect is strong, and the outward shift in the IS curve modest, the overall effect of the devaluation may be contractionary. Although this objection to devaluations may often be relevant, Dornbusch (1996) reports a number of examples where devaluations have apparently succeeded in expanding aggregate demand without adverse effects on interest rates.

There are two effects on the foreign exchange reserves:

1. *The portfolio composition effect*: after the devaluation the public wishes to rebalance its portfolio. When $F_{p0} > 0$ they have had a capital gain, part of which they want to reinvest in kroner. Thus they sell foreign exchange to the central bank, as explained in more detail in chapter 1 (p. 20). This effect is the same in all three monetary regimes.
2. *The effect through the risk premium*: if M is exogenous, the interest rate goes up. Reduced expectations of further depreciation may also contribute to a higher risk premium. The increased risk premium brings an increase in reserves. If i is exogenous, the increase in the risk premium is smaller. If B is exogenous, we do not know whether the interest rate goes up. Still we can prove that reserves must go up. Since the new equilibrium is below the old LM curve, M must have increased. The only way the public can get more money is by selling foreign currency to the central bank.

The initial positive impact of a devaluation on the trade balance is dampened by the ensuing increase in Y, which leads to increased import demand. If there are strong positive wealth effects of a devaluation, it is even possible that the total effect is an increased trade deficit. This can also happen if a devaluation leads to a reduced interest rate, and hence to increased investment demand. In this connection it is useful to remember that the current account is equal to the discrepancy between saving and real investment.

Changes in price levels

The foreign price level P_* enters the *IS* equation through the real exchange rate. It does not enter the financial side of the model. When the foreign price level increases, net exports go up, and this shifts the *IS* curve to the right. Thus, inflation abroad has an expansionary effect on the domestic economy. Because of the nominal rigidity in price formation, prices of home goods are unaffected.

The price of home goods P affects the *IS* equation through the real exchange rate, through real wealth and through real interest income. As long as $W_p > 0$ and $F_* < 0$, all effects are contractive. The *IS* curve shifts to the left. An increase in P also increases the demand for money at the expense of the demand for kroner bonds. This means that the *LM* curve shifts to the left. P thus has a contractionary effect on Y when there is full sterilization. The effect on the interest rate is ambiguous.

6.4 Floating exchange rate

The solution of the model can be depicted in an *IS-LM* diagram in this case too. However, we have to take account of the fact that the *IS* curve depends on the exchange rate and that the exchange rate depends on the interest rate. The latter relationship is given by the equilibrium condition for the foreign exchange market, which after (6.14) has been inserted in (6.15) can be written

$$F_g + \frac{P}{E}f\left(i - i_* - e_e(E), \frac{M_0 + B_0 + EF_{p0}}{P}\right) = -F_*$$

The solution of this for E can be written

$$E = E(i - i_*, P, F_g) \tag{6.20}$$

where $E_1 < 0$, since an increase in the interest rate differential leads to appreciation. Imagine that this function is inserted for E in the equation defining the *IS* curve. We then get an equation which tells us which (i, Y) combinations are compatible with equilibrium in both the goods market and the foreign exchange market. I call this the *ISFX* curve: *FX* for foreign exchange market equilibrium. It combines the *IS* equation and the *FX* equation (6.20) into a single equation between just two endogenous variables, i and Y.

IS shows the combinations of i and Y that yield equilibrium in the goods market for a given exchange rate. *ISFX* shows the combinations of i and Y which are consistent with equilibrium in both the goods market *and the foreign exchange market* when F_g is given.[50] The reason why the *ISFX* curve is flatter, as in figure 6.4, is: an increase in the interest rate leads to an appreciation of the domestic currency. The appreciation means that demand is shifted away from home goods and towards foreign goods. It also means a reduction in the wealth of the private sector ($F_p > 0$), and this again means reduced consumer demand. Thus an increase in the interest rate has a more contractionary effect when the exchange rate is floating than when it is fixed.

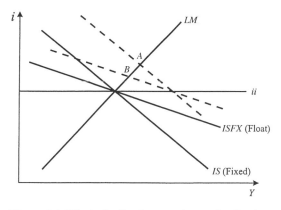

Figure 6.4 Effect of a fiscal expansion under fixed and floating exchange rates.

More formally, by differentiating the equation for the *ISFX* curve, we find that its slope is

$$\left.\frac{dY}{di}\right|_{ISFX} = \frac{C_\rho + I_\rho + \Delta_E E_1}{1 - C_Y - X_Y} < 0 \tag{6.21}$$

Compared to the corresponding derivative of the *IS* curve (6.16) there is an extra term in the numerator. We recognize Δ_E as the impact of a depreciation on demand for home goods (cf. (6.19)). This is assumed to be positive. Thus, since $E_1 < 0$, the last term is negative like the others. This means that a given increase in the interest rate has a stronger effect on aggregate demand when the exchange rate is floating than when it is fixed.

Since the demand for money does not depend on E, the *LM* curve is not affected by whether the exchange rate is fixed or floating. With floating exchange rates the *BB* curve coincides with the *LM* curve since keeping M constant and keeping B constant is equivalent, as discussed in section 3.1.

Fiscal policy

An expansionary fiscal policy shifts the *ISFX* curve to the right. If we keep the interest rate fixed at the initial level, the exchange rate does not change. Thus, at the initial interest rate the expansionary policy produces a shift of equal size in the *IS* and *ISFX* curve. When the interest rate is fixed, fiscal policy has the same effect on Y irrespective of whether the exchange rate is fixed or floating. When the money supply is given, this means that the fiscal expansion has more effect on aggregate demand when the exchange rate is fixed than when it is floating. The economy ends up at point A in figure 6.4 when the exchange rate is fixed, at point B when it is floating. With a given money supply, a fiscal expansion produces an increase in the interest rate. When the exchange rate is floating, this leads to an appreciation which dampens the expansionary effect.

As under fixed rates, the trade balance deteriorates. Under floating rates this is the combined effect of increased imports owing to an increase in Y and a real appreciation. Over time an increased trade deficit may lead to depreciation of the domestic currency, but this effect is beyond the short run that we study here. However, if people realize that the currency is going to depreciate, that will have an immediate effect on exchange rate expectations, which will dampen the initial appreciation and possibly reverse it. This example shows that our treatment of expectations may be a limitation when we discuss policy questions.

Monetary policy

As usual, an expansionary monetary policy shifts the *LM* curve to the right. As can be seen from figure 6.5, the expansionary effect is stronger when the exchange rate is floating than when it is fixed. The difference is between points *A* and *B* in figure 6.5. The reason is that the reduced interest rate causes a depreciation which again leads to more demand for home goods.

The effect of capital mobility

The degree of capital mobility affects the *ISFX* curve through the *FX* part, the function $E(i - i_*, P, F_g)$. Higher capital mobility means that the exchange rate reacts more strongly to an increase in the interest rate. An increase in the interest rate then has a stronger contractionary effect on aggregate demand. The *ISFX* curve is flatter the higher the degree of capital mobility. This means that with floating rates fiscal policy

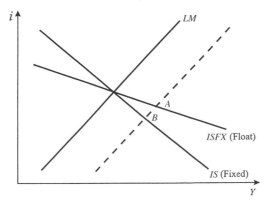

Figure 6.5 Effect of a monetary expansion under fixed and floating exchange rates.

has *less* effect on aggregate demand the higher capital mobility is. This is the opposite of the result under fixed rates when B is kept constant.

   Some authors even claim that fiscal policy has no effect if capital mobility is perfect. This is based on a case where e_e is exogenous and constant. Then the *ISFX* curve approaches a horizontal straight line as capital mobility goes to infinity. The reason is that the effect of the interest rate on the exchange rate goes to infinity. However, as long as e_e is a decreasing function of E, the *ISFX* curve will remain negatively sloped even with perfect capital mobility.[51]

   With a floating exchange rate high capital mobility does not prevent the central bank from controlling the quantity of money. A given increase in the money supply has a stronger effect on aggregate demand the higher capital mobility is. The reason is that a small decrease in the interest rate then leads to a large depreciation and this stimulates demand for the domestic good.

   In comparison with fixed rates (and B exogenous) we can summarize the results as follows: when the exchange rate is fixed, more capital mobility means that fiscal policy gets more effective, monetary policy less effective. When the exchange rate is floating, it is the other way around: fiscal policy gets less effective, monetary policy more effective.

Further comparisons with fixed rates

   A systematic comparison of how the economy responds to shocks under fixed and floating exchange rates can get messy because of the multiplicity of possible monetary regimes. We shall limit the discussion to two comparisons: one between fixed and floating rates when capital mobility is low and M is exogenous in both regimes, and one when capital mobility is perfect. In the latter case, the money supply is treated as endogenous under fixed rates and exogenous under floating rates. In making the comparison we use the results we have already derived for the effects of fiscal and monetary policy as representative for the effects of real demand shocks and money demand shocks, respectively.

   In the case where capital mobility is low and the money supply is exogenous under both fixed and floating rates, we find:

- Real demand shocks, like fiscal policy, have stronger effect on output when the exchange rate is fixed.
- Monetary shocks, like monetary policy, have a stronger effect on output when the exchange rate is floating.
- Foreign exchange shocks have no effect on output when the exchange rate is fixed.

If we are interested in automatic stabilization of output, the choice between the two regimes must depend on the magnitude of the different kinds of shocks. Strong money demand and exchange rate shocks are favouring fixed rates, while strong real demand shocks are favouring floating rates.

If we then turn to the case with perfect capital mobility and B exogenous, the first two points on the list of comparisons are the same. However, their quantitative importance is increased. High capital mobility increases the impact of real demand shocks under fixed rates, and reduces the impact of real demand shocks under floating rates, as it does for fiscal policy. For money demand shocks (as for monetary policy) it is the opposite. This strengthens the case for floating rates if real demand shocks are important, and weakens it if money demand shocks are important.

Exchange rate shocks are reflected directly in the domestic interest rate when the exchange rate is fixed. Thus, the fixed rates policy loses the advantage of insulating against such shocks. The same exchange rate shocks have opposite output effects under fixed and flexible exchange rates. Consider an exogenous increase in expected depreciation. When the exchange rate is fixed, the interest rate increases, and the economy moves up along the IS curve to a lower output. When the exchange rate is floating, the $ISFX$ curve shifts to the right, because at the initial interest rate the expected future depreciation causes an actual depreciation now, and this gives a boost to demand. The resulting intersection between the new $ISFX$ curve and the LM curve has higher output than before. Whether the absolute effect on output is greater with a fixed or a floating E depends on a whole set of elasticities.

If money demand shocks are not particularly important, it would seem that high capital mobility strengthens the case for floating exchange rates.

A comparison should also be made of fixed and flexible rates with respect to active stabilization. We can then note that irrespective of whether the exchange rate is fixed or floating the authorities have in principle the same number of instruments at their disposal. Thus, normally they should by the active use of these instruments be able to reach the same outcome. If a particular exchange rate regime also means a prohibition against the use of one instrument (as a free float means a prohibition on the use of F_g) then, of course, that regime entails less possibility for active stabilization.

One recipe for active stabilization is to meet each shock with the policy instrument which is most directly related to it. This means meeting real demand shocks by fiscal policy (G or T), monetary shocks by monetary policy (M) and foreign exchange shocks by sterilized foreign exchange interventions (F_g). Keeping the exchange rate fixed can be seen as an application of this principle to the foreign exchange market. If capital mobility is low, we have effective policy instruments which can be used to counter the effects of the three types of shocks. If they were actually used to this end, the exchange rate would turn out to be independent of the shocks, and thus constant also in the floating rate regime. Thus, the difference between fixed and floating rates in a sense disappears in this hypothetical scenario of perfect active stabilization.

When capital mobility is perfect (or close to perfect), the authorities lose one instrument. Sterilized interventions are no longer effective. There is then no instrument which can be used as a direct answer to foreign exchange shocks, neutralizing their effect. If we then keep the exchange rate fixed, foreign exchange shocks must be fully accommodated in the domestic interest rate. We either have to accept the effect this has on output, or use fiscal policy to counter it. If the exchange rate is floating, we can use monetary policy to choose how the effect should be distributed between changes in the exchange rate and changes in the interest rate. If there are increased depreciation expectations, there must be some monetary policy which distributes the effect between an increase in the interest rate and a depreciation in such a way that the total effect on aggregate demand is zero. There is then no effect on output either. In this sense monetary policy can be of more use when we have floating exchange rates.

However, the above may give a too rosy picture of the advantages of floating rates when capital mobility is high. We have discussed policy as if output was the only target of interest. A fixed exchange rate gives the economy a nominal anchor. If it is strictly adhered to, and inflation abroad is acceptable, that takes care of the economy's inflation target, and gives a focus for inflation expectations. Furthermore, if the fixed rate policy is strictly adhered to and credible, the foreign exchange shocks may be few and small and little to worry about. In the floating rate system just described, with an activist monetary policy, there is no obvious nominal anchor, and one may worry about the stability of expectations. If a fixed money supply is used as a nominal anchor, then the possibility for activist monetary policy disappears. Monetary policy is then no longer available as an answer to foreign exchange shocks. Furthermore, there is no instrument available as a direct answer to money demand shocks either. Their output consequences would then have to be accepted or met with fiscal policy. The advantage of floating rates with respect to active stabilization under perfect capital mobility thus seems to vanish if M is used as a nominal anchor.

It should be borne in mind that these conclusions are derived within the confines of our model. We have not discussed supply shocks (they are treated in section 10.1), nor have we looked properly at the question of long-run price stability. Expectations may depend on the policy regime. We have looked only at how shocks are transmitted in the economy under the various systems, and not discussed whether the choice of system may have consequences for the frequency and magnitude of shocks. This is conceivable if one or the other system creates more uncertainty about future price levels and exchange rates.

6.5 Some observations on real interest rates, expected inflation and the choice of deflator

In this section we first discuss briefly the relationship between different measures of real interest rates in models with home and foreign goods. We then look at how our conclusions are modified if we include inflationary expectations that are consistent with a short-run Phillips curve. Finally we look at some consequences of deflating with a price index instead of with the price of home goods.

Relationships among real interest rates

In our model there are two interest bearing assets and two goods. We can define real interest rates for each of the four combinations of goods and assets. The law of one price holds for each commodity. This means that for each asset the real return in terms of a given commodity is the same at home and abroad. It also means that measured in terms of the same commodity, the only difference in the real returns of domestic and foreign bonds is the risk premium. Thus, as long as we calculate real returns in terms of the same commodities, the relationships between real interest rates are as in section 5.1. However, we get the additional possibility that real interest rates can differ simply because we measure them in terms of different goods.

As an example we can look at the interest rates in terms of home goods. The expected real return to a domestic investor is $i - p_e$ on an investment in domestic currency and $i_* + e_e - p_e$ on an investment in foreign currency $(p_e = (\dot{P}/P)_e)$. The difference between the two is the risk premium $r = i - i_* - e_e$. On an investment in our currency a foreign investor receives an expected nominal return of $i - e_e$. The price increase she should expect on our home goods is $p_e + e_e$. Thus her expected real return is $i - p_e$, just as for the domestic investor.

The question now is how to define the real interest rates in our model. In (6.9) we defined ρ as $i - p_e$ – i.e. as the real rate on domestic currency in terms of home goods. A natural choice would seem to be also to define ρ_* in terms of home goods. This would imply that

$$\rho_* = i_* + e_e(E) - p_e \tag{6.22}$$

If we adopt this definition, it means that ρ_* cannot properly be treated as exogenous, since it depends on a variable, E, which is endogenous when the exchange rate is floating.

Most models simply leave out ρ_*. If foreign currency has a small share in the portfolio, and if the foreign debt is low, this may be justified, as the effects of ρ_* are then probably minor. Another simple way out is to define ρ_* in terms of foreign goods – i.e. as $\rho_* = i_* - p_*$. Then it can safely be assumed exogenous, but we no longer consistently deflate everything by the price of home goods.

The choice of deflator

The money demand function (6.12) is based on the fact that transaction needs can be measured by Y and P alone. Prices on imported goods have no influence. Nor has the level of absorption (domestic demand). One simple reformulation of the demand for money is to deflate by a price index instead of by the price of home goods. Let the price index be $P_c = P^\alpha (EP_*)^{1-\alpha}$ where $0 < \alpha < 1$ is the weight on home goods. Then the money demand and function is

$$\frac{M}{P^{\alpha}(EP_*)^{1-\alpha}} = m(i, Y) \tag{6.23}$$

This has one important consequence: the *LM* curve becomes dependent on the exchange rate. Under floating exchange rates this increases indirectly the interest elasticity of money demand. To see why, remember that an increase in i leads to a lower E. Money demand is reduced not only because of the usual effect from an increased alternative cost, but also because the appreciation lowers the price of imports and thus lowers the general price level.

A more elastic money demand means a flatter *LM* curve. Keeping the money stock constant then contributes less to dampening the output effect of real demand shocks. We may say that in this respect a regime with floating exchange rates and a fixed money supply is less different from a regime with a fixed exchange rate and a fixed interest rate than it appeared in section 5.4.

Another consequence is that the efficiency of monetary policy under floating exchange rates is reduced in the sense that a given increase in the money supply has a smaller impact on interest rates and output. The dependence of money demand on import prices also provides another channel for foreign exchange shocks to influence the interest rates and the real economy. An increase in i_* will shift the *LM* curve upwards because of the induced depreciation which raises money demand. This implies a tendency for the domestic interest rate to move more in pace with the foreign interest rate even if M is constant.

The use of the price of home goods as the deflator for the income and wealth arguments in the consumption function is not as arbitrary as it may first seem. Let Y_N and W_N stand for nominal income and nominal wealth, respectively – i.e. $Y_N = PY - \rho_* EF_*$ and $W_N = M + B + EF_p$. Let $P_c = P_c(P, EP_*)$ be a general price index, C_N total nominal consumer expenditure, and $C_R = C_N/P_c$. C_R is what we usually think of as total consumption in real terms. It is then reasonable to write the aggregate consumption function as

$$C_R = g\left(\frac{Y_N}{P_c}, \frac{W_N}{P_c}, \rho, \rho_*\right) \tag{6.24}$$

However, consumption in the *IS* equation (6.6) is not C_R: it is nominal consumption expenditure deflated by P. In other words,

$$C = \frac{C_N}{P} = \frac{C_R P_c}{P}$$

or

$$C = \frac{P_c}{P} g\left(\frac{Y_N}{P_c}, \frac{W_N}{P_c}, \rho, \rho_*\right)$$

This is equivalent to the consumption function we have used if, and only if, g is homogeneous of degree one in income and wealth. In that case, we can write

$$C = g\left(\frac{Y_N}{P}, \frac{W_N}{P}, \rho, \rho_*\right)$$

Thus, homogeneity makes it permissible to deflate with the price of home goods as long as we do it consistently. Standard life-cycle models (which assume homothetic utility functions) imply that a proportional increase in income and wealth results in a proportional increase in consumption. In long time series there has often been observed a tendency to proportionality between income, consumption and wealth. Thus, there is a defence for the way income and wealth is deflated in our consumption function.[52]

The consumption function (6.24) may be used to throw some light on the nature of the wealth effect arising from a depreciation. If we use the same price index as when we deflated money demand above, the wealth argument in (6.24) can be written

$$\frac{M_0 + B_0 + EF_{p0}}{P^\alpha(EP_*)^{1-\alpha}} = \frac{M_0 + B_0}{P^\alpha(EP_*)^{1-\alpha}} + \frac{E^\alpha F_{p0}}{P^\alpha P_*^{1-\alpha}}$$

Suppose all three components of wealth are positive. Then the increase in import prices following a depreciation reduces the real value of the initial stocks of domestic currency assets, just as it did in chapter 5. On the other hand, it increases the real value of the initial stock of foreign currency. Which effect dominates depends on the weight of imports in the price index and on the shares of the two currencies in the portfolio. The point is that, as in chapter 5, a depreciation reduces the real value of the domestic debt of the government, even if this is not immediately obvious when we deflate everything by P instead of P_c.[53] The difference between the wealth effects in the two chapters is smaller than it appears on the surface.

We may also deflate by the price index P_c instead of P in the demand function for foreign currency. This may change the magnitude of the portfolio composition effect, but not its sign (unless F_p and $M + B$ happen to be of opposite signs). In the important special case where asset demands are proportional to wealth, the choice of deflator has, of course, no effect at all.

Endogenous inflation expectations: the Walters effect

One weakness of the Mundell–Fleming–Tobin model is the exogeneity of expected inflation. One way to endogenize expectations is to add a Phillips curve to the model and assume that expected inflation is equal to the inflation predicted by the Phillips curve. A suitable expectations augmented Phillips curve may in this case be

$$\frac{\dot{P}}{P} = \left(\frac{\dot{E}}{E}\right)^e + \frac{\dot{P}_*}{P_*} + \gamma(Y - \bar{Y}) = e_e(E) + p_* + \gamma(Y - \bar{Y}) \tag{6.25}$$

where $\gamma > 0$ is a constant parameter and $\bar{Y}$ is the equilibrium level of output (corresponding to equilibrium unemployment). A brief justification for this Phillips curve is given in section 6.6. Model-consistent expectations of domestic inflation means that

$p_e = p = \dot{P}/P$. Note that expectations here are not fully rational, since expected depreciation is not necessarily model-consistent.

Expected inflation enters the model through the real interest rate ρ in the *IS* curve, and in principle also through the real interest rate on foreign currency loans, ρ_*. With expectations consistent with (6.25), the two real interest rates are

$$\rho = i - p_e = i - e_e(E) - p_* - \gamma(Y - \bar{Y}) \tag{6.26}$$

$$\rho_* = i_* + e_e(E) - p_e = i_* - p_* - \gamma(Y - \bar{Y}) \tag{6.27}$$

Equation (6.26) replaces (6.9) in the original model, while (6.27) may be added to endogenize ρ_*. Note that ρ_* is independent of e_e because the direct effect of e_e and the effect through p_e cancel out.

Both real interest rates depend on the level of output. The domestic real interest rate also depends on the expected rate of depreciation. Thus, there are now two new effects to discuss.

An increased activity level tends, *ceteris paribus*, to reduce the real interest rates. This is because a high activity level produces more inflation. When deriving the *IS* curve, (6.26) and (6.27) should be inserted in (6.6). The effect of Y on expectations reinforces the standard multiplier process in the goods market. An exogenous increase in demand not only leads to a further increase in demand because of the income effect on consumption, but also because it reduces the expected real interest rates. Thus, for a given interest rate and a given exchange rate any demand shock has a stronger effect on output. This is the *Walters effect* (Walters, 1986).

The Walters effect makes both the *IS* and *ISFX* curves flatter.[54] The impact of an increase in i is reinforced under both fixed and floating exchange rates, as are the impacts of other demand shocks. A given *LM* curve then contributes more towards dampening the output effect of demand shocks.

Walters used this as an argument against British participation in the European Exchange Rate Mechanism. He reasoned that a credible commitment to a fixed exchange rate would make i equal to i_* and thus independent of British demand shocks. There would then be no monetary mechanism to dampen the effect of demand shocks on output. Because the effect on expected inflation gives demand shocks a strong impact on output, the ability to raise interest rates in booms and lower them in recessions would be badly needed. Hence floating rates were to be preferred.

However, the Phillips curve (6.25) has another consequence for the *ISFX* curve that Walters apparently neglected. A depreciation now leads to an expected appreciation in the future, since e_e' is negative. Since an expected appreciation contributes to lower inflation, this means a higher real interest rate, ρ. Thus, the expansionary effect of a depreciation is reduced when expected inflation is endogenized. One consequence is a steeper *ISFX* curve. This reduces the efficacy of monetary policy as a tool for stabilizing aggregate demand under floating exchange rates.

At this point it may be helpful to focus on the case with perfect capital mobility. Then $i = i_* + e_e$, and if this is inserted in (6.26) we get

$$\rho = i_* - p_* - \gamma(Y - \bar{Y}) = \rho_*$$

Any increase in the domestic interest rate is exactly offset by an increase in the expected rate of depreciation and the real interest rate is unaffected. Monetary policy then affects aggregate demand only through the exchange rate, not the real interest rate.

The last conclusions should be treated with some caution, though. They rely heavily on the forward-looking nature of both inflationary expectations and price setting.

6.6 From short- to long-run equilibrium: the price–specie–flow mechanism

So far in chapter 6 we have focused entirely on the short run. However, after a shock or a change in policy, the process of asset accumulation (or decumulation) will gradually move the equilibrium. This means that after a while the effects of an exogenous event may be quite different from the initial impact. The economy will also move over time as the current state of demand leads to gradual changes in the price level. In the present section we shall give an example of how these dynamics may move the economy from short-to long-run equilibrium.[55] The emphasis is on a case with fixed exchange rates, while floating rates are treated in sections 6.7–6.8. Unlike in sections 6.2–6.5 the focus is now on the effects of permanent shocks.

The basic structure of our model is this: at every moment of time there is a temporary (or 'short-run') equilibrium described by the model from section 6.2. To this model are added two differential equations: one which relates the growth of foreign debt to the current account and one which relates inflation to aggregate demand through a Phillips curve. The two differential equations move the temporary equilibrium over time towards a final stationary state called the stationary or 'long-run' equilibrium. This is characterized by both 'external' and 'internal' balance – i.e. by a balanced current account and a balance between aggregate supply and demand at home. Our aim is to study the process which leads from short-run imbalances to long-run balance.

Thus, the model is comparable to that in section 5.7, but with the important difference that there is now a link from foreign debt through aggregate demand to output and inflation. The specie–flow mechanism still works, but in a more indirect manner than in chapter 5. Increased wealth raises domestic demand and output, and through that the demand for imports. But increased output also raises inflation. The real exchange rate appreciates, and this leads to further reductions in the trade surplus. This is the price–specie–flow mechanism. The model highlights the role that the real exchange rate plays in the adjustment process that leads to current account balance.[56]

Compared to section 6.2 we make some simplifications. We assume away real investment,[57] and we assume that the government budget is balanced in the sense that $\dot{W}_g = 0$. Including investment and government deficits would have made the analysis too complicated at this stage. Since we are looking at the effects of permanent shocks, the assumption of a balanced budget also seems appropriate. We focus on just one monetary regime, namely the one with an exogenous interest rate. An alternative interpretation is that we have perfect capital mobility.

For simplicity we assume a non-inflationary background – i.e. we assume that $p_* = 0$ and that $e = e_e = 0$. There is no inflation abroad and the exchange rate is kept constant. This means that in the long run domestic inflation must also approach zero. Otherwise the real exchange rate would diverge, and this would make it impossible to balance the current account. For simplicity, and because of the non-inflationary background, real interest rates are set equal to nominal rates ($\rho = i$ and $\rho_* = i_*$).

The model consists of three equations:

$$Y = C\left(Y - i_*\frac{EF_*}{P} - G, -\frac{EF_*}{P} - W_g, i, i_*\right) + G + X\left(\frac{EP_*}{P}, Y, Y_*\right) \tag{6.28}$$

$$\dot{P} = P\gamma(Y - \bar{Y}) \tag{6.29}$$

$$\dot{F}_* = i_*F_* - \frac{P}{E}X\left(\frac{EP_*}{P}, Y, Y_*\right) \tag{6.30}$$

Equation (6.28) describes the *IS* curve. Note that $T = G$ in line with the assumption that $\dot{W}_g = 0$. (6.29) is a Phillips curve. Inflation ($\dot{P}/P$) is proportional to the gap between actual and equilibrium output ($Y - \bar{Y}$); $\gamma > 0$. We return to this shortly. Equation (6.30) is the equation for the accumulation of the foreign debt. The right-hand side is the current account deficit, which is the sum of net interest payments to abroad and the trade deficit, all measured in foreign currency this time.

Equations (6.28)–(6.30) determine the time paths of Y, P and F_* given the time paths of the exogenous variables, and given the initial conditions $P(0) = P_0$, $F_*(0) = F_{*0}$ and $W_g = (-M_0 - B_0 + E(0)F_{g0})/P_0$. The exogenous variables are i_*, P_*, Y_*, E, G and i.

From (6.30) it may appear that the current account is determined in an entirely different way than in chapter 5. However, if (6.28) is used to substitute for X in (6.30), one sees that the direct relationship between savings and the current account is actually the same. The present model and the Phillips curve model in section 5.7 are closely related. The main difference is that savings behaviour here affects output and prices.

Interpreting the Phillips curve

The connection between the Phillips curves in chapter 5 and the Phillips curve here (6.29) needs explanation. The former was a relation between real wage growth and (un)employment of the type

$$\frac{\dot{W}}{W} - \left(\frac{\dot{P}_c}{P_c}\right)^e = \gamma'(N - \bar{N})$$

N and $\bar{N}$ can be replaced by Y and $\bar{Y}$ if we assume that labour productivity, A, is constant. This means that $Y = AN$, and we can define $\bar{Y} = A\bar{N}$. Furthermore, with constant productivity and mark-up pricing P is proportional to W, and their growth rates are the same. Under these assumptions the expectations augmented Phillips curve can be written

$$\frac{\dot{P}}{P} - \left(\frac{\dot{P}_c}{P_c}\right)^e = (\gamma'/A)(Y - \bar{Y})$$

By definition

$$\frac{\dot{P}_c}{P_c} = \alpha\frac{\dot{P}}{P} + (1 - \alpha)\left(\frac{\dot{E}}{E} + \frac{\dot{P}_*}{P_*}\right)$$

When this is substituted for expectations in the Phillips curve above, we get

$$\frac{\dot{P}}{P} = \frac{\dot{E}}{E} + \frac{\dot{P}_*}{P_*} + \frac{\gamma'}{A(1 - \alpha)}(Y - \bar{Y})$$

Given our assumption of a non-inflationary environment and a fixed exchange rate, this is the same as (6.29) with $\gamma = \gamma'/A(1 - \alpha)$. Note that a high share of imports reduces the slope of this 'reduced form' augmented Phillips curve. Note also that a positive import share combined with the fixed exchange rate makes it possible to have rational expectations even when Y is different from $\bar{Y}$. This would not be possible in a similar closed economy.

Implicit in the derivation of the Phillips curve here is the assumption of model-consistent expectations. It can then be argued that we should have included the Walters effect in the interest rates in (6.28). However, this would not have changed the nature of the dynamics we are studying as long as the IS curve still slopes downwards.

The temporary equilibrium

The temporary equilibrium is described by (6.28), which for given levels of P and F_* determines Y. The solution can in principle be written

$$Y = Y(P, F_*, x) \tag{6.31}$$

where $x = (i_*, P_*, Y_*, G, i, E, W_g)$ is the vector of exogenous variables. It will be of particular interest to us how P and F_* influence Y. By differentiating (6.28) we find that the effect of F_* on Y is

$$\frac{\partial Y}{\partial F_*} = \frac{(-i_* C_Y - C_W)E/P}{1 - C_Y - X_Y} < 0 \tag{6.32}$$

A higher foreign debt reduces consumption demand both through an income effect and a wealth effect, and this has the standard multiplier effect on aggregate demand.

The effect of an increase in the price level is

$$\frac{\partial Y}{\partial P} = \frac{(i_* C_Y + C_W)W'_* - X_R R}{1 - C_Y - X_Y}\frac{1}{P} \tag{6.33}$$

where $W'_* = EF_*/P$ is the real value of the foreign debt measured in terms of home goods. The first term in the numerator is the wealth effect. An increase in P reduces the real value of F_*. This raises aggregate demand if $F_* > 0$, lowers aggregate demand if $F_* < 0$. The second term in the numerator is the effect of a real appreciation. It shifts demand away from home goods, and thus always has a negative impact on aggregate demand. If the country is a net creditor – i.e. if $W'_* < 0$ – both terms are negative. A price increase then has a contractionary effect. If the country is a net debtor – i.e., if $W'_* > 0$ – the first term is positive. If the debt is large, the first term may dominate the expression. Then a price increase on home goods is expansionary. However, the standard assumption is that the real exchange rate effect dominates and thus that $\partial Y/\partial P < 0$. In other words, we assume that the aggregate demand curve slopes downwards.

The stationary equilibrium

If we insert for Y from (6.31) in (6.29) and (6.30) we get a system of two differential equations which in compact form can be written

$$\dot{P} = \phi_1(P, F_*, x) \tag{6.34}$$

$$\dot{F}_* = \phi_2(P, F_*, x) \tag{6.35}$$

The stationary solution of this system is defined by

$$\dot{P} = \phi_1(P, F_*, x) = 0 \Leftrightarrow Y = Y(P, F_*, x) = \bar{Y} \tag{6.36}$$

$$\dot{F}_* = \phi_2(P, F_*, x) = 0 \Leftrightarrow X(EP_*/P, Y, Y_*) = i_* EF_*/P(= i_* W'_*) \tag{6.37}$$

These two equations determine the stationary values of F_* and P. Equation (6.36) is the condition for internal balance, (6.37) the condition for external balance. Internal balance means that output (and presumably also unemployment) is at its equilibrium value. Thus, in the long-run equilibrium output is determined from the supply side. External balance means that the current account is balanced – i.e. that the trade surplus is just sufficient to cover the interest payments on the foreign debt.

If we insert $Y = \bar{Y}$ in (6.28), we find that internal balance requires (cf. (6.36)) that

$$C(\bar{Y} - i_* W'_* - G, -W'_* - W_g, i, i_*) + G + X(R, \bar{Y}, Y_*) = \bar{Y}$$

With $Y = \bar{Y}$ external balance requires (cf. (6.37))

$$i_* W'_* = X(R, \bar{Y}, Y_*) \tag{6.38}$$

If we insert this in the condition for internal balance above, we get

$$C(\bar{Y} - i_* W'_* - G, -W'_* - W_g, i, i_*) + G = \bar{Y} - i_* W'_* \tag{6.39}$$

This is the same stationary equilibrium condition as we had for the foreign debt in chapter 5. Total consumption should be equal to national income. The only endogenous variable in this equation is W'_*. Thus, in the long run both Y and W'_* are determined in the same way here as in chapter 5. In particular, the long-run value of the foreign debt depends only on savings behaviour. W'_* is not affected by the X function.

Where the difference between chapters 5 and 6 appears is in the determination of relative prices. In chapter 5 all relative prices were given exogenously. In chapter 6 the relative price of foreign and home goods, R, is determined by (6.38). The higher the foreign debt is, the lower the relative price of home goods must be in order that we shall sell enough of our goods to pay the interest on the debt and balance the current account. In chapter 5 a low price on exports was unnecessary, because foreign demand was infinitely elastic.

We can also compare the two chapters from the point of view of wage determination. Since prices and wages are proportional in the present section, (6.38) also determines the equilibrium wage level. Because of the wealth effect in the consumption function, the current account can be balanced at any level of Y. Both here and in chapter 5 the role of long-run wage flexibility is to make sure that the balancing takes place at the level of Y which corresponds to equilibrium employment. Here it means that the wage level has to be low enough that a sufficient share of world demand is directed towards home goods. In chapter 5 it means that wages have to be low enough that domestic producers are willing to supply a sufficient share of world demand for the single good. Hence, the new element relative to chapter 5 is that the equilibrium wage rate also depends on domestic demand conditions.

Since $R = EP_*/P$ and E is exogenous, the absolute price level, P, follows when R has been determined.

Stability conditions

In order to study the stability of the system around the stationary state, the mathematical theory of differential equations tells us to form the Jacobian matrix

$$A = \begin{bmatrix} \phi_{11} & \phi_{12} \\ \phi_{21} & \phi_{22} \end{bmatrix}$$

where the elements are the derivatives of (6.34) and (6.35). A set of necessary and sufficient conditions for local asymptotic stability of the stationary state is that

$$\text{tr}(A) = \phi_{11} + \phi_{22} < 0$$

and

$$|A| = \phi_{11}\phi_{22} - \phi_{12}\phi_{21} > 0$$

where the trace and determinant of A are to be evaluated at the stationary state.

In order to check the stability conditions we must compute the derivatives involved. By differentiating (6.29) and (6.30) taking account of (6.28) and inserting $Y = \bar{Y}$ we find

$$\phi_{11} = \frac{\partial \dot{P}}{\partial P} = P\gamma \frac{\partial Y}{\partial P} \tag{6.40}$$

$$\phi_{12} = \frac{\partial \dot{P}}{\partial F_*} = P\gamma \frac{\partial Y}{\partial F_*} \tag{6.41}$$

$$\phi_{21} = \frac{\partial \dot{F}_*}{\partial P} = (-X + X_R R)\frac{1}{E} - X_Y \frac{P}{E}\frac{\partial Y}{\partial P} \tag{6.42}$$

$$\phi_{22} = \frac{\partial \dot{F}_*}{\partial F_*} = i_* - X_Y \frac{P}{E}\frac{\partial Y}{\partial F_*} \tag{6.43}$$

Of the elements in the Jacobian only ϕ_{12} can be signed unambiguously. Since $\partial Y/\partial F_* < 0$, it follows that $\phi_{12} < 0$. We need extra assumptions to sign the three other derivatives.

We shall argue that a plausible combination of signs is:

$$\phi_{11} < 0 \quad \phi_{12} < 0$$
$$\phi_{21} > 0 \quad \phi_{22} < 0$$

This shall be our *standard case*. It is easily checked that in this case both the trace and the determinant condition are satisfied. Thus, the stationary equilibrium is stable. After having argued for the standard case, we discuss the requirements for stability more generally. They turn out to be quite mild, and resemble conditions we have seen earlier. The ensuing discussion of the dynamics is focused on the standard case, while other cases are given as exercises.

That $\phi_{11} < 0$, follows directly if we assume that the aggregate demand curve slopes downwards. It is always true if the foreign debt is not too large. That $\phi_{12} < 0$ is, as already mentioned, a general result following from the fact that higher indebtedness reduces aggregate demand.

Now to the current account effects of prices and foreign debt. $\phi_{21} > 0$ is the effect on the current account deficit of a price increase on home goods. The direct effect of an increase in P on the trade balance is measured by the first term in (6.42). If trade is balanced initially and the Marshall–Lerner condition holds, this effect is positive (i.e. leading to an increased deficit). However, we have already assumed that an increase in P is contractionary. There is then an offsetting effect as a reduced Y leads to reduced demand for imports. If we insert for dY/dP from (6.33) in (6.42), we find after some reorganization[58] that

$$\phi_{21} = \frac{1}{1 - C_Y - X_Y}\frac{1}{E}\{X_R R(1 - C_Y) - [i_*(1 - C_Y)(1 - X_Y) + C_W X_Y]W'_*\}$$

The two terms inside the braces correspond to two different effects of a price increase. First there is the competitiveness effect, which always leads to a larger current account deficit. Thus, the first term inside the braces is always positive. The second term is more complicated and more difficult to sign. It combines the effect that a price increase has on real wealth and the revaluation effect which arises when trade is not balanced in the initial equilibrium. The sign clearly depends on whether W_*' is positive or negative. It also depends on the sign of the expression in brackets, which is ambiguous. However, if the stationary value of W_*' is not too far from zero, the last term is small. The standard case, ϕ_{21}, is based on that the competitiveness effect dominates.

ϕ_{22} is the effect of foreign debt on the current account deficit. Conceptually it is similar to the effect of W_* on $\dot{W}_*$ that we discussed in chapter 5. Not surprisingly, we find that the ambiguity in sign has the same cause in the two cases. If we substitute for dY/dF_* from (6.32) in (6.43) we get

$$\phi_{22} = \frac{i_*(1 - C_Y)(1 - X_Y) + C_W X_Y}{1 - C_Y - X_Y} \tag{6.44}$$

The first term in the numerator is positive, the second negative. The first term tells us how much the current account deteriorates because of higher interest payments when foreign debt is higher. The second term tells us how much the current account improves because higher foreign debt means lower private wealth and lower consumption. As in chapter 5, the question of the sign boils down to the question of which is the stronger: the interest rate effect or the wealth effect; only their relative strength is somewhat affected by the fact that the relation between consumption and net exports is less direct. As was standard in chapter 5, we assume that the wealth effect is the stronger, and thus that $\phi_{22} < 0$[59]. Note that $\phi_{22} < 0$ implies $\phi_{21} > 0$ when $W_*' \geq 0$.

The trace condition requires that the sum of the two direct feedback effects must be negative. A sufficient condition for this is that each of them are negative – i.e. that a larger foreign debt leads to a smaller current account deficit, and that a higher price level leads to less aggregate demand and less inflation. Neither assumption is necessary, but at least one of them must hold for stability.

Given that the direct feedback effects are negative and thus stabilizing, the determinant condition can be interpreted as a condition that the two cross-effects shall not destabilize the system. A straightforward, but tedious, calculation shows that

$$|A| = \gamma X_R R \frac{-i_*(1 - C_Y) + C_W}{1 - C_Y - X_Y}$$

Thus, the requirement that $|A| > 0$ is equivalent to that $C_W > i_*(1 - C_Y)$ or that the wealth effect on consumption dominates over the interest rate effect. This is the same stability condition as for the extremely open economy in section 5.3. It can be shown that if $\phi_{22} < 0$, then $C_W > i_*(1 - C_Y)$. Thus, in the present case instability can arise only if one of the direct feedbacks is positive – i.e. if $\phi_{11} > 0$ or $\phi_{22} > 0$. Instability must then be due either to a large foreign debt, which makes $\partial Y/\partial P > 0$, or a weak wealth effect on consumption.

Dynamics: the standard case

The movement from short- to long-run equilibrium can best be illustrated by a phase diagram such as that drawn in figure 6.6. The diagram is drawn for the standard case where all the sign assumptions that we just made on the elements of A are satisfied.

The curve marked $\dot{P} = 0$ shows the locus of (P, F_*) combinations which yield internal balance. It is defined by

$$\dot{P} = \phi_1(P, F_*, x) = 0$$

or $Y = \bar{Y}$ (cf. (6.36)). The locus for internal balance slopes downwards, since a high price level P is compatible with aggregate demand equal to $\bar{Y}$ only if the foreign debt is low. More formally, by implicit differentiation of $\phi_1(P, F_*, x) = 0$ we find that the slope of the $(\dot{P} = 0)$ curve is

$$\left.\frac{dF_*}{dP}\right|_{\dot{P}=0} = -\frac{\phi_{11}}{\phi_{12}} = -\frac{\partial Y/\partial P}{\partial Y/\partial F_*} < 0$$

To the right of the locus for internal balance the price level is high. Since $\phi_{11} < 0$, this means that the demand for home goods is low ($Y < \bar{Y}$) and prices are falling ($\dot{P} < 0$). To the left of the locus home goods are relatively cheaper, demand for them is above $\bar{Y}$ and prices are rising ($\dot{P} > 0$). The direction of movement for P is also indicated by the horizontal arrows, which point towards the locus for internal balance from both sides.

Similarly the curve marked $\dot{F}_* = 0$ shows the locus of (P, F_*) combinations which yield external balance. It is defined by (cf. (6.37))

$$\dot{F}_* = \phi_2(P, F_*, x) = 0$$

Its slope is

$$\left.\frac{dF_*}{dP}\right|_{\dot{F}_*=0} = -\frac{\phi_{21}}{\phi_{22}} > 0$$

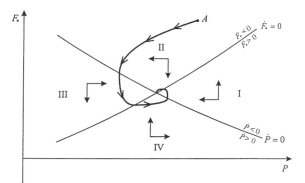

Figure 6.6 Transition from short- to long-run equilibrium: a cyclic path.

Since $\phi_{22} < 0$, a large foreign debt, which also means a large private sector debt, tends to produce a current account surplus as consumers save to reduce their indebtedness. A high price on home goods tends on the other hand to produce a current account deficit, since $\phi_{21} > 0$. Thus, if there is going to be external balance, a high foreign debt F_* must be combined with a high price on home goods P. This explains why the locus for external balance slopes upwards. Above the curve the foreign debt is high, which means that domestic demand is low and savings are high. There is a surplus on the current account, and the foreign debt is declining ($\dot{F}_* < 0$). Below the curve there is a current account deficit and $\dot{F}_* > 0$. The direction of movement for F_* is also indicated by the vertical arrows. They point towards the locus for external balance.

The stationary equilibrium is of course where the two loci meet. The two loci divide the plane into four regions where the foreign debt and the price level move in different directions. If we are at a point in one of the regions, the equilibrium moves with time in a direction which is intermediate between the two arrows in that region.

Suppose that initially the economy is at point A in figure 6.6. The location is determined by the historically given initial values of P and F_*. Point A is in region II which combines a current account surplus with high unemployment. This leads to a gradual decline in the foreign debt and a gradual decline in the price level. The path leading from A is marked with arrows. As the citizens pay off their debts, domestic demand begins to pick up. After a while the locus for internal balance is reached. At that point the price level is stationary while the foreign debt continues to decline. Thus, domestic demand increases further and we go into a period of 'over-full' employment, where the pressure from demand makes prices rise again (region III). The real exchange rate appreciates. Domestic demand continues to increase owing to the steady decline in debt. This, in addition to the real appreciation, means that the current account deteriorates. After a while the economy hits the locus for external balance. At this point the foreign debt is stationary, while prices are still rising and the real exchange rate still appreciating. The real appreciation means that the current account goes into deficit, and that the foreign debt starts to increase. We are then in region IV.

Real appreciation and accumulation of debt both reduce the demand for home goods, and after a while the path again hits the locus for internal balance. Then inflation stops, competitiveness begins to improve again, and after a while in region I we are back to region II, where we started. However, we are closer to the stationary equilibrium, as we should be when it is stable. After going a full circle, the economy starts on another and then on yet another, and in this way spirals towards the stationary solution.

However, the solution need not be cyclic. Figure 6.7 illustrates the case where the economy moves straight towards the stationary equilibrium at the first opportunity.

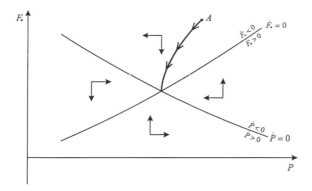

Figure 6.7 Transition from short- to long-run equilibrium: a direct path.

An expansionary shock to domestic demand

Figure 6.8 illustrates how the model can be used to analyse the effects of a domestic demand shock. By this is meant either a positive shift in the consumption function or a fiscal expansion (within a balanced budget).

A domestic demand shock shifts the locus for internal balance to the right. A higher price level is required to keep demand down to $\bar{Y}$. The locus for external balance shifts to the left. A lower price level – i.e. better competitiveness – is required in order to balance the current account when domestic demand is higher. As we can see from figure 6.8, the new stationary equilibrium (B) obviously has higher foreign debt than the old (A), since both curves shift upwards. Whether P will go up or down, depends on the relative size of the shifts. One can prove that the shift in the curve for external balance is the greater and, thus, that in the new long-run equilibrium P has gone down.

The easiest way to prove this is to look at the condition for external balance given that $Y = \bar{Y}$ (6.38). Taking account of that $W_*' = EF_*/P$, this can be written

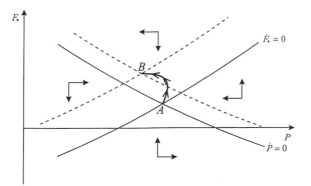

Figure 6.8 Effects of a domestic demand shock.

$$i_*F_*/P_* = (1/R)X(R, \bar{Y}, Y_*) \tag{6.45}$$

We know that the left-hand side – interest payment on the foreign debt – must increase, since F_* has increased. Then the right-hand side – the trade surplus measured in foreign goods – must also increase. Since both output levels are given, this requires a real depreciation.[60] The price of home goods must be reduced in order to increase the market share enough that the higher interest payments can be covered. Thus, we know that the new stationary equilibrium not only has a higher F_* but also a lower P. In other words, the new equilibrium must be above and to the left of the old, as in figure 6.8. This can happen only if the shift in the locus for external balance is the greater.

Alternatively we can find the effects on the stationary equilibrium by differentiating the equilibrium conditions (6.36) and (6.37). The stability conditions and the other assumptions we have made about the Jacobi matrix A can then be used to sign the effects.

In figure 6.8 we have assumed that the initial equilibrium was at the old stationary state. The initial effect of the domestic demand shock is an increase in Y, which means 'overfull' employment and a current account deficit. Thus the old stationary state is in a region where both P and F_* grow. There is an immediate boom. However, as competitiveness deteriorates and the public gets more indebted, Y declines. After a while we enter the region with unemployment and downward pressure on prices. Competitiveness is restored, and the economy moves towards the new stationary state (either directly, as in the figure, or in cycles as in figure 6.6).

Since we have assumed a unique equilibrium level for Y, the expansionary effect of a domestic demand shock is short-lived. The boom necessarily turns into bust. The competitiveness which is lost during the boom needs to be regained. That can be done only by going through a period of low employment. Not only that: because the foreign debt grows in the process, in the end we need to be more competitive than before. This means that even if prices go as easily down as up, the 'depression' must be stronger than the boom. Countries which have deregulated their credit markets have often experienced an initial boom accompanied by a large current account deficit. This has usually been followed by a strong recession, just as we should expect from the model.

One may be tempted to conclude from the above analysis that using fiscal policy as a weapon against unemployment is a bad idea. However, that conclusion needs to be qualified. What we have shown is that a permanent fiscal expansion may be a bad idea if we already have internal balance. The use of fiscal policy as a countercyclical tool is quite another matter, and in fact the above analysis may be used as a support for some fiscal activism.

Suppose that there is a *temporary* positive shift in the consumption function. If the government does nothing, the economy first goes into a boom as a result of the increase in consumer demand. This leads to increased inflation and a loss of international competitiveness. At the same time there will be a current account deficit.

Through the dynamic mechanisms described above, this gradually tends to reduce output and employment. Output and employment is reduced further when the shift in the consumption function is reversed. Before an equilibrium can be reached, the country will need to go through a period of high unemployment in order to depress prices and regain competitiveness. The government can in principle avoid this by responding to the initial positive shock with a fiscal contraction. In that way the effect of the demand shock is neutralized, and the economy remains in equilibrium. There is no boom, no inflation and no loss of competitiveness. When the shock is reversed, fiscal policy should also be reversed. Aggregate demand is then kept constant. The economy avoids a possibly painful and protracted period when unemployment is high while the competitiveness lost during the boom is regained.

A devaluation

The effect of a once-and-for-all devaluation is shown in figure 6.9. Equation (6.28) shows that it is the ratio P/E which matters for aggregate demand, not P and E separately. Hence, only P/E matters for internal balance. Equation (6.30) shows that the same is true for external balance. A first guess would therefore be that if P increases in the same proportion as E, that restores both external and internal balance after a devaluation. This would mean that both the $\dot{F}_* = 0$ locus and the $\dot{P} = 0$ locus shift to the right by the same magnitude, and that the stationary level of F_* is unaffected by a devaluation. This is the case depicted in figure 6.9.

However, we should know from the discussion of the specie–flow model in chapter 5 that a devaluation causes an initial redistribution of wealth. It changes W_g which is one component in the x vector which is an argument in the conditions for internal and external balance. By definition $W_{g0} = (-M_0 - B_0 + EF_{g0})/P$. Only when $F_{g0} = 0$, is there no initial jump in W_g, and only then is the shift in the two curves of the same size, as in figure 6.9. With this reservation in mind, we shall first focus on the simple case

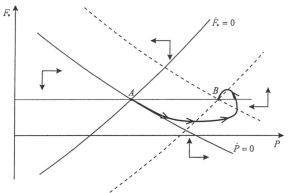

Figure 6.9 Effect of a devaluation.

depicted in figure 6.9, where W_g is assumed constant, and comment on the more general case later.

The immediate effect of a devaluation is an expansion of output and an improvement of the current account. The old equilibrium A is in the region where there is a current account surplus and overfull employment. Immediately after the devaluation the economy enters a period with an increasing price level and a declining foreign debt. The increase in P gradually reduces the surplus on the trade balance, though, and after a while the economy enters a region where foreign debt is accumulating again. This, together with the increased price level, has a depressing effect on domestic demand, and implies a gradual reduction in output. This may lead the economy straight to the new equilibrium in B, where everything is as in A except that the price level and the exchange rate has increased by the same percentage. The approach to B may also go through several phases, as indicated in figure 6.9. A devaluation improves the current account and employment, but only temporarily. The current account even goes into deficit after a while, and we may also get a period with relatively high unemployment later.

As indicated, the long-run effect is somewhat different if we have an initial change in W_g. If $F_{g0} > 0$, a devaluation leads to an immediate increase in W_g. By assumption, W_g is kept constant after that. As can be seen from the stationarity condition (6.39), the long-run effect of an increase in W_g is a reduction in the real value of the foreign debt, W_*'. This is the same result, and for the same reasons as in chapter 5. Consumers save to keep private wealth in a certain relation to income. When government wealth is increased, this adds to national wealth in the long run.

Since W_*' is reduced, it follows from the condition for external balance (6.38) that the real exchange rate must be appreciated. We can afford lower net exports when there is less interest to pay. Thus, the long-run effect of a *nominal* depreciation is a *real* appreciation. This means that P increases more than proportionally with E.

What does this mean for the long-run value of F_*? This we can find from another version of the condition for external balance, (6.45). If a real appreciation reduces the trade surplus measured in foreign goods, then the right-hand side of that equation goes down. F_* on the left-hand side must then also go down.

The upshot of all this is that the new equilibrium is not like point B in figure 6.9, but instead somewhere to the south-east of this, where F_* is reduced and P has increased more than proportionally with E. It can be shown by differentiating the stationarity conditions that the curve for external balance shifts somewhat more to the right than in figure 6.8, while the curve for internal balance shifts somewhat less. The dynamics leading towards the equilibrium will essentially be of the same kind. However, since the foreign debt is bound to go down in the long run, it is not absolutely necessary that the country goes through a period with a current account deficit.

The consequences of the change in W_g owing to a devaluation should not be overstated. F_{g0} is usually small relative to total wealth, and the capital gain of the government small relative to the short-run current account effects that a devaluation causes.

By this measure, the picture in figure 6.9 may not be too misleading even if F_{g0} is not exactly zero. (It was another matter in chapter 5, where the government's kroner debt was the basis for the capital gain.)

A stationary equilibrium is probably not a typical starting point for a devaluation. A more common starting point may be like A in figure 6.10. At A there is high unemployment and a deficit in the current account. The currency is 'overvalued' in the sense that the real exchange rate is too low compared to its long-run equilibrium value. The economy is initially on its way to a point like B. A devaluation moves the stationary equilibrium to C. Point A suddenly becomes a point of high employment and current account surplus. The devaluation has been strong enough to change the real exchange rate from being below to being above its long-run equilibrium value. This means that the approach to long-run equilibrium can be made through a period of high employment and inflation instead of through low employment and deflation. In figure 6.10 the devaluation is somewhat excessive. A smaller devaluation with C closer to A would have produced less inflation and a faster approach to the long-run equilibrium.

Figure 6.10 shows how exchange rate policy can be used under ideal circumstances to shorten the way to long-run equilibrium after the economy has been hit by a shock. The road to long-run equilibrium can also be made more comfortable, at least if one regards unemployment as a greater evil than inflation.

In particular, devaluations may be useful when there is an adverse shift in the demand for a country's products (a negative shift in the net export function X). As we saw from (6.39) the long-run equilibrium value of W'_* is independent of X. From (6.38) a negative shift in X then requires a real depreciation in the long run (an increase in $R = EP_*/P$). Without a devaluation, P has to fall. With a devaluation, some unemployment can be avoided.

However, there are some snags. If the environment is non-inflationary, an economy which systematically uses devaluations to adjust to various adverse shocks gets an inflationary bias. This will affect expectations of inflation and of depreciation. When capital mobility is high, the economy will be forced to keep higher nominal interest

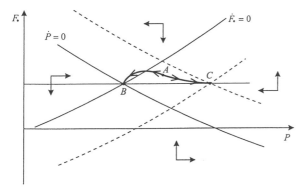

Figure 6.10 A devaluation starting from a disequilibrium.

rates on average. *Ex post* real rates may become highly variable depending on whether a devaluation actually takes place. Whenever there is an adverse shock, a devaluation will be expected. This will induce a flight from the currency, and the government may not have much discretion on when to devalue.

Furthermore, frequent use of devaluations may lead to indexing of prices and wages which greatly reduces the potential for devaluation to influence aggregate demand. In the models we have looked at in the present chapter the short-run rigidity of the nominal price of home goods is after all the major reason that a devaluation has real effects.

6.7 Floating rate dynamics and overshooting

The model from section 6.6 can also be extended to cover the case of floating exchange rates. However, before we do that we shall look at a drastically simplified model where wealth effects and foreign debt dynamics are excluded. As in section 6.6 we combine a simplified version of the Mundell–Fleming–Tobin (MFT) model from section 6.2 with two dynamic equations – this time one for prices and one for the exchange rate. We assume perfect capital mobility and a non-inflationary environment. Exchange rate expectations are rational in the sense that $e_e = e$. We also assume, as an inessential simplification, that the interest rate has no effect on aggregate demand. We then end up with the famous 'overshooting' model first presented by Dornbusch (1976). The model can be seen as an extension of the monetary approach to a case where there is nominal price rigidity (most likely caused by nominal wage rigidity). A similar extension was made in section 5.7 on wage rigidity in the extremely open economy. The difference is that now relative prices are no longer given from the world market and aggregate demand matters for output and employment.

The original motivation for the overshooting model was that the simple monetary model of chapter 4 seemed unable to explain the large swings in exchange rates that were observed after several countries began floating their exchange rates in the 1970s.

The equations of the model are

$$Y = C(Y) + X(EP_*/P, Y, Y_*) \tag{6.46}$$

$$\frac{M}{P} = m(i, Y) \tag{6.47}$$

$$\dot{P} = P\gamma(Y - \bar{Y}) \tag{6.48}$$

$$\dot{E} = E(i - i_*) \tag{6.49}$$

Equations (6.46) and (6.47) are simple *IS* and *LM* curves. Equation (6.48) is the same Phillips curve relation as in section 6.6. Equation (6.49) is the same dynamic equation for the exchange rate as in chapter 4. As we remember, it is just another way of writing the interest rate parity condition when actual and expected depreciation are equal.

The endogenous variables are Y, i, P and E. The exogenous variables are Y_*, P_*, i_* and M. The initial value of P, P_0, is given. P is a state variable that can change only gradually over time. E may in principle jump at any time. Thus, the initial value of E has to be determined endogenously, as in chapter 4. However, there can be no expected jumps in the exchange rate. Thus the expected time path of E after the initial jump is continuous as described by our model.

Solving the model

The model is solved through the same steps as in section 6.6. For given values of P and E (6.46) and (6.47) define a temporary equilibrium for Y and i. The two equations can be solved to yield

$$Y = Y(EP_*/P, Y_*) \tag{6.50}$$

$$i = i(M/P, EP_*/P, Y_*) \tag{6.51}$$

As we learned from the model in section 6.2, both a real depreciation and an increase in foreign output raise domestic output. The domestic interest rate then also increases, since the money supply is given. An increased real money supply will, of course, lower the interest rate.

The solution for the temporary equilibrium can be inserted in (6.47) and (6.48) to yield the two differential equations

$$\dot{P} = \phi_1(P, E, Y_*, P_*) \tag{6.52}$$

$$\dot{E} = \phi_2(P, E, M, Y_*, P_*) \tag{6.53}$$

The stationary equilibrium is defined by

$$\dot{P} = 0 \Leftrightarrow Y = Y(EP_*/P, Y_*) = \bar{Y} \tag{6.54}$$

$$\dot{E} = 0 \Leftrightarrow i = i(M/P, EP_*/P, Y_*) = i_* \tag{6.55}$$

These equations determine the stationary values of P and E.

If one checks the stability conditions, one will find that the determinant condition is not satisfied. Thus the system is unstable. This means that if we choose an arbitrary starting point, the economy does not move towards the stationary state.

The dynamics of the model is illustrated by a phase diagram in figure 6.11. The locus for internal balance ($\dot{P} = 0$) defined by (6.54) is a straight line sloping upwards from the origin. The reason is that Y depends only on the ratio E/P, not E or P separately. There is a unique real exchange rate, EP_*/P which is compatible with internal balance. To the left of the $\dot{P} = 0$ locus the price of home goods is low, demand for home goods is high, ($Y > \bar{Y}$), and the price is rising ($\dot{P} > 0$). To the right of the locus for internal balance, it is the opposite. The horizontal arrows indicate that the direction of movement for P is towards internal balance.

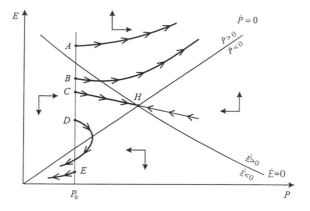

Figure 6.11 Alternative time paths for E and P.

The $\dot{E} = 0$ curve is the locus of points where the exchange rate is constant. Since $\dot{E} = 0$ is equivalent to $i = i_*$, it is also the locus of points where the two interest rates are equal. By implicit differentiation (6.55) its slope is found to be

$$\frac{dE}{dP}\bigg|_{\dot{E}=0} = -\frac{di/dP}{di/dE} \tag{6.56}$$

The denominator of this expression is positive since a depreciation leads to an increase in Y and this raises the domestic interest rate. The numerator is more ambiguous. A price increase reduces the supply of real balances, M/P, but it also reduces Y and thereby reduces money demand. The net effect on the interest rate depends on which is the greater: the reduction in money supply or in money demand. Behind figure 6.11 is the assumption that the supply effect dominates and that a price increase thus raises the interest rate. This means that the numerator in (6.56) is positive. The whole expression is then negative. We return to the slope of the $\dot{E} = 0$ locus towards the end of this section.

Above the $\dot{E} = 0$ locus the high exchange rate means high economic activity and thus a high interest rate. With rational expectations and perfect capital mobility the domestic interest rate can be above the foreign interest rate only if the domestic currency is depreciating. That $i > i_*$ and $i = i_* + e$ implies $e > 0$. Hence, the exchange rate depreciates ($\dot{E} > 0$) if we are above the $\dot{E} = 0$ locus, appreciates if we are below. As the vertical arrows indicate, when we are outside the $\dot{E} = 0$ locus, the exchange rate moves away from it. This is the same destabilizing mechanism as in chapter 4.

Suppose that the initial price level on home goods is equal to P_0 in figure 6.11. Then we know that the initial equilibrium must be somewhere along the vertical line which starts from P_0. However, $E(0)$ is not given.[61] As a step towards determining $E(0)$ we shall examine the different paths which start from P_0. In the figure five qualitatively different paths are shown:

- *Path A* starts with a relatively high exchange rate. Behind the high exchange rate is expectations of further depreciation, which have produced a high interest rate. Since actual and expected depreciation are equal, this means that the path is towards a higher E. The depreciated exchange rate also means that the demand for home goods is high, and that there is thus upward pressure on prices. Along the path from A there is inflation and depreciation 'forever'.
- *Path B* starts with a somewhat lower exchange rate. An exchange rate this low can only come about if an appreciation is expected. The exchange rate is still high enough to produce excess demand for home goods and inflationary pressure. To begin with, therefore, prices rise while the exchange rate appreciates. After a while, however, the exchange rate hits the $\dot{E} = 0$ locus. After that the path enters the region where there is both inflation and depreciation and path B continues like path A.
- *Path C* starts out like path B, but it happens to hit the $\dot{E} = 0$ locus exactly at the stationary equilibrium. There the process of appreciation and inflation stops.
- *Path D* also starts out like path B, but instead of hitting the $\dot{E} = 0$ locus, it hits the $\dot{P} = 0$ locus. The gradual appreciation and inflation has then appreciated the real exchange rate so much that we enter a period of excess supply of home goods. This means that the price level and the exchange rate begin to decline together. Path D continues with appreciation and deflation forever.
- *Path E* starts out with a strongly appreciated currency. The reason is that further appreciation is expected, and as expectations are rational this actually happens. The appreciated exchange rate also means that the demand for home goods is below equilibrium and this produces deflation. As along path D, this continues forever.

The five paths which are depicted exhaust all possibilities which are qualitatively different. There is just one path which leads to the stationary equilibrium – namely, the one starting from C. All other paths diverge. Between B and D somewhere there must always be a unique path which leads to the stationary equilibrium. This is the *saddle path*. The presumption is that the public chooses to believe in the saddle path for the same reasons as they chose in chapter 4 to believe in the stationary solution rather than in one of the diverging paths that were equally consistent with the model. The same principle was also used to select the solution in the case of floating rates in section 5.7.

In an unstable model like the one we have studied, there is a unique saddle path which leads into the stationary equilibrium from each side. The path coming in from the right-hand side is also indicated in figure 6.11.

The prescription for determining $E(0)$ is then: start by locating the stationary equilibrium. Find the unique saddle path which leads into this point from the direction of the initial price level. Follow this path backwards until you hit today's price level. Read off the exchange rate at this point, and that will be today's equilibrium exchange rate. Read off the rate of depreciation along the saddle path at this point, and that is the rate of depreciation you should expect today. This also determines today's interest rate since $i = i_* + e$. In figure 6.11 the prescription means that we should start at point H, find the saddle path that leads into H from the left, and follow this back to point C, where the initial exchange rate can be read off.

Note that the slope of the saddle path implies that on the left branch inflation is accompanied by appreciation, and by low interest rates (because $i = i_* + e$). On the right branch there is deflation accompanied by depreciation and high interest rates.

A monetary expansion

Figure 6.12 illustrates the effect of an increase in M. Since in this simple model aggregate demand is independent of the money supply, the locus for internal balance is unaffected. The $\dot{E} = 0$ locus shifts to the right. An increase in the money supply tends to lower i. If i is to be kept equal to i_*, the price level must go up so that the demand for money increases with the same amount as the supply.

The old stationary equilibrium was at A, the new one is at C. A stationary equilibrium is characterized by $Y = \bar{Y}$ and $i = i_*$. Thus it is also characterized by

$$\frac{M}{P} = m(i_*, \bar{Y})$$

This means that the real money supply is unchanged. Thus, in the end the percentage increase in P must be the same as the percentage increase in M. Since internal balance means that the real exchange rate, $R = EP_*/P$, is the same in the new equilibrium as in the old, the percentage increase in E must also be the same as in M. Thus, in the long run we will have the same effect on P and E of an increase in M as we had in chapter 4.

However, the short-run effect is different. Suppose the original equilibrium were at A. Then the new short-run equilibrium must be where the vertical line passing through

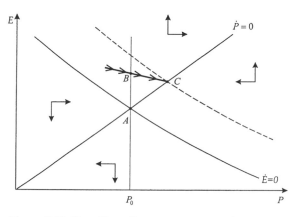

Figure 6.12 The effect of a monetary expansion.

A hits the saddle path leading to *C* – i.e. at point *B*. We know from the discussion above that the saddle path from the left slopes downwards. This means that before we get to *C* we have to go through a period of appreciation. The only way that can happen is if the exchange rate initially depreciates more than in proportion to the increase in the money supply. This is the reason that point *B* is above point *C*. The initial effect on the exchange rate *overshoots* the final effect.

At B $i < i_*$. The expansionary monetary policy thus succeeds in bringing down the interest rate in spite of perfect capital mobility. This is possible because an appreciation is expected ($e_e = e < 0$). The immediate depreciation of the exchange rate produces excess demand for home goods. That starts off price increases on home goods.

A comparison with chapter 4 shows that the overshooting comes about because the price of home goods is rigid in the short run while the exchange rate is free to jump. If the price of home goods were also free to jump, we could move immediately from *A* to *C* in one step. Short-run price rigidity thus results in more instability in the exchange rate. *Price* rigidity seems to be important. In section 5.7, where we had *wage* rigidity, we got no overshooting. The difference is that in section 5.7 a wage increase lowered the interest rate, while the overshooting here occurs when a price increase raises the interest rate. The price level has a direct positive effect on nominal money demand, the wage level has not, at least according to our assumptions.

A shock to the trade balance

Figure 6.13 illustrates the effect of a negative trade balance shock (a downward shift in the net export function *X*). The original equilibrium is at *A*. The two equilibrium loci shift upwards with the same amount. The reason is that they both depend on *E* only through the trade balance. Measured vertically the shifts are equal to the increase in *E* that is necessary to keep the trade balance constant after the *X* function has had a negative shift. When *X* is kept constant, *Y* is also constant, and thus internal balance is preserved. Since *Y* is constant, there is no change in the demand for money, and thus *i* remains constant. But then the foreign exchange market remains in equilibrium too. Thus, the new stationary equilibrium is at *B* right above the old one. Initially the exchange rate jumps to the saddle path which leads to the new stationary equilibrium. In the present case this means that the exchange rate jumps directly from the old equilibrium to the new one, or from *A* to *B*. Both internal and external balance are preserved automatically.

Insulation against the output and trade balance effects of shocks to export or import demand has been seen as a main advantage of flexible exchange rate systems. However, the insulation property here is derived in a highly simplified model where the trade balance is the only channel for real effects from the exchange rate. As we shall see in section 6.8, the insulation property does not always carry over to more general models.

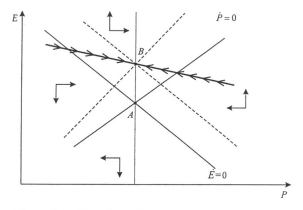

Figure 6.13 The effect of a negative trade balance shock.

Upward-sloping $\dot{E} = 0$ locus

So far we have focused on the case where the $\dot{E} = 0$ locus slopes downwards – i.e. on the case where a price increase has a stronger effect on the supply than on the demand for real balances. If the locus slopes upwards, it is easy to show that it can never be steeper than the $\dot{P} = 0$ locus. Furthermore, the saddle path slopes upwards. This means that the initial depreciation is smaller than the final depreciation. There is no overshooting. Since a further depreciation is expected, the domestic interest rate initially increases after a monetary expansion.[62] This was also the result in section 5.7 where we had nominal wage rigidity. Although it may at first seem counter-intuitive, the possibility that a monetary expansion leads to higher interest rates should not be dismissed. The key is that the monetary expansion leads to an expected future depreciation. Only if there is initial overshooting will there be a reduction in the interest rate.

The different conclusions in the two cases warrants a closer examination of the slope of the $\dot{E} = 0$ locus. From the discussion of (6.56) we remember that the locus slopes downwards if, and only if, $di/dP > 0$. This is then the condition for overshooting. By implicit differentiation of (6.46) and (6.47) we find that

$$\frac{di}{dP} = \frac{1}{m_i}\left[-\frac{M}{P^2} + m_Y \frac{dY}{dR}\frac{EP_*}{P^2}\right] = \frac{M}{P^2 m_i}[-1 + \text{El}_Y m \cdot \text{El}_R Y] \tag{6.57}$$

where $dY/dR = X_R/(1 - C_Y - X_Y)$. ($\text{El}_X Y$ is the elasticity of Y with respect to X.) The first term in brackets is negative, the second term is positive. The first term represents the reduced supply of real balances when prices go up, the second represents the reduced demand for real balances. The assumption leading to overshooting is that the first term dominates or that $\text{El}_Y m \cdot \text{El}_R Y < 1$. Then a higher price level means a higher interest rate.

The product $\text{El}_Y m \cdot \text{El}_R Y$ measures the effect of a real depreciation on real money demand. Money demand is affected because output is affected, and only for that reason. Both empirical results and theoretical considerations indicate that $\text{El}_Y m$ is smaller than one. The other elasticity, $\text{El}_R Y$, depends on the strength of the trade balance response to a real depreciation and on the size of the multiplier. If the Marshall–Lerner condition is just barely fulfilled, the elasticity will be small. Thus, if the sum of the demand elasticities for imports and exports is not too much above one, it is likely that $\text{El}_R Y < 1$, that $\text{El}_Y m \cdot \text{El}_R Y < 1$ and that there is overshooting. If export and import demand elasticities are high, overshooting is less likely.[63]

Consequences for the Mundell–Fleming–Tobin model

In the light of the present section, should we revise our conclusions about floating exchange rates in section 6.4?

In the present model the long-run equilibrium exchange rate $\bar{E}$ is determined by (6.54) and (6.55) – or, equivalently, by inserting $Y = \bar{Y}$ and $i = i_*$ in (6.46) and (6.47). Equation (6.46) then gives us the equilibrium real exchange rate $\bar{R}$. Equation (6.47) gives us the equilibrium price level as $P = M/m(i_*, \bar{Y})$. By definition the nominal exchange rate is related to the real exchange rate by $E = RP/P_*$. This means that the equilibrium exchange rate is

$$\bar{E} = \frac{\bar{M}}{\bar{P}_* m(\bar{i}_*, \bar{Y})} \bar{R} \tag{6.58}$$

where the bar over M, P_* and i_* underlines that it is the long-run expected values of these variables that should be inserted.

One suggestion for improving on the expectations mechanism in section 6.4 is then to assume that $e_e = e_e((E - \bar{E})/\bar{E})$ where $e'_e < 0$ and $\bar{E}$ is given by (6.58). This mimics rational expectations as they appear in the Dornbusch model. When M, P_* or i_* is changed, one would have to consider if the change is permanent, implying that $\bar{E}$ should be changed. A permanent change in Y_* will affect $\bar{E}$ through $\bar{R}$. With imperfect capital mobility and wealth effects on consumption the determination of $\bar{E}$ will be more complicated.

An increase in the money supply which is expected to be permanent is more expansionary than one which is expected to be temporary. Suppose capital mobility is perfect. A permanent increase in the money supply then induces an increase in $\bar{E}$ of the same relative size. For a given i there is then an immediate depreciation equal to the increase in $\bar{E}$, since $i = i_* + e_e((E - \bar{E})/\bar{E})$. This shifts the *ISFX* curve in figure 6.5 to the right together with the *LM* curve. The result is a stronger increase in Y. The effect on i is ambiguous for the same reason as Dornbusch's model does not always give overshooting and a fall in the interest rate.

6.8 A more general dynamic model

This section sketches how the models of sections 6.6 and 6.7 can be combined in a more general model that covers both fixed and floating exchange rates. As we shall see, many of the results from the previous analysis are preserved. For simplicity perfect capital mobility is assumed.

The momentary equilibrium is described by the *IS* and *LM* curves:[64]

$$Y = C(Y - \rho_* RW_* - G, -RW_* - W_g, \rho_*) + G + X(R, Y, Y_*) \tag{6.59}$$

$$\frac{M}{EP_*/R} = m(i, Y) \tag{6.60}$$

The *IS* equation is the same as in section 6.6, only written differently. $W_* = F_*/P_*$ is the real value of the foreign debt measured in foreign goods ($W_* = RW_*'$, when W_*' is the foreign debt measured in terms of home goods, as in section 6.6). The *LM* equation is the same as in section 6.7, since $EP_*/R = P$.

The laws of motion for P and F_* are essentially the same as in section 6.6. However, since we allow E and P_* to change over time, it is convenient to rewrite the dynamic equations in terms of R and W_*. In section 6.6 we derived the Phillips curve

$$\frac{\dot{P}}{P} = \frac{\dot{E}}{E} + \frac{\dot{P_*}}{P_*} + \gamma(Y - \bar{Y})$$

Since $R = EP_*/P$, this can also be written as

$$\frac{\dot{R}}{R} = -\gamma(Y - \bar{Y}) \tag{6.61}$$

Since $W_* = F_*/P_*$, its rate of growth is by definition

$$\dot{W_*} = \rho_* W_* - X(R, Y, Y_*)/R \tag{6.62}$$

where ρ_* is the real interest rate on the foreign debt.

The last equation of the model is the interest parity condition from section 6.7:

$$\frac{\dot{E}}{E} = i - i_* \tag{6.63}$$

The initial values of P and W_* are given. When the exchange rate is fixed, the five equations (6.59)–(6.63) determine the time paths of R, W_*, Y, i and M. When the exchange rate is floating, E is free to jump, but we assume that a saddle path is chosen. The five equations then determine the time paths of R, W_*, Y, i and E, while M is exogenous.

Note that the three equations (6.59), (6.61) and (6.62) form a closed subsystem with three unknowns, R, W_* and Y. Neither E nor i enter in these equations. Hence, for given initial values of R and W_*, (6.59), (6.61) and (6.62) determine the whole time path for R, W_* and Y. This means that the dynamics of the current account and the real exchange rate are the same irrespective of whether the exchange rate is fixed or floating. In fact, when we start from the same initial point, the evolution of all real variables is the same irrespective of exchange rate system. Furthermore, the subsystem for the real variables is equivalent to the system we studied in section 6.6. The stability conditions are the same. We can use the same phase diagrams, except that on the vertical axis we should put W_*, on the horizontal axis $1/R = P/EP_*$. The loci for external and internal balance are the same. However, they should be relabelled $\dot{W}_* = 0$ and $\dot{R} = 0$, respectively.

The difference between fixed and floating exchange rates comes in when there is an exogenous shock. Then a floating exchange rate takes an initial jump. This changes the initial values of R and W_g. The simplified model in section 6.7 also indicates the nature of the solution for the exchange rate in the present case. There is a saddle path leading to the stationary equilibrium, and initially the exchange rate jumps onto that path. Unfortunately it is not possible to draw the phase diagram since that requires three dimensions. If we want to find the effects of exogenous shifts, the analysis of section 6.6 is still of some help. The real effect of an exogenous shock under floating rates is equal to the effect of the same shock under fixed rates plus the effect of a devaluation/revaluation equal to the initial jump in the exchange rate. However, the size and even the direction of the jump is often difficult to deduce without a numerical model.

The conditions for long-run equilibrium are the same as in section 6.6 ((6.38) and (6.39)). This means that the level of the foreign debt *measured in terms of home goods* is determined by savings behaviour, while the real exchange rate ensures that enough demand is directed towards home goods to make a balanced current account consistent with equilibrium employment.

When the exchange rate is floating, the absolute price level in long-run equilibrium is determined by the money supply in the usual way. Stationarity in the nominal exchange rate requires $i = i_*$, which inserted in the *LM* equation (6.60) yields

$$\frac{M}{P} = m(i_*, Y) \tag{6.64}$$

which determines P. The nominal exchange rate then follows from $E = RP/P_*$.

In the special case where W_g is unaffected by a devaluation ($F_{g0} = 0$) the effect of a trade balance shock is the same as in the Dornbusch model. Suppose the economy is in a stationary state before the shock. Afterwards it then jumps directly to the new stationary equilibrium. P and $W'_* = RW_*$ stay constant. A jump in E ensures that R jumps to the level where current account balance is preserved with output at the equilibrium level.

Suppose that initially the exchange rate is overvalued in the sense that R is above its equilibrium level. There is a current account deficit and unemployment is high. As we saw in connection with figure 6.10, a devaluation may then be used to ease the path to stationary equilibrium. Under floating exchange rates the same can be achieved with a one-time increase in the money supply, since it makes the exchange rate jump.

These two examples illustrate two points. Floating exchange rates can sometimes help to dampen the real effects of shocks and, hence, reduce the amount of disequilibrium that they create. However, once a disequilibrium has arisen, there is less difference between fixed and floating rates. Then it is more important whether the monetary target (the exchange rate or the money supply) is kept fixed forever, or whether it can be changed by policy decisions.

Trade balance shocks are a special case, though. Floating exchange rates cannot provide full insulation against other types of shocks. The worry about floating exchange rates is that shocks to the money market or shocks to expected future exchange rates (or expected future monetary policy) will drive the economy out of equilibrium. There are also reasons to suspect that a floating exchange rate does not always insulate fully against the effects of trade balance shocks. In the present model, if jumps in E affect W_g, there is not complete insulation. Furthermore, the jump in the exchange rate causes a jump in the average price level even if the price of home goods is constant. If money demand depends on the average price level, a trade balance shock will affect output and the current account also under floating. If there is more than one production sector, a trade balance shock may also necessitate adjustments of the capital stock.

Exercises

1. The export surplus can be measured in domestic currency, in foreign currency and in real terms by deflating with the price index for exports or for imports. Compare the partial effect of a devaluation on the four different measures of the export surplus. Can you give a set of conditions which are sufficient for a devaluation to improve all four measures of the export surplus?

2. Compare the immediate effects on Y and i of an increase in Y_* in the different regimes discussed in sections 6.3 and 6.4.

3. Use the Mundell–Fleming–Tobin model of section 6.2 and assume that the exchange rate is fixed:

    (a) Compare the immediate effects on Y, i and F_g of an upward shift in e_e with and without sterilization.

    (b) Compare also the effects on the current account. Discuss how these effects may alter the equilibrium over time.

4. Assume that the *IS* curve, instead of (6.6), has the simpler form:

    $$Y = C(Y, W_p, \rho) + I(\rho) + G + X(R, Y, Y_*)$$

    Suppose that capital mobility is perfect, and that exchange rate expectations are determined by $e_e = e_e(E)$ with $e'_e < 0$. Reformulate the model of section 6.2 for the case of perfect capital mobility. Compare the effect of an increase in the foreign interest rate on the domestic activity level under fixed and floating exchange rates. What options do the government have if it wants to avoid the increased foreign interest rate having an effect on the activity level?

5. Assume that the *IS* curve is simply $Y = C(Y) + I(i) + X(EP_*/P, Y, Y_*)$.
   (a) Assume that i is constant. Find the effect of E on Y and X. Compare the size of the two effects. Why is the marginal propensity to save crucial?
   (b) Assume now that there is perfect capital mobility $(i = i_* + e_e(E))$. Discuss what this means for the relative strength of the effects of a devaluation on Y and X.

6. Assume that the exchange rate is fixed and that the government budget is balanced continuously. How does an increased propensity to save in the private sector affect the level of activity and the current account in the short and in the long run? How is the shape of the transition path?

7. The standard assumptions of section 6.6 are violated if $\phi_{11} > 0$. Explain how this can happen. Draw two phase diagrams for this case, one where the equilibrium is stable, one where it is unstable. Do they look different? Which stability condition may be violated? Illustrate how the time paths from an arbitrary starting point differ in the two diagrams. Assume that the stationary equilibrium is stable. Starting from a full equilibrium, what does the time path after a domestic demand shock look like? Compare it to the time path shown in section 6.6.

8. Suppose the overshooting model of section 6.7. What is the effect on the time path of the exchange rate of (a) an increase in Y_* and (b) an increase in i_*.

9. In the model of section 6.7, suppose the money demand function is

$$\frac{M}{P^\alpha (EP_*)^{(1-\alpha)}} = m(i, Y) \qquad 0 < \alpha < 1$$

What is the condition for overshooting to take place?

10. Compare the model in section 6.6 with its closest relative from chapter 5 – i.e. the differential equation for foreign debt in section 5.3 combined with the differential equation for wages in section 5.7 (the case with nominal wage rigidity and a fixed exchange rate). You may assume a non-inflationary environment in both cases, and in the model with home and foreign goods you may assume that wages and prices grow at the same speed $(\dot{W}/W = \dot{P}/P)$. Compare in particular:

   (a) the structure of the Jacobian matrix
   (b) the conditions for stability
   (c) the co-movement of wages and foreign debt in the process towards long-run equilibrium
   (d) the effect of a positive demand shock
   (e) The effect of a devaluation.

11. Assume the exchange rate is floating. Compare the immediate effects on Y, i, E and X of an increase in i_* when it is expected to be temporary and when it

is expected to be permanent. In the latter case the expected equilibrium exchange rate is revised according to (6.58).

12. In section 6.7 we saw that flexible exchange rates may neutralize the effects of a trade balance shock on output and on the trade balance itself. Make a list of possible channels for real effects of exchange rates. Discuss how taking account of these channels may change the conclusions from the overshooting model on the real effects of a trade balance shock. Modify the overshooting model to include the same money demand function as in exercise 9. What does this mean for the real effects of a trade balance shock?

13. Show that the elasticity $\mathrm{El}_R Y$ from the Dornbusch model can be written

$$\mathrm{El}_R Y = \frac{1}{1 - C_Y - X_Y} \frac{Z}{Y} (\check{Z} + \check{Z}_* - 1)$$

when trade is balanced initially. Discuss the likely size of the elasticity in the light of this expression and section 6.1.

14. Write down the expression for the real interest rate on a foreign currency loan in terms of home goods and in terms of foreign goods. Show that the difference between them is equal to the expected rate of *real* depreciation. What is the difference between the real interest rate on domestic loans measured in domestic goods and the real interest rate on foreign loans measured in foreign goods equal to?

7   Traded and non-traded goods

In chapter 6 there were two goods, one produced at home and one produced abroad. In the present chapter there are also two goods. However, both goods are produced at home *and* abroad. The distinction is instead between goods which have to be consumed in the country where they are produced, and goods which can be exported or imported. The former are called *non-traded goods* (*n*-goods), the latter *traded goods* (*t*-goods). For *t*-goods we assume that there is a competitive world market. A small open economy has to take the prices at this market as given. For *n*-goods there is also a competitive market, but this is confined to the single country.

The reason why some goods are not traded internationally may be transport costs or trade regulations. Some services have to be produced on the spot. However, the obstacles to international trade are seldom absolute. Transport costs do not prevent trade if the price differential between two countries becomes large enough. Only if the domestic price stays in the interval defined by the foreign price plus/minus transport costs, will there be no international trade. Other costs of trade, such as tariffs, may enlarge this interval.[65] Transport costs depend mainly on distance. Tariffs and the costs of customs clearance may produce a discontinuity in the costs of trade at the border. However, the distance between supplier and consumer is sometimes shorter across the border than within the country. This means that, except for some government services, it is hard to find goods which are not traded at all. The traded and non-traded goods in our models are extremes. In one case the international competition is total, in the other it is absent. However, in reality the degree of exposure to international competition varies between industries. By focusing on the extreme cases, we are able to study how the effects of macro policies and of exogenous shocks differ between industries which are more or less exposed to international competition.

Throughout this chapter we assume that the exchange rate is fixed. In the background there must also be a given real interest rate – e.g. as a result of perfect capital mobility. We also disregard wealth effects on consumption, which played such a prominent role in chapters 5 and 6. It is possible to include flexible exchange rates, endogenous interest rates and wealth effects in the models here. However, one advantage of two-sector models is that they are better suited to discuss supply-side issues than the one-sector models in chapters 5 and 6. Hence, the focus is now more on the supply side.

Section 7.1 describes the basic static model where nominal wages are rigid and employment is determined by demand. In section 7.2 we discuss six extensions: real wage rigidity, consumption demand which depends on the income distribution, VAT and payroll taxes, government employment, terms-of-trade changes and imported raw materials. In section 7.3 wages are endogenized by adding a Phillips curve to the model, and we also study some long-run effects of various policies. In section 7.4 we endogenize real investment and the capital stock in the t-industry. In section 7.5 we take a brief look at the consequences of extending the model to include the use of capital and the production of investment goods in both industries. This is followed in section 7.6 by a discussion of the Scandinavian model of inflation and its foundations.[66]

7.1 The basic static model

There are two goods:

- *traded goods* (subscript t), which can be exported and imported freely
- *non-traded goods* (subscript n), which cannot be traded internationally.

Corresponding to the two goods there are two industries. The model describes how output, employment and prices in the two industries are determined in the short run when the nominal wage and the capital stocks are predetermined. Perfect competition is assumed in the goods markets. The exchange rate is fixed and world market prices of t-goods are exogenous. Before we discuss the model in more detail, it is convenient to list the symbols and equations. There are twelve equations and twelve endogenous variables.

Symbols

Symbols relating to industry/commodity i ($i = n, t$)

$N_i =$ employment
$K_i =$ capital stock
$Y_i =$ output
$C_i =$ private consumption
$G_i =$ government consumption
$D_i =$ domestic demand
$P_i =$ price
$\Phi_i =$ production function
$c_i =$ consumer demand function

Economy aggregates:

$Y_p =$ private disposable income (nominal)

C = private consumption (nominal)
X = trade surplus (real)
N = total employment

Other

W = wage rate
E = exchange rate
P_* = foreign currency price of traded goods
τ = tax rate on income
σ = savings rate

Equations

Production functions:

$$Y_i = \Phi_i(N_i, K_i), \ \ i = n, t \tag{7.1}$$

First-order conditions for maximum profit:

$$P_i \Phi'_{iN}(N_i, K_i) = W, \ \ i = n, t \tag{7.2}$$

Domestic private demand functions:

$$C_i = c_i(P_n, P_t, C), \ \ i = n, t \tag{7.3}$$

Equilibrium conditions:

$$Y_n = C_n + G_n \tag{7.4}$$

$$P_t = EP_* \tag{7.5}$$

Definition of disposable income:

$$Y_p = (1 - \tau)(P_n Y_n + P_t Y_t) \tag{7.6}$$

Consumption function:

$$C = (1 - \sigma)Y_p \tag{7.7}$$

Trade surplus:

$$X = Y_t - C_t - G_t \tag{7.8}$$

Total employment:

$$N = N_n + N_t \tag{7.9}$$

Endogenous variables:

$N_n, N_t, Y_n, Y_t, P_n, P_t, C_n, C_t, Y_p, C, N, X$

Exogenous variables:

$E, P_*, W, K_n, K_t, G_n, G_t, \tau$

The production functions (7.1) are assumed to have standard neo-classical proper-ties. They are homogeneous of degree one,[67] concave and have positive marginal productivity. Real capital is sector-specific – i.e. it cannot be moved between industries in the short run. Labour is mobile and homogeneous. Hence the same wage applies in both industries. Since the nominal wage is exogenous, there is nominal wage rigidity. Employment is determined by the demand for labour, which follows from the first-order conditions for maximum profits (7.2).

The demand functions (7.3) are also assumed to have standard neo-classical proper-ties. They should be interpreted as resulting from the maximization of a utility function $U = u(C_n, C_t)$ given the budget equation $P_n C_n + P_t C_t = C$. Both goods are assumed to be normal – i.e., $c_{iC} > 0$ for $i = n, t$. Among the standard properties which apply to the demand functions is the Slutsky equation (see, for example, Varian, 1993, ch. 8):

$$c_{ij} = s_{ij} - C_j c_{iC}, \quad i = n, t, \quad j = n, t \tag{7.10}$$

where s_{ij} is the Slutsky derivative for commodity i with respect to a change in the price of commodity j. Other standard properties are $s_{ii} < 0$ and, since we are looking at a two-good case, $s_{ij} > 0$ for $j \neq i$. In words, the direct substitution effects are negative, and the cross-substitution effects are positive, which means that the two goods are substitutes.

The equilibrium condition for n-goods (7.4) is the usual one, that domestic supply equals domestic demand. Since we look at a small country which takes P_* as given, the equilibrium condition for t-goods (7.5) simply says that measured in the same cur-rency the domestic and the international price should be equal.

In (7.6) it is assumed that all income is earned by the private sector, and that there is a proportional income tax. In (7.7) we have assumed the simplest possible macro consumption function with a constant savings rate. The savings rate and the tax rate are, of course, between zero and one – i.e. $0 < \sigma < 1$ and $0 < \tau < 1$. (7.8) defines the trade surplus as the discrepancy between output and consumption of t-goods. Interest payment on the foreign debt is disregarded. Thus, the current account surplus is equal to the trade surplus. Equation (7.9) just defines total employment.

Solving the model

The solution of the model can be illustrated in two standard supply and demand diagrams, as in figure 7.1. They are drawn with the *real prices* $\Pi_t = P_t/W$ and $\Pi_n = P_n/W$ on the vertical axes. The two real prices are measured in units of labour. The solution proceeds in the following steps:

1. The price of t-goods, P_t, follows immediately from (7.5). It is determined by the exogenous world market price and the exchange rate policy. The real price of t-goods then follows as $\Pi_t = EP_*/W$. In figure 7.1 this is represented by the horizontal price line for t-goods.

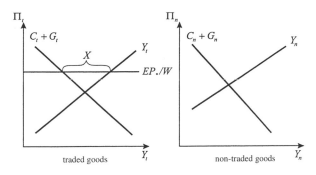

Figure 7.1 Short-run equilibrium.

2. For t-goods we can solve (7.1) and (7.2) to yield the standard supply function[68]

$$Y_t = Y_t(\Pi_t, K_t), \quad Y_{t1} > 0, \quad Y_{t2} > 0 \tag{7.11}$$

The output of t-goods is determined by the intersection of the supply curve and the price line, as depicted in Figure 7.1.

3. Output of n-goods is determined by the intersection of supply and demand. In figure 7.1 we have drawn a supply curve

$$Y_n = Y_n(\Pi_n, K_n), \quad Y_{n1} > 0, \quad Y_{n2} > 0 \tag{7.12}$$

similar to the one for t-goods and derived from (7.1) and (7.2). The macro demand curve for n-goods is defined implicitly by the equation

$$c_n(P_n, P_t, (1 - \sigma)(1 - \tau)(P_n Y_n + P_t Y_t)) + G_n = Y_n$$

In order to derive this, first insert from (7.3) with $i = n$ in (7.4). Then substitute for C from (7.7) and for Y_p from (7.6). Because the demand function is homogeneous of degree zero, the equation above can be rewritten as

$$c_n\left(\frac{P_n}{W}, \frac{P_t}{W}, (1 - \sigma)(1 - \tau)\left(\frac{P_n}{W} Y_n + \frac{P_t}{W} Y_t\right)\right) + G_n = Y_n$$

or

$$c_n(\Pi_n, \Pi_t, (1 - \sigma)(1 - \tau)(\Pi_n Y_n + \Pi_t Y_t)) + G_n = Y_n \tag{7.13}$$

This equation implicitly defines Y_n as a function of Π_n. All other variables in it have already been determined. Equation (7.13) has the same general form as the equation which defines the aggregate demand curve in standard macro models with one commodity. Thus, the macro demand curve for n-goods takes account of the Keynesian multiplier mechanism that operates in the n-industry. Higher demand for Y_n generates higher income, which again generates higher demand.

A price increase on n-goods has three immediate effects on the demand for these goods:

- a *negative* substitution effect, because demand shifts from n- to t-goods
- a *negative* income effect, because the real value of a given nominal income has declined
- a *positive* income effect, because nominal income from the production of n-goods has increased.

The negative income effect is proportional to the consumption of n-goods, C_n. The positive income effect is proportional to the real income derived from the production of n-goods and spent on consumption, $(1 - \sigma)(1 - \tau)Y_n$. The income effects cancel if $C_n = (1 - \sigma)(1 - \tau)Y_n$. Then consumers automatically receive full compensation for the price increase on n-goods through increased revenue from the production of the same goods. Normally we assume that the two income effects are close to cancelling each other, and that the substitution effect dominates. The demand curve then slopes downward, as in figure 7.1. The negative effect of Π_n on the demand for n-goods is enhanced by the multiplier. A more formal analysis of the slope of the demand curve is given towards the end of this section.

Equilibrium is found at the intersection between the demand and supply curves. Thus, Π_n and Y_n are determined jointly by (7.12) and (7.13). By inserting (7.12) into (7.13) we can also write the equilibrium condition as

$$c_n(\Pi_n, \Pi_t, (1 - \sigma)(1 - \tau)(\Pi_n Y_n(\Pi_n, K_n) + \Pi_t Y_t)) + G_n = Y_n(\Pi_n, K_n) \qquad (7.14)$$

This is one equation in one unknown, Π_n. When this is solved, Y_n follows from (7.12) or (7.13). Since W is given, P_n follows from $\Pi_n = P_n/W$.

4. Contingent on the now given levels of Y_t, Π_n and Y_n we can draw the demand curve for t-goods. Formally it is given by

$$D_t = C_t + G_t = c_t(\Pi_n, \Pi_t, (1 - \sigma)(1 - \tau)(\Pi_n Y_n + \Pi_t Y_t)) + G_t \qquad (7.15)$$

Unlike in the demand curve for n-goods, we do not have to take account of the multiplier effect, since domestic production of t-goods is unaffected by domestic demand. We still have the substitution and income effects of a price increase which we listed for n-goods. Again we assume that the two income effects are close to cancelling and that the substitution effect dominates. Thus the demand curve slopes downward.

5. The trade surplus, X, is the difference along the price line between the demand and supply curves for t-goods in figure 7.1. Since domestic supply exceeds demand, there is an actual surplus in the example.

6. The solutions for the remaining variables (N_n, N_t, N, Y_p, C) can be derived one by one from suitable equations.

Note that (7.11)–(7.15) depend only on Π_t, not on its individual components E, P_* or W. *For the real variables in the model only the ratio EP_*/W matters.* The absolute levels of E, P_* and W have no independent influence. This is the result of the basic homogeneity property of the model. If we look back at (7.1)–(7.9) we find that these can all be written in terms of real prices, real income and real total consumption by dividing by W in appropriate places.

We are now ready to discuss the effects of fiscal policy, devaluations and shifts in other exogenous variables.

Fiscal policy

Government consumption of t-goods, G_t, does not enter until the fourth step in the solution. This means that it has no effect on prices, production, employment or income. In figure 7.1 the only shift is a rightward one in the demand curve for t-goods. It reduces the trade surplus with the same amount as the purchase.

Government consumption of n-goods, G_n, enters in the third step of the solution procedure. As in figure 7.2, it shifts the demand for n-goods to the right and raises prices and production of n-goods. The multiplier is at work and tends to make the increase in Y_n greater than the increase in G_n. The increase in Π_n dampens the increase in Y_n, however.

As before, we assume that the direct income effects of the increase in Π_n cancel. The increase in Y_n, however, raises real income and shifts the demand curve for t-goods to the right. In addition there is a cross-substitution effect; n-goods have become relatively more expensive. This also shifts the demand curve for t-goods to the right. The result is a decline in the trade surplus, as figure 7.2 shows.

Devaluation

A devaluation (an increase in E) raises the price line for t-goods in figure 7.3. Supply of t-goods responds positively, and Y_t is increased. As before, we assume that the direct income effects of increased prices cancel. However, there is a positive shift in

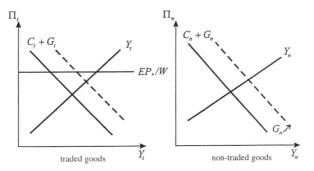

Figure 7.2 Increased government consumption of non-traded goods.

the demand for n-goods both because of the increase in real income owing to higher Y_t, and because of the substitution towards n-goods induced by the higher price of t-goods. The result is also higher prices and higher output in the n-industry.

As figure 7.3 is drawn, there is an initial trade deficit. The direct effects on the trade balance of a devaluation are those we get if we keep the demand curve for t-goods fixed. Then we see from figure 7.3 that supply increases, demand declines (because of substitution towards n-goods) and the trade surplus improves (the deficit is reduced). However, there is also an indirect effect owing to a rightward shift in the demand curve. This shift comes about both because of the extra income generated by the increase in Y_t and Y_n, and because of the cross-substitution effect which results from the increase in the price of n-goods. The effect of the increase in Y_t is smaller than the increase in Y_t itself, since some of the extra income is taxed away, some is saved and some is spent on n-goods.

When everything is taken into account, could the indirect effect possibly make the current account worse after a devaluation than before? This is impossible to answer from figure 7.3 alone. However, if one remembers that in this model with no real investment the current account surplus is by definition equal to total savings, the answer is not so difficult. Real income has gone up, because production in both sectors has gone up. This means higher private savings, and also, because tax revenue has increased, higher public savings. The current account must then improve. A formal derivation is given below. Again we assume that the direct income effects of price changes cancel.

Initially a devaluation means an increase in the price of t- relative to n-goods. However, the final effect on the relative price of t-goods may go in either direction. That the final effect may be an increase in the relative price of t-goods is rather obvious. Just think of the limiting case where the supply curve for n-goods is horizontal. Then the price of n-goods does not increase at all, while the price of t-goods goes up. For the price of n-goods to increase more than the price of t-goods, a relatively steep supply curve for n-goods is obviously needed. But this is not enough. Demand for n-goods must go up in spite of a relative price increase on the same goods. This can

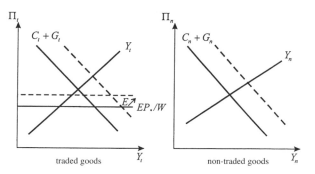

Figure 7.3 A devaluation.

happen only if increased output of t-goods has produced a substantial increase in real income and a large share of the increased income is spent on n-goods. There is then a large outward shift in the demand for n-goods in figure 7.3. This raises the price of n-goods more than the price of t-goods if the supply curve for n-goods is steep. Thus, for the relative price of t-goods to decline after a devaluation the supply of t-goods must be sufficiently elastic, the supply of n-goods sufficiently inelastic and the savings rate not too high. The common presumption in the literature is the opposite, that a devaluation raises the relative price of t-goods. This presumption may be justified if the supply of n-goods is not too inelastic compared to the supply of t-goods.

Effects of other exogenous variables

Table 7.1 lists the qualitative effects of changes in all the exogenous variables. A useful exercise is to derive these effects either in graphs like figures 7.1–7.3 or by differentiation of the equations of the model. Note in particular that since the solution for the real variables depends only on Π_t, not on E, P_* or W separately, a 10 per cent devaluation, a 10 per cent increase in world market prices and a 10 per cent wage cut all have the same real effects. The ambiguity in the effect of W on P_n has the same cause as the ambiguity in the effect of a devaluation on the relative price of t- and n-goods. Since the real effects of a depreciation and a wage cut are the same, a wage cut must raise P_n in the same circumstances as a depreciation raises the relative price of n-goods. Obviously special circumstances are required for this result, and the normal expectation is that a wage increase raises the price of n-goods. It will always do so if the supply curve for n-goods is horizontal.

A more formal analysis of the slopes of the demand curves

Let us first look at the slope of the macro demand curve for n-goods. By differentiating (7.13) we find

$$\frac{dY_n}{d\Pi_n} = m_n[c_{nn} + (1-\sigma)(1-\tau)Y_n c_{nC}] \tag{7.16}$$

where

$$m_n = \frac{1}{1-(1-\sigma)(1-\tau)\Pi_n c_{nC}} \tag{7.17}$$

is the usual multiplier. Remember that because expenditures on the two goods add up to C, $\Pi_n c_{nC} = 1 - \Pi_t c_{tC}$. Since output of t-goods is constant, $\Pi_t c_{tC}$ is the marginal propensity to import (or to reduce exports). Since both goods are normal, $0 < \Pi_n c_{nC} < 1$. Thus the value of the multiplier is reduced by the three usual terms: the savings rate, the tax rate and import leakage. Still $m_n > 1$.

By substituting in (7.16) from the Slutsky equation (7.10) we get

Table 7.1   *Effects of exogenous variables*

Increase in	Effect on					
	Y_t	Y_n	N	X	P_t	P_n
G_t	0	0	0	−1	0	0
G_n	0	+	+	−	0	+
τ	0	−	−	+	0	−
E, P_*	+	+	+	+	+	+
W	−	−	−	−	0	?
K_t	+	+	+	+	0	+
K_n	0	+	?	+	0	−

$$\frac{dY_n}{d\Pi_n} = m_n\{s_{nn} + [(1-\sigma)(1-\tau)Y_n - C_n]c_{nC}\} \tag{7.18}$$

We recognize the negative direct substitution effect and the two opposing income effects. The income effects cancel when

$$C_n = (1-\sigma)(1-\tau)Y_n \tag{7.19}$$

What this condition requires is that private consumption of n-goods is equal to the share that is spent on private consumption of the real income generated in the non-traded industry.

By a similar derivation from (7.15) we get that the slope of the demand curve for t-goods is

$$\frac{dD_t}{d\Pi_t} = s_{tt} + [(1-\sigma)(1-\tau)Y_t - C_t]c_{tC} \tag{7.20}$$

The condition for the two income effects to cancel is now

$$C_t = (1-\sigma)(1-\tau)Y_t \tag{7.21}$$

The two conditions (7.19) and (7.21) are actually equivalent. In order to see this, remember that because of the consumers' budget equation

$$\Pi_n C_n + \Pi_t C_t = (1-\sigma)(1-\tau)(\Pi_n Y_n + \Pi_t Y_t)$$

or

$$\Pi_n[C_n - (1-\sigma)(1-\tau)Y_n] = -\Pi_t[C_t - (1-\sigma)(1-\tau)Y_t]$$

If one side is equal to zero, the other side is too. Conditions (7.19) and (7.21) can also be written

$$\frac{C_n}{Y_n} = \frac{C_t}{Y_t} = (1-\sigma)(1-\tau) \tag{7.22}$$

In fact the only assumption we need is the first equality in (7.22). The second equality then follows from the budget equation above. Thus, *all direct income effects of price increases cancel if, and only if, the share of private consumption in production is the same in both sectors.*

The condition for the income effects to cancel can be looked at from another angle which reveals how it can be violated. A set of sufficient condition for (7.22) to hold is that trade is balanced ($X = 0$) and that the government consumes the same share of the output of each industry:

$$\frac{G_n}{Y_n} = \frac{G_t}{Y_t} \tag{7.23}$$

To see this, just recall that when $X = 0$ we have that $C_t + G_t = Y_t$ and, as usual, $C_n + G_n = Y_n$. When government consumption is the same share of output in both sectors, this must also be true of private consumption.

Disregard government consumption for a moment. If there is an export surplus, it means that domestic residents sell more t-goods than they buy. A price increase on t-goods then raises their real income. If there is a trade deficit, the result is the opposite. Only when trade is balanced are the real incomes unaffected by a price increase on t-goods.

In the present model the government's tax revenue is the same percentage of output in both industries. Condition (7.23) means that government consumption is also the same share of output in both industries. (The consumption shares and tax shares are not necessarily equal, though.) Together this means that the government's real income is not directly affected by price changes. If a price increase is going to affect the real income of the private sector, it must affect the real income of the foreign or the government sector in the opposite direction. Looked at from this perspective we see that important income effects from price changes are likely if trade is highly imbalanced, or if there is a great discrepancy between the goods the government taxes and the goods the government buys.

Formally (7.22) is a sufficient condition for the model to give the conclusions summarized in table 7.1. Unless substitution effects are weak, though, all conclusions go through even if (7.22) is satisfied only approximately. Most conclusions will go through even if demand curves slope the wrong way, provided a price increase does not increase demand more than supply.

However, it is possible to give examples of conclusions that change if income effects of price changes work in the opposite direction of, and are stronger than, substitution effects. The most important example is perhaps that a devaluation may be contractionary when there is a large initial trade deficit. Unless the deficit is created by high government purchases, a trade deficit must mean that consumers spend more on t-goods than the income they receive from the t-industry. Thus a large deficit probably means that $C_t > (1 - \sigma)(1 - \tau)Y_t$. A price increase on t-goods then depresses real income and reduces demand for n-goods. However, there are still two effects in the opposite direction, the substitution effect and the positive income effect from increased output of t-goods. Only if both these effects are weak can the overall result of a devaluation be a negative shift in the demand for n-goods, and lower output and employment in the n-industry. But if this happens there is also a possibility that total employment decreases.

There were important *if*s in this story. It may still be relevant for some developing countries where the t-industry is based on a natural resource which limits output and imports consist of manufactured goods with no close domestic substitutes.

The current account and savings

As already indicated, it is sometimes easier to derive the effects on the current account and the trade surplus by looking at savings than by looking more directly at the balance between demand and supply of t-goods. Private and government savings are, respectively,

$$S_p = \sigma(1 - \tau)(P_n Y_n + P_t Y_t)$$

$$S_g = \tau(P_n Y_n + P_t Y_t) - (P_n G_n + P_t G_t)$$

In the absence of real investment the current account surplus is by definition equal to total savings. Measured in t-goods this means

$$X = \frac{S_p}{P_t} + \frac{S_g}{P_t}$$

or, after inserting for S_p and S_g from above,

$$X = [\sigma(1 - \tau) + \tau]\left(\frac{P_n Y_n}{P_t} + Y_t\right) - \left(\frac{P_n G_n}{P_t} + G_t\right) \tag{7.24}$$

The trade surplus is equal to the economy's marginal propensity to save, $\sigma(1 - \tau) + \tau$, times real income and then minus government consumption, all measured in t-goods.[69] Above we concluded that a devaluation improves the trade balance because both Y_n and Y_t increase. However, the devaluation also changes P_n/P_t. By taking the derivative of X with respect to P_n/P_t keeping quantities constant, one finds that the price effects cancel if $[\sigma(1 - \tau) + \tau]Y_n - G_n = 0$. This is the same condition as (7.19). In order to see that, just substitute for G_n from (7.4). This means that, when (7.19) holds, we need to look only at what happens to Y_n and Y_t in order to determine the effect on the current account. In this case a devaluation is always expansionary. Production in both sectors goes up, savings go up and the current account is improved. Note that since the aggregate propensity to save, $\sigma(1 - \tau) + \tau$, is below one, the effect of a devaluation on the trade balance is smaller than the effect on GDP. For realistic values of σ and τ the effect is *much* smaller.

Even if (7.19) does not hold exactly, a devaluation is bound to improve the current account in most cases. A contractionary devaluation always improves the current account. The contraction means a reduction in the price and output of n-goods. Both shift the demand curve for t-goods to the left, and the demand for t-goods must decline relative to supply. The trade balance thus improves in spite of the first impression one may get from (7.24). The reason is that the same condition which caused the contraction in output also ensures that there are strong relative price effects working in the direction of an improved current account in (7.24).

7.2 Alternatives and extensions

Real wage rigidity

Wage contracts often index wages to prices. Even when no formal index clause is at work, wages may respond rapidly to changes in prices. Bruno and Sachs (1985) explained the different performance of the United States and Europe after the oil price shocks of 1973–4 and 1979–80 by the United States having nominal wage rigidity and Europe real wage rigidity.[70] It may thus be of interest to see what happens if we replace the given nominal wage in the model of section 7.1 with a given real wage. As we shall see, real wage rigidity means that devaluations cease to have real effects. It may also mean that an expansion of demand has a negative effect on total employment.

Define the consumer price index as $P_c = P_n^\alpha P_t^{1-\alpha}$, where α is the weight on n-goods. The real wage from the consumer's point of view is then $\omega = W/P_c$ or

$$\omega = \frac{W}{P_n^\alpha P_t^{1-\alpha}} \tag{7.25}$$

If we combine (7.25) with (7.1)–(7.9) and make W endogenous, ω exogenous, we have a model of how the economy works under real wage rigidity.

Equation (7.25) is called the *real wage constraint*. It is a constraint on the two real prices, $\Pi_n = P_n/W$ and $\Pi_t = P_t/W$. By dividing by W in both the numerator and denominator, (7.25) can be written

$$\omega = \frac{1}{\left(\frac{P_n}{W}\right)^\alpha \left(\frac{P_t}{W}\right)^{1-\alpha}} = \frac{1}{\Pi_n^\alpha \Pi_t^{1-\alpha}}$$

or

$$\Pi_n^\alpha \Pi_t^{1-\alpha} = \frac{1}{\omega} \tag{7.26}$$

In figure 7.4 we have drawn this relation between the two real prices as the curve marked *RWC*. If the real wage is to be constant, a high price in terms of work hours on one commodity has to be compensated by a low price on another. Hence, the *RWC* curve slopes downwards. One implication is that changes originating on the demand side of the economy must move production in the two industries in opposite directions, since if one real price goes up, the other must go down.

The equilibrium condition for the market for n-goods (7.14) also implies a relationship between the real prices in the two sectors. This time the relationship slopes upwards, as the curve marked NTE for non-traded equilibrium in figure 7.4. It shows the combinations of Π_n and Π_t which yield equilibrium in the market for n-goods. A higher Π_t raises the demand for n-goods, and this in turn leads to a higher Π_n as we saw when discussing a devaluation in section 7.1.

The intersection of the two curves in figure 7.4 determines the equilibrium real prices. In other words, the two real prices are determined by the real wage constraint (7.26) and the equilibrium condition for n-goods (7.14). The nominal wage then follows from the fact that $\Pi_t = P_t/W$.

The exchange rate enters nowhere in (7.14) or (7.26). This means that the two curves in figure 7.4 are unaffected by devaluations or revaluations. A devaluation has no effect on the two real prices. The initial impact of E on $\Pi_t = EP_*/W$ is neutralized because W increases in the same proportion as E as a result of indexation. Since supply depends only on the real prices, this means that the exchange rate has no effect on output of t-goods either. There can then be no further real effects on the n-sector. The only effect of a devaluation is that all nominal variables increase proportionally. A devaluation of 10 per cent leads to a 10 per cent increase in all prices and wages. That is it.

An expansion of demand for n-goods (which may be caused by an increase in G_n or a decrease in τ) shifts the NTE curve upwards, as illustrated in figure 7.4. More demand for n-goods means a higher Π_n for every level of Π_t. As we can see from figure 7.4, the effect is an increase in the real price of n-goods and a decrease in the real price of t-goods.

What happens can be described like this: more demand for n-goods means higher prices on those goods. Because of the real wage constraint this leads to a higher nominal wage. The higher nominal wage again means that the real price of t-goods goes down, since the nominal price on those goods is in effect exogenous. The lower real price on t-goods owing to the increase in wage costs means that the suppliers of t-goods reduce their output. Thus, an expansion of the demand for n-goods, which

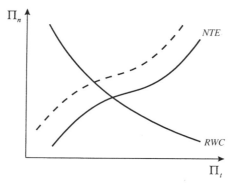

Figure 7.4 Equilibrium with a real wage constraint.

increases production and employment in the n-industry, actually reduces output and employment in the t-industry.

Whether the effect on total employment will be positive or negative depends on the elasticities of demand and supply in all markets. An elastic supply of n-goods is favourable to employment, because then the price increase on n-goods is relatively small. This means a modest increase in the nominal wage. If the supply of t-goods is *in*elastic, the wage increase has only a small negative effect on output and employment in the t-industry. Thus an *elastic* supply of n-goods combined with an *inelastic* supply of t-goods are the most favourable conditions if we want a fiscal expansion to improve employment. If the actual case is the reverse of this – inelastic supply of n-goods and elastic supply of t-goods – then a fiscal expansion reduces total employment.

The effect of an increase in G_n with a real wage constraint is like the effect of a simultaneous increase in G_n and W in section 7.1. The former is expansionary, the latter contractionary. The positive effect on employment in the n-industry is always weaker than when W is constant. As we know from section 7.1, an increase in G_n and an increase in W both reduce the trade surplus. Thus, the trade-off between employment and current account balance is made worse by the real wage constraint.

In the special case where the supply of n-goods is infinitely elastic, the *NTE* curve is horizontal. This means that the price of n-goods is independent of demand. An increase in G then has no effect on P_n and, hence, does not lead to any increase in W. Thus, in this special case an expansion of demand has the same effect irrespective of whether the wage rigidity is nominal or real.

Income distribution effects

So far we have assumed that demand is independent of the income distribution *within* the private sector. However, there is reason to believe that in the short run the propensity to consume is higher out of wage income than out of profits. A devaluation, or a wage cut, redistributes income away from wages and towards profits in the t-goods sector. Thus, a devaluation, or a wage cut, may reduce aggregate demand if the marginal propensity to consume out of wages is higher than out of profits. This may lead to a contraction in the production of n-goods, and eventually to a decline in total employment.

In order to investigate how income distribution effects may change our conclusions, we shall take the argument to its extreme and replace the definition (7.6) of the disposable income which motivates consumption by

$$Y_p = (1 - \tau)WN \tag{7.6a}$$

In other words: only wage income matters for consumption.

In order to solve the revised model we have to go through the same steps as in section 7.1. Prices and output in the t-industry are determined in the same way as before. The supply function for n-goods is also the same as before. However, the demand function is now defined by

$$c_n(\Pi_n, \Pi_t, (1-\sigma)(1-\tau)(N_n + N_t)) + G_n = Y_n$$

Remember that N_n depends on Y_n. If we invert the production function, we can write the demand for labour as

$$N_i = N_i(Y_i, K_i) \quad i = n, t \qquad \qquad (7.27)$$

When this is inserted in the definition of the demand curve, we get

$$c_n(\Pi_n, \Pi_t, (1-\sigma)(1-\tau)(N_n(Y_n, K_n) + N_t(Y_t, K_t))) + G_n = Y_n \qquad (7.28)$$

This equation implicitly defines the demand for n-goods, Y_n, as a function of the real price Π_n. There is no longer any ambiguity about the slope of the demand curve. It is negative. The reason is that workers do not get compensated for price increases on n-goods. A price increase on n-goods always has a negative impact on the real income of the workers. Thus, c_{nn}, which is negative, measures the impact of an increase in Π_n.[71]

The effect of a devaluation is the same as the effect of an increase in Π_t. The positive effect on the output of t-goods is the same as in section 7.1. However, the impact on the demand for n-goods is somewhat different. As is evident from (7.28), Π_t affects the demand for n-goods through two channels: (1) The income effect from increased employment in the t-industry. (2) The cross-price effect on consumption. When Π_t is increased, the former effect is always positive. The latter effect can be viewed as a sum of two opposing terms. An increase in Π_t induces substitution towards n-goods. On the other hand, the price increase has a negative income effect which reduces demand for n-goods. Since profits are not part of the relevant income concept here, this income effect is not compensated by the corresponding increase in profits. If the income effect is sufficiently strong, the demand for n-goods is reduced. An increase in Π_t then shifts the demand curve to the left, and the result is a decline in the output of n-goods.

It follows that a devaluation, which raises Π_t, may lead to decreased employment in the n-industry. A wage increase, which reduces Π_t, may lead to increased employment in the n-industry. A devaluation always has a positive, and a wage increase a negative, effect on employment in the t-industry. If the income effect on the demand for n-goods is sufficiently negative, however, the effect on total employment could be the opposite.

More formally, if we want to find out in what direction an increase in Π_t shifts the demand for n-goods, we can calculate the derivative of the consumer demand $C_n = c_n(\Pi_n, \Pi_t, (1-\sigma)(1-\tau)(N_n + N_t))$ with respect to Π_t keeping Π_n and Y_n constant. This is

$$\frac{dC_n}{d\Pi_t} = c_{nt} + c_{nC}(1-\sigma)(1-\tau)\frac{dN_t}{d\Pi_t}$$

$$= s_{nt} - C_t c_{nC} + c_{nC}(1-\sigma)(1-\tau)\Pi_t Y_{t1}$$

where in the last line we have used the fact that $dN_t/d\Pi_t = \Pi_t dY_t/d\Pi_t$ because of the first-order condition, and then inserted from the Slutsky equation (7.10). Compared to what we would have got in section 7.1, a positive income effect is missing. If the middle term, $C_t c_{nC}$, is sufficiently large, a devaluation or a wage cut reduces the demand for n-goods. In order to clarify further the conditions for this to happen, it is useful to rewrite the expression above as

$$\frac{dC_n}{d\Pi_t} = s_{nt} - [C_t - (1-\sigma)(1-\tau)Y_t]c_{nC} + c_{nC}(1-\sigma)(1-\tau)[\Pi_t Y_{t1} - Y_t] \qquad (7.29)$$

(We have added and subtracted $(1-\sigma)(1-\tau)Y_t c_{nC}$.) As in section 7.1, we may disregard the second term since it is probably close to zero. Then a necessary condition for the whole expression to be negative is that the last term is negative, which requires $\Pi_t Y_{t1} - Y_t < 0$ or

$$\frac{Y_{t1}\Pi_t}{Y_t} < 1$$

In other words: a necessary condition for an increase in Π_t to have a negative impact on the demand for n-goods is that the supply of t-goods is inelastic. Only then may a devaluation or a wage cut have a contractionary effect.

As an example of an increase in Π_t we may think of a wage cut. The immediate redistribution effect of a wage cut is very different in the two industries. In the n-industry we expect that the first-round effect of a wage cut is a proportional reduction in prices. In the t-industry prices are given, and the wage cut immediately distributes real income away from wages and towards profits. However, if the increase in output and employment in the t-industry is great, workers gain income anyway. Hence the condition that supply in the t-industry must be inelastic, which means that a wage cut reduces the wage bill there. This condition is not sufficient to produce reduced demand for n-goods, however, because the income redistribution effect needs to overcome the substitution effect. If we are to see a decline in total employment, even more is required, since the contractionary effect in the n-industry needs to be strong enough to overcome the expansionary effect in the t-industry.

The conditions for a wage cut or a devaluation to have a negative employment effect may seem stringent. However, if we think of a country whose t-industry is based on a natural resource which is in limited supply, the supply elasticity could indeed be low.

VAT and payroll taxes: 'internal devaluations'

A devaluation in the model of section 7.1 works through two channels: (1) It raises the prices of t-goods relative to wage costs, and thus induces increased supply of t-goods. (2) Initially it also raises the relative price of t-goods in terms of n-goods, and thus leads consumers to substitute non-traded for traded goods. The same changes in relative prices can be achieved by reducing the payroll tax and increasing the general value added tax (VAT). This policy is sometimes called an *internal devaluation*. In addition to their use in internal devaluations, the payroll tax and VAT are worth studying in their own right.

In order to include these taxes in the model from section 7.1 we must modify (7.2), (7.3) and (7.6). Let θ be the rate of VAT and τ_W the rate of payroll tax. Let P_n and P_t be the two producer prices. The consumer prices are then $P_n(1 + \theta)$ and $P_t(1 + \theta)$. The modified equations are

$$P_i \Phi'_{iN}(N_i, K_i) = W(1 + \tau_W), \qquad i = n, t \tag{7.2b}$$

$$C_i = c_i(P_n(1 + \theta), P_t(1 + \theta), C), \qquad i = n, t \tag{7.3b}$$

$$Y_p = (1 - \tau)(P_n Y_n + P_t Y_t - \tau_W WN) \tag{7.6b}$$

Factor income (income at producer prices) is $P_n Y_n + P_t Y_t$. The amount of payroll tax, $\tau_W WN$, is subtracted from this in order to find taxable income. When this is multiplied with $(1 - \tau)$ we get disposable income as in (7.6b).

The supply functions (7.11) and (7.12) are unchanged, provided we take care to define Π_t and Π_n as real *producer* prices – i.e., $\Pi_i = P_i/W(1 + \tau_W)$, $i = n, t$.

The demand function for n-goods is defined implicitly by

$$c_n(P_n(1 + \theta), P_t(1 + \theta), (1 - \sigma)(1 - \tau)(P_n Y_n + P_t Y_t - \tau_W WN)) + G_n = Y_n$$

Because of the homogeneity property we can divide all arguments in c_n by $(1 + \theta)$ $W(1 + \tau_W)$ to get

$$c_n(\Pi_n, \Pi_t, (1 - \sigma)Y_r) + G_n = Y_n \tag{7.30}$$

where

$$Y_r = \frac{1 - \tau}{1 + \theta}\left(\Pi_n Y_n + \Pi_t Y_t - \frac{\tau_W}{1 + \tau_W} N\right) \tag{7.31}$$

expresses real disposable income measured in units of labour.

As we can see, the basic structure of the model is unchanged. Π_t is determined directly by exogenous variables. Y_t is then determined by supply. Π_n and Y_n are determined simultaneously by supply and demand functions of the same general form as before.

An increase in VAT has exactly the same effect on real disposable income as an increase in the income tax. Since θ does not enter the equations determining supply and demand except through Y_r, an increase in θ has the same real effects as an increase in τ – i.e. it reduces output and employment in the n-industry and improves the trade balance. However, θ has the additional effect of raising nominal consumer prices.

A reduction in the payroll tax increases Π_t in the same way as a devaluation does. As discussed in section 7.1, this raises output of both goods and improves the balance of trade. In addition, however, a cut in τ_W has the same effect on domestic demand as an ordinary tax reduction, as can be seen from the expression for Y_r. This means a further positive effect on non-traded output, while the positive trade balance effect is dampened and may even be reversed.

Suppose the government reduces τ_W and increases θ in such a way that $(1 + \theta)$ $(1 + \tau_W)$ is constant. This is what is called an 'internal devaluation'. It obviously reduces Π_t in the same way as an ordinary devaluation. It also raises the nominal consumer price $P_t(1 + \theta)$ in the same way. Since one tax is reduced and another increased, we can as a first approximation assume that the tax change has no direct impact on disposable income. Then the only shift in the demand and supply curves in the n-sector are those caused by the increase in Π_t. Hence the effect on Π_n and Y_n are the same as for an ordinary devaluation. This must then also be the case for the effect on the consumer price $P_n(1 + \theta)$, since the decrease in τ_W compensates for the increase in θ.

In practice, an internal devaluation has a direct impact on real disposable income. The reason is that the tax base is different for the two taxes. One is based on the total wage bill, the other on consumption. Which is larger of the two formal tax bases determines whether the immediate impact of the internal devaluation is to raise or lower the recorded nominal tax revenues of the government. However, as we can see from (7.31), it is not the formal base for VAT which matters for aggregate demand. An increase in θ also reduces the real value of that part of income which is saved. Hence, the effective base for VAT in this sense is the sum of wages and profits (total income after payroll tax has been subtracted). The effective base for VAT then exceeds the base for the payroll tax by the amount of profits. Consequently an internal devaluation means a small increase in the overall tax burden. However, this can be compensated by a reduction in τ if one wants to duplicate the effect of an ordinary devaluation. Alternatively one can increase the VAT somewhat less and still get the same real effect as from an ordinary devaluation, but somewhat smaller nominal increases in consumer prices.

Small internal devaluations were used by Norway and Sweden in 1992 in futile attempts to avoid actual devaluations. What is the point of making these complicated tax changes when an ordinary devaluation can do the same? The answer must be that there are important effects which are not included in the present model and where the two policies differ. One difference is that an internal devaluation is neutral with respect to the returns on investment in foreign and domestic currencies. Foreigners who have invested in the domestic currency are unaffected by an internal devaluation. Domestic residents are affected in the same way irrespective of which currency they have invested their money in. While active use of ordinary devaluations as a policy instrument may induce currency speculation, internal devaluations entail no such problem.

In practice there are limits to the size of internal devaluations. Reducing the rate of payroll tax below zero – i.e. introducing a payroll subsidy – may violate international trade agreements and may be politically infeasible. A high rate of VAT may create problems of tax avoidance. Thus, it seems difficult to replace large or repeated ordinary devaluations by internal devaluations.

Real wage rigidity made ordinary devaluations ineffective. How about internal deva-luations? In order to answer that we can return to figure 7.4. If we assume that τ is used to compensate for the direct impact on real disposable income, the *NTE* curve is unaffected by an internal devaluation. The *RWC* curve is now defined by

$$\frac{W}{[P_n(1+\theta)]^\alpha [P_t(1+\theta)]^{1-\alpha}} = \omega$$

or

$$\Pi_n^\alpha \Pi_t^{1-\alpha}(1+\theta)(1+\tau_W) = \frac{1}{\omega}$$

Since an internal devaluation keeps $(1+\tau_W)(1+\theta)$ constant, the *RWC* curve is unaf-fected, and the internal devaluation has no real effect.

It is probably of more interest that we can soften the real wage constraint by redu-cing the payroll tax only. This means that workers can obtain the same real wage with lower wage costs for the firms. If the immediate income effect of a reduction in τ_W is neutralized by an increase in τ, while θ is constant, the *RWC* curve shifts outwards. We get higher real producer prices and increased output in both sectors. This kind of supply-side policy thus seems to be an effective instrument for increasing employment when there is a real wage constraint.

There is one snag, however. We have assumed that the constraint is on real wages before income tax. Although this may be an adequate description of certain indexing schemes that have been used, it seems rather irrational to have real wage constraints where taxes have asymmetric effects. A more consistent treatment of taxes would imply that the real wage constraint is either a constraint on after-tax wages or on the wage costs of employers. A constraint on the real after-tax wage would make it irrelevant whether the cut in the payroll tax is financed by increased VAT or increased income tax.

A cut in the payroll tax which is not compensated by an increase in one of the other tax rates, shifts both curves in figure 7.4 upwards (remember that the *NTE* curve is now defined by (7.12) and (7.30)). We are certain to get an increase in production of *n*-goods, while the effect on the production of *t*-goods could go either way.

Government employment

When we have discussed the effects of government consumption, we have so far assumed that the government buys goods from the business sector. However, the government is also a major employer in most economies. Government employment has a double effect: it increases employment directly and it increases the disposable income of the private sector. The latter effect is equivalent to the effect of a tax reduc-tion.

Government employment, N_g, can be included in our model by modifying (7.6) and (7.9) to

$$Y_p = (1 - \tau)(P_n Y_n + P_t Y_t + W N_g) \tag{7.6c}$$

$$N = N_n + N_t + N_g \tag{7.9c}$$

We can treat N_g as exogenous.

If we neutralize the income effect of increased government employment by an appropriate tax increase, the only effect of an increase in government employment of, say 10,000 man years is to increase total employment by 10,000 man years. There are no further repercussions to the private sector as long as the nominal wage rate is given. In this sense, the famous 'balanced budget theorem' from a closed economy holds also in an open economy as long as the increased government expenditure is concentrated on government employment.

Suppose the government considers two alternative policies: either spend 1 billion kroner on reducing taxes, or spend 1 billion kroner on increasing government employment. By spending 1 billion kroner we mean that this is the initial cost of the programme after the income tax paid by those in the programme has been subtracted, but before taking account of any further repercussions on the tax base. Both programmes have the same impact on private disposable income, and they thus have the same effect on the two industries. The difference is that the employment programme gives an extra employment effect equal to the number of man years the government can buy for 1 billion kroner (calculated on the basis of what the employees receive net of tax).

If increased government employment is fully financed by an increase in τ, the increase in total employment is equal to the increase in government employment. This is true even if there is a real wage constraint. Since there are no repercussions on the private sector, there will be no change in prices and no need for wage adjustments. The crucial assumption behind this result is that the real wage constraint relates to wages before income tax.

There are of course objections to the active use of government employment as a tool for keeping total employment at some target level. An increase in government employment could be difficult to reverse quickly. The point here is merely that it may be a powerful tool in the short run.

This may be the place to mention one objection to our discussions of the effects of government consumption. We have assumed that G_n, G_t and N_g are exogenous. We have proceeded as if these quantities can be set independently. However, government agencies are usually left considerable discretion on how to spend the money they are allocated. This means that in advising a government one should probably assume that the exogenous variable is the size of the budget, and that the commodity distribution of government consumption is determined by the behaviour of the lower levels of government. Then the difference in impact between a tax reduction and an increase in government expenditure depends on the difference in demand behaviour between private consumers and government agencies. If on the margin government agencies tend to save less (which is reasonable) and consume a larger share of n-goods or direct labour, expenditure on government consumption tends to have a larger employment effect than tax reductions.

Exports, imports and changes in terms of trade

So far, we have reasoned as if there is only one traded good. As long as the relative world market prices of different t-goods are constant, nothing is lost by this. The standard *composite commodity theorem* tells us that. Since the relative prices on different t-goods are exogenous, it is legitimate to assume that they are constant whenever we analyse the effects of shocks originating at home. However, if relative prices in the world market change for some external reason, a more disaggregated approach is necessary. An example is an oil price shock.

There are two simple ways to incorporate changes in the *terms of trade* (the relative price between imports and exports). One is to divide the t-industry in two: one import and one export industry. The other is to assume that the imports are raw materials which go into the production of both t- and n-goods.

First to the case with one export and one import industry. Each has its own output price, production function and domestic demand function. Consider a partial increase in import prices with export prices constant. The analysis goes through the same steps as in section 7.1. First we notice that output increases in the import-competing industry and remains constant in the export industry. The next step is to find out how the demand curve for n-goods shifts. There are three effects:

1. The increased output in the import-competing industry has a positive income effect on the demand for n-goods.
2. Since consumption exceeds output for the imported good, the price increase on imports has a negative direct effect on the real incomes of the consumers. This shifts the demand curve for n-goods to the left.
3. If imports and n-goods are substitutes, there is a positive substitution effect towards n-goods. However, if the two goods are complements, there is a substitution effect away from n-goods.

The three kinds of effects were also present when we discussed the effects of a general increase in the prices of t-goods in section 7.1. However, there are some important differences. In section 7.1 we chose to ignore the direct income effects of a price change (item 2 above). The two opposing effects were assumed to cancel out. This assumption is not reasonable when we look at imports and exports separately. By definition, we consume relatively more than we produce of imports. In section 7.1 we had only two commodities, which meant they had to be substitutes. When there are three goods, two of them may be complements. Broad commodity groups are usually believed to be substitutes. However, it is conceivable that imports and n-goods are complements if a large share of the n-industry consists of retail services related to imports. On the whole, then, we cannot tell in which direction the demand for n-goods shifts. It depends on the quantitative strength of the different effects. Increased import prices may thus have a contractionary effect on the n-sector and on total employment. If the import-competing industry is small, or non-existent, this seems to be the likely case. Then the positive effect from output in that industry is probably small, and the negative real income effect is strong.

If export prices go up, output in the export industry increases, while output in the import-competing industry stays constant. There are the same three channels for spillovers to the n-sector as above. However, since output exceeds consumption for the export, the direct income effect of the price increase is positive. An expansionary effect on the n-sector is thus more likely. Only if exports and n-goods are strong complements are there reasons to expect a contractionary effect. Exports and imports cannot both be complements to n-goods. It seems difficult to come by good examples where exports and n-goods are complements.

The main lesson is that relative to a general increase in the prices of t-goods, a partial increase in import prices is likely to be more contractionary, a partial increase in export prices is likely to be more expansionary.

The effect on the trade balance can, as before, be analysed by considering the effect on savings. Again, changes in output are a major influence. However, price effects cannot be dismissed as easily as in section 7.1. An increase in import prices has a direct negative effect on real income and, hence, a direct negative effect on savings and the trade balance (for given output levels). The direct effect of an increase in export prices is the opposite. Thus, when all effects are taken into consideration, increased export prices improve the current account. The effects of increased import prices are more ambiguous. If the price increase calls forth a large increase in output from the import-competing industry, or if there is strong substitution towards n-goods, a positive effect on the trade balance cannot be excluded.

Imported inputs

Now to the case where all imports are raw materials for domestic production. Suppose that the input–output coefficients are constant: i.e. that raw material inputs in each industry are proportional to output. Think first of the case where the raw materials are used only in the t-industry. Let the world market price of the output of that industry be P_*, the world market price of raw materials P_m and the input coefficient for raw materials b_t (units of input per unit of output). Then the net output price in the t-industry is $P_* - b_t P_m$, or in domestic currency $P'_t = E(P_* - b_t P_m)$. Thus, the effect of an increase in P_m on t-goods output is the same as the effect of a decrease in P_t, which we have analysed earlier.

However, the demand effects are different. The demand functions can be written

$$C_i = c_i(P_n, P_t, (1 - \sigma)(1 - \tau)(P_n Y_n + (P_t - Eb_t P_m)Y_t)) \quad i = n, t$$

Here, $P_t = EP_*$ is the price the consumer pays, while $P_t - Eb_t P_m = P_t'$ is the net price which accrues to the producer after subtraction of the costs of raw materials. In this case an increase in P_m for a given P_t has a negative income effect which reduces demand for both n- and t-goods. This adds to the negative shift in the demand curve for n-goods which already follows from the decline in t-goods output. The result is lower output also of n-goods, lower real income, lower saving and a lower trade surplus.

In the present case we are looking at a non-competitive import which is neither a substitute nor a complement to n-goods. The direct income effects of the price change are the same as if we had been importing a consumer good. That the import is instead a raw material introduces an additional negative effect on real income due to the decline in t-goods output.

Note that a terms of trade improvement in the form of an increase in P_* for an unchanged P_m now has a positive income effect aside from its effect on t-goods output. In order to see this, just remember that if trade is balanced, C_t is now smaller than Y_t, since part of Y_t must be used to pay for the imported raw materials.

If the imports were raw materials for n-goods instead, the output of t-goods would of course not be affected by an increase in P_m. In the n-industry both the demand and supply curves would shift to the left after an increase in P_m. Supply would be reduced owing to increased costs of raw materials. Demand would be reduced, because for a given P_n an increase in the cost of raw materials would reduce the net income from the n-industries. The result is reduced output of n-goods, reduced real income, reduced savings and reduced trade surplus.

7.3 Wage dynamics

As in chapters 5 and 6 we shall supplement the basic static model by adding on relations for wage growth, first a Phillips curve and then a union wage equation.[72] We start with

$$\frac{\dot{W}}{W} = \frac{\dot{P}_t}{P_t} + \gamma(N - \bar{N}), \quad \gamma > 0 \tag{7.32}$$

This can be interpreted as an ordinary expectations augmented Phillips curve where equilibrium employment is $\bar{N}$. Expected inflation is set equal to the inflation that is imported from abroad, or created through continuous exchange rate changes. One way of defending this assumption is to say that people know that in the long run inflation in a small open economy with a fixed exchange rate cannot differ from the imported rate of inflation. When forming expectations they do not find it worthwhile to collect information about what temporary deviations there may be from this.

Alternatively (7.32) may be interpreted as a Phillips curve with fully rational expectations. Suppose for simplicity that the production function in the n-industry is

$$Y_n = A_n N_n \qquad (7.1f)$$

where A_n is the exogenous average (=marginal) productivity of labour. Equation (7.1f) means that there is no real capital in the n-industry. The marginal productivity condition is replaced by the condition that the price equals average costs:

$$P_n = \frac{W}{A_n} \qquad (7.2f)$$

This means that the supply of n-goods is infinitely elastic at an exogenously given real price $\Pi_n = P_n/W = 1/A_n$. We assume that A_n is constant, and thus $\dot{P}_n/P_n = \dot{W}/W$.

Suppose the Phillips curve relation is not (7.32) but

$$\frac{\dot{W}}{W} = \frac{\dot{P}_c}{P_c} + \gamma'(N - \bar{N}) \qquad (7.32f)$$

where we have assumed that actual and expected consumer price inflation are equal. By definition, the rate of change of the consumer price index is

$$\frac{\dot{P}_c}{P_c} = \alpha \frac{\dot{P}_n}{P_n} + (1 - \alpha)\frac{\dot{P}_t}{P_t} = \alpha \frac{\dot{W}}{W} + (1 - \alpha)\frac{\dot{P}_t}{P_t}$$

If we insert this in the Phillips curve (7.32f), we get

$$\frac{\dot{W}}{W} = \alpha \frac{\dot{W}}{W} + (1 - \alpha)\frac{\dot{P}_t}{P_t} + \gamma'(N - \bar{N})$$

or

$$\frac{\dot{W}}{W} = \frac{\dot{P}_t}{P_t} + \frac{\gamma'}{1 - \alpha}(N - \bar{N})$$

This is the same as (7.32) with $\gamma = \gamma'/(1 - \alpha)$.[73]

In this section we stick to the assumption contained in (7.1f). This may seem rather restrictive. However, in the case of nominal wage rigidity the analysis and the conclusions are essentially the same if we retain a more general production function.

In section 7.1 we showed how total employment depends on the exogenous variables of the model there. That discussion can be summarized in a reduced form equation for total employment:

$$N = N(\omega_t, \ G_n, \ \tau, K_t) \qquad (7.33)$$
$$\quad - \quad + \ - \ +$$

where $\omega_t = W/P_t = 1/\Pi_t$ is the real wage in terms of t-goods. The signs beneath the arguments show the signs of the partial derivatives.

If (7.33) is inserted into (7.32), we have one differential equation to determine the time path of the wage rate. Instead of the nominal wage we focus below on the real wage in terms of t-goods, ω_t. From the definition of ω_t it follows that

$$\frac{\dot{\omega}_t}{\omega_t} = \frac{\dot{W}}{W} - \frac{\dot{P}_t}{P_t}$$

or, after insertion from (7.32) and (7.33):

$$\frac{\dot{\omega}_t}{\omega_t} = \gamma\left[N(\omega_t, G_n, \tau, K_t) - \bar{N}\right] \tag{7.34}$$

This differential equation for the real wage is similar to the one we studied in section 5.7. The only difference is that the demand variables G_n and τ now have an effect on employment and indirectly on wages. The phase diagram for the equation is shown in figure 7.5, which should be compared to figure 5.5. As in chapter 5, the relationship between the level of the real wage and its rate of change (marked (7.34)) slopes downward, since a high real wage means low employment and thus low wage increases. Clearly our differential equation is stable.[74] Irrespective of which level of ω_t we start at, we move in the long run towards the stationary equilibrium at A where $\dot{\omega}_t = 0$. The real wage there, $\bar{\omega}_t$, is defined by $N(\bar{\omega}_t, G_n, \tau, K_t) = \bar{N}$.

The initial real wage is by definition $\omega_{t0} = W_0/P_{t0}$. When there is nominal wage rigidity, W_0 is given by past history. Since P_{t0} is given by the exchange rate and international prices, the initial real wage then follows.

As long as A_n is constant, there is a unique positive relationship between the real wage in terms of t-goods, ω_t and the average real wage, ω. This follows from (7.26), which says that

$$\omega = \Pi_n^{-\alpha}\Pi_t^{-(1-\alpha)} = A_n^\alpha\omega_t^{1-\alpha}.$$

A given ω is the same as a given ω_t. If one is given by past history, so is the other. If ω goes up, ω_t goes up too. This means that when A_n is constant, the analysis is the same irrespective of whether it is ω or ω_t which is rigid. Hence, real wage rigidity means that ω_{t0} is given by past history alone. If there is real wage rigidity and P_{t0} changes, W_0 changes in the same proportion.

Figure 7.5 also shows the effect of a fiscal expansion (an increase in G_n or a reduction in τ). For every ω_t there is more demand for labour and, thus, more rapid wage increases. The Phillips curve shifts upwards. The economy initially moves from the old equilibrium A to B. Then it moves gradually towards the new long-run equilibrium at C, which has a higher real wage in terms of t-goods. The positive employment effect

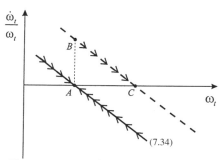

Figure 7.5 Wage dynamics with a Phillips curve.

from the fiscal expansion is only temporary. It is eroded by gradually declining competitiveness. After the initial increase in employment in the n-industry employment starts to decline in both industries. In the new stationary equilibrium total employment is back to its old level, $\bar{N}$. The industrial distribution of employment is changed, however. More workers are producing n-goods, fewer are producing t-goods. This also means that the trade surplus has decreased.

Suppose we try to use fiscal policy to peg employment at some level greater than $\bar{N}$. In a closed economy this would lead to accelerating inflation (or there would be no rational expectations equilibrium). In an open economy with a fixed exchange rate this does not happen. Instead, as we can see from (7.34), it means that ω_t grows at a constant rate. Wage increases and price increases on n-goods are higher than price increases on t-goods. The country loses international competitiveness. Employment in the t-industry declines continuously. In order to keep employment constant a more and more expansionary fiscal policy is required – i.e. a continuous increase in G_n or reduction in τ. The current account deficit gets wider and wider as the government deficit increases. Obviously the authorities will have to stop keeping employment above its equilibrium level, or give up the fixed exchange rate. If the government sticks to its employment policy and gives up pegging the exchange rate, the road is open to accelerating inflation. However, it is conceivable that if a country initially has a current account surplus, it can go on with N above $\bar{N}$ for a long while. Inflation will then be higher than abroad, but not accelerating. The fixed exchange rates keeps a lid on inflation.

The effects of a devaluation are essentially the same as in chapter 5.7. A devaluation does not change the relationship between the real wage and its rate of increase, and if there is real wage rigidity nothing happens, except that all nominal prices increase proportionally. If there is nominal wage rigidity, a devaluation reduces the initial real wage, since P_t goes up while W is given. This gives a temporary boost to employment, but over time the real wage moves towards the same stationary equilibrium as before. The devaluation has no real effect in the long run.

The wage curve and bargaining

In chapter 5 we looked at the effect of replacing the unique equilibrium level of employment by a wage curve derived from bargaining. Introducing wage bargaining in the two-sector model is more difficult. Suppose, as in section 5.9, that bargaining takes place at the firm level. With two industries the parties will be concerned with the real wage in terms of different goods. Producers in each industry are concerned with the real wage in terms of the goods they produce (producer real wages). Union utility presumably depends on real wages in terms of the average basket of consumer goods (the consumer real wage). Even with homogeneous labour we cannot expect wage bargaining at the firm level to yield the same nominal wage in the two sectors, except under rather special conditions.

For the moment we shall leave these complications aside. We assume, as has been traditional in the Nordic countries, that the t-industry is a wage leader and the n-industry a follower setting the same wage. Furthermore, we stick to the assumption that productivity is constant in the n-industry. As explained above, there is then a unique relation between ω and ω_t. This means that the discrepancy between the producer and consumer real wage in the t-industry need not concern us. In section 8.5 we look more closely at the impact of relative prices on the wage bargain.

Assume then that in equilibrium the outcome of the wage bargaining can be described by the wage curve

$$\omega_t = g(N) \quad g' > 0 \tag{7.35}$$

The higher employment is, the higher is the equilibrium real wage resulting from the wage bargain. If the equilibrium real wage, $g(N)$, is above the actual real wage, ω_t, the real wage increases. Thus the real wage moves gradually according to

$$\frac{\dot{\omega}_t}{\omega_t} = \gamma \left[g(N) - \omega_t \right] \tag{7.36}$$

The wage equation (7.36) replaces the Phillips curve (7.32)

As in chapter 5, wage bargaining brings in an extra stabilizing element in wage growth. The stability condition now becomes

$$\frac{\partial \dot{\omega}_t / \omega_t}{\partial \omega} = \gamma (g' N_\omega - 1) < 0$$

where N_ω is the derivative of the labour demand function (7.33) with respect to ω_t. Obviously, the -1 at the end helps for stability, and stability is possible even if wage increases have an expansionary effect on employment.

According to (7.36) $\dot{\omega}_t = 0$ when $\omega_t = g(N)$. The stationarity condition is thus that the economy will be on the wage curve. The economy must also be on the labour demand curve. The two curves are shown in figure 7.6. The stationary equilibrium is at (N_0, ω_0) where they intersect.

Figure 7.6 also illustrates what happens when G_n is increased. The original equilibrium is at (N_0, ω_0). An increase in G_n shifts the labour demand curve outwards. Employment increases immediately to N_1, while the wage remains at ω_0. The economy is at A. Since we are now below the wage curve, the real wage starts to increase. As it increases, labour demand declines. In this way the economy moves along the labour demand curve towards the wage curve and the new long-run equilibrium (N_2, ω_2) at B. The new long-run equilibrium has both a higher real wage and higher employment than before.

If there were a unique equilibrium level of employment, as in the simple Phillips curve model, the wage curve would be a vertical line at $N_0 (= \bar{N})$. After the increase in G_n there would still be a movement towards the wage curve. Since it is vertical, however, the end result would be just an increased real wage, not increased employment. The real wage would continue to increase beyond ω_2 until labour demand was back at N_0.

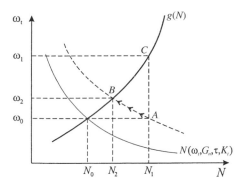

Figure 7.6 Wage dynamics with a wage curve.

Suppose the government keeps employment constant at N_1 in figure 7.6 by increasing G_n further as ω_t increases. The real wage then increases gradually towards ω_1, but it stops there. The economy comes to rest at C. There is no further deterioration of international competitiveness, and no further injections of government demand are needed. Since nominal wages at C increase at the same rate as t-goods prices and the exchange rate is kept constant, inflation is at the international level. We do not get accelerating inflation, and we do not get a continuing loss of competitiveness from keeping employment high.

This rosy picture may seem too good to be true. Indeed two long-run problems should be mentioned. One is that if the fiscal expansion creates a budget deficit, it may not be sustainable in the long run. The other is that a high level of the real wage may harm investment, and through this channel reduce employment at a later stage. Another qualification is that the wage curve may become vertical at high levels of employment. A bargaining solution may require that there is some unemployment. If this is the case, there is an upper limit to the level of employment that can be sustained through an expansion of aggregate demand. This upper limit may be lower than the equilibrium level of employment in a hypothetical competitive labour market.

7.4 Capital stock dynamics

In this section the models from section 7.3 are extended with an investment equation and capital stock dynamics. We continue to assume that only the t-industry uses real capital. We also assume that capital goods are t-goods. The aggregate demand effect of real investments thus affects only the balance of trade and not the demand for n-goods and labour. These assumptions limit the applicability of the model. However, they make it possible to focus on the important connection between competitiveness, investment and the size of the t-industry. In section 7.4 we comment briefly on the more general case.

The model is also an extension of the models with an endogenous capital stock in chapter 5. The difference is that employment is now affected by domestic demand because there is a non-traded sector. The Phillips curve version of the model is, except for a minor modification, the same as in Kouri (1979). The model consists of three equations:

$$N = N(\omega_t, G_n, \tau, K_t) \tag{7.37}$$
$$\quad - \quad + \ - \ +$$

$$\frac{\dot{\omega}_t}{\omega_t} = \gamma h(\omega_t, N, \bar{N}), \quad \gamma > 0 \tag{7.38}$$

$$\frac{\dot{K}_t}{K_t} = I(\rho_t(\omega_t) - \rho_*) \tag{7.39}$$

Equation (7.37) is the same labour demand function as before. Equation (7.38) is a wage equation which encompasses both alternatives in section 7.3. With a Phillips curve $h(\omega_t, N, \bar{N}) \equiv N - \bar{N}$, with a union wage equation $h(\omega_t, N, \bar{N}) \equiv g(N) - \omega_t$. Hence, $h_\omega \leq 0$ and $h_N > 0$. Equation (7.39) is the same investment function as in chapter 5. We assume $I' > 0$, $\rho'_t < 0$ and $I(0) = 0$. The rate of investment depends on the discrepancy between the real rate of return achieved in the t-industry and an exogenous rate of return, ρ_*, which can be achieved on international financial markets. The higher the rate of return differential in favour of real capital, the more is invested. If the rate of return differential is zero, net investment is zero. That $\rho'_t < 0$ follows from the standard theory of the firm (see Appendix B, p. 359).

Equations (7.37)–(7.39) constitute a dynamic model with three endogenous variables: N, ω_t and K_t. The initial values of K_t and ω_t are given. We assume nominal wage rigidity.

By inserting (7.37) in (7.38) the model can be reduced to a system of two differential equations in two unknowns: ω_t and K_t. The stationary solution is defined by:

$$\dot{\omega}_t = 0 \Leftrightarrow h(\omega_t, N, \bar{N}) = 0 \tag{7.40}$$

$$\dot{K}_t = 0 \Leftrightarrow \rho_t(\omega_t) = \rho_* \tag{7.41}$$

Equation (7.40) is the condition for internal balance. With a Phillips curve it simply says that $N = \bar{N}$. With a union wage equation it says that the economy should be on the wage curve, $\omega_t = g(N)$. Equation (7.41) is the stationarity condition for the capital stock.

In figure 7.7 we have drawn a phase diagram for the system. The stationarity condition for real capital (7.41) defines a unique stationary value for the real wage, $\bar{\omega}_t$. Only this real wage makes the return on real capital equal to the return obtained in the international financial markets, and only at this real wage is net investment equal to zero. Thus the locus for $\dot{K}_t = 0$ is a horizontal line in the diagram. Above the line real wages are high, profits low and the capital stock is shrinking. Below the line the capital stock is expanding, as the horizontal arrows indicate.

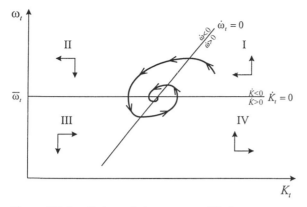

Figure 7.7 A path towards long-run equilibrium.

The locus for internal balance is defined by (7.37) and (7.40) together – i.e. by the equation $h(\omega_t, N(\omega_t, G_n, \tau, K_t)) = 0$. As in chapter 5, the locus is an increasing curve. A higher capital stock is beneficial for employment and needs to be balanced with a higher real wage if the labour market is going to be in equilibrium. Above the curve the real wage is high and employment low. This puts downward pressure on wages. Below the curve the real wage is low, employment high, and there is upward pressure on wages, as the vertical arrows indicate.

The long-run equilibrium is where the two loci in figure 7.7 intersect. Let the values of ω_t, N and K_t in the long-run equilibrium be respectively $\tilde{\omega}_t$, $\tilde{N}$ and $\tilde{K}_t$. The structure of the long-run equilibrium is this: $\tilde{\omega}_t$ is determined in (7.41) by the required international return and the production technology (reflected in the ρ_t function). $\tilde{N}$ is then determined by the supply side of the labour market in (7.40). With a Phillips curve, $\tilde{N}$ is simply equal to $\bar{N}$, with a wage curve $\tilde{N} = g^{-1}(\tilde{\omega}_t)$. Since $\tilde{N}$ and $\tilde{\omega}_t$ have already been determined, $\tilde{K}_t$ follows from the labour demand function (7.37). As in section 5.9, the equilibrium real wage is independent of eventual union wage pressures and equilibrium (un)employment is independent of aggregate demand.

Figure 7.7 also shows one possible path from an arbitrary starting point towards the stationary equilibrium. The path is stable and cyclic.

The Jacobian of the system is

$$A = \begin{bmatrix} \frac{\partial \dot{\omega}_t}{\partial \omega_t} & \frac{\partial \dot{\omega}_t}{\partial K_t} \\ \frac{\partial \dot{K}_t}{\partial \omega_t} & \frac{\partial \dot{K}_t}{\partial K_t} \end{bmatrix} = \begin{bmatrix} \omega_t \gamma (h_N N_\omega + h_\omega) & \omega_t \gamma h_N N_K \\ K_t I' \rho' & 0 \end{bmatrix}$$

Hence, the trace and determinant conditions are

$$\mathrm{tr}(A) = \omega_t \gamma (h_N N_\omega + h_\omega) < 0$$
$$|A| = -\omega_t K_t \gamma h_N N_K I' \rho' > 0$$

They are always satisfied. In general we cannot tell whether the approach to the equilibrium is cyclic or not. As in chapter 5, a direct approach is likely if the adjustment speed for real wages is fast relative to the adjustment speed for real capital.

In figure 7.8 we have illustrated the effect of a devaluation starting from the initial stationary equilibrium at A. The level of the exchange rate enters nowhere in our equation system. This means that the two curves defining long-run equilibrium are unaffected by the devaluation. The initial capital stock is of course also unaffected. The real wage is reduced immediately, and a momentary effect of the devaluation is to move the temporary equilibrium to B, where there is upward pressure on wages. They start to rise faster than prices. Because of the low real wage, profitability is high, and the capital stock also begins to rise.

After a while, the real wage is back to its initial level. With a larger capital stock employment is still above $\tilde{N}$. Wages continue to rise faster than prices, but the capital stock now declines. Employment must also decline since the economy is getting both less competitive and less equipped with capital. After a while internal balance is reached, and we enter a period where there is downward pressure on real wages. The capital stock is still decreasing. This phase may lead us straight to the stationary equilibrium or the economy may go for a cyclic approach. In the final equilibrium the devaluation has of course had no real effect.

The boost a devaluation gives to employment is temporary. However, with a Phillips curve it is worse than that. After the initial decline the real wage rises above the long-run equilibrium. Then it has to decline, and the only way this can come about is if $N < \bar{N}$. In other words, a devaluation starting from equilibrium leads to reduced employment in a later period. The initial reduction in unemployment is paid for with increased unemployment later. It is the temporary increase in K_t which makes the real wage overshoot the long-run equilibrium.

Matters are slightly more complicated with a wage curve, because then a high real wage in itself is enough to create downward pressure on wages. Thus, employment

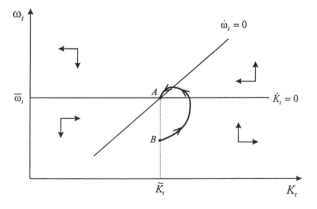

Figure 7.8 The effect of a devaluation.

need not be below $\tilde{N}$ even if we are above the $\dot{\omega}_t = 0$ locus. The possibility that employment falls below $\tilde{N}$ for a while is still there, but it need not happen.

In figure 7.9 we have shown the effects of a fiscal expansion – e.g. a permanent increase in G_n. The locus for internal balance shifts upwards. For a given capital stock employment has increased and a higher real wage is needed to keep the labour market balanced. If the initial equilibrium was at the old stationary point A, wages start to rise faster than prices. Soon the real return in the t-industry is too low, and its capital stock begins to shrink. The economy goes through a phase where the real wage increases, the capital stock shrinks and employment declines. This reduces the upward pressure on wages, and after a while the path enters a region where there is downward pressure on wages. Then competitiveness improves again, while the capital stock still declines as we move towards the new long-run equilibrium, B.

Again we note that a policy which benefits employment in the short run may have negative consequences in a future period (and is certain to have that if wage dynamics are governed by a Phillips curve). The reason is the need to regain the competitiveness lost during the initial expansion. A fiscal expansion had a similar effect and for similar reasons in section 6.6. We also note that in the long run the real wage is back to its old level, while the capital stock has declined. This means that employment in the t-industry has declined. Employment in the n-industry must have increased with the same amount.

If macro policies of the kind we have discussed are to be of more use, they must be applied when the economy is out of equilibrium. They may also be combined to bring the economy from one equilibrium to another in the least painful way.

One example is given in figure 7.10. The economy is initially at A. This is a stationary equilibrium, but it is not sustainable because there is a government deficit and a corresponding current account deficit. The government wants to improve on this by permanently reducing government expenditure on n-goods. That shifts the curve for internal balance downwards. If nothing else is done, moving from A to C requires the

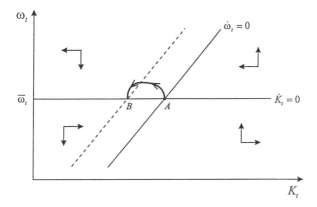

Figure 7.9 The effect of a fiscal expansion.

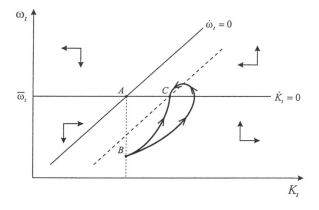

Figure 7.10 Fiscal contraction and devaluation combined.

economy to go through a period of high unemployment first. However, if the government combines the fiscal contraction with a sufficiently large devaluation, it can move the initial equilibrium down to B. From B there may be a path leading directly to C. The approach is made through a period of high employment and inflation. The devaluation then removes the need to go through a period of deflation first.

However, as the alternative path in figure 7.10 indicates, the real wage may also overshoot the equilibrium. Then employment may be below equilibrium in a later period, as in the earlier examples. Still the period with low employment is likely to be shorter and less painful than if we started with deflation right away.

7.5 Real capital in both industries

In actual economies real capital is used to produce both t- and n-goods, and investment goods are usually produced both by t- and n-industries. In fact, it may be the need for non-traded inputs in the investment process which prevents the capital stock from jumping immediately to its long-run equilibrium level. The limited supply of necessary domestic inputs means that the investment process must take time.

Based on the Kouri model (the Phillips curve version of the model in section 7.4) it is fairly simple to write down a dynamic model where real capital is produced and applied in both industries (or produced in a separate investment goods industry with inputs of both t- and n-goods in addition to labour and capital). However, such a model, even if conceptually simple, is too complicated to solve by analytic techniques.[75]

Still, it is possible to say something about the initial impact of exogenous shocks and about the stationary states. Below we make some informal comments based on the fact that real capital is used in both industries in accord with the production functions of section 7.1. Real investment in each industry depends on the difference between the rate of return on real capital in the industry and in international financial markets. The investment functions are thus of the same kind as in the Kouri model. We discuss two cases: one where investment goods are traded, one where they are non-traded. The short-run equilibrium is described by the model of section 7.1 amended with investment functions for each industry and with aggregate investment inserted in either (7.4) or (7.8) as part of the end use of either t- or n-goods.

We measure the international real rate of interest in terms of t-goods, as before. This means that the rates of return on real capital in each industry should also be calculated in terms of t-goods for comparison. In the Kouri model we wrote the marginal productivity of capital in the t-industry as a function of the real wage there – i.e. as $\rho_t = \rho_t(\omega_t)$. We can do the same in the n-industry – i.e. we can write $\rho_n = \rho_n(\omega_n)$. If capital goods are t-goods, the real rates of return on capital in the two industries are, respectively,

$$\rho_t(\omega_t) \quad \text{and} \quad \frac{P_n}{P_t}\rho_n(\omega_n)$$

In the last expression $P_n\rho_n$ is the value of the marginal product of capital. When we divide by P_t, we get the return per krone invested. If real capital is produced in the n-industry, the comparable expressions are

$$\frac{P_t}{P_n}\rho_t(\omega_t) + \frac{\dot{P}_n}{P_n} - \frac{\dot{P}_t}{P_t} \quad \text{and} \quad \rho_n(\omega_n) + \frac{\dot{P}_n}{P_n} - \frac{\dot{P}_t}{P_t}$$

Again the values of the marginal products are divided by the prices of capital goods to get the return per krone invested. In addition we have to add the gain that is obtained from an eventual increase in the price of n- relative to t- goods.

Stationary states

Suppose that all exogenous real variables are stationary. This means that in the long run equilibrium all relative prices are constant, and the real rates of return in both industries are equal to ρ_*. The cost of capital is then $\rho_* P_t$ if capital is produced in the t-industry, $\rho_* P_n$ if capital is produced in the n-industry.

One important feature of the stationary equilibrium in the Kouri model is that all relative prices are determined by technology alone. Aggregate demand does not matter for relative prices. This turns out to be true also in the more general case, as long as the production functions are homogeneous of degree one in labour and capital.

Homogeneity of the production functions means that we can write down unit cost functions for each industry. Competition means that in equilibrium prices must equal unit costs. Thus, if investment goods are produced in the t-industry

$$P_t = h_t(W, \rho_* P_t) \tag{7.42}$$
$$P_n = h_n(W, \rho_* P_t) \tag{7.43}$$

where h_t and h_n are the two unit cost functions. These are homogeneous of degree one, which means that we can divide by W on both sides to get

$$\Pi_t = h_t(1, \rho_* \Pi_t) \tag{7.44}$$

$$\Pi_n = h_n(1, \rho_* \Pi_t) \tag{7.45}$$

Equation (7.44) alone determines Π_t; (7.45) then determines Π_n. As we see, both real prices are determined by the two cost functions – i.e. by technology and ρ_* alone. Because of the homogeneity, (7.44) can also be written as $h_t(\omega_t, \rho_*) = 1$, which shows that there is just one real wage compatible with equilibrium. The condition is equivalent to $\rho_t(\omega_t) = \rho_*$.

If investment goods are produced in the n-industry, P_n replaces P_t in the last argument of the unit cost functions (7.42)–(7.43), which means that instead of (7.44)–(7.45) we get

$$\Pi_t = h_t(1, \rho_* \Pi_n) \tag{7.46}$$

$$\Pi_n = h_n(1, \rho_* \Pi_n) \tag{7.47}$$

Now the order of causation is reversed: first (7.47) determines Π_n, then (7.46) determines Π_t. The relative prices are still determined by the cost functions. This also means that there is just one $\omega_t = 1/\Pi_t$ compatible with equilibrium. However, the equilibrium ω_t now depends on the production technology in the n-industry, which takes part in determining the cost of capital. A high level of productivity in the n-industry means low capital costs in the t-industry. This again means that there is room for a higher real wage in terms of traded goods. This is a special case of a more general phenomenon: if the t-industry uses inputs from the n-industry, low prices on n-goods means that there is room for higher wages in the t-industry.

With relative prices determined on the supply side and the absolute price level determined from abroad, the demand side determines the sectoral composition of the economy, as in the Kouri model. More domestic demand means an expansion of the n-industry and a contraction of the t-industry.

The momentary equilibrium

Allowing t-goods to be invested in the n-industry does not change the basic nature of the momentary equilibrium described in section 7.1. An expansion of the demand for n-goods increases the rate of return on capital in the n-industry. This means a higher rate of investment in that industry. Since investment goods are t-goods, this has no effect on output or employment. It just means a (temporary) decline in the trade surplus.

An increase in ω_t has an ambiguous effect on investment in the n-industry. To see why, think of a reduction in P_t with W constant. On the one hand, capital goods (t-goods) become cheaper relative to n-goods, and this increases the real return on investment in the n-industry. On the other hand, the demand for n-goods falls because of both income and substitution effects, as we saw in section 7.1. This reduces the marginal productivity of capital in the n-industry and, hence, reduces the return on capital there. The net effect may go either way. If the first effect dominates, a decline in international competitiveness may lead to a (temporary) increase in investment in the n-industry.

If instead we assume that real capital is produced in the n-industry, things get slightly more complicated. As above, an expansion of the demand for n-goods increases the rate of return in the n-industry. The upshot is higher investment there, which by itself contributes to a further increase in demand and in the rate of return. One might fear that this leads to an expansion without limit. However, there are two countervailing forces:

- *In the long run prices are independent of demand.* This means that the price increase caused by higher demand must be temporary. Thus, there is reason to expect that prices on n-goods will decline again as the capital stock is built up. This fall in prices will inflict a loss on the owners of real capital, and is a disincentive on investment now. Another way to put the argument is that while the rate of return on capital is increased, the capital cost is also increased because of an expected decline in the relative price of capital goods.
- *Investment in the t-industry declines.* One reason is that investment goods (n-goods) have got relatively more expensive compared to t-goods. The other reason is the increase in the cost of capital caused by the expected future decline in the relative price of n-goods.

These countervailing forces rely on the fact that there is, after all, an increase in the price of n-goods. Thus, they will dampen, but not prevent, the increase in the price of n-goods.

In the Kouri model increased demand for n-goods would harm investment in t-goods production because of the ensuing increase in wages and loss of competitiveness, as we saw in the discussion of a fiscal expansion in section 7.4. When capital goods are produced by the n-industry, there is an additional immediate negative effect on investment in the t-industry. The industry loses competitiveness because its real capital becomes more expensive.

A decline in ω_t, brought about, for example, by an increase in P_t, has a positive direct impact on investment in t-goods production. However, there is a negative indirect effect. The ensuing expansion in the n-industry raises the relative price of capital goods (temporarily), and this dampens the increase in investment. In this case there is even a theoretical possibility that investment in t-goods production goes down although, judging from experience, this seems to be an unlikely case.

Dynamics

Adding real capital and investment in the *n*-industry brings in a third state variable in the model, K_n. In addition P_n enters the model both in levels and through the cost of capital in rate of change form. Effectively this means that we end up with a dynamic system with four equations (two for capital accumulation, one for wages and one for *n*-goods prices).[76] The wage equation should also take account of the fact that *n*-goods inflation is not equal to wage increases. General stability results seem impossible to derive. Nor can we depict the dynamics in phase diagrams. We are left to do numerical simulations, which will not be done here.

We may note, however, that an increase in K_n reduces P_n (see table 7.1) and, thus, reduces the rate of return on capital in the *n*-industry. This lowers investment there. Thus, there is a negative feedback from K_n on itself, which should promote stability.

7.6 The Scandinavian model of inflation

Section 7.4 focused on the time paths of real variables. Long-run developments of nominal variables are also of interest and the model there has implications for these too. Before we go through those implications, we shall present the Scandinavian model of inflation. This was used in Scandinavia from the 1960s onwards for predicting the course of inflation in the long run, and for setting norms in wage negotiations.[77] The model distinguished between *t*- and *n*-goods and assumed a fixed exchange rate. Thus we are on the same ground as in the earlier parts of this chapter.

The model consists of four equations:

$$p_t = e + p_* \tag{7.48}$$

$$w = p_t + a_t \tag{7.49}$$

$$p_n = w - a_n \tag{7.50}$$

$$p = \alpha p_n + (1 - \alpha)p_t \tag{7.51}$$

where the symbols are

p_t = Traded goods inflation $\dot{P}_t/P_t$

p_n = Non-traded goods inflation $\dot{P}_n/P_n$

p_* = Traded goods inflation abroad $\dot{P}_*/P_*$

p = Average rate of inflation

e = Rate of depreciation $\dot{E}/E$

w = Rate of wage increases $\dot{W}/W$

a_t = Rate of growth of the average productivity A_t of labour in the *t*-industry $\dot{A}_t/A_t$

a_n = Rate of growth of the average productivity A_n of labour in the non-traded goods industry $\dot{A}_n/A_n$

α = Weight on non-traded goods in the consumer price index

Equation (7.48) is the familiar $P_t = EP_*$ transformed to rates of change. Equation (7.49) is derived from the assumption that the labour share in the t-industry is constant. The labour share can be written

$$\alpha_t = \frac{WN_t}{P_t Y_t} = \frac{W}{P_t A_t}$$

where A_t is the average productivity of labour in the t-industry. If α_t is constant, simple differentiation of this equation with respect to time gives us (7.49). The same procedure applied to the n-industry gives us (7.50). Thus, the labour share in the n-industry is also constant. Observe that we assume that wage increases in the two sectors are the same. Equation (7.51) just defines the change in the price index.

The model determines four endogenous variables: p_t, p_n, p and w. The exogenous variables are p_*, e, a_t and a_n. The model has a very simple recursive structure. The rate of depreciation and the international rate of inflation first determine t-goods inflation in (7.48). Then t-goods inflation and productivity growth in the t-industry determines wage inflation in (7.49). Non-traded goods inflation is determined by the growth in average production costs – i.e. by wage increases minus productivity increases in (7.50). Finally, in (7.51), we can calculate the price index.

The recursive structure means that the model can be solved by successive insertions. (7.48) in (7.49) gives

$$w = e + p_* + a_t \tag{7.52}$$

This in (7.50) yields

$$p_n = e + p_* + a_t - a_n \tag{7.53}$$

This together with (7.48) inserted in the index formula (7.51) yields

$$p = e + p_* + \alpha(a_t - a_n) \tag{7.54}$$

Overall inflation is determined by imported inflation and by the difference in productivity growth between the t- and n-industries. The effect of the productivity growth differential is proportional to the share of n-goods in the price index. Higher productivity growth in the t-industry raises inflation, because it makes wages increase more, and this raises production costs and prices in the n-industry. On the other hand, productivity increases in the n-industry lower production costs there and, thus, lower prices on n-goods. The productivity growth rates in the two industries affect inflation differently because in one industry prices are given from abroad, in the other they are determined by domestic production costs.

Let us now go back to section 7.4. The long-run solution for prices and wages there has the same recursive structure as the Scandinavian model. First, t-goods prices are determined by $P_t = EP_*$. Then, the wage rate is determined by the profitability condition $\rho_t(W/P_t) = \rho_*$, and the prices of n-goods are determined by the horizontal supply curve $P_n = W/A_n$. Furthermore, if we differentiate these conditions and assume constant productivity and a constant real interest rate, we get the same equations as in the Scandinavian model of inflation. Thus, the Scandinavian model of inflation may be seen as the equilibrium outcome of the Kouri model. This is also the case if we allow for productivity growth in the Kouri model. Suppose productivity growth is labour augmenting, and let the productivity factors in the two industries be A_n and A_t. The cost per efficiency unit of labour in the t-industry is then W_t/A_t, and the long-run equilibrium condition for capital is $\rho_t(W_t/A_t P_t) = \rho_*$. With a constant ρ_* differentiation of this yields (7.49).

Note that the Kouri model determines the absolute levels of prices and wages. There is a potential danger in using the Scandinavian model as a norm for wage-setting. For the rate of return on capital to be at a competitive level in the t-industry, it is not enough that wage increases are equal to the norm $p_t - a_t$; the wage *level* must also be right.

Note also that on one point the Kouri model and the Scandinavian model start from different assumptions. The Kouri model assumes a constant real interest rate, which implies a constant real rate of return on capital in long-run equilibrium. The Scandinavian model assumes a constant wage share in the t-industry. The result is the same, because a constant rate of return implies a constant wage share when there is constant returns to scale.[78] However, if we believe the Kouri model, the Scandinavian model gives a false prediction of the rate of inflation when the real interest rate is changing, and it is then also misleading as a norm for wage-setting.

It can be shown that an increase in the real interest rate lowers the wage share in long-run equilibrium if the elasticity of substitution between labour and capital is smaller than one; increases the wage share if the elasticity is greater than one.[79] Thus, if we believe in the Kouri model, and if the elasticity of substitution is smaller than one, an increase in the interest rate should mean a lower wage share. Then the Scandinavian model exaggerates the room for wage increases in periods where the interest rate is rising.

Alternatively the room for wage increases can be related to the growth of wage costs abroad. An equation analogous to (7.49) must hold also for the rest of the world. As $w = p_t + a_t$, $w_* = p_* + a_*$. If we combine these two equations with (7.48) $p_t = e + p_*$, we get

$$w - a_t = e + w_* - a_* \tag{7.55}$$

which says that measured in a common currency the increase in unit wage costs should be equal at home and abroad. It can be shown that this condition holds in long-run equilibrium even if the real interest rate is changing provided that the wage shares and the elasticities of substitution between labour and capital are the same in both countries. Then the effect of interest rates on production costs in the countries cancel. This is the basis for the use of (7.55) as a tool for calculating the room for wage increases.

There is a close link between the Scandinavian model of inflation and the so-called *Balassa–Samuelson effect.*[80] There is a well known tendency for the absolute price levels to be higher in rich countries. Balassa and Samuelson suggested that the explanation is that the relative difference in productivity between rich and poor countries is higher in t-industries than in n-industries. The large productivity differential in the t-industries causes the wage levels in rich countries to be higher. This combined with lower productivity differentials in the n-industries makes prices of n-goods high in rich countries. This is in accord with what comes out of the long-run equilibria we have studied here. The effect of $a_n - a_t$ on inflation is just the Balassa–Samuelson effect translated to rates of change. Empirical support for the Balassa–Samuelson effect therefore also supports the Scandinavian model of inflation. Some support of this kind is provided by Rogoff (1996) and by a number of studies surveyed by him. However, it is also clear that the productivity differences between n- and t-industries are not the only factors that create fairly persistent differences in price levels. The Balassa–Samuelson effect is most visible when one compares countries which are at very different income levels or which have had very different productivity growth such as the United States and Japan (Marston, 1987). Still the effect has been found to contribute significantly to the explanation of inflation differences between European countries (Gregorio, Giovannini and Wolf, 1994). Aukrust (1977) showed that even if the model performed fairly well in explaining the trends in wages and prices in Norway, the assumption of constant wage shares in the long run was not tenable. On the whole, the conclusion from the empirical literature must be that the mechanisms described by the Scandinavian model are present, but they alone are not sufficient to give very accurate predictions. Among the possible reasons for deviations are: not all technical progress is of the simple labour-augmenting kind. The empirical counterparts of the n- and t-industries have many sub-sectors with different wages shares, and the distribution on sub-sectors changes over time. Competition is not always perfect.

Exercises

1. Check the signs of the effects of a tax increase in table 7.1 (p. 226).
2. In the model of section 7.1, a devaluation and a wage cut has the same real effect. Can you think of some reasons why in a more general model a devaluation and a wage cut will have different effects?
3. Compute by implicit differentiation of (7.14) the elasticity

$$\frac{d\Pi_n}{d\Pi_t}\frac{\Pi_t}{\Pi_n}$$

Discuss its sign and whether it is greater than one. What are the implications for the effects of a devaluation on relative prices?

4. Make a list of reasons why a devaluation may be contractionary. Try to make the list as exhaustive as possible, and not limited to the models of the present chapter.

5. Suppose that there is real wage rigidity and that the exchange rate is fixed. What is the effect of a cut in the real wage on employment in the two industries?

6. Suppose the government wants to improve its budget balance by 1 billion kroner. Does it matter for employment whether the government does this by raising the income tax, the value added tax or the payroll tax? You can assume nominal wage rigidity and that the exchange rate is fixed.

7. (a) Suppose the savings rate σ in the model of section 7.1 depends positively on the domestic rate of interest. What is then the short-run effect on output in the two industries of an increase in the interest rate?

   (b) Suppose that the exchange rate is floating and that the central bank keeps the domestic interest rate constant. How would you modify the model of section 7.1 to cover this case? What is now the effect on the level of production in the two industries of an increase in the domestic interest rate?

   (c) Compare also the effect on the current account in (a) and (b).

8. Assume a fixed exchange rate and nominal wage rigidity. What is the effect on the time paths of employment in the two industries of an increase in the savings rate in the private sector? Does the time path differ if we have real wage rigidity? What is the effect on the trade surplus in the short and in the long run?

9. The government gets a yearly gift from abroad equal in value to X_0 units of t-goods. (Alternatively X_0 can be interpreted as the proceeds from sales of a natural resource.) The gift is used to increase government expenditure with an equal amount:

   (a) What is the immediate effect of the introduction of the gift on employment? Compare the cases where the gift is spent on t-goods, n-goods and as a transfer to households. Compare also the effects on the trade balance.

   (b) Discuss the effect of the gift on the sectoral distribution of employment and on the current account in long-run equilibrium. Assume in this case that the gift is spent exclusively on a transfer to households.

   (c) Sketch a path from the short to the long-run equilibrium in case (b). Emphasize what happens to ω_t, N and N_t.

10. What would the long-run equilibrium of section 7.4 look like if private consumption also depended positively on wealth? Would any of the conclusions about relative prices or total employment change? How is the current

account determined? Suppose that the government increases G_t. The increase is financed by a lump-sum tax. How does that affect the current account and the sectoral composition of the economy? For simplicity you can assume that $G_t = G_n = \tau = 0$ initially.

8 Alternative market structures, purchasing power parity and monopolistic competition

Chapters 5–7 were distinguished by different assumptions about market structure. In chapters 5 and 6 all goods were traded internationally, while chapter 7 allowed for non-traded goods. In chapters 5 and 7 all internationally traded goods had exogenously given world market prices, in chapter 6 export prices were affected by domestic cost and demand conditions. These approaches should not be seen as mutually exclusive and competing. In going from chapter 5 to chapter 7 we also went from the simple to the more general. An even more general and realistic model would combine chapters 6 and 7 and include non-traded goods, some traded goods where the home country is a price taker and some traded goods where it has market power. Quantitative macroeconomic models of open economies are often of this kind. However, such models usually require numerical solutions. One purpose of the present book is to give insight into the different mechanisms that are at work in such models, and in the real economy, by treating them more in isolation.

The demand and supply elasticities in international markets and the extent to which industries are sheltered against foreign competition are important for the quantitative effects of domestic demand and domestic wage costs. We saw that already in connection with the Marshall–Lerner condition. In general, domestic demand has a stronger effect on output and a weaker effect on the trade balance the less elastic export demand and import supply are, the larger the non-traded sector is and the less substitution there is between traded and non-traded goods. For the effects of domestic wage costs or exchange rates, it is the opposite.

One purpose of the present chapter is to review briefly some empirical results on market structure in international trade. An important part of the literature is tests of different versions of purchasing power parity (PPP), and it is convenient to start there (section 8.1). This also gives us an opportunity to look at some evidence on the existence of nominal rigidities.

For traded goods the assumptions in chapters 5 and 6 are extreme opposites. In the former prices are given from abroad and unaffected by local costs, in the latter prices are based on costs with no regard for what competitors charge. In the theory of monopolistic competition these two extremes are endpoints on a continuum where the weight on own costs and competitors' prices can differ. Some elements of this theory, which forms a basis for many empirical studies of market structure, is presented in section 8.2. In section 8.3 the model of monopolistic competition is extended to take account of price discrimination, which empirical studies suggest can be important. In section 8.4, we look at some other aspects of monopolistic competition. Monopoly power may be a result of investment in market shares. Market power usually belongs to corporations, not countries. Multinationals may choose to exploit their market power by producing in different locations, but moving production may require investment.

In the last section of the chapter (section 8.5) we combine monopolistic competition with wage bargaining. This gives us opportunity to discuss the effects of relative prices on wage bargaining and to see how wage bargaining and monopolistic competition together change some of the results from chapter 6.

8.1 Purchasing power parity, the law of one price and nominal rigidities

The concept of *purchasing power parity (PPP)* has been mentioned several times throughout the book, but we never went deeply into it. Actually the expression 'PPP' is used with different meanings. There are two main alternatives:

1. *Absolute PPP* prevails if the same broad basket of goods costs the same. Let P_A and P_B be the price of the basket in the local currency in countries A and B, respectively. Let E be the price of country B's currency in terms of the currency of country A. Absolute PPP then prevails when $P_A = EP_B$.

2. *Relative PPP* prevails if the ratio between two broadly defined price indices, one from country A and one from country B, stays constant when corrected for changes in the exchange rate. Let P_A and P_B be the two price indices. Relative PPP then prevails between the two countries if the ratio EP_B/P_A is constant. In other words, relative PPP prevails if the real exchange rate in terms of two broad price indices is constant.

The two concepts are deceptively similar. By appropriate choice of units we can also write relative PPP as $P_A = EP_B$, making the constant ratio equal to one. One distinction is that absolute PPP is based on comparing the same basket of goods, while relative PPP is based on comparing two baskets which may differ from country to country – e.g. their consumer price indices. If the same basket is used in all comparisons, absolute PPP implies relative PPP. The converse is not true: the absolute price levels may differ even if the ratio between them stays constant.

PPP is related to the law of one price. If the law of one price holds for every commodity, then there is *absolute* PPP. Thus, absolute PPP prevails both in the extremely open economy of chapter 5 and in the economy with home and foreign goods in chapter 6. Measured in the same currency, all commodities there have the same price at home and abroad. The existence of non-traded goods in chapter 7 means that absolute PPP in general does not hold there. The law of one price is not necessary for absolute PPP, since the basket may cost the same even if the prices of individual goods differ.

The law of one price is not sufficient for relative PPP, since the weights in the relevant price indices may differ. The law of one price is not a necessary condition for relative PPP, either. Relative PPP would obviously hold if the *ratios* between individual prices were constant between countries. An example may be when tariffs make prices in two countries stand in fixed relations to each other.

Whether relative PPP, holds for the consumer price indices in chapter 6 depends on whether the composition of consumption differs from country to country. Relative PPP clearly does not hold for the producer price indices there, since they measure the prices of different goods (home and foreign goods respectively). This is the reason why it is often said that Mundell–Fleming-type models do not assume PPP, although strictly speaking there is absolute PPP.

The assumption that the law of one price holds for traded goods is less important in the earlier chapters than it may appear. In chapters 4, 5 and 7 the key assumption is that the foreign currency prices of traded goods are given exogenously. If they differ from prices in other countries because of tariffs, transport costs, etc. that does not matter as long as they are exogenous. In chapter 6 nothing is changed as long as the prices of the same goods at home and abroad stands in a fixed relation to each other.

PPP is sometimes referred to as a *theory of exchange rate determination*. By itself the statement that $P = EP_*$ is just a relation between three variables and not sufficient to say anything about exchange rate determination. The PPP theory of exchange rate determination proposed by Cassel (1921) is a version of the monetary theory presented in chapter 4, and this term seems preferable.

Sometimes it is claimed about a theoretical model that PPP holds in the long run, but not in the short run. This statement can be misleading. What is meant is usually that the model in question has a certain homogeneity property: the relative prices in long-run equilibrium are independent of monetary policy. The Dornbusch overshooting model may be a case in point. There a monetary expansion leaves the real exchange rate constant in the long run. Thus, if we compare two long-run equilibria which differ only with respect to the money supply, relative PPP appears to hold (there is always absolute PPP). However, long-run equilibria could differ for other reasons – for example, because of a shift in export demand. Then the real exchange rate will not be constant.

If we are interested in the effects of a certain exogenous event, and there is reason to believe that this event will not affect relative prices, a model where relative PPP is assumed can give valid predictions even if PPP does not hold as a general proposition. In this respect there is a difference between the long-run equilibria of chapters 6 and 7. In chapter 6 the real exchange rate depends on the demand functions. In chapter 7 all relative prices are determined from the supply side alone. In the latter case, relative PPP would be a tenable assumption when examining the long-run impacts of all kinds of demand disturbances. However, as we saw in sections 7.5 and 7.6, differences in productivity may create deviations from relative (and absolute) PPP even when we compare long-run equilibria.

As there are two definitions of PPP, there are also two approaches to empirical studies of PPP. One compares the prices of individual goods across countries, and uses this to test the law of one price and absolute PPP. The other investigates whether there is a tendency for the ratio between official price indices and exchange rates to approach a constant as time goes by, thereby testing long-run relative PPP.[81]

International price comparisons invariably show that prices on most goods differ greatly from country to country. For non-traded goods this is to be expected, and in that respect the studies seem to confirm that it is important to include non-traded goods in the model. It is more worrying that the law of one price does not seem to hold in international trade either.[82] This goes against a maintained assumption in all the preceding chapters. If the deviations from the law of one price were caused solely by transport costs and tariffs, our models could still be valid. However, there are indications that for a wide range of goods price differences are too large to be explained in this way. A likely cause is monopolistic price discrimination, which is discussed in section 8.3.

Most studies of relative PPP have looked at real exchange rates in terms of consumer price indices. In the short run there are large deviations also from relative PPP. However, as reported in the survey by Rogoff (1996), a number of recent studies have provided fairly persuasive evidence that real exchange rates tend towards relative PPP in the long run. This means that after a deviation the real exchange rate tends to return towards a constant level. The speed of convergence is quite low, though; the estimated half-life of deviations from relative PPP is typically around four years. In other words, deviations tend to dampen out at a rate of roughly 15 per cent per annum. Such slow convergence is difficult to detect unless one uses very long data series or panel data.[83]

The finding that relative PPP holds in the long run is apparently at odds with the results we reported in chapter 7 which gave support to the Scandinavian model of inflation. We also know that different goods have different weights in the consumer price indices from country to country. It is hard to believe that over long periods there are no systematic changes in relative prices. One reason why long-run relative PPP is still found may be that the studies often compare rich countries which are at roughly the same income level. The weights in the consumer price indices and the productivity growth differentials may have been fairly similar, implying that there is only a weak trend in the real exchange rate. Because of the large short-run fluctuations in the real exchange rate, econometric methods which test whether it tends towards a constant may fail to detect that the 'constant' is not quite constant after all. Not all studies using long data series show convergence to relative PPP (see Edison and Klovland, 1987).

The long-run effect of aggregate demand on relative prices in chapter 6 is also at odds with long-run relative PPP. A possible explanation, which saves some of the results from chapter 6, is that international competition is more intense in the long run. It is possible to charge higher prices than competitors for a while and still retain a significant market share; however, one cannot charge higher prices forever and still remain in the market (see section 8.4). Studies which estimate the effects of govern-

Table 8.1 *Exchange rate variability versus the US dollar, selected countries, 1976–1990, yearly data*

	Germany	Italy	Japan	Argentina	Chile	Peru	Uruguay	Singapore
μ_p	0.03	0.11	0.03	1.48	0.30	1.10	0.47	0.03
σ_p	0.02	0.05	0.03	0.87	0.26	1.23	0.13	0.03
σ_e	0.13	0.15	0.13	0.94	0.25	1.20	1.20	0.03
σ_r	0.13	0.13	0.13	0.37	0.13	0.19	0.17	0.03
ρ_{re}	0.99	0.98	0.98	0.33	0.16	−0.11	0.72	0.49

Notes: μ_p = average log rate of inflation; σ_p, σ_e, σ_r = standard deviation of the log rates of inflation, nominal depreciation and real depreciation, respectively; ρ_{re} = coefficient of correlation between real and nominal depreciation.

ment or current account deficits on real exchange rates have sometimes found effects that last fairly long, though (see Rogoff, 1996).

After the major countries moved from fixed to floating exchange rates in the early 1970s, the short-run volatility of both real and nominal exchange rates increased. Furthermore, the correlation between real and nominal exchange rates became very high. An extensive documentation was given in Mussa (1986). According to Mussa, nominal price levels exhibit similar smooth paths under both fixed and floating exchange rates, and most of the variability in real exchange rates can be accounted for by variations in nominal exchange rates.

The figures for Germany, Italy and Japan relative to the United States in table 8.1 give some examples of results which are typical for countries with floating exchange rates. The standard deviations are an order of magnitude higher for the rate of depreciation than for the rate of inflation. The coefficient of correlation between the real and the nominal exchange rate is 0.98 or higher. The real exchange rate may be computed in terms of consumer prices (as in table 8.1), producer prices or wages, but the results are similar. The simplest explanation is that there is nominal wage or price rigidity. In particular the models of chapters 6 and 7 can explain a high correlation between real and nominal exchange rates when nominal wages are slow to adjust. Krugman (1989) and Frankel (1993) argue strongly in support of this interpretation.

Economists adhering to the research programme 'new classical macroeconomics' have as a goal to explain the observed facts with models where all markets clear and there are no nominal rigidities. They have attempted alternative explanations. One is that the price levels show little variability because the central banks use monetary policy to keep them stable, while the exchange rates vary because shocks to technology and preferences warrant large changes in relative prices (see, for example, Stockman, 1990). However, this does not explain the increase in real exchange rate variability when one goes from fixed to floating exchange rates. If real shocks drive real exchange rate movements, it is hard to see why a change in monetary policy should make such a great difference. In principle, one can argue that the transition from fixed to floating rates happened because of increased volatility in technology and preferences. Given the historical record and the many instances of the same phenomenon, this explanation seems rather far-fetched however.

The evidence in support of nominal rigidity is not universal. Table 8.1 shows some examples of countries which had high and variable inflation in the observation period (Argentina, Chile, Peru, Uruguay). For these the volatility of the price level and the exchange rate was of the same order of magnitude, while the volatility of the real exchange rate was much lower in three of them. The correlation between real and nominal depreciation differed, but was lower than in the examples discussed above, and even negative in one case. One interpretation is that nominal rigidities are reduced when inflation is high and variable. Money loses its function as a standard of value. The economies are dollarized and indexation may be widespread in many types of contracts. Whether nominal rigidity is then replaced by real wage rigidity is another matter. Edwards (1989), in a study of 29 devaluations in developing countries, found that in most cases they had significant effects on the real exchange rate. The effects appeared to erode completely beyond the third year. However, in chronic inflation countries the effects were much smaller.

In table 8.1 Singapore was the country that came closest to keeping the exchange rate versus the US dollar fixed. For Singapore the volatility of inflation and of the exchange rate was the same. The correlation between nominal and real exchange rates was positive, but much lower than for the major floating currencies. Austria and the Netherlands, which kept their currencies tightly fixed to the German mark, show a similar picture in table 8.2. Sweden formally fixed its exchange rate to a basket where Germany counted heavily, but undertook some large devaluations. This form of exchange rate flexibility also gave a coefficient of correlations between real and nominal exchange equal to 0.98.

When the correlation between real and nominal exchange rates is high, movements in real exchange rates also tend to show a high degree of persistence. This is a corollary

Table 8.2 *Exchange rate variability versus the German mark, selected countries, 1976–1990, yearly data*

	Sweden	Austria	Netherlands
μ_p	0.08	0.04	0.04
σ_p	0.03	0.02	0.03
σ_e	0.07	0.01	0.01
σ_r	0.07	0.01	0.01
ρ_{re}	0.98	0.72	0.43

Notes: μ_p = average log rate of inflation; σ_p, σ_e, σ_r = standard deviation of the log rates of inflation, nominal depreciation and real depreciation, respectively; ρ_{re} = coefficient of correlation between real and nominal depreciation.

of the slow convergence to relative PPP. In the models with nominal rigidity in chapters 5–7 this must mean that the adjustment speeds in the dynamic wage equations are low. Once they have been displaced by a shock, real wages are slow to adjust. Persistent deviations of the real exchange rate from its long-run equilibrium are often called *misalignments*, especially if it is believed that they are not part of the normal adjustment to a real shock. Marston (1988) reviews some cases where floating exchange rates are believed to have been seriously misaligned, and discusses the merits of different interventions in the foreign exchange market on this basis.

8.2 Monopolistic price-setting

In chapter 6 we studied a model where home and foreign goods were imperfect substitutes and where there was short-run price rigidity. A standard interpretation of that model is that the price rigidity results from a combination of nominal wage rigidity, constant returns to scale and monopolistic price-setting. In this section we first give a more detailed underpinning of that interpretation, and then discuss more generally how the prices of home and foreign goods may be determined.

Suppose that in the home country there are a large number of firms which produce differentiated products. Each firm faces a demand function which is downward-sloping in the prices of its own product. Monopolistic price-setting means that each firm equates marginal revenue to marginal costs. With labour being the only variable factor of production and constant returns, this means (see, for example, Varian, 1993, ch. 23)

$$P_i \left(1 - \frac{1}{\epsilon_i} \right) = \frac{W}{A_i} \tag{8.1}$$

where P_i is the output price of firm i, $\epsilon_i > 1$ is the absolute value of the price elasticity of the firm's demand, W is the wage rate common to all firms and A_i is labour productivity in firm i ($A_i = Y_i / N_i$). In general ϵ_i depends on P_i and on the prices of all competitors, foreign as well as domestic. This means that P_i depends not just on producer i's unit costs W/A_i but also on the prices of all competitors. However, a common simplification is to assume that ϵ_i is constant. Then P_i is a constant times unit wage costs. When productivity is also constant, relative prices between domestic firms are constant, and there is no aggregation problem. For illustrative purposes, aggregation is still usually done by assuming that $A_i = A$ and $\epsilon_i = \epsilon$ for all i. Then $P_i = P$ for all i, and we get

$$P = \frac{\epsilon}{\epsilon - 1} \frac{W}{A} \tag{8.2}$$

Note that prices depend on domestic costs only and are independent of the prices of competing imports. This is a consequence of the constant demand elasticity.

In empirical macro models it is quite common to allow both domestic costs and the prices of foreign competitors to influence the price of home goods. Price-setting equations are often of the form

$$P = B(W/A)^\alpha (EP_*)^{1-\alpha} \tag{8.3}$$

where $B > 0$ and $0 \leq \alpha \leq 1$ are constant parameters. The special case $\alpha = 1$ corresponds to (8.2) above, while $\alpha = 0$ corresponds to the case where domestic producers are price takers in the world market.

The price-setting equation (8.3) can be derived from the optimum condition (8.1) if we assume that the price elasticity depends on the different goods prices, as in

$$\epsilon_i = \frac{1}{1 - \Lambda(P_i/P)^{\lambda_1}(P_i/EP_*)^{\lambda_2}} \tag{8.4}$$

where Λ, λ_1 and λ_2 are positive constants. Thus, the elasticity is increasing in the firm's price relative to that of both domestic and foreign competitors (P and EP_* respectively). We may think of it in this way: if the firm's price is relatively low, it loses only a small fraction of its many customers by raising the price. If the price is already high, a price increase of the same relative size is a greater absolute price increase and will drive away a larger fraction of the now lower number of customers. For simplicity we have assumed the same function for all firms. The relative size of λ_1 and λ_2 indicates the relative importance of competition from foreign and domestic firms. The amount of competition depends on the number of competitors and on how close substitutes their products are to the products of firm i. Together with Λ the sum $\lambda_1 + \lambda_2$ determines how quickly the demand elasticity increases with the own price. If there are many close substitutes available, $\lambda_1 + \lambda_2$ may be high.

If we insert (8.4) in (8.1), we get

$$P_i \Lambda \left(\frac{P_i}{P}\right)^{\lambda_1} \left(\frac{P_i}{EP_*}\right)^{\lambda_2} = \frac{W}{A_i}$$

which can be solved to yield

$$P_i = \Lambda^{\frac{1}{1+\lambda_1+\lambda_2}}(W/A_i)^{\frac{1}{1+\lambda_1+\lambda_2}} P^{\frac{\lambda_1}{1+\lambda_1+\lambda_2}}(EP_*)^{\frac{\lambda_2}{1+\lambda_1+\lambda_2}}$$

To make aggregation easy, assume again that $A_i = A$ for all i. This gives the same price in every firm. By setting $P_i = P$ and solving for P we then get

$$P = \Lambda^{\frac{1}{1+\lambda_2}}(W/A)^{\frac{1}{1+\lambda_2}}(EP_*)^{\frac{\lambda_2}{1+\lambda_2}}$$

which is the same as (8.3), only with a different parametrization. Note that $\alpha = 1/(1 + \lambda_2)$, which means that strong competition from foreign firms implies a low weight on domestic costs in the price-setting equation. When λ_2 goes to infinity, α goes to zero, and we get the price taking behaviour of chapters 5 and 7.

If we do the same exercise for foreign firms, we get an equivalent price-setting equation for foreign goods:

$$P_* = B_*(W_*/A_*)^{\beta}(P/E)^{1-\beta} \tag{8.5}$$

Goldstein and Kahn (1985) surveys a number of studies of the pass-through of exchange rates to prices and of export pricing equations similar to (8.3) and (8.5). They show that both domestic unit costs and competitors' prices matter, but the estimated weights differ strongly from country to country and from study to study. Goldstein and Khan find a consistent pattern, though:

> The smaller and more open countries apparently base their export prices on competitors' export prices; conversely, the larger, less-open countries apparently use domestic factor costs or prices as the prime mover of export prices. (p. 1091).

In other words α is smaller for small countries, which must be because λ_2 is larger. This means that the demand elasticity, ϵ_i, increases rapidly when the producers in a small country raise their prices relative to those of foreign competitors. This is also what we should expect. Producers in small countries more often find their closest competitors abroad. Hence, for them λ_2 should be high.

The two pricing equations (8.3) and (8.5) are interdependent. They can be solved, for example, by inserting (8.5) in (8.3), to yield

$$
\begin{aligned}
P &= C(W/A)^{\alpha/(\alpha+\beta-\alpha\beta)}(EW_*/A_*)^{(\beta-\alpha\beta)/(\alpha+\beta-\alpha\beta)} \\
P_* &= C_*(W/AE)^{(\alpha-\alpha\beta)/(\alpha+\beta-\alpha\beta)}(W_*/A_*)^{\beta/(\alpha+\beta-\alpha\beta)}
\end{aligned} \tag{8.6}
$$

where C and C_* are constants which depend on all the parameters in the original equations. If $\beta = 1$, P_* depends only on W_*/A_*. Note that whenever both α and β are strictly positive, the weight on W/A is always greater for home goods than for foreign goods. Conversely, the weight on W_*/A_* is always greater for foreign goods. Thus, a producer's costs has a stronger effect on his own prices than on the prices of his competitors.

If $\alpha = \beta = 1$, we are back to the previous case where $P = W/A$ and $P_* = W_*/A_*$. This is what we would expect if there is strong specialization between countries. Then close substitutes mainly come from the same country, and the price ratio to foreign competitors is not so important for the demand elasticity. In the models with home and foreign goods, the foreign country is interpreted as the rest of the world. We should then expect that most foreign producers also find their closest competitors abroad. Thus, if the home country is small, we expect β to be close to one. Hence, a possible definition of the limiting case of a small open economy is that $\beta = 1$, or that it has no influence on the prices set by foreign producers. A country which is 'small' in this sense may still influence the prices set by its own producers. Sometimes we find small countries which are specialized in branches where they have significant shares of world output, and where these products constitute the bulk of their exports. Then we would expect to find α relatively high even for a small country.

From (8.6) we can also derive the real exchange rate in terms of producer prices:

$$R = \frac{EP_*}{P} = \frac{C_*}{C}\left(\frac{EW_*A}{WA_*}\right)^{\frac{\alpha\beta}{\alpha+\beta-\alpha\beta}} \tag{8.7}$$

R is a function of relative unit labour costs. The elasticity is between zero and one. In the small country case ($\beta = 1$) the elasticity is simply equal to α. The elasticity is zero if the domestic country is a price taker ($\alpha = 0$).

The price equations (8.6) can easily be appended to the models of chapter 6. The basic structure of the model is not fundamentally altered, and qualitatively most of the results are still valid. However, when $0 < \alpha < 1$ and $0 < \beta < 1$ the effect of a nominal depreciation on the real exchange rate and on the trade balance is smaller. Hence, a depreciation appears less expansionary. The likelihood that the overall effect of a depreciation is contractionary is increased also because a depreciation leads to an increase in P which has a negative effect on the real value of private wealth. Hence, there is a negative effect on consumer demand. If the overall effect of a depreciation is contractionary, a wage increase is expansionary. When the effect of E on aggregate demand is reduced, the gap between the *IS* and *ISFX* curves narrows. In this sense, the difference between fixed and floating exchange rates is reduced.

8.3 Pricing to market

Price discrimination between different national markets is profitable if firms face different price elasticities in different countries. For such price discrimination to be possible it must be costly or impossible to re-export the goods.

Fortunately the apparatus from section 8.2 is easily extended to allow for price discrimination. Let us first look at a domestic producer indexed by subscript i. He faces demand elasticities ϵ_h and ϵ_f in the home and foreign markets, respectively, and charges prices P_{ih} and P_{if} (measured in the domestic currency). The first-order condition for maximum profit is (see, for example, Varian, 1993, ch. 24)

$$P_{ih}\left(1 - \frac{1}{\epsilon_h}\right) = P_{if}\left(1 - \frac{1}{\epsilon_f}\right) = \frac{W}{A_i} \tag{8.8}$$

If the demand elasticities are constant but at different levels, the prices in the different markets will be proportional. The more interesting case is when the demand elasticities depend on prices, as in (8.4). By the same aggregation procedure, we then end up with price equations identical to (8.3), except that the parameters differ between markets. Hence,

$$P_{hj} = B_{hj}(W/A)^{\alpha_j}(EP_{fj})^{1-\alpha_j} \quad j = h, f \tag{8.9}$$

where the first subscript denotes the country of origin and the second the destination. A common presumption, which has some empirical support, is that the weight on unit costs is higher in the home market than for exports – i.e. that $\alpha_h > \alpha_f$. Since $\alpha = 1/(1 + \lambda_2)$, $\alpha_h > \alpha_f$ requires that λ_2 is greater for the foreign market. In other words, competition from foreign producers must be more intense in the foreign market. Why this should be the case is not obvious, but the cost of establishing a 'beachhead' discussed in section 8.4 may be one reason.

There are similar equations for the foreign currency prices charged by foreign producers:

$$P_{fj} = B_{fj}(W_*/A_*)^{\beta_j}(P_{hj}/E)^{1-\beta_j} \quad j = h, f \tag{8.10}$$

If foreign producers also experience more intense competition abroad than at home, $\beta_f > \beta_h$.

The four equations (8.9) and (8.10) determine the four goods prices given the wage rates, productivity and the exchange rate. Since the interdependence between prices is limited to each market, the system can be solved separately for the prices in the home and foreign markets. The solution is the same as (8.6), except that the weights on W/A and W_*/A_* differ from market to market:

$$P_{hj} = C_{hj}\left(\frac{W}{A}\right)^{a_{hj}}\left(\frac{EW_*}{A_*}\right)^{1-a_{hj}} \quad j = h, f$$

$$P_{fj} = C_{fj}\left(\frac{W}{EA}\right)^{a_{fj}}\left(\frac{W_*}{A_*}\right)^{1-a_{fj}} \quad j = h, f \tag{8.11}$$

where

$$a_{hj} = \frac{\alpha_j}{\alpha_j + \beta_j - \alpha_j\beta_j} \quad a_{fj} = \frac{\alpha_j(1-\beta_j)}{\alpha_j + \beta_j - \alpha_j\beta_j} \quad j = h, f \tag{8.12}$$

Suppose that $\alpha_h > \alpha_f$ and $\beta_f > \beta_h$ (competition with producers from a given country is always most intense in their home market). As can be seen from (8.12), a similar property then carries over to the reduced form coefficients: $a_{hh} > a_{hf}$ and $a_{fh} > a_{ff}$. For *each producer the weight on domestic costs is highest in his home market.*

The degree of exchange rate pass-through is defined as the elasticity of import prices with respect to the exchange rate. For the home country the degree of exchange rate pass-through in our model is $1 - a_{fh}$. Kreinin (1977), in a case study of the 1971 currency realignment, estimated the pass-through to the United States to be 50 per cent, to Germany 60 per cent, to Japan 70 per cent, to Canada and Belgium 90 per cent and to Italy 100 per cent. In their survey Goldberg and Knetter (1997) report that later studies have often found an average exchange rate pass-through of around 60 per cent to the United States, but that it varies greatly across different goods.

Kreinin's finding that pass-through in import prices is greater for small countries gets some support from Knetter (1989). It has a natural explanation within our model of price discrimination. In a small country there are fewer domestic firms which produce close substitutes to imports. Hence, the demand elasticity depends less on the relative price between imports and domestic products (λ_2 is smaller). The result is greater exchange rate pass-through. However, the finding of strong exchange rate pass-through for imports to small countries has not always been repeated. For example, Naug and Nymoen (1996) find that the exchange rate pass-through is 0.6 for manufactured imports to Norway.

Other studies attack the same subject from the point of view of export pricing. In this connection the results on export prices summarized by Goldstein and Kahn (1985) and referred to in section 8.2 are relevant. As will be recalled, they claimed that the smaller, more open economies base their export prices on competitors' prices, while the larger, more closed economies base their export prices more on domestic costs. Knetter (1993) finds that destination-specific price adjustments offset 48 per cent of the impact of exchange rate changes on price in the buyers' currency for Japanese exports, 36 per cent for German and UK exports and 0 per cent for US exports. However, he attributes the difference between countries more to a different commodity composition of exports than to country size. The study by Marston (1990) of Japanese exports gives a direct measure of the degree to which exchange rate changes create differences between prices in different markets. He estimates the elasticity of the ratio between Japanese export and home market prices with respect to the exchange rate ($a_{hh} - a_{hf}$ in our model) to be between 30 and 100 per cent for different goods. The conclusion is then that in the case of Japan domestic costs play a much greater role for price-setting in the home market than in the export markets.

In earlier models the real exchange rate in terms of producer price indices, the relative price of foreign goods and the terms of trade have been the same. This is no longer the case. The relative price of foreign goods is EP_{fh}/P_{hh} at home, EP_{ff}/P_{hf} abroad. Both relative prices can be expressed as functions of relative unit labour costs, as in (8.7). Naturally the parameters differ between the home and the foreign market. However, as long as all αs and βs are between zero and one, the elasticities of the relative prices with respect to relative unit labour costs are also between zero and one. This means that the two relative prices always move in the same direction. Hence, the difference from chapter 6 is more quantitative than qualitative.

The *terms of trade* is the price of imports relative to exports, or

$$\frac{EP_{fh}}{P_{hf}} = \frac{C_{fh}}{C_{hf}} \left(\frac{EW_*A}{WA_*} \right)^{a_{hf}-a_{fh}} \tag{8.13}$$

In the exponent a_{fh} is the elasticity of our import prices (measured in foreign currency) with respect to the exchange rate, while a_{hf} is the elasticity of our export prices (measured in foreign currency). In chapter 6 the assumption was that $a_{fh} = 0$ and $a_{hf} = 1$, which implies that a devaluation raises the relative price of imports (worsens the terms of trade). In general a devaluation worsens the terms of trade if $a_{hf} > a_{fh}$. This is always the case when producers place more weight on their own costs than on competitors' prices – i.e. when $a_{hf} > 0.5$ and $a_{fh} < 0.5$. For a large country which bases its export prices mainly on domestic costs, while it receives imports that are priced to market, both a_{hf} and a_{fh} could be close to one. This means that its terms of trade are not much affected by the exchange rate. Nor is it much affected for a small country which is close to being a price taker in all markets. In that case both a_{hf} and a_{fh} are close to zero. A devaluation *improves* the terms of trade if $a_{hf} < a_{fh}$. This may happen if the home country is small, exports standardized goods to a highly competitive market, and imports finished goods with close domestic substitutes. It is then close to being a price taker in the export market, which means that a_{hf} is close to zero. Presumably its imports are priced to market to a considerable extent. In this case a devaluation reduces the price of imports relative to exports in spite of the fact that the relative price of foreign goods is increased in both markets. If a devaluation improves the terms of trade, there is no need for the Marshall–Lerner condition.

Pricing to market combined with nominal wage rigidity can explain two observed phenomena: (i) A country's price level sometimes appears to be less sensitive to devaluations than one would expect on the basis of its import share. (ii) Trade flows sometimes also seem to be quite insensitive to devaluations. A high degree of pricing to market, means that α_f and β_h are close to zero, α_h and β_f close to one. This makes the prices in each market depend primarily on the costs of the producers who reside there, while the exchange rate has little influence. Since nominal prices even on imports are not much affected by exchange rates, the consumer price index is not much affected either. Since relative prices in each market remain fairly constant, trade flows need not be much affected either. Where exchange rate changes show up in this case is in the terms of trade. Measured in domestic currency, the price of exports rises, the price of imports is fairly unchanged. A devaluation thus improves the terms of trade.

The extent of pricing to market is probably greatest in countries which produce many close substitutes to the commodities they import. In such cases the effect of a devaluation on the price level is likely to be small. However, this does not necessarily mean that the effect on the imported quantities is small.

Without price discrimination we defined a small country as a country where $\beta = 1$ – i.e. as a country which has no influence on the prices set by foreign competitors. With price discrimination we have two βs. A natural suggestion is then to define a small country as a country for which $\beta_f = 1$. This means that a small country is a country which has no influence on the prices set by foreign producers *in foreign markets*. A country which is small in this sense is an insignificant competitor in foreign markets, but may still be significant in its home market, in the sense that $\beta_h < 1$.

Since there is a unique relationship between all relative prices and relative unit wage costs, the models of chapter 6 can easily be extended to allow for price discrimination. The recipe is the same as the one that was given at the end of section 8.2, and the consequences similar. Increasing marginal costs of production, as in chapters 5 and 7, can also be included by replacing A and A_* with marginal productivities that depend on output. With an appropriate disaggregation into sectors we are then on the track to a model which encompasses all the cases discussed previously.

8.4 Customer markets, 'beach-head' effects and multinational firms

An important difference between the long-run equilibria in chapters 6 and 7 is that in the former aggregate demand had effects on relative prices, while in the latter relative prices were determined by the supply side alone. In chapter 6, and in the models with monopolistic competition in the present chapter, increases in domestic production costs are shifted to the prices of traded goods partly or fully. A small country can go on producing forever even if it has higher costs than other countries.

This may be too optimistic. Is it realistic to assume that the monopoly power exploited by the producers is permanent, or is it only temporary? Is the monopoly power truly national, or can the firms continue to exploit their monopoly power while moving production to countries with lower costs?

When products are differentiated, what prevents firms in countries with lower wage costs from producing exactly the same good? Among the standard reasons offered are patents, lack of know-how, lack of established brand name and the need to invest in physical capital that is specialized for the commodity in question. Patents are temporary. The other obstacles have in common the fact that they can be overcome by investment. Usually they are also a product of previous investment. If the capital needs to be renewed, the monopoly power is temporary. It is bounded, since if cost differences become too high, producers with lower wage costs will find it profitable to enter the market.

Furthermore, domestic producers can choose to move production abroad. Patents, brand names and know-how are then less of an obstacle, and specialized machinery can be moved at a cost. If the owners remain residents of the home country, their monopoly power still contributes to national income. If the accounts are kept properly, their monopoly rents will be recorded as property revenue from abroad. However, the direct relationship between product demand and domestic output is cut. The demand for domestic labour must be distinguished from the demand for the brands and designs owned by domestic firms. As an extreme case, one can envisage a world where owners of brands and designs farm out production to whoever offers to do it in the cheapest way. As far as the determination of domestic output of traded goods is concerned, the price taker model of chapters 5 and 7 may then be better suited than the monopolistic competition model.

In the macroeconomic literature the above arguments have so far not been extensively treated. However, there are two strands of literature – customer markets and 'beach-head' effects – that explicitly allow the degree of market power to be different in the short and the long run. They will be treated below.

Market power can also be had from the ownership of a significant share of the world supply of a natural resource. When the resource is found inside the country, the market power is then truly national, and the country has market power even if the industry in question is competitive. A crucial distinction is between countries which in the long run can balance their current accounts with natural resource based industries only, and those which have to engage also in other, footloose industries. In the former a whole range of different real wages may be compatible with long-run equilibrium. This holds irrespectively of whether the countries have monopoly power, since higher wage costs can just be absorbed in lower resource rents.

For countries which also depend on footloose industries where they have no long-run monopoly power the situation is entirely different. In those countries there will be a single real wage which gives capital the international real rate of return. This determines the long-run equilibrium real wage in those industries independently of aggregate demand, as we have seen in chapters 5 and 7.

When there are important externalities in production, these may create a kind of national market power similar to the one given by natural resources. If there are positive externalities between firms which are located together, individual firms need not have incentives to move to other locations even if it would be profitable for the whole group of firms if everybody moved together. There may also then be a range of possible long-run equilibria with different real wages.

Customer markets

The basic idea of the literature on customer markets is this: firms have a customer base which is inherited from the past. Customers are to some extent loyal to their suppliers, or at least they do not check the prices of alternative suppliers too often. However, if a firm charges higher prices than its competitors, customers gradually find out and switch to other suppliers. In this way monopoly power is greater in the short run than in the long run.[84]

The way it works can be learned from figure 8.1. The variables on the axis are the firm's output y_i and price p_i. The short-run demand curve, given the customer base the firm has inherited from the past, is D. The corresponding marginal revenue curve is MR. The price charged by the firm's competitors is p, the firm's marginal production costs are MC. If the firm maximizes short-run profits, it charges the monopoly price

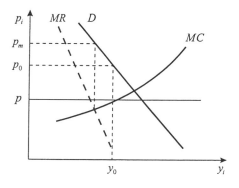

Figure 8.1 Price-setting in customer markets.

p_m, which makes marginal cost equal to marginal revenue. However, since this price is higher than p, the firm then gradually loses customers. A firm which values future profit should then set a somewhat lower price – for example, p_0. This price is still above the price charged by competitors and above marginal costs. Customers are still lost, but not as rapidly as with p_m. The advantage of the lower price is a larger customer base to be exploited in the future.

However, as long as the firm charges more than its competitors, its customer base shrinks. The short-run demand curve moves to the left, as illustrated in figure 8.2. The firm will then find it optimal to reduce its price from p_0 to p_1, then to p_2 and so on. All the time the margin between p_i and p is reduced. In the end, the price approaches the competitive level p, and output is where price equals marginal cost (y). Thus, in the long run the firm behaves like a price taker.

'Customer markets' provides a bridge between the different approaches in the earlier chapters. For a small open economy monopolistic price-setting may be relevant for the short run, price taking for the long run.

In customer markets the real interest rate is important for price-setting. A higher interest rate means that the gain from having a larger customer base in the future is discounted more heavily. The firms then raise their prices towards the short-run monopoly price. This is a central element in Phelps' (1994) theory of 'structural slumps' where the increased margins over wage costs charged by the producers inter-act with a wage curve of the kind we are going to describe in section 8.5 to produce an equilibrium with lower employment.

'Beach-head' effects

The focus in this approach, pioneered by Baldwin (1988) and Dixit (1989), is on the need to invest in order to be present in a market. Suppose a firm in country A wants to sell its products to country B. In order to get into country B it may have to

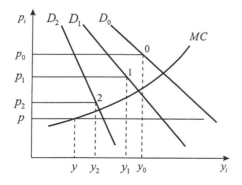

Figure 8.2 Price movement over time in a customer market.

invest in a sales organization there. The investment may include physical capital, training of employees, market research, etc. In order to build a brand name and a reputation in the new country it may have to invest in advertising. To begin with it may also have to sell with a loss in order to build up a customer base, as in the models of customer markets. The essence is that to capture the 'beach-head' from which to invade a new market is costly. An important point is that the costs are lumpy: the firm must make a minimum investment to 'win the beach-head'. The costs are also irreversible.

The need to invest gives those who are already in a market a protected position, which they to some extent can exploit. Hence, there is some limited scope for mono-polistic price-setting. However, the main focus in the beach-head literature has been on the effects of exchange rate movements on trade flows. Suppose there is a small real appreciation. Perhaps it is not expected to last very long either. Imports may then not be much affected, because foreign firms do not find it worthwhile to incur the invest-ment costs necessary to get into the market. Exporters who have already incurred the fixed costs of entering a foreign market will also remain there. The conclusion is then that small exchange rate changes have little effect on trade flows.

However, if the appreciation is large and expected to last for some time, many foreign firms will find it worthwhile to invest in beach-heads in our country. This could mean a surge in imports that is proportionally larger than the size of the appre-ciation. Furthermore, if there is also a fixed cost to being continually present in a country, a large appreciation may induce proportionally more domestic producers to withdraw from the foreign market.

The conclusion that large appreciations have proportionally larger effects can be criticized. Initially there may be a number of foreign firms which are on the verge of deciding to break into the market. A small appreciation can be enough to make them go for it. Thus, even when the appreciation is small, some firms can find it profitable to invest in a beach-head. However, Baldwin and Krugman (1989) argues that there is a difference between small and large appreciations that does not get smoothed away when there are many industries.

When there are fixed costs of entry, the effects of changes in real exchange rates on trade flows may depend strongly on how long they are expected to last. Also exchange rate uncertainty by itself reduces the response of trade flows to exchange rates (see Dixit, 1989). When there are fixed costs, uncertainty makes firms more reluctant to enter new markets, and to leave old markets. They will adopt a wait-and-see strategy. Krugman (1989) argues that the high volatility of floating exchange rates has substan-tially reduced the response of trade flows to exchange rates, and hence made exchange rate flexibility less useful for policy purposes.

As Dixit (1989) shows, the degree of exchange rate pass-through can be close to zero when exchange rate movements are within the interval where there are no entries or exits. The pass-through can be close to one when entries or exits take place. Exchange rate movements that are known to be temporary can have long-lasting effects on trade if they trigger entries or exits.

8.5 Wage bargaining: the wedge

The purpose of this section is to sketch how the basic model from chapter 6 can be extended to allow for monopolistic competition (as in section 8.2 of the present chapter) and for wage bargaining (as in section 5.9). For simplicity, and for comparability with chapter 6, we assume that the capital stock is constant. Price discrimination could have been included without changing the qualitative conclusions.

An important difference from section 5.9 is that there is now a *wedge* between consumer and producer real wages. The producer real wage is $\omega = W/P$, the consumer real wage $W(1 - \tau)/P_c$ where τ is a (proportional) tax rate on labour income and P_c is the consumer price index; $P_c = P^a(EP_*)^{1-a}$, $0 < a < 1$. The wedge, θ, is the ratio between the real wage from the point of view of the producer and the consumer:

$$\theta = \frac{W/P}{W(1 - \tau)/P_c} = \frac{P_c}{P}\frac{1}{1 - \tau} = \left(\frac{EP_*}{P}\right)^{1-a}\frac{1}{1 - \tau} = R^{1-a}(1 - \tau)^{-1}$$

Thus, the wedge depends positively on the relative price of imports and on the tax rate. The consumer real wage can be expressed as ω/θ. An increase in the wedge reduces the consumer real wage for a given producer real wage.

The model of wage-setting is the same as in section 5.9 except for one modification. Workers are supposed to care about the consumer real wage, which means that the utility of an employed union member and the reference utility are, respectively, $v(\omega/\theta)$ and $v_0(\Omega/\theta)$, where Ω is the average real wage in the economy. Since we neglect real capital, we can write the (real) profit function simply as $\Pi(\omega)$.

If, as in section 5.9, we write down the Nash product, derive the first-order condition and let $\Omega = \omega$, we find (compare (5.60), and recall that $\Pi'(\omega) = N$)

$$\beta\frac{v'(\omega/\theta)\omega/\theta}{v(\omega/\theta) - v_0(\omega/\theta, U)} = (1 - \beta)\frac{\omega N}{\Pi(\omega)} \tag{8.14}$$

This yields a wage curve which depends on the wedge. It is often claimed that an increase in the wedge raises wage pressure. However, this does not necessarily follow from our theory.

The effect of an increase in the wedge depends on how it affects the union side of (8.14), which can conveniently be rewritten:

$$\frac{v'(\omega/\theta)\omega/\theta}{v(\omega/\theta) - v_0(\omega/\theta, U)} = \frac{v'(\omega/\theta)\omega/\theta}{v(\omega/\theta)}\frac{v(\omega/\theta)}{v(\omega/\theta) - v_0(\omega/\theta, U)} \tag{8.15}$$

The first term on the right-hand side is the elasticity of the utility function. The second term is the utility of an employed member relative to the difference between this and the reference utility. We do not know how either of the two terms are affected by ω/θ. As for the last term, the numerator is obviously increased by an increase in ω/θ. Both terms in the denominator also increase, and whether the fraction goes up or down, we cannot tell. An interesting special case is when the income elasticities of v and v_0 are constant and equal. In that case ω/θ drops out of the expression above. The union side of the wage equation is then unaffected by the wedge – and, hence, the wage curve is independent of the wedge.

The presumption that an increase in the wedge raises wage pressure could be due to a false generalization from micro to the aggregate level. Suppose the elasticity of v is constant, so the first term on the right-hand side of (8.15) is constant. From the point of view of the local union v_0 is given from outside. An increase in θ lowers $v(\omega/\theta)$. This obviously raises the second term on the right-hand side of (8.15), and thus the whole expression. For a given v_0 an increase in the wedge causes more aggressive wage demands. The main cause of the ambiguity in the aggregate effect is that an increase in the wedge not only reduces v, but also the reference utility v_0. A reduction in the reference utility reduces wage pressure.

Bargaining models which produce a positive effect of the wedge on wage pressure usually include an assumption which serves to reduce the dependency of v_0 on θ. One example is that $v = (\omega/\theta)^\sigma$ while $v_0 = q(\omega/\theta)^\sigma + (1 - q)b^\sigma$ where b is an untaxed unemployment benefit that is indexed to consumer prices; q, which depends on U, is the probability of reemployment for a union member who loses his job; and σ is a positive constant. As can be seen from (8.15), this makes wage pressures increase with θ. The reason is that an increased wedge makes unemployment relatively more attractive.

A closer look at the employer side of (8.14) is also warranted. Assume as in section 8.2 that average labour productivity, A, is constant. The ratio of wage costs to profits, which measures 'employer resistance' to wage increases (8.14), is then

$$\frac{\omega N}{\Pi(\omega)} = \frac{\omega N}{Y - \omega N} = \frac{\omega N}{AN - \omega N} = \frac{\omega}{A - \omega} \tag{8.16}$$

Thus, the right-hand side of (8.14) is an increasing function of ω.

The wage curve defined by (8.14) can be written $\omega = g(U, \theta(R, \tau))$ – or, if we take account of that U is determined by Y and θ by R and τ:

$$\omega = g(Y, R, \tau) \tag{8.17}$$

As usual, $g_Y > 0$. For the reasons explained above, the signs of g_R and g_τ are ambiguous, but in the sequel we investigate the consequences of the hypothesis that $g_R > 0$ and $g_\tau > 0$.

The price-setting equation (8.3) yields another relationship between ω and R. From section 8.2

$$P = B(W/A)^\alpha (EP_*)^{1-\alpha}$$

By dividing with $P = P^\alpha P^{1-\alpha}$ on both sides:

$$1 = B(W/AP)^\alpha (EP_*/P)^{1-\alpha} = B(\omega/A)^\alpha R^{1-\alpha}$$

When this is solved for ω, we get

$$\omega = AB^{-1/\alpha} R^{-(1-\alpha)/\alpha} \equiv \omega(R) \qquad \omega' < 0 \tag{8.18}$$

Price-setting thus implies a negative relation between ω and R, which we write as $\omega(R)$. Given the way prices are set, a higher producer real wage can come only through a real appreciation.

Just as a union wage equation replaced the Phillips curve in section 5.9, the Phillips curve in chapter 6 can be replaced by

$$\frac{\dot{\omega}}{\omega} = \gamma\left[g(Y, R, \tau) - \omega(R)\right] \tag{8.19}$$

Real wage growth depends positively on the discrepancy between the equilibrium real wage, $g(Y, R, \tau)$, and the actual real wage, $\omega(R)$. There are then some significant changes both to the long-run equilibrium and the dynamics.

In addition to (8.17) and (8.18) the long-run equilibrium must satisfy the conditions for zero private saving and for a balanced current account from section 6.6

$$C(Y - \rho_* W'_* - G, -W'_* - W_g, \rho_*) = Y - \rho_* W'_* - G \tag{8.20}$$

$$X(R, Y, Y_*) - \rho_* W'_* = 0 \tag{8.21}$$

There are four variables to be determined in the long-run equilibrium: W'_*, R, ω and Y. In chapter 6 both Y and ω were in effect given exogenously, the latter because the pricing equation sets it equal to productivity times a fixed mark-up.

In chapter 6 the long-run equilibrium could be solved recursively. This is no longer the case. In order to find the solution one can take as a starting point that the wage curve and the price equation represent aggregate supply, while the two other equations represent the demand side. The supply equations (8.17) and (8.18) can be solved to give one supply-side relation between the real exchange rate and output. Similarly, the savings and the current account equations (8.20) and (8.21) can be solved to give one demand-side relation between output and the real exchange rate. Then we can combine the two to find the full equilibrium. For convenience we use the names 'supply' and 'demand' for the two curves, although they are of course not the standard type of demand and supply curves.

First to the supply side. Figure 8.3 depicts the wage-setting curve (8.17) and the price equation (8.18) in a diagram with R and ω on the axes. Behind the increasing wage-setting curve is the assumption that $g_R > 0$, or that a real depreciation increases wage pressure. The price-setting curve is falling, because a real depreciation means an increase in the margin between price and production costs. An increase in Y shifts the wage-setting curve upwards. Since unemployment is reduced, the union wage pressures increase. The equilibrium moves from A to B. The result is a real appreciation. The relative price of home goods increases. From the supply side there is thus a falling relation between output and the real exchange rate, which is carried over to figure 8.4. Since $R = EP_*/P$, the falling curve in figure 8.4 shows that the supply side responds to an increased demand for output by setting higher prices on home goods.

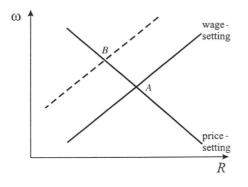

Figure 8.3 Price- and wage-setting.

On the demand side the relationship between Y and R is slightly more complicated. This derives from the fact that according to (8.20) an increase in Y leads to a lower foreign debt. When we then go to (8.21), Y has two opposing effects on the current account. The reduction in foreign debt improves the current account. On the other hand, the direct effect of Y on the trade balance worsens the current account. The net effect is ambiguous and, thus, we do not know whether a real appreciation or a real depreciation is required to keep the balance at zero. If the direct effect dominates, we need a real depreciation, and this case is shown in figure 8.4, where the curve representing the demand side is upward sloping. When figure 8.4 looks like the inverse of the usual AS–AD diagram, it is because R is inversely related to P.

The models of long-run equilibrium here and in Layard, Nickell and Jackman (1991, ch. 8) are similar. The wage- and price-setting curves are the same, except that in Layard, Nickell and Jackman the price-setting curve also depends on the level of output (because of increasing costs). The representation of the demand side in Layard, Nickell and Jackman is simplified. Their long-run equilibrium condition is just that trade should be balanced, which means that they neglect wealth accumulation.

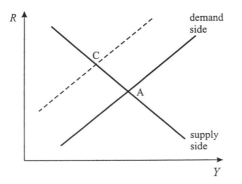

Figure 8.4 Equilibrium with wage
bargaining and monopolistic competition.

Figure 8.4 also illustrates the effect of an inward shift in the demand curve. Such a shift could be caused by a negative shift in net exports, or in savings. Both worsen the current account, and for any given Y a real depreciation is needed to restore balance. The equilibrium moves from A to C. Thus, the final effect is a real depreciation, which is the same result as in chapter 6. The new result is that output declines. The reason is that the real depreciation increases the wedge, and this increases wage pressure. Higher unemployment is thus required to restore balance in the labour market and prevent wages from rising further.

Increased union wage pressure shifts the wage-setting curve in figure 8.3 upwards. As figure 8.3 shows, this raises ω and reduces R for a given Y. Thus, the supply curve shifts downwards, as illustrated in figure 8.5. The equilibrium there moves from A to D, which means that increased wage pressure results in a real appreciation and lower output in the long run. This time the effect on output (and employment) is in line with what we found in section 5.9. The new result is that increased wage pressure actually has a lasting positive effect on the real wage, since a reduction in R means an increase in ω. The consumer real wage increases even more because when there is a real appreciation it means that the wedge is reduced.

The reason for the different result is that the long-run demand curve for labour is not infinitely elastic as in section 5.9. There the infinite elasticity was owing to the combination of infinitely elastic output demand from the world market and an endogenous capital stock. Since the demand for home goods is not infinitely elastic, making the capital stock endogenous is not enough to give a constant real wage. If the country has market power, it is possible for more militant unions to raise the real wage permanently, but at the cost of a higher equilibrium rate of unemployment. However, the conclusion depends on the fact that the home country also has market power in the long run. If its market power erodes over time for the reasons described in section 8.4, we are back to the results from section 5.9.

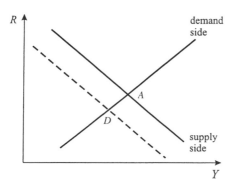

Figure 8.5 The effect of increased wage pressure.

One possible cause of increased wage pressure is an increase in the wedge owing to an increased tax rate. This raises the real producer wage and leads to lower output and employment. However, since the wedge has also increased, the consumer real wage may go down. Another possible cause of an increase in the wedge is an unfavourable exogenous change in relative prices in international markets. The oil shocks of 1973–4 and 1989–90 increased the wedge in oil-importing countries, and it has been claimed that this was a major cause of the increase in unemployment that followed (see, for example, Bruno and Sachs, 1985).

At this point, a warning is warranted. When we see a change in τ as just another shift in wage pressure, we neglect the fact that the tax rate may have an effect on aggregate demand. The hidden assumption is that this effect is removed by appropriate changes in other taxes and transfers. A similar warning is warranted against the analysis of a demand shift. The price elasticity of demand is a crucial variable in determining the coefficients in the price equation. When there is a shift in the demand functions X or C, this may also shift the demand elasticity, and thus shift the supply curve. These two examples illustrate a general problem with shift analysis in models with monopolistic competition and wage bargaining. Supply and demand becomes intertwined in a complicated way. The only remedy for this is to make structural models where the relationship between the parameters that enter the supply and demand curves is explicit.

The special case where domestic producers set their prices only on the basis of domestic costs deserves a comment. Recall that this is the case where the price elasticity of demand is constant and $\alpha = 1$. The pricing equation (8.18) then uniquely determines the producer real wage, ω. In figure 8.3 the price-setting curve is horizontal. Wage bargaining has no long-run effect on the producer real wage. This is the same result as in chapter 5, but for different reasons. Then it was owing to capital mobility. Now it is owing to monopolistic price-setting, constant productivity and a constant demand elasticity. However, other results still differ. As above, increased union wage pressure still leads to a real appreciation, a higher consumer real wage and lower employment.

Now to stability. The basic structure of the dynamic model is as in section 6.6 with one dynamic equation for foreign debt and one for prices or wages. The latter can most favourably be expressed as an equation for the real exchange rate. From (8.18)

$$\frac{\dot{R}}{R} = -\frac{\alpha}{1-\alpha}\frac{\dot{\omega}}{\omega}$$

Insert into this the equation for real wage growth (8.19), and you get

$$\frac{\dot{R}}{R} = \frac{\alpha}{1-\alpha}\gamma\big[g(Y, R, \tau) - \omega(R)\big] \tag{8.22}$$

Stability depends on the feedback effects from the levels R and W_* to their rates of growth. Qualitatively, three out of four feedbacks are the same here as in chapter 6. The equation for the accumulation of foreign debt is unaffected by the supply side. The level of foreign debt affects wage formation only through output, as before. The difference is in the feedback from the price level to price growth – or, as we have written it now, from the level of the real exchange rate to its rate of growth. Looking at (8.22), R has an effect through Y, which is the same effect that was included in section 6.6. In addition there are two new and more direct effects. When $g_R > 0$, both are stabilizing. The effect through $\omega(R)$ is the same stabilizing effect from the level of the real wage to real wage growth that we found in the union model of section 5.9. The new effect through g comes in because a depreciated real exchange rate means a relatively high wedge and, hence, leads to upward pressure on wages. As wages rise, the real exchange rate appreciates. The upshot is that wage bargaining in this case promotes stability.

As the surveys by Layard, Nickell and Jackman (1991, ch. 4.7) and Bean (1994) make clear, the empirical evidence in favour of the hypothesis that the wedge shifts the long-run wage curve is weak at best. Thus, there are reasons to doubt that the wedge has any effect on unemployment and the real wage in long-run equilibrium. However, many studies find relatively large short-run effects of changes in the wedge on real wage growth. A satisfactory representation of such effects requires a more complicated dynamic model.

Part 3

Policy issues

9 International interactions

In the earlier chapters we have focused on a single open economy. Now it is time to look at how countries interact in the world economy. Again we start at the financial side and take a look at the international monetary system in section 9.1. In section 9.2 we go on to the real side and study shock transmission in a model based on chapter 6. Then we take a brief look at the arguments for international policy coordination in section 9.3, before we conclude (section 9.4) with some comments on the theory of optimal currency areas and on monetary unions.

9.1 The international monetary system

An exchange rate is a *relative price between two currencies*. Thus, both central banks cannot set the exchange rate independently. Furthermore, they both affect the exchange rate through interest rates and interventions. There has to be some division of labour between central banks; this division of labour, which must be based on some mutual understanding, is the international monetary system.[85] It has taken many different forms during the twentieth century.

In the portfolio model of chapter 1 the foreign central bank played no explicit role. Before we go on, it is useful to extend the balance sheet from chapter 1 by dividing the foreign sector in two: the foreign private sector (subscript p_*) and the foreign government/central bank (subscript g_*), as is done in table 9.1. We have also included one new asset, gold (G), in order to be able to discuss the gold standard and other commodity standards. Otherwise, the symbols are the same as in chapter 1. For simplicity it is assumed that gold is held only by the central banks. The price of gold in terms of kroner is E_1, in terms of dollars E_2.

Private sector behaviour can be described by the same portfolio demand functions as in chapter 1:

$$\frac{EF_p}{P} = f(r, W_p) \tag{9.1}$$

$$\frac{F_{p*}}{P_*} = W_{p*} - b(r, W_{p*}) \tag{9.2}$$

Let us first neglect gold. Equilibrium in the foreign exchange market requires

$$F_g + F_p + F_{g*} + F_{p*} = 0 \tag{9.3}$$

Table 9.1   *Net financial assets, by sector*

	Domestic		Foreign		
Assets	Government	Private	Government	Private	Sum
Kroner assets	B_g	B_p	B_{g*}	B_{p*}	0
Dollar assets	F_g	F_p	F_{g*}	F_{p*}	0
Gold	G_g	0	G_{g*}	0	$\bar{G}$
Real wealth	W_g	W_p	W_{g*}	W_{p*}	$E_1\bar{G}/P$

or, after inserting from the portfolio demand functions,

$$F_g + F_{g*} + \frac{P}{E}f(r, W_p) + P_*\left[W_{p*} - b(r, W_{p*})\right] = 0 \qquad (9.4)$$

Earlier we have used this equation to determine either F_g or E. However, there is now a new variable, F_{g*}, in the equation. We have two countries, but only one exchange rate E. Interventions by either country (F_g and F_{g*}) affect the exchange rate symmetrically. This illustrates two general features of international monetary systems based entirely on national paper money. Since the exchange rate is a relative price, the number of independent exchange rates is one less than the number of countries *('the n − 1 problem')*, and interventions by all countries affect the exchange rate equally. In the past we have assumed that the home country can fix the exchange rate unilaterally. Implicitly we have also assumed that foreign governments do not intervene by buying or selling our currency. Thus, B_{g*} has been assumed constant, and in the short run this also implies that F_{g*} is constant.

In a *pure float* no country intervenes in the foreign exchange market. In the short run both F_g and F_{g*} are constant, and (9.4) determines E. No country has any target for E. Changes in interest rates affect the exchange rate symmetrically.

If the exchange rate is fixed, we can ask four key questions: What is the exchange rate fixed in relation to? Who sets the exchange rate? In what form are foreign exchange reserves kept? Who is responsible for the necessary interventions? Depending on the answers to these questions, we can distinguish three prototypes which cover most fixed rate paper standards which have been practised.

In a *key currency system* the $n − 1$ problem is solved by singling out one key country. The remaining $n − 1$ countries, the periphery, fix their exchange rates relative to the key currency. Each peripheral country keeps reserves in the key currency and buys or sells the key currency in the amounts necessary to defend its own exchange rate. The key country does not intervene, and does not need to have foreign exchange reserves. The historical example which comes closest to a key currency system is the Bretton

Woods system in which most countries participated from 1945 to 1971, and where the US dollar was the key currency.[86]

In the Bretton Woods system changes in exchange rates were in principle a matter to be decided collectively in the International Monetary Fund (IMF), the organization set up to oversee the system. However, nations who wished to change their exchange rates were usually allowed to do so. In principle, the exchange rate between dollar and gold was fixed, and the United States kept gold reserves. However, since there was a mutual understanding between the majority of the participating central banks that they would not exchange their dollar reserves for gold, gold played no significant role in the day-to-day operations of the system.

Our discussion of fixed exchange rates in earlier chapters fits a peripheral country in a key currency system, but not the key country. The latter does not have to worry about its foreign exchange reserve. This means greater freedom in setting interest rates. If the key country lowers its interest rate, it does not lose reserves. Instead the peripheral countries get increased reserves. Similarly, a current account deficit in the key country does not mean that it loses reserves. Instead the peripheral countries, which have a corresponding current account surplus, get increased reserves.[87] Thus, a key currency system confers an advantage on the centre. However, in return for its greater freedom in monetary policy, the key country is expected to provide price stability. This then translates into price stability also in the periphery if the exchange rates are kept constant. The pursuit of price stability then constrains monetary policy in the centre in much the same way as the pursuit of fixed exchanges rates constrains monetary policy in the periphery. This removes some of the advantage that the key country would otherwise have. The Bretton Woods system broke down after there had been an increase in inflation in the United States.

A country may adopt a *unilateral peg*. This is not very different from being the peripheral country in a key currency system. The country can choose to peg to a single foreign currency, or to a basket of currencies. The currency composition of reserves does not need to match the currency composition of the basket. Because of the $n-1$ problem, not all countries can adopt a unilateral peg simultaneously. If many countries peg to different baskets, it is necessary to check that the exchange rates are consistent. Unilateral pegs are mainly an option for relatively small countries. Other countries may choose not to care, and the $n-1$ problem is then solved implicitly. After the final breakdown of the Bretton Woods system in 1973 the major economies have had floating exchange rates *vis-à-vis* each other. In this environment unilateral pegs by small countries have been common and readily accepted. However, if one of the major countries had tried to peg *vis-à-vis* another major country, that could hardly have been done without explicit agreement.

A third possibility is a *symmetric multilateral peg*. Then a number of countries jointly agree on a set of exchange rate parities. There is also a joint responsibility for interventions. The currencies in the club are used as reserves, possibly together with other currencies. The best example of a symmetric multilateral peg is the Exchange Rate

Mechanism (ERM) in which a varying number of members of the European Union participated from 1978 to 1998.[88]

In principle, two countries which cooperate can always beat speculators and keep the exchange rate fixed between them. Together they have unlimited reserves. Suppose the exchange rate is fixed between France and Germany, and that speculators sell French francs in order to buy German Marks. The French National Bank may run out of D-Mark reserves, but the German Bundesbank never will. Literally it can print more D-Marks if necessary. Thus, if there is speculation against the French franc, the two central banks can create vast profits for themselves by keeping a positive interest rate differential in favour of francs. Speculators who move from francs to D-Marks then lose interest income, and the central banks gain. Clearly, a multilateral peg is unbreakable when all the central banks involved are fully committed to defend it without limits. A multilateral peg should thus have an unusually high degree of credibility. This should lead to high capital mobility (see chapter 2) and near-equalization of interest rates. At least this should happen if exchange rates are never adjusted, as for most ERM members in the 1988–91 period. If the exchange rates are adjusted now and then, as in the early ERM period (1978–88), interest rates must of course differ.

As the breakdown of the ERM in 1992–93 showed, however, it is difficult to establish an unlimited commitment to fixed parities, and systems are not always as symmetric as they appear on paper. Suppose in our example that the Bundesbank bought a large amount of French francs. If France actually devalued, the Bundesbank would suffer a large capital loss, and France obtain a similar gain. The mutual obligation to intervene was limited in ERM. In practice this meant that the burden of intervention fell more than proportionally on the countries whose currencies were weak – i.e. in danger of devaluing.

An interesting question is: Who sets the general level of interest rates in a multilateral peg? The answer to this is closely related to how the burden of defending the parities by interventions is distributed. The less responsibility for intervening, the more freedom in setting the domestic interest rate (cf. the key currency system). Suppose there are only two countries in the system. Assume that the costs of intervention are shared equally between the two countries, and that there are no effective constraints on the size of interventions. Capital mobility is imperfect. Initially interest rates are equal. Then the larger country raises its interest rate, while the smaller country keeps its rate constant. This leads investors to sell the currency of the smaller country, and the two central banks have to buy. Owing to the interest rate differential, the central banks lose from this. This loss is shared equally. The government of the larger country can better afford the loss, however. The larger country can thus afford to give greater priority to the domestic effects of interest rate changes, while the smaller country is forced to give higher priority to the foreign exchange market. In this way countries get an influence over interest rates which is proportional to country size.

Size is less important, however, if the responsibility for interventions rests mainly with the country with the weak currency. Instead the system is then biased in favour of high interest rates. A country which raises its interest rate gets a strong currency, and does not have to intervene. Instead the other countries are left with the choice of either to intervene or to raise their own interest rates. A country which lowers its interest rate, however, will have to intervene and cannot expect help from the others. The upshot is that the country wanting the highest interest rate (corrected for expected depreciation) sets the trend for the whole group.

In the case of the ERM Germany had the biggest economy and has generally been considered as the most inflation averse country. These factors combined to give Germany the leadership in setting interest rates. In fact, some have argued that ERM was more like a D-Mark zone than the symmetric multilateral system it was supposed to be. This is disputed, though.[89]

So far we have looked at systems which are based on paper money only. In a *commodity standard* each country sets the price of the commodity in terms of its own paper currency. In the example of table 9.1, where the commodity is gold, the home country sets E_1 in kroner per gramme of gold and the foreign country sets E_2 in dollars per gramme of gold. The exchange rate between the two currencies then follows in kroner per dollar by dividing the two gold prices – i.e. $E = E_1/E_2$. Both central banks keep reserves in the commodity (gold), and both central banks intervene by buying or selling their currencies against gold.[90] The best historical example of a commodity standard is the classical gold standard which was practised by most countries from the 1870s until the outbreak of the First World War.

The gold reserves of the home country are determined by the private demand for foreign currency in much the same way as the foreign exchange reserves in other fixed rate systems. We can derive the equilibrium gold reserves by starting from (9.3) and adding $E_2(G_g + G_{g*} - \bar{G})$ on the left-hand side. This yields

$$E_2(G_g + G_{g*} - \bar{G}) + F_g + F_p + F_{g*} + F_{p*} = 0$$

By solving for G_g we get

$$G_g = \bar{G} - \frac{1}{E_2}(F_g + F_p + F_{g*} + F_{p*}) - G_{g*}$$

By inserting the portfolio demand functions (9.1) and (9.2), and the definitional relationship $P_* W_{g*} = F_{g*} + E_2 G_{g*} + B_{g*}/E$ we get

$$G_g = \bar{G} - \frac{1}{E_2}F_g - \frac{P}{E_1}f(r, W_p) - \frac{P_*}{E_2}[W_{p*} - b(r, W_{p*})] - \frac{P_*}{E_2}\left[W_{g*} - \frac{1}{EP_*}B_{g*}\right]$$

$$(9.5)$$

Here all the variables on the right-hand side are either exogenous or predetermined. Equation (9.5) tells how the gold reserves are distributed between the two central banks depending on the demand for foreign currency by the private sector. In a *pure* gold standard $F_g = B_{g*} = 0$. The risk premium has the same effect on G_g here as it had on F_g in (9.4). A redistribution of wealth from foreign to domestic residents also has the same effect on reserves irrespective of in which form they are held.

The gold standard is a symmetric system. Every country is responsible for its own gold price and its own interventions. In principle, every country is also free to set its own interest rate. However, if a country lowers its interest rate, gold moves out of that country and into the foreign central bank. A country which lowers the interest rate too much loses all its gold reserves. Increased gold reserves are less of a problem. Thus, a commodity standard may be biased towards high interest rates in the same way as ERM. Suppose countries normally keep gold reserves in proportion to the size of their economies. Because the absolute changes in gold reserves sum to zero, a change in the interest rate by a large country has a smaller relative impact on the gold reserves of that country. Thus, a large country tends to have more influence on the general level of interest rates. Britain, with its empire, was considered the most influential country during the gold standard period.

During the gold standard many countries had legal limits on the amount of currency in circulation related to the volume of gold reserves. This resembles the currency board system discussed in section 3.4. A central bank that lost reserves might then be compelled to reduce its money supply. This would raise interest rates. However, to the extent that the gold parities were credible, capital mobility was high and a small increase in interest rates sufficed to stop the loss of reserves.

The gold standard has some inherent drawbacks. Gold has alternative uses. There is therefore a real cost to keeping gold in reserve in the vaults of the central banks. When economic growth is strong, the available stock supply of gold tends to increase less than the output of goods and services in general. If the price level was constant, this would mean that the demand for money and other nominal quantities tended to increase more than the gold reserves available to the central banks. In the long run this would make reserves insufficient. Each central bank would have an incentive to raise interest rates in order to boost its own reserves. Since this does not increase the total reserves available, the result would instead be slack aggregate demand and downward pressure on prices. Thus, the gold standard could easily have a deflationary bias. In fact, this seemed to be the case during a large part of the classical gold standard period.

In principle, gold could be replaced by a paper reserve currency issued by an international body. The issuer would have to determine the volume in circulation of this 'paper gold', and could let it increase in order to allow for economic growth. If every country fixed their exchange rates to 'paper gold', the international body would determine through its issue of 'paper gold' the baseline for inflation and interest rates around the world. The 'paper gold' would give rise to seigniorage income which would have to be distributed somehow. In fact, during the Bretton Woods era a kind of 'paper gold' was created in the form of Special Drawing Rights (SDRs) at the International Monetary Fund. However, these were never created in sufficient volume to take over for the dollar as the main form of international reserves. It is difficult for an international body to agree on the appropriate speed of reserve creation and on the distribution of seigniorage.

9.2 The international transmission of shocks

Cyclical variations in output, prices and interest rates in one country are transmitted to the rest of the world through the balance of trade and through capital movements. An expansion of aggregate demand and output in one country leads through the trade balance to increased demand for the output of other countries. Their output then expands. In a second round this raises the demand for the output of the first country, which expands again. Another increase in the output of the rest of the world results, and in this way a *multiplier process* continues. In broad outline this is how shocks are transmitted through the trade balance.

The other channel, capital movements, is more complicated. An expansion in one country usually leads to increased interest rates there. Depending on the exchange rate system and the degree of capital mobility, the increased interest rate leads to an appreciation of the domestic currency or to increased interest rates abroad. In the first case the demand for foreign goods is stimulated, in the second case it is dampened.

A formal model is necessary to keep track of the different international repercussions. The present section extends the Mundell–Fleming–Tobin (MFT) model of chapter 6 to a 'world' model. This is done by putting together MFT models for two countries which together comprise the world.[91]

We approach the question of international interactions in several steps. First, we focus exclusively on the goods market and on transmission through the trade balance. This is done by assuming that both interest rates and the exchange rate are kept constant. Next we bring in money markets with 'flexible' interest rates, then the foreign exchange market and flexible exchange rates. Lastly, we discuss shock transmission in fixed rate systems when capital mobility is high. Throughout this section we shall be concerned with three types of questions: (1) To what extent do the results we derived for small countries in chapter 6 hold also when we allow for international repercussions and for countries which are 'large'? (2) To what extent are the effects of macroeconomic shocks transmitted to other countries? (3) To what extent will output in the two countries move in parallel?

Case A: fixed interest rates, fixed exchange rate

As mentioned, we build on the MFT model from section 6.2. The symbols are the same, except that the two countries are identified with subscripts a and b, respectively. The two *IS* equations are simplified to:

$$Y_a = C_a(Y_a) + I_a(i_a) + G_a + X(EP_b/P_a, Y_a, Y_b) \tag{9.6}$$

$$Y_b = C_b(Y_b) + I_b(i_b) + G_b - X(EP_b/P_a, Y_a, Y_b)P_a/EP_b \tag{9.7}$$

Note that the exchange rate E and the trade surplus X are seen from the point of view of country a. In this sense, country a is the home country. In (9.7) we need the trade balance measured in the same units as country b's output. Hence, X is divided by the real exchange rate $R = EP_b/P_a$. G_a and G_b may now be interpreted alternatively as government expenditure or as generic variables which can be used to represent real demand shocks. The endogenous variables are Y_a and Y_b, while the remaining variables are treated as exogenous. That includes the interest rates and the exchange rate. This does not necessarily mean that we are in a fixed exchange rate regime. If both interest rates are set independently, the exchange rate would follow from the equilibrium condition in the foreign exchange market, and be exogenous relative to the output markets. If we are in a fixed exchange rate regime, capital mobility must be so low that each country is free to set its own interest rate.

The first thing to note is that the global effect of a demand shock is the same as in a closed economy. World output measured in a-goods is from (9.6) and (9.7)

$$Y_a + RY_b = C_a(Y_a) + RC_b(Y_b) + I_a(i_a) + RI_b(i_b) + G_a + RG_b \tag{9.8}$$

If we assume for a moment that $C_a' = C_b' = C'$, and differentiate, we find that

$$\frac{d(Y_a + RY_b)}{dG_a} = \frac{1}{1 - C'}$$

which is the same as the familiar closed-economy multiplier. Indeed the only difference between (9.8) and the standard closed-economy IS equation is an aggregation problem in the consumption function.

Let us then look at how the effect of a demand shock in country a is divided between the two countries. By differentiating (9.6) and (9.7) (now permitting C_a' and C_b' to differ), we find:

$$\frac{dY_a}{dG_a} = \mu\left[1 - C_b' + X_b\right] > 0 \tag{9.9}$$

$$\frac{dY_b}{dG_a} = -\mu X_a > 0 \tag{9.10}$$

where

$$\mu = \frac{1}{[1 - C_a' - X_a][1 - C_b' + X_b] + X_a X_b}$$

and $-X_a$ and X_b are shorthand for the marginal import propensities, $X_a = dX/dY_a < 0$ and $X_b = dX/ \, dY_b > 0$. (We have simplified the expressions for the derivatives by reporting them for $R = 1$, and continue to do so throughout this section.)

In order to interpret the results it is useful to take one step back. If we disregard the international repercussions, we get what we may call the *national multipliers*. By differentiating (9.6) with respect to G_a holding Y_b constant, and similarly differentiating (9.7) with respect to G_b holding Y_a constant, we find the standard open-economy multipliers

$$\mu_a = 1/(1 - C_a' - X_a) \quad \text{and} \quad \mu_b = 1/(1 - C_b' + X_b) \tag{9.11}$$

We can use μ_a and μ_b to write (9.9) and (9.10) in an illuminating way. Divide through the numerator and denominator in (9.9) by $(1 - C'_a + X_a)(1 - C'_b + X_b)$. This yields

$$\frac{dY_a}{dG_a} = \frac{1}{1 - \dfrac{-X_a X_b}{(1 - C'_a - X_a)(1 - C'_b + X_b)}} \frac{1}{1 - C'_a - X_a}$$

The last term is the national multiplier μ_a. The first term must then represent the international repercussion effects. Hence, we define

$$\mu_i = \frac{1}{1 - \dfrac{-X_a X_b}{(1 - C'_a - X_a)(1 - C'_b + X_b)}} = \frac{1}{1 - \mu_a \mu_b (-X_a) X_b} \tag{9.12}$$

as the *international multiplier*. Obviously $\mu_i > 1$, since we subtract a number which is between zero and one in the denominator. We can now write

$$\frac{dY_a}{dG_a} = \mu_i \mu_a > 0 \tag{9.13}$$

The international repercussions increase the multiplier, as explained in the introduction to this section.

If we transform (9.10) in the same way, we get

$$\frac{dY_b}{dG_a} = \mu_i \mu_b (-X_a) \mu_a > 0 \tag{9.14}$$

It is instructive to read this expression from the end. μ_a measures the impact of G_a on Y_a for a given level of Y_b. This is multiplied by $(-X_a)$ to get the impulse that is transmitted to aggregate demand in country b. Multiplied by the national multiplier there, μ_b, we get the first-round effect on output in country b. Then, repercussions go back and forth between the two countries. The increase in Y_b raises demand for country a's goods and, hence, it raises Y_a. Which leads to another increase in the demand for country b's goods and so on. We get the final effect by applying the international multiplier. Note that $\mu_b(-X_a)$ is the effect of Y_a on Y_b that we would have found in chapter 6 where we disregarded the international repercussions.

Qualitatively the results we got in chapter 6 by disregarding international repercussions still hold. The only difference is that the effects are larger to the extent that μ_i is greater than 1. This immediately raises the question of how much larger? First, however, we shall look at figure 9.1, which illustrates the different multipliers. The curve marked aa shows the combinations of Y_a and Y_b which are consistent with equilibrium in the goods market in country a. The curve marked bb does the same for country b. In other words, the two curves represent (9.6) and (9.7), respectively. Both curves have a positive slope since increased output in one country raises the demand for the other country's products. The aa curve is steeper because relative to Y_b, Y_a has a stronger effect on the excess supply of a-goods than on the excess supply of b-goods. Thus, for a

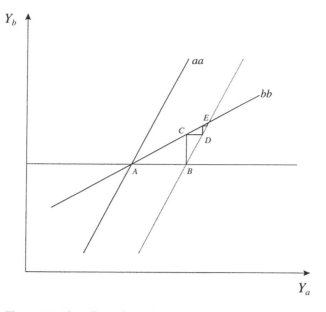

Figure 9.1 The effect of a real demand shock in country a when interest rates and exchange rates are fixed.

given increase in Y_a, a greater increase in Y_b is required to keep the market for a-goods balanced. This can be proved by differentiating (9.6) and (9.7).

In figure 9.1 the initial equilibrium is at A. Then there is an increase in G_a, dG_a. Initially the output of country a goes up by $dY_a = \mu_a dG_a$. The move is from A to B. The impact of this on country b's output is $dY_b = \mu_b(-X_a)dY_a$, or from B to C. In the second round this raises output in country a from C to D. In this way it continues. The final equilibrium is at E, and the movement from C to E is the result of the international multiplier.

The size of the international multiplier depends crucially on the marginal import propensities X_a and X_b. When discussing these, it is useful to start with the corresponding average import propensities (imports/output). Suppose trade is balanced, and let $R = 1$ for simplicity. Balanced trade means that output and domestic demand are equal, and that there is a common level of imports, Z. Suppose that in both countries demand is distributed on the two goods in the same way. Then it must be true that

$$Z = \frac{Y_a}{Y_a + Y_b} Y_b = \frac{Y_b}{Y_a + Y_b} Y_a$$

Each country's import is equal to its output (= demand) level times the share that the other country has in total output. Thus, the average import propensities are

$$\frac{Z}{Y_a} = \frac{Y_b}{Y_a + Y_b} \quad \text{and} \quad \frac{Z}{Y_b} = \frac{Y_a}{Y_a + Y_b}$$

In other words, a country's average propensity to import is equal to the share of the rest of the world in world output. The two import propensities sum to one.

In practice there is a substantial bias towards consuming goods produced at home.[92] This implies that the import propensities sum to less than one. We can measure home bias, h, by the extent to which the sum of the two import propensities fall short of one. If home bias is the same in both countries, the average import propensities are

$$\frac{Z}{Y_a} = (1 - h)\frac{Y_b}{Y_a + Y_b} \quad \text{and} \quad \frac{Z}{Y_b} = (1 - h)\frac{Y_a}{Y_a + Y_b} \tag{9.15}$$

In other words, a country's average import propensity is equal to $(1 - h)$ times the share of the rest of the world in total output. We should expect marginal import propensities to be of the same magnitude, although there may be deviations for countries which produce goods that have income elasticities far from one.

An example may indicate the likely size of the international multiplier. Assume that the marginal propensity to consume is 0.6 for both countries, that home bias is 0.4 and that the marginal import propensities are equal to the average import propensities in (9.15). Then μ_i varies from 1.01 when the country in focus has 1 per cent of world GDP to 1.17 when it has 25 per cent (roughly the share of the United States). With a home bias of 0.6, which is perhaps more realistic, the range is from 1.00 to 1.09. Thus, the international multiplier means a relatively minor adjustment of the national multiplier.

That the international multiplier is close to one does not mean that the impact of G_a on Y_b is small, only that the second-round effects are not very important. The ratio of the effects on the two countries is

$$\frac{dY_b/dG_a}{dY_a/dG_a} = \mu_b(-X_a) = \frac{-X_a}{1 - C_b' + X_b}$$

The higher the import propensity of a country, the less of the total effect comes in that country. With the same assumptions as above and a home bias of 0.4, 50 per cent of the effect comes abroad when country a has 1 per cent of world GDP, 45 per cent when a has 25 per cent of world GDP.

A more general framework

So far, we have looked at a specific model and a specific shock, but the decomposition of total effects into national and international multipliers can be made general. The equation system (9.6)–(9.7) is a special case of

$$Y_a = D_a(Y_a, Y_b, s) \tag{9.16}$$

$$Y_b = D_b(Y_a, Y_b, s) \tag{9.17}$$

where D_a and D_b are demand functions including both consumption demand, investment demand and net exports, while s is a shift parameter which can represent any exogenous variable. The models of other monetary regimes in the remaining part of this section can also be concentrated in two equations that are special cases of (9.16) and (9.17). If interest rates and/or exchange rates are endogenous, the equilibrium conditions for the financial markets can be used to eliminate i_a, i_b and E from (9.6) and (9.7) which then become congruent with (9.16) and (9.17). The procedure is in principle the same as for deriving aggregate demand curves in *IS–LM* models.

Thus, the different cases we are going to discuss can be compared within the general framework given by (9.16) and (9.17). It is then useful to have general expressions for the effects of exogenous shocks in this framework and general definitions of national and international multipliers.[93]

By differentiating (9.16) and (9.17) we get

$$\frac{dY_a}{ds} = \mu_i \mu_a D_{as} + \mu_i \mu_a D_{ab} \mu_b D_{bs} \tag{9.18}$$

$$\frac{dY_b}{ds} = \mu_i \mu_b D_{ba} \mu_a D_{as} + \mu_i \mu_b D_{bs} \tag{9.19}$$

where the national and international multipliers are now defined by

$$\mu_a = \frac{1}{1 - D_{aa}}, \quad \mu_b = \frac{1}{1 - D_{bb}}$$

$$\mu_i = \frac{1}{1 - \mu_a \mu_b D_{ab} D_{ba}}$$

μ_a measures the impact on country a's output of an exogenous increase in aggregate demand in country a ($D_{as} = 1$) for a given level of Y_b. The interpretation of μ_b is symmetric. μ_i is the ratio between the total effect on a country's output of an exogenous increase in aggregate demand there and the partial effect when output in the rest of the world is kept constant. Thus, μ_i tells us to what extent the repercussions back and forth between countries change the total effects. The partial derivatives D_{ab} and D_{ba} represent the initial demand *spillovers* from one country to the other. D_{ba} is the initial effect of an increase in Y_a on the demand for country b's output. The spillovers play a central role in the sequel.

In the case with fixed interest rates, the expressions for μ_a and μ_b of course specialize to those in (9.11). The initial spillovers in that case are $D_{ab} = X_b$ and $D_{ba} = -X_a$. Other examples of multipliers and spillovers are summarized in table 9.2. We shall go through each case in turn (Case E in section 9.4). The appendix (p. 319) shows how the derivatives of D_a and D_b can be derived. In table 9.2 it is assumed that trade is balanced initially ($X = 0$).

The national multipliers and spillovers were the subject of sections 6.3–6.5. What we learned there is still valid. The role of the international multiplier is to scale up or down all effects of exogenous shocks in the same proportion. As long as $\mu_i > 0$ – i.e. as long as $\mu_a \mu_b D_{ab} D_{ba} < 1$ – it does not change any signs. $\mu_a \mu_b D_{ab} D_{ba} < 1$ is also a condition for the international multiplier process to converge. Above we saw that it is satisfied in the case with fixed interest rates and fixed exchange rates.

Table 9.2   *National multipliers and demand spillovers*

A: Fixed interest rates, fixed exchange rate

$$\mu_a = \frac{1}{1 - C_a' - X_a} \qquad\qquad D_{ab} = X_b$$

$$\mu_b = \frac{1}{1 - C_b' + X_b} \qquad\qquad D_{ba} = -X_a$$

B: Fixed money supplies, fixed exchange rate

$$\mu_a = \frac{1}{1 - C_a' + I_a' \frac{m_{aY}}{m_{ai}} - X_a} \qquad\qquad D_{ab} = X_b$$

$$\mu_b = \frac{1}{1 - C_b' + I_b' \frac{m_{bY}}{m_{bi}} + X_b} \qquad\qquad D_{ba} = -X_a$$

C: Flexible exchange rate, fixed money supplies

$$\mu_a = \frac{1}{1 - C_a' + I_a' \frac{m_{aY}}{m_{ai}} - X_a + X_R E_i' \frac{m_{aY}}{m_{ai}}} \qquad\qquad D_{ab} = X_b + X_R E_i' \frac{m_{bY}}{m_{bi}}$$

$$\mu_b = \frac{1}{1 - C_b' + I_b' \frac{m_{bY}}{m_{bi}} + X_b + X_R E_i' \frac{m_{bY}}{m_{bi}}} \qquad\qquad D_{ba} = -X_a + X_R E_i' \frac{m_{aY}}{m_{ai}}$$

D: Country *a* fixes the exchange rate to *b*[1]

$$\mu_a = \frac{1}{1 - C_a' - X_a} \qquad\qquad D_{ab} = X_b - I_a' \frac{m_{bY}}{m_{bi}}$$

$$\mu_b = \frac{1}{1 - C_b' + I_b' \frac{m_{bY}}{m_{bi}} + X_b} \qquad\qquad D_{ba} = -X_a$$

E: Monetary union

$$\mu_a = \frac{1}{1 - C_a' + I_a' \frac{m_{aY}}{m_{ai} + m_{bi}} - X_a} \qquad\qquad D_{ab} = X_b - I_a' \frac{m_{bY}}{m_{ai} + m_{bi}}$$

$$\mu_b = \frac{1}{1 - C_b' + I_b' \frac{m_{bY}}{m_{ai} + m_{bi}} + X_b} \qquad\qquad D_{ba} = -X_a - I_b' \frac{m_{aY}}{m_{ai} + m_{bi}}$$

Note: 1. Country *b* fixes M_b.

D_{as} and D_{bs} represent the *direct impact* of a shock on aggregate demand in *a* and *b*, respectively. By this, we mean the impact before there has been any change in Y_a and Y_b. When we look at the effects of G_a, *s* represents G_a and $D_{as} = 1$, $D_{bs} = 0$. Thus, from (9.18) and (9.19)

$$\frac{dY_a}{dG_a} = \mu_i \mu_a, \qquad \frac{dY_b}{dG_a} = \mu_i \mu_b D_{ba} \mu_a \qquad\qquad (9.20)$$

Another interesting case is a demand shift from country *b* to country *a* ($ds = dG_a = -dG_b > 0$). Then $D_{as} = 1$ and $D_{bs} = -1$. The effects of a demand shift towards country *a* are thus from (9.18) and (9.19)

$$\frac{dY_a}{ds} = \mu_i\mu_a(1 - D_{ab}\mu_b), \quad \frac{dY_b}{ds} = -\mu_i\mu_b(1 - D_{ba}\mu_a) \tag{9.21}$$

In case A above $0 < D_{ab}\mu_b < 1$ and $0 < D_{ba}\mu_a < 1$. Hence, the effect on Y_a is positive, on Y_b negative. When the marginal import propensities decrease with country size, $D_{ab}\mu_b$ also decreases with country size. In the numerical example above, if $h = 0.6$ and country a has 1 per cent of world GDP, $1 - D_{ab}\mu_b$ is equal to 0.99. If it instead has 25 per cent of world GDP, $1 - D_{ab}\mu_b$ is equal to 0.8. In the latter case $\mu_i(1 - D_{ab}\mu_b)$ is 0.87. This indicates the bias one gets by neglecting all international repercussions.

Case B: Fixed money supplies, fixed exchange rate

The difference from Case A is that interest rates are now flexible. Capital mobility must be low enough that complete sterilization is a viable option. A determinate model for the endogenous variables Y_a, Y_b, i_a and i_b now consists of the two IS equations (9.6) and (9.7) and the LM equations:

$$\frac{M_a}{P_a} = m_a(i_a, Y_a) \tag{9.22}$$

$$\frac{M_b}{P_b} = m_b(i_b, Y_b) \tag{9.23}$$

The latter can be used to eliminate i_a and i_b from the IS equations. We then get two equilibrium conditions which are of the same form as (9.16) and (9.17). The familiar national multipliers in this case are reported in table 9.2. Naturally, they are lower than when the interest rate is constant. As we saw in section 6.3, a fixed money supply makes the interest rate increase when there is a positive demand shock, and this dampens the effect on output. The only channel for the international transmission of shocks is still the trade balance. Thus, the demand spillovers are the same as when interest rates were fixed. Lower national multipliers mean a lower international multiplier, closer to 1. The world-wide impact of the demand shock is reduced because of the interest rate response. However, as long as capital mobility is low and exchange rates are fixed, the transmission mechanism between countries is not fundamentally altered from the case with fixed interest rates.

When do real demand shocks in the two countries have the same effect on world output? This turns out to be when $C_a' = C_b'$ and $I_a'm_{aY}/m_{ai} = I_b'm_{bY}/m_{bi}$ (see Exercise 4, p. 322). In other words, an increase in output must have the same effect on consumption demand and investment demand in both countries. In this case, the world-wide effect is given by the familiar closed-economy multiplier from the IS–LM model.

Case C: Flexible exchange rate, fixed money supplies

In this case, we need to extend the model with an equilibrium condition for the foreign exchange market. As in section 6.4, we can solve the equilibrium condition for the exchange rate (9.4) and write it as

$$E = E(i_a - i_b, \bar{E}) \qquad (9.24)$$

We know that $E_i = E_1' < 0$. $\bar{E}$ can be thought of as an expected future exchange rate, or simply as a shift parameter ($E_E = E_2' > 0$). In the special case of perfect capital mobility the E function is derived from the interest parity condition $i_a = i_b + e_e(E)$. If capital mobility is imperfect, (9.24) contains a number of suppressed arguments: the initial asset stocks, the price levels, P_a and P_b and the foreign exchange reserves, F_a and F_b. These are either exogenous or predetermined.

The equations of the model are now (9.6), (9.7), (9.22), (9.23) and (9.24), while the endogenous variables are Y_a, Y_b, i_a, i_b and E. Shocks are transmitted from country to country through a new channel, the exchange rate. However, a change in the exchange rate merely redistributes demand. The positive effect on the trade balance in one country is matched by an equally large negative effect in the other country. The 'world' *IS* equation (9.8) does not contain the exchange rate. The exchange rate affects world demand only to the extent that there are behavioural differences between the countries. As shown in the appendix, if $C_a' = C_b'$ and $I_a' m_{aY}/m_{ai} = I_b' m_{bY}/m_{bi}$, then aggregation is possible and the geographical distribution of demand is irrelevant for the determination of world output. Since our main interest is in comparing policy regimes, not in the aggregation problem, we maintain this assumption. World output is then determined in the same way as in case *B* and exchange rate flexibility is irrelevant for the world-wide effect of demand shocks.

With the relations between interest rates and activity levels from (9.22) and (9.23) inserted in (9.24), E can be related to Y_a and Y_b, and this can be used to eliminate E from the *IS* equations. We then get two aggregate demand equations that are special cases of (9.16)–(9.17). When there is a positive demand shock in country a, Y_a goes up, i_a increases and the currency appreciates. The appreciation shifts demand to the rest of the world, and this dampens the increase in Y_a. Similarly for country b. Thus, as we learned in chapter 6, the national multipliers are lower when the exchange rate is floating (see table 9.2). For the very same reason, demand spillovers:

$$D_{ab} = X_b + X_R E_i m_{bY}/m_{bi} \quad \text{and} \quad D_{ba} = -X_a + X_R E_i m_{aY}/m_{ai} \qquad (9.25)$$

are greater. In D_{ba} the effect of the appreciated exchange rate, $X_R E_i m_{aY}/m_{ai}$, comes in addition to the direct effect of Y_a on import demand. Both add to the aggregate demand for country b's products. The international multiplier is increased. Remember that μ_i is increasing in $\mu_a D_{ba} \mu_b D_{ab}$. If you compare cases B and C in table 9.2, you will see that both $\mu_a D_{ba}$ and $\mu_b D_{ab}$ are greater in case C. The exchange rate term raises the numerator and the denominator by the same amount in each of $\mu_a D_{ba}$ and $\mu_b D_{ab}$, and this makes the fraction increase towards 1.

Is the increase in the international multiplier quantitatively important? This depends on $X_R E_i m_{aY}/m_{ai}$ and $X_R E_i m_{bY}/m_{bi}$. Thus, we need to know how much an increase in output affects the interest rates, how much an increase in interest rates affects the exchange rate and how much the exchange rate affects the trade balance. However, there is reason to believe that X_R is related to home bias and country size in the same way as X_a and X_b. Thus, when country a is small relative to the world economy, μ_i is still not likely to be much above one. Already in the first round the increase in output in country b is likely to be so small relative to total output that it has virtually no effect on the interest rate there. The chain of international repercussions is quickly broken.

In essence the conclusion is: *Exchange rate flexibility does not change the total effect of a real demand shock, but it shifts more of the effect from where the shock originated to the rest of the world.* This can be an advantage. If countries are hit by independent shocks, flexible exchange rates work as a kind of insurance or burden-sharing. If aggregate demand in the two countries shifts in opposite directions, as when $dG_a = -dG_b$, flexible exchange rates dampen the reactions in both countries. This can be seen from (9.21). On the other hand, if shocks affect aggregate demand in both countries in the same direction, there is less to gain from exchange rate flexibility.

Countries may use exchange rate flexibility to shift too much of the effects of a shock to other countries. This is called 'beggar-thy-neighbour policies'. Countries which can 'export' the effects of shocks have less incentive to stabilize the economy by other means, even if that would have contributed to stabilizing world output. We return to these kinds of externalities in section 9.3 on policy coordination.

Case D: Country a fixes the exchange rate to b

Above we compared floating exchange rates to a case where the exchange rate was fixed while each country retained monetary independence. Although instructive, this comparison does not apply to a world where capital mobility is high (or foreign exchange reserves low). When capital mobility is perfect and the exchange rate is fixed, the two interest rates are tied together. Then, fixing the exchange rate has three consequences: (1) The exchange rate channel for the transmission of shocks is closed. (2) Instead, a new interest rate channel is opened, but this is a one-way street from the centre to the periphery. (3) The peripheral country loses its interest rate flexibility. Its interest rate does not respond to its activity level, except in so far as the activity level abroad changes in the same direction.

The model consists of the same five equations as with floating exchange rates. The only difference is that the exchange rate has become exogenous while the money supply is endogenous in the peripheral country, which we take to be a. The model applies equally well to a key currency system where b is the centre and to the case where country a fixes its exchange rate unilaterally. The model can be solved by first solving the LM equation for country b for i_b as a function of Y_b, then inserting the solution in the equilibrium condition for the foreign exchange market to find i_a as a function of Y_b and finally inserting for both i_a and i_b in the equilibrium conditions for the goods market.

The national multiplier for the peripheral country, μ_a, is the same as in the case where both the exchange rate and the interest rate are fixed. The national multiplier for the centre country, μ_b, is the same as in the case where the interest rate is flexible, while the exchange rate is fixed. Relative to the case with a floating exchange rate, the national multipliers are increased, but more so in the peripheral country.

The initial demand spillover from a to b is $D_{ba} = -X_a$. In the other direction the transmission also runs through the interest rate. Thus, $D_{ab} = X_b - I'_a m_{bY}/m_{bi}$. The new second term is negative. When Y_b goes up, so does i_b. Perfect capital mobility means i_a has to follow, and this reduces investment demand in country a. Whether D_{ab} is positive or negative depends on the strength of the two opposing effects. It is possible that an expansion in country b has a contractionary effect on country a.

Compared to the case with a floating exchange rate, the international multiplier is reduced. That fixing the exchange rate reduces the international multiplier has already been explained. The opening of the interest rate channel has the same effect. As we have just seen, the interest rate effect reduces further the impact of an expansion in country b on aggregate demand for country a's products. In fact, if $I'_a m_{bY}/m_{bi} > X_b$, the international multiplier is smaller than one, since then an expansion in country b leads to a contraction in country a.

Because of the asymmetry in the exchange rate system, the effect of fixing the exchange rate depends strongly on where a shock hits. As for the world-wide response, remember that it is interest rate flexibility which is important. Flexible exchange rates only redistribute demand. This means that the world-wide effect of a positive demand shock in the periphery (an increase in G_a) is greater than under floating rates, since i_a does not respond directly to Y_a. The average interest rate in the world goes up less than in the case of floating exchange rates. If instead G_b increases, the world-wide effect is reduced. The reason is that the increase in i_b is transmitted directly to i_a. The world average of interest rates increases more than under a floating exchange rate.

In both cases, more of the total effect comes in the country where the shock originates. This is a direct consequence of the closing of the exchange rate channel. In addition, when the increase is in G_b, the interest rate channel means that relatively less of the effect is transmitted to country a. The net effect there may even be negative, and in that case the effect on output in country b is greater than on world output.

A case in point may be the German unification in 1990. As mentioned in section 9.1, many have looked upon the European Exchange Rate Mechanism (ERM) as a key currency system with Germany as the centre. After unification, aggregate demand in Germany increased. This led to increased interest rates which had a negative effect on output in other member countries of the ERM. The ERM countries closest to Germany, which also had strongest trade links to Germany, fared better than countries further away, where the interest rate link was more important.

Table 9.3   *Direct impacts on aggregate demand from different shocks*

C: Flexible exchange rate, fixed money supplies

Shock (s)	Impact on a (D_{as})	Impact on b (D_{bs})
dG_a	1	0
dG_b	0	1
$d\bar{E}$	$X_R E_E$	$-X_R E_E$
dM_a	$(I'_a + X_R E_i)/m_{ai}$	$-X_R E_i/m_{ai}$
dM_b	$-X_R E_i/m_{bi}$	$(I'_b + X_R E_i)/m_{bi}$
dP_a	$-I'_a/m_{ai} - X_R(1 + E_i m_a/m_{ai})$	$X_R(1 + E_i m_a/m_{ai})$
dP_b	$X_R(1 + E_i m_b/m_{bi})$	$-I'_b/m_{bi} - X_R(1 + E_i m_b/m_{bi})$

D: Country a fixes the exchange rate to b

Shock (s)	Impact on a (D_{as})	Impact on b (D_{bs})
dG_a	1	0
dG_b	0	1
$d\bar{E}$	$-I'_a E_E/E_i$	0
dM_b	I'_a/m_{bi}	I'_b/m_{bi}
dP_a	$-X_R$	X_R
dP_b	$-I'_a m_b/m_{bi} + X_R$	$-I'_b m_b/m_{bi} - X_R$

Source: Appendix (p. 319)

Shocks from other sources

So far, we have investigated only the effects of real demand shocks. Something also needs to be said about demand shifts, supply shocks and shocks originating in the financial markets. We limit the discussion to a comparison of fixed and floating rates under high capital mobility (cases *C* and *D* in table 9.3). An overview of the direct impacts of different shocks is given in table 9.3. It is assumed that trade is balanced initially.

Equation (9.21) (p. 300) contains general expressions for the effects of demand shifts on output in the two countries. We still assume that behaviour is similar in the sense that $C'_a = C'_b$ and $I'_a m_{aY}/m_{ai} = I'_b m_{bY}/m_{bi}$. World output is then not affected by a demand shift when the exchange rate system is symmetric as in case *C*. A demand shift always means an expansion in one country, a contraction in the other. The expansion is dampened because of reduced import demand from the contracting country. The contraction is dampened because of increased import demand from the expanding country. When behaviour is similar and the exchange rate system symmetric, a demand shift has the same absolute effect on the outputs level of both countries. This intuitive proposition can be proved by inserting in (9.21) the relevant expressions from table 9.2. One implication is that the relative effects on output in the two countries are inversely proportional to their GDP levels. Exchange rate flexibility serves to dampen the effects of demand shifts on both countries output levels.

In a key currency system with high capital mobility (Case D) a demand shift between the key country and the rest of the world affects world output. The reason is the asymmetric reaction of interest rates. The more demand that is directed towards the key country, the higher will interest rates be, and the lower is world output. This also means that in absolute terms the output effects of a demand shift are greater in the periphery than in the key country. The changes in interest rates which dampen the effect in the centre also exacerbate the effect in the periphery. The interest rate moves in the same direction, while the shocks are in opposite directions. Thus, demand shifts are particularly problematic for the peripheral countries in key currency systems with high capital mobility.

Now to a *shock to the foreign exchange market*, say an upward shift in $d\bar{E}$. Under floating exchange rates the direct impact is a depreciation which shifts demand from b to a. This is just like any other demand shift. The final result is an expansion of output in a and a contraction in b, while the world-wide effect is zero. If the same shock occurs under fixed exchange rates, there is no direct impact in the centre (country b). In the periphery (a), the interest rate goes up in order to keep the exchange rate constant. By reducing investment this works exactly like a negative real demand shock in country a. Output in both countries is reduced. Thus speculation against the peripheral currencies has negative effects on the world as a whole. Note that the output effect in the periphery is the opposite of that under floating.

Now to *shocks which originate in the money market*. Focus first on floating exchange rates. Take an exogenous increase in M_a. This lowers i_a and causes a depreciation of a's currency. The direct impact on aggregate demand then consists of two components: a demand shift from b to a owing to the depreciation, and a positive demand shock in country a owing to the effect of the lower interest rate on investment. World demand goes up, as does the output of country a. The effect on b's output is more ambiguous. The direct impact owing to the appreciation is negative, but then there is a positive spillover from the expansion in country a. The demand shift component of the shock reduces Y_b, the component that is equivalent to a positive demand shock in country a increases Y_b. In general, we cannot tell which component dominates. The effects of a monetary shock in b are, of course, symmetric.

With fixed exchange rates monetary shocks in the periphery (a) has no effect. The direct impact of an increase in the money supply in the centre, M_b, is to reduce interest rates in both countries equally. It is as if positive real demand shocks happen in both countries at the same time. The world-wide effect is, of course, greater than for a shock to M_b under floating rates. The effect on Y_b is positive, since both components of the shock work in the same direction there. The effect on Y_a may seem ambiguous, since a positive demand shock in the centre has a negative spillover on the periphery, as explained. However, it can be shown that in this case the total effect is also positive on Y_a. A negative effect on Y_a would have required an increase in the common interest rate, but this is impossible when the origin of the shock is an increase in the money supply. In general, we cannot tell whether the effect on Y_b is greater or smaller than under floating, since b does not benefit from a demand shift.

Supply shocks in the present model must be interpreted as exogenous shocks to the price levels P_a and P_b. There is some similarity between shocks to the price level and shocks to the money supply, since they both appear in the ratio M/P. However, the price levels have an additional effect through the real exchange rate in the trade balance function. This reinforces the demand shift effects in the case of floating exchange rates. An increase in P_a leads to a real appreciation of a's currency, for *two* reasons: It has a direct negative effect on $R = EP_b/P_a$ and in addition it raises i_a, which leads to a reduction in E. Thus a negative supply shock in country a (an increase in P_a) has a negative direct impact on aggregate demand in that country, while the direct impact on the other country is positive, but smaller. World output is reduced, as is output in country a. Country b experiences a positive direct impact, but also a negative spillover from country a. Since the demand shift component is stronger than for a monetary shock, an expansion in b is more likely. Naturally there is symmetry with an increase in P_b.

Under fixed exchange rates a negative supply shock in a has no direct impact on i_a. Thus, it works like a demand shift from a to b. Output in a declines, output in b expands. The effect in country a is smaller than under floating. A similar shock in country b has an additional negative direct impact on demand in both countries because of higher interest rates. The result is a stronger decline in world output than under floating. The impact on Y_a is more likely to be negative, since in addition to a possibly negative spillover from b, the direct impact is smaller and more likely to be negative. The latter is a result of the fact that the demand shift is smaller (it is not reinforced by an appreciation) and that there is a negative direct impact on investment demand.

Conclusions and some further points

In the introduction to this section we asked three questions. It is time to summarize the answers. The international repercussions from the second round onwards require an (often minor) proportional adjustment of the quantitative effects on output of all kinds of shocks, but do not change any qualitative conclusions. Hence, for shocks which have a direct impact only in one country, the qualitative results for small countries in chapter 6 hold also for large countries and when we take full account of the international repercussions. However, many shocks have a direct impact both at home and abroad. Examples are demand shifts, exchange rate shocks and, when capital mobility is high, also monetary shocks. Even then most qualitative results are the same as in chapter 6. One lesson, though, is that exogenous changes in the foreign variables (Y_* and i_* in chapter 6) are not independent, but result from the same underlying shocks. For the key country in a key currency system we should use a version of the model where M is exogenous even if capital mobility is high.

Not surprisingly, the difference between small and large countries is quantitative, not qualitative (except for key countries). The relevant international multiplier tends to deviate more from one for large countries, which means that it is more important to take account of the international feedbacks from the second round onwards. On the other hand, the first-round effect of a demand shift is more subdued in a large country.

Exchange rate flexibility does not by itself change the effect of shocks on world output, except when there are important behavioural differences between countries. However, eventual asymmetries in fixed exchange rate systems are important. In a key currency system the effect on world output of real demand shocks in the periphery is strengthened, the effect of real demand shocks in the centre is weakened. The opposite is true for monetary shocks. Monetary shocks in the periphery, of course, have no output effects if capital mobility is perfect.

The exchange rate regime is important for the distribution of the effects of a given shock. More of the effects of a real demand shock in one country is 'exported' to the other when exchange rates are floating. Shocks in the financial markets and supply shocks often affect output in the two countries in opposite directions, and it is difficult to establish general rules about how the exchange rate regime affects the distribution of their effects.

To what extent will output move in tandem in the two countries under the different exchange rate regimes? This depends on which shocks dominate. If independent real demand shocks dominate, the output levels will be more correlated under floating. The opposite is true for exchange rate shocks. Monetary shocks tend to produce more covariation of output under fixed than under floating exchange rates. If supply shocks are important, the comparison is more ambiguous.

Our comparison may exaggerate the difference between fixed and floating rates somewhat. In section 6.5 we saw that if the money supply is fixed and money demand is deflated with the consumer price index, interest rates respond positively to a depreciation. For the regime with floating this means that an expansion in country a in the first round still leads to higher interest rates and an appreciation of a's currency, but the response in both variables is weaker. Thus, the national multipliers are higher. More importantly, there is a new channel for demand spillovers. When country a appreciates, country b, whose currency depreciates, responds by raising its interest rate. Accordingly, when Y_a goes up this has opposing effects on the demand for country b's products: a positive direct effect on exports, another positive effect because of the depreciation and a negative effect because of the increased interest rate. Thus, the spillover is smaller when interest rates respond to exchange rates, and may even be negative (compare a key currency system). The same mechanisms also ensures that a monetary expansion in country a has a negative direct impact on interest rates in country b. Thus, interest rates will be more closely tied together.

Above we assumed that when a country has monetary independence, the money supply is fixed exogenously. This is not crucial. All we need for the qualitative conclusions is that the interest rate responds positively to output, and does not respond to the exchange rate (except to the extent that output has been affected). The first assumption seems innocuous. The second assumption is more dubious, and the only reason for maintaining it is that it makes the contrast between fixed and floating exchange rates sharper. As we just saw, dropping the assumption would yield an intermediate case. The more the interest rate depends positively on the exchange rate, the closer we are to a system of fixed rates. However, it is a symmetric fixed rate system where both countries take part in stabilizing the exchange rate. If monetary policy is somehow geared towards stabilizing the consumer price index, interest rates will respond positively to both an increase in the activity level and to a depreciation.

In earlier chapters exchange rates had wealth effects. Wealth was redistributed between different sectors of the world economy, and this led to a redistribution of the demand for goods and services. In that respect, the wealth effects are similar to the trade balance effects discussed above. The wealth effects matter for the global result only to the extent that behaviour differs between sectors. Some potential effects of redistribution were studied in chapters 5 and 6. For the global effects of a shock the eventual redistribution of wealth between the private and government sectors are probably most important.

Above, it was assumed that economic policy does not respond in any way to imbalances in the current account. In chapter 5 we saw that there are several self-correcting mechanisms for the current account. However, it is a fact that governments are sometimes concerned with avoiding too large current account deficits. This was common during the Bretton Woods era when low capital mobility made the financing of deficits difficult (see Artis and Bayoumi, 1990).[94] If one country expanded, it would then tend to ease the current account constraints of others, which would respond by easing fiscal or monetary policy. The result was to make output movements more synchronized. In such circumstances the United States, which did not have the same reason to worry about current account deficits, would often lead the business cycle. Conflicting targets for the current account and the implications for policy cooperation are discussed in section 9.3.

The discussion above was based on the assumption that trade was balanced initially. If $X \neq 0$, there is an additional effect of the real exchange rate. Formally it comes from the last term in (9.7), and it breaks the symmetry between the effects of the real exchange rate on the two countries. It is in principle straightforward to include the additional effect in the analysis. However, this may be to take the model one step too far. There is an underlying problem which we touched upon in section 6.5 – namely, that the technique for deflation in MFT models is somewhat arbitrary. A change in the real exchange rate is in the present model also a change in the terms of trade. This may redistribute real income between the two countries, and that may in turn affect the distribution of aggregate demand. But it is not obvious that these effects are well represented in the present model. The extra effect of R when $X \neq 0$ is related to the income effect of R in such a way that a discussion of the former without the latter is hardly worth pursuing. If there is a redistribution of income, it should be in favour of the appreciating country whose export goods become relatively more expensive. Given that there is some home bias, this means that there is less redistribution of demand towards the depreciating country. As long as the substitution effects are sufficiently strong, the qualitative conclusions above should still be valid.

Although the formal model has only two countries, the same principles obviously apply to a multicountry world. However, some care should be taken. Suppose the world is divided in different currency blocs which have fixed exchange rates internally but floating rates against the rest of the world. The countries with key currencies then get a special position. What happens there will immediately influence interest rates for the whole currency bloc. This gives them a disproportionate influence in the world economy. This especially is true for monetary shocks originating in the key countries. The influence of the key countries may also be strengthened if their currencies are used as parallel currencies and standards of value in countries with rapid inflation. The practical consequence at the moment is primarily to make the United States more important in the world economy than would follow merely from its size.

Transmission and shock absorption in practice

The above models are highly stylized. One important feature of the world is the great variety of monetary and exchange rate policies. There exist a number of simulation models for the world economy. These are more or less detailed in their representation of the economic structure, and more or less based on extensive econometric work. Some of them are run by international organizations (OECD, IMF), others by individual researchers or small research groups. An overview of a number of world models is given in Bryant (1989). Other useful sources are Bryant *et al.* (1989); Masson and Knight (1990); Taylor (1993).

Table 9.4, excerpted from an article by McKibbin and Sachs (1989), shows a fairly representative example of the output of simulation studies.[95] The model differs from ours by including explicit intertemporal considerations on the demand side, but otherwise it is fairly similar. Unlike us, the policy experiment is a *permanent* increase in US government spending. Since it is permanent, it is financed with tax increases. This explains why the effect on US output is rather small compared to what we would expect from the numerical examples above. The effect on other countries is considerable. Note the marked appreciation of the US dollar, which is a result of increased US interest rates. Interest rates in other countries follow by about half as much as US rates. The decline in US inflation is a result of a decline in import prices caused by the appreciation. The effect is rather small because the model includes some 'pricing to market' of the type we discussed in section 8.3. Prices on domestic goods show short-run nominal rigidity.

Table 9.4 *First-year effect of a permanent increase in US government spending equal to 1 per cent of GDP (effect measured in per cent)*

	US	Japan	Germany	REMS[1]	ROECD[2]	Dev[3]	Oil[4]
GDP	0.56	0.18	0.21	0.29	0.17	NA	NA
Trade balance[5]	−0.39	0.43	0.37	0.36	0.40	0.10	−0.17
Short interest rate	1.17	0.44	0.56	0.56	0.50	NA	NA
Consumer prices	−0.11	0.27	0.26	0.31	0.24	NA	NA
Exchange rate (US$)	NA	−4.99	−4.29	−4.28	−4.03	NA	NA

Notes: 1. EMS members except Germany.
2. OECD countries except those mentioned earlier.
3. Developing countries.
4. Oil exporting countries.
5. Effect in per cent of GDP.
Source: McKibbin and Sachs (1989).

In the same study a monetary expansion in the United States has a small negative impact on GDP in the other regions in the first year. The reason is that the depreciation of the US dollar shifts demand towards the United States. This is more important than the spillover from increased activity in the United States. An interesting feature of the simulations is that the exchange rate initially overshoots, as in the Dornbusch model.

Frankel (1988) gives an interesting overview of the effects of fiscal and monetary expansion in 12 different world models. Qualitatively the results for the United States and the rest of OECD are in accord with case *C* above, but the numerical effects vary greatly. The estimated percentage effects on output are in most cases several times higher in the regions where the shocks occur than in the other regions. The simulation models disagree on whether an increase in the money supply has a positive or a negative effect on output abroad. An interesting feature is that in many of the models US monetary policy has a strong effect on interest rates in the rest of the OECD, while the effect in the other direction is much smaller.

Unfortunately developing countries are given only rudimentary treatment in world models. However, in Beenstock (1988) and Muscatelli and Vines (1989) the focus is explicitly on North–South interdependence. One result in the latter is that a fiscal expansion in the 'North' has a contractionary effect in the 'South' because of higher interest rates.

Model simulations have also been used to study the volatility of macroeconomic variables under different exchange rate regimes. Two examples are given in table 9.5. The exogenous shocks are identified with the error terms in the estimated equations, and these are assumed to follow the same distributions irrespective of policy regime. The resulting standard deviations of the macroeconomic variables of interest are then computed for different policy rules. According to Taylor (1989), flexible exchange rates reduce output volatility by almost one-half, while according to Frenkel, Goldstein and Masson (1989), flexible exchange rates do not make much difference. The different

Table 9.5   *Standard deviations of log output under fixed and flexible exchange rates*

	US	Germany	Japan
Taylor[1] :			
Fixed	3.5	6.0	8.0
Flexible	2.1	2.8	4.6
Frenkel *et al.*[2]			
Fixed	5.0	3.8	5.8
Flexible	5.1	5.1	5.2

Notes: 1. The real interest rate is set to stabilize the price level in each country (floating) or the average price level (fixed).
2. A constant money growth rule in each country (floating) or just in the United States (fixed).
Source: Bryant *et al.* (1989).

results may be due to differences in model specification, estimation technique or the details of the policy rules. Frenkel, Goldstein and Masson (1989) used OECD's MULTIMOD, which is a true world model. Taylor's (1989) model is a multicountry model, which means that some parts of the world are missing, and that there is no adding-up constraint on trade balances. A serious empirical problem behind most simulation studies is that the number of observations is too low to get good estimates of the covariances between shocks. Since flexible exchange rates have fewer advantages when all countries are subject to the same shocks, the covariances are crucial for the results. Under floating rates Frenkel, Goldstein and Masson used monetary policy to stabilize the money supply, while Taylor used it to stabilize the price level. The same policies were followed by the nth country (United States) when exchange rates were fixed. However, other simulations reported in the same book (Bryant *et al.* 1989) seem to indicate that this is not so important for the results.

For a country that does not fix its exchange rate there are, of course, infinitely many possible monetary policies. Bryant, Hooper and Mann (1993) report simulations from eight multicountry or world models for a number of policy rules. The results seem to support the view that came out of Frenkel, Goldstein and Masson (1989) that it is difficult to tell which regime gives the most stable output: fixed exchange rates or fixed money supplies. However, according to the editors' summary both these rules are outperformed by policies which are more directly geared to stability in output and prices. These are different versions of nominal GDP targeting, and they give more of both output and price stability. The editors still indicate that fixed exchange rates may perform better in certain circumstances: if the openness of the economy is great (Germany being the example), if supply shocks are important, or if stable interest rates are desired. We return to some of these questions in chapter 10 on exchange rate policy.

There are also empirical studies of the relationships between exchange rate volatility and volatility in real variables. Flood and Rose (1995) find no correlation between exchange rate volatility and output volatility in a panel of nine industrial countries over the period 1960–91. This seems to support Frenkel, Goldstein and Masson against Taylor. However, a large number of studies have found that real exchange rates have been much more volatile under floating exchange rates (see Mussa, 1979). Frenkel, Goldstein and Masson does not find much difference in real exchange rate volatility between fixed and floating rates. This suggests that important aspects of the history are not captured by the simulation studies. One potential problem is the assumption that shocks follow the same distribution irrespective of regimes. If, as Flood and Rose seem to suggest, floating exchange rates introduce extra noise, the model simulations are biased in favour of floating. On the other hand, the actual experience with floating encompasses a great variety of monetary policies. Had the sensible policy rules assumed in the simulations been followed, the actual outcome might have been better.

9.3 Policy coordination

The international spillovers raise the question of whether countries can gain by coordinating their economic policies. By 'coordination' we here mean agreements about instrument setting. In this section we illustrate the question of policy coordination with a simple example, and then briefly describe some other cases where cooperation may be useful.[96]

The example is a case where countries a and b have inconsistent targets for the trade balance, X. The targets are $\bar{X}_a$ and $\bar{X}_b$, respectively, where $\bar{X}_a > \bar{X}_b$. The two countries also have output targets equal to the equilibrium output levels $\bar{Y}_a$ and $\bar{Y}_b$. The governments want to minimize quadratic loss functions

$$L_a = \frac{1}{2}\left[(Y_a - \bar{Y}_a)^2 + \xi(X - \bar{X}_a)^2\right] \quad \text{and} \quad L_b = \frac{1}{2}\left[(Y_b - \bar{Y}_b)^2 + \xi(X - \bar{X}_b)^2\right] \quad (9.26)$$

Thus, the loss increases with the distance from the targets. The parameter ξ measures the weight that the governments attach to the trade balance relative to the output target. The higher ξ, the more the instruments are directed towards meeting the trade balance target. On reduced form, the model of the economy can be written as:

$$Y_a = Y_{a0} + \gamma_{aa}G_a + \gamma_{ab}G_b \tag{9.27}$$

$$Y_b = Y_{b0} + \gamma_{ba}G_a + \gamma_{bb}G_b \tag{9.28}$$

$$X = X_0 - \alpha_a G_a + \alpha_b G_b \tag{9.29}$$

Here G_a and G_b are the policy instruments, which we can think of as fiscal instruments. The γs, the αs, Y_{a0}, Y_{b0} and X_0 are constant parameters. The γs and the αs are positive. Equations (9.27)–(9.29) can be seen as the reduced form of a linearized version of the first model in section 9.2 (the one with fixed exchange rate and fixed interest rate). Increased government expenditure in country a raises output in both countries. The trade surplus of country a decreases – which, of course, means an equally large increase in the surplus of country b. The effects of an increase in G_b are symmetric.

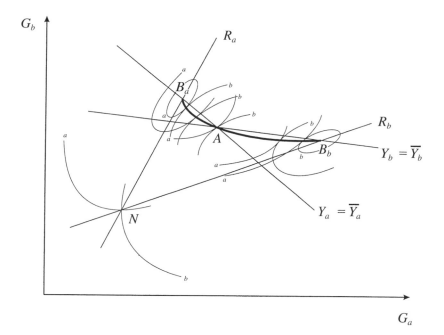

Figure 9.2 A two-country game about external and internal balance.

The resulting game is illustrated in figure 9.2 in what Currie (1990) has labelled a Hamada diagram. The two downward-sloping lines, marked $Y_a = \bar{Y}_a$ and $Y_b = \bar{Y}_b$, show the combinations of G_a and G_b which yield goods market equilibrium in countries a and b, respectively. The two lines intersect at A, where both goods markets are in equilibrium. The countries' 'bliss points' are marked B_a and B_b. At B_a country a reaches both its targets. At B_b country b does the same. The bliss points differ because a wants a higher X than b. We have assumed that $\bar{X}_a > X > \bar{X}_b$ at A. Hence, country a wants to be at a point along $Y_a = \bar{Y}_a$ to the left of A, where more demand comes from b. Similarly, country b wants to be to the right of A along $Y_b = \bar{Y}_b$. Around the bliss points we have drawn indifference curves (marked with as and bs). These are derived from the loss functions after inserting the reduced form. The linear-quadratic form of the model ensures that the indifference curves are ellipses around the bliss points. Naturally, the further away from the bliss point, the greater the loss.

Without cooperation each country takes the instrument setting of the other as given and then maximizes its own utility. This means that for a given level of G_b, say G_{b0}, country a chooses the tangency point between the horizontal line at G_{b0} and an indifference curve. In other words, it chooses a point where the gradient of its indifference curve is horizontal. At this point $\partial U_a/\partial G_a = 0$. The curve joining all points where a's indifference curves are horizontal is drawn in figure 9.2 and marked R_a. This is country a's *reaction function*, which tells how G_a is set for given levels of G_b. Similarly, country b's reaction function is R_b, which joins the points where b's indifference curves are vertical. In figure 9.2, the two reaction functions have a positive slope. This means that if G_b is reduced, country a responds by reducing G_a and vice versa. The response to contraction is contraction, and the response to expansion is expansion. This is not a necessary consequence of the model. If G_b is reduced, the immediate effect for country a is a reduction in Y_a and in X. Country a's opportunity set is reduced, and it cannot attain the same utility level. Because the economy is linear, country a still faces the same trade-off between Y_a and X as before. The utility function implies that both goods are normal in the relevant range. Country a is thus going to accept a reduction in both Y_a and X. Whether it is going to reduce G_a or not, depends on whether it thinks the initial reduction in Y_a was too small or too large relative to the initial reduction in X. If ξ, the weight on the trade balance in the utility function, is high enough, country a prefers a smaller reduction in X and accepts a larger reduction in Y_a. Thus, if the governments are sufficiently concerned with the trade balance, they respond to a fiscal contraction abroad with a fiscal contraction at home. Their reaction functions then slope upwards.

The Nash equilibrium is at N where the two reaction functions meet. At this point each country's instrument setting is optimal given the other country's instrument setting. Neither country has any reason to change its behaviour. Without cooperation the economies end up in N.

The Nash equilibrium is not a Pareto-optimum. Any point to the north-east of N between the two indifference curves that run through N is better for both parties. This shows that there is room for cooperation. Pareto-optimal policies are policies where the indifference curves are tangent to each other. As one can see from figure 9.2, at such points it is not possible to increase the utility of one country without reducing the utility of the other. The solid curve which runs from B_a to B_b joins all Pareto-optimal points. It is called the *contract curve*. Note that the point where both output levels are in equilibrium, A, is on the contract curve. At this point a marginal change in output in either country does not affect the loss functions. Then only the trade balance matters. But the trade balance can be improved from the point of view of one country only if it is worsened from the point of view of the other. Hence, A is a Pareto-optimum, and therefore on the contract curve.

In a Pareto-optimum the output levels of the two countries cannot deviate from equilibrium in the same direction. If output levels in both countries are above their equilibrium levels, it is always possible to change G_a and G_b in such a way that demand is reduced in both countries while the trade balance is constant. This would be a Pareto-improvement. A similar argument applies when output is below equilibrium in both countries. Hence, the contract curve runs between the lines where $Y_a = \bar{Y}_a$ and $Y_a = \bar{Y}_a$.

If countries cooperate, one would expect them to exploit all possibilities for Pareto-improvements. This means that they end up along the contract curve. Where they end up depends on the bargaining strength of each country. By withdrawing from cooperation each country is able to block solutions which it finds worse than the Nash equilibrium.

Without cooperation and with sufficient weight on the trade balance target, the conflict over the trade balance results in a Nash equilibrium with low output and employment in both countries. However, cooperation may be difficult to achieve. If the two countries have agreed on a Pareto-optimal point, each country has an incentive to cheat. As long as the other party sticks to the agreement, the government that cheats will be better off by reducing domestic demand. Since there is usually no outside authority that can enforce contracts between independent countries, it may be difficult to achieve cooperation in practice.

The problem we just discussed is obviously much more general than the particular model. It does not depend on the chosen functional forms, and it may arise with any number of countries. The conflict does not go away if we allow for monetary policy and floating exchange rates. The root of the problem is the strong concern for the inconsistent trade balance targets. However, one may ask whether countries should have targets for the current account, and whether they actually do have such targets. We saw in chapter 5 that there are many self-correcting mechanisms for the current account. Concern with the trade balance was strong in the early post-war period when capital mobility was low and current account deficits difficult to finance. After the increase in oil prices in 1973 (OPEC I) the main oil-exporting countries got huge current account surpluses. The oil-importing countries seemed reluctant to accept the corresponding deficits at the same time as unemployment rose. To many observers, there seemed to be a conflict of the kind described above, and it is probably no coincidence that much of the literature on conflicts over the current account is from the following period (see Johansen, 1982 and Hamada, 1979, for examples).

A number of other conflicts have been analysed within a similar theoretic framework:

- In order to obtain full employment and price stability, countries may attempt a combination of *expansionary fiscal and contractionary monetary policy*. The purpose of the latter is to achieve stability of the average price level through appreciation of the currency. However, when all countries do this, the result may be that fiscal policy is too expansionary, monetary policy too contractionary and interest rates higher than desirable. This theory found some favour in the 1980s when most OECD countries had relatively high government deficits and high interest rates.

- Suppose only *monetary policy* is available for stabilization purposes. If the economies are hit by a common stagflationary shock (a shock which raises prices and lowers aggregate demand in both countries), monetary policy may be too contractionary in the Nash equilibrium because both countries want to avoid the extra inflation caused by depreciation. If the shock is in the opposite direction, monetary policy will be too expansionary, because with a tendency to falling prices the governments do not fear depreciation (see Persson and Tabellini, 1995).[97]

- Eichengreen (1984) suggested that in the inter-war period, when several attempts were made to revive the gold standard, the central banks had inconsistent targets for the shares of the world gold stocks in their reserves. In order to increase their reserves the central banks raised their discount rates, and this contributed to the *general tendency to depression* in the period.

In all these cases policy coordination may be useful. However, according to the survey by Currie, Holtham and Hughes Hallett (1989) most studies find the gains from policy coordination to be 'small', on the order of magnitude of 0.5–1 per cent of GDP. It has even been suggested by Rogoff (1985a) that international cooperation can be harmful. Rogoff's result is based on the assumption that countries have target output levels that exceed equilibrium output. They would thus tend to pursue too expansionary policies if it were not for balance of payments considerations. Oudiz and Sachs (1985) suggested that most of the advantages of policy coordination could be obtained by fixing exchange rates. However, this clearly depends on the cause of the policy conflict (balance of payments concerns or concerns over inflation) and on the kind of shocks that hit the economy, as simulation studies in Bryant *et al.* (1989) confirm. Exchange rate flexibility can be useful to both parties when the economies are hit by asymmetric shocks. It is when they are hit by the same shocks that fixing the exchange rate to avoid 'beggar-thy-neighbour' policies may be adequate.

9.4 Monetary union and optimal currency areas

A monetary union differs from a regime of fixed exchange rates in that there is a common central bank and a common monetary policy. There is no exchange rate ($E = 1$ permanently), and no exchange rate shocks. Presumably the union's monetary policy depends on conditions in both countries. In line with what we did in section 9.2, we can assume that the money supply at the level of the union is exogenous. The equilibrium condition for the money market is then

$$M = P_a m_a(i, Y_a) + P_b m_b(i, Y_b) \qquad (9.30)$$

where the common interest rate i has replaced i_a and i_b in the old money demand equations. Equation (9.30) together with (9.6) and (9.7) determine Y_a, Y_b and i. Equation (9.30) can be solved for i as a function of Y_a and Y_b. When this is inserted for i_a and i_b in (9.6) and (9.7) we get a system equivalent to (9.16) and (9.17). The resulting national multipliers and cross-country impacts are shown as Case E in table 9.3 (p.304). The main difference from the case with fixed exchange rates discussed in section 9.2 is the greater symmetry, which results when interest rates respond positively to output in both countries. The national multiplier is lower in country a, higher in country b. The cross-country impacts include opposing balance of trade and interest rate effects in both directions. Since the interest rate responds less to an increase in Y_b than in a key currency system, it is less likely that a positive demand shock in country b has a negative impact on output in country a. From the point of view of the periphery, a monetary union seems clearly preferable to a key currency system where the exchange rates are never adjusted. It is less clear that the centre can gain.

Optimal currency areas

Which countries or regions would benefit from having their own currencies and which would benefit from having a common currency? This is the subject of the theory of optimum currency areas founded by Mundell (1961) and McKinnon (1963). Mundell and subsequent writers made the following observations:

1. Countries that are subject to *asymmetric shocks* may benefit from having their own currencies. The shocks Mundell had in mind were mainly demand shifts, where exchange rate flexibility stabilizes output in both countries. Exchange rate flexibility can then be used to reduce unemployment in the contracting country and inflationary tendencies in the expanding country.
2. *Wage flexibility* in both countries reduces the need for exchange rate flexibility. With complete wage flexibility output and employment in both countries stay at their equilibrium levels. The real exchange rate adjusts through a jump in the price level.
3. *Mobility of labour* between the regions reduces the need for exchange rate adjustments. Equilibrium can be preserved with movements of people instead of movements in relative prices.
4. *Automatic fiscal stabilizers* reduce the national multipliers and hence reduce the need for exchange rate flexibility. However, if the government finances of each region are completely separate, strong automatic stabilizers mean that a demand shift has a strong negative impact on the budget surplus in the contracting region, and a correspondingly strong positive impact in the expanding region. This may make it difficult to let the automatic stabilizers work. If a central government collects taxes from all regions and distributes transfers, then there are fewer budgetary problems. Thus, a large 'federal' budget with strong built-in stabilizers reduces the need for exchange rate flexibility.

The last point means that two regions that have a common government with a substantial budget are better suited to having a common currency than two regions which are separate jurisdictions. In most cases the point about labour mobility probably works in the same direction, although steps can be taken to reduce the obstacles to labour mobility that are created by national borders. A common claim is that the European Union is less suited to have a common currency than the United States, because in the European Union wages are less flexible, labour is less mobile and the 'federal' budget is much smaller.[98]

One obvious point is sometimes forgotten in expositions of the theory of optimum currency areas: the national multipliers in a monetary union and the effects of demand shifts also depend on how integrated the regions are through trade. The more trade, the higher the marginal import propensities and the lower the effects of demand shifts. High import propensities also means that the effects of other asymmetric shocks are distributed more evenly between the countries. Furthermore, high trade implies that exchange rate shocks or asymmetric shocks to monetary policy have greater impact on the distribution of demand between the two countries. Thus, a high level of mutual trade seems to favour a common currency, quite apart from the fact that with a high level of trade the reduction in transaction costs caused by monetary union will also be large.

In connection with the movement towards monetary union in Europe a number of empirical studies have tried to find out the extent to which European countries are subject to asymmetric shocks. A method often used is to check how much the industrial structure differs from the average. These studies tend to find that small countries on the outskirts of Europe (Finland, Norway, Greece) are less suited for monetary union than larger and more central countries. One objection is that small countries often tend to be specialized in relatively few industries. But this also means that they depend strongly on foreign trade. It is not obvious that they have less to gain (or more to lose) from a common currency than the larger and more diversified countries. If one picks regions of comparable size within larger countries, one can obviously find some regions which are as specialized and as subject to asymmetric shocks as the small countries. In fact, if we make the regions smaller, we are bound to find even more asymmetric shocks, but it would be ridiculous to suggest that each firm or each village should have its own currency.

The analogy between regions and countries should not be drawn too far, however. Regions within a large country benefit from automatic stabilization through a common budget, and migration is usually easier within a country.

A monetary union removes two sources of asymmetric shocks – namely, shocks which originate in the money market and in the foreign exchange market. Attitudes towards monetary union may depend on one's judgement about the importance of this type of shock. A monetary union may also solve or reduce some of the policy coordination problems discussed in section 9.3.

A two-country model may be misleading when the discussion is about the benefits of a common currency for a limited region. Then the amount of trade within the region versus with the outside world must obviously be important. The same goes for the amount of competition that domestic producers face from within the region and from outside. The more the members of a bloc trade with each other, the more the effects of asymmetric shocks are spread among the members through demand effects. Different trade relations to third countries may be a source of asymmetric shocks, which makes a common currency less attractive. If the external exchange rate of the bloc is subject to shocks, countries which produce goods that have close substitutes from third countries may be more exposed than countries which have its main competitors within the bloc.

Appendix: deriving the properties of the aggregate demand functions

9A.1 Equations of the model

The equations of the model are:

$$Y_a = C_a(Y_a) + I_a(i_a) + G_a + X\left(\frac{EP_b}{P_a}, Y_a, Y_b\right) \tag{9A.1}$$

$$Y_b = C_b(Y_b) + I_b(i_b) + G_b - X\left(\frac{EP_b}{P_a}, Y_a, Y_b\right)\frac{P_a}{EP_b} \tag{9A.2}$$

$$\frac{M_a}{P_a} = m_a(i_a, Y_a) \tag{9A.3}$$

$$\frac{M_b}{P_b} = m_b(i_b, Y_b) \tag{9A.4}$$

$$E = E(i_a - i_b, \bar{E}) \tag{9A.5}$$

Total differentiation of all the equations yields

$$dY_a = C_a'dY_a + I_a'di_a + dG_a \tag{9A.6}$$
$$+ X_R(dE + dP_b - dP_a) + X_a dY_a + X_b dY_b$$

$$dY_b = C_b'dY_b + I_b'di_b + dG_b - X_R(dE + dP_b - dP_a) \tag{9A.7}$$
$$- X_a dY_a - X_b dY_b$$

$$dM_a = m_a dP_a + m_{ai}di_a + m_{aY} dY_a \tag{9A.8}$$

$$dM_b = m_b dP_b + m_{bi}di_b + m_{bY} dY_b \tag{9A.9}$$

$$dE = E_i(di_a - di_b) + E_E d\bar{E} \tag{9A.10}$$

After differentiation P_a, P_b and E have been set equal to one and X equal to zero in order to simplify the expressions.

9A.2 Case C: Flexible exchange rates

From reorganizing (9A.8) and (9A.9):

$$di_a = -\frac{m_{aY}}{m_{ai}} dY_a + \frac{1}{m_{ai}} dM_a - \frac{m_a}{m_{ai}} dP_a \tag{9A.11}$$

$$di_b = -\frac{m_{bY}}{m_{bi}} dY_b + \frac{1}{m_{bi}} dM_b - \frac{m_b}{m_{bi}} dP_b \tag{9A.12}$$

Inserting (9A.11) and (9A.12) in (9A.10) yields:

$$dE = E_i\left(-\frac{m_{aY}}{m_{ai}}dY_a + \frac{1}{m_{ai}}dM_a - \frac{m_a}{m_{ai}}dP_a\right)$$

$$-\left(-\frac{m_{bY}}{m_{bi}}dY_b + \frac{1}{m_{bi}}dM_b - \frac{m_b}{m_{bi}}dP_b\right) + E_E d\bar{E} \tag{9A.13}$$

Insert (9A.11) and (9A.13) in (9A.6), (9A.12) and (9A.13) in (9A.7):

$$dY_a = \left(C_a' - I_a'\frac{m_{aY}}{m_{ai}} + X_a - X_R E_i \frac{m_{aY}}{m_{ai}}\right)dY_a \tag{9A.14}$$

$$+ \left(X_b + X_R E_i \frac{m_{bY}}{m_{bi}}\right)dY_b + dG_a + X_R E_E d\bar{E}$$

$$+ \frac{1}{m_{ai}}(I_a' + X_R E_i)dM_a - X_R E_i \frac{1}{m_{bi}}dM_b$$

$$- \left(I_a'\frac{m_a}{m_{ai}} + X_R\left(1 + E_i\frac{m_a}{m_{ai}}\right)\right)dP_a + X_R\left(1 + E_i\frac{m_b}{m_{bi}}\right)dP_b$$

$$dY_b = \left(-X_a + X_R E_i \frac{m_{aY}}{m_{ai}}\right)dY_a \tag{9A.15}$$

$$+ \left(C_b' - I_b'\frac{m_{bY}}{m_{bi}} - X_b - X_R E_i \frac{m_{bY}}{m_{bi}}\right)dY_b + dG_b - X_R E_E d\bar{E}$$

$$- X_R E_i \frac{1}{m_{ai}}dM_a + \frac{1}{m_{bi}}(I_b + X_R E_i)dM_b$$

$$+ X_R\left(1 + E_i\frac{m_a}{m_{ai}}\right)dP_a - \left(I_b'\frac{m_b}{m_{bi}} + X_R\left(1 + E_i\frac{m_b}{m_{bi}}\right)\right)dP_b$$

All derivatives of D_a and D_b can be read out of (9A.14) and (9A.15). Case A and B fall out as special cases by deleting irrelevant terms.

By adding (9A.14) and (9A.15):

$$dY = dY_a + dY_b = \left(C_a' - I_a'\frac{m_{aY}}{m_{ai}}\right)dY_a + \left(C_b' - I_b'\frac{m_{bY}}{m_{bi}}\right)dY_b + dG_a$$

$$+ dG_b + I_a'\frac{1}{m_{ai}}(dM_a - m_a dP_a) + I_b'\frac{1}{m_{bi}}(dM_b - m_b dP_b) \tag{9A.16}$$

When $C_a' - I_a'\frac{m_{aY}}{m_{ai}} = C_b' - I_b'\frac{m_{bY}}{m_{bi}} = \Delta_Y$ this aggregates to:

$$dY = \Delta_Y dY + dG_a + dG_b$$

$$+ I_a'\frac{1}{m_{ai}}(dM_a - m_a dP_a) + I_b'\frac{1}{m_{bi}}(dM_b - m_b dP_b) \tag{9A.17}$$

from which the world-wide effects on output can be derived. The effects of dG_a and dG_b on world output are the same.

9A.3 Case D: fixed exchange rates, b centre, a periphery

From (9A.10) and since $dE = 0$:

$$di_a = di_b - \frac{E_E}{E_i} d\bar{E} \tag{9A.18}$$

After inserting for di_b from (9A.12), which still holds:

$$di_a = -\frac{m_{bY}}{m_{bi}} dY_b + \frac{1}{m_{bi}} dM_b - \frac{m_b}{m_{bi}} dP_b - \frac{E_E}{E_i} d\bar{E} \tag{9A.19}$$

(9A.12), (9A.19) and $dE = 0$ in (9A.6) and (9A.7) yields:

$$dY_a = (C_a' + X_a)dY_a + \left(X_b - I_a'\frac{m_{bY}}{m_{bi}}\right)dY_b + dG_a \tag{9A.20}$$

$$+ I_a'\frac{1}{m_{bi}} dM_b - X_R dP_a + \left(X_R - I_a'\frac{m_b}{m_{bi}}\right)dP_b$$

$$- I_a'\frac{E_E}{E_i} d\bar{E}$$

$$dY_b = -X_a dY_a + \left(C_b' - I_b'\frac{m_{bY}}{m_{bi}} - X_b\right)dY_b + dG_b \tag{9A.21}$$

$$+ I_b'\frac{1}{m_{bi}} dM_b + X_R dP_a - \left(X_R + I_b'\frac{m_b}{m_{bi}}\right)dP_b$$

All derivatives of D_a and D_b can be read out of (9A.20) and (9A.21) in case D. By adding (9A.20) and (9A.21) we get:

$$dY = dY_a + dY_b = C_a'dY_a + \left(C_b' - (I_a' + I_b')\frac{m_{bY}}{m_{bi}}\right)dY_b + dG_a$$

$$+ dG_b + \frac{1}{m_{bi}}(I_a' + I_b')(dM_b - m_b dP_b) - I_a'\frac{E_E}{E_i} d\bar{E} \tag{9.A22}$$

This shows why the world-wide effects depend on where the shocks originate. No reasonable assumptions make the coefficient in front of dY_a and dY_b equal.

Exercises

1. Find the global effect of an increase in G_a by adding equations (9.6) and (9.7). Show that it can be written

$$\frac{d(Y_a + Y_b)}{dG_a} = \frac{1}{1 - C_a'}\frac{1 - C_b' - X_a + X_b}{1 - C_b' - \frac{1 - C_b'}{1 - C_a'} X_a + X_b}$$

   Discuss to what extent this may differ from the closed-economy multiplier and why. Which has the greater effect, an increase in G_a or in G_b?

2. Suppose exchange rates are fixed. Country a is the periphery while country b is the centre. Suppose the central bank of the centre uses monetary policy to keep Y_b stable at $\bar{Y}_b$. Explain why a positive demand shock in country b then always has a negative impact on the level of activity in country a. Show that a positive demand shock in country a has a *smaller* effect on Y_a when we take

account of the feedbacks through country b than when we neglect these feedbacks.

3. The first priority of country a is to avoid an increase in the trade deficit. If necessary, it will tighten fiscal policy to achieve that. The exchange rate is floating and the money supply is fixed. There is a negative demand shock in country b. What will be the effects on output in the two countries? How do they compare to the effects when there is no concern about the trade balance? What happens if country a instead uses monetary policy to achieve its target for the trade deficit?

4. (a) Explain why the world-wide effect of G_a can be written $\mu_i\mu_a(1 + \mu_b D_{ba})$, and that of G_b, $\mu_i\mu_b(1 + \mu_a D_{ab})$. (b) Apply this to case B (fixed exchange rate, fixed money supply) in section 9.2. (c) Show that the multipliers are identical if $C_a' = C_b'$ and $I_a' m_{aY}/m_{ai} = I_b' m_{bY}/m_{bi}$.

10   Exchange rate policy

Previous chapters have shown that exchange rate flexibility can be useful in many circumstances. Still a large number of countries attempt to keep their exchange rates fixed. The present chapter discusses the choice between fixed and floating exchange rates from the perspective of a single open economy.

The choice of exchange rate regime is part of a wider question: What should the target(s) for monetary policy be? The number of targets which can be met is at most equal to the number of independent instruments available. We may think of the central bank as having two instruments: the rate of interest (i) and the foreign exchange reserve (F_g).[99] With two instruments the central bank can reach at most two independent targets. If capital mobility is perfect, one instrument (F_g) is ineffective, and it can reach just one target.

Targeting the exchange rate ties up one instrument. Traditionally it has been assumed that the foreign exchange reserve is used to keep the exchange rate fixed. An alternative is to use the interest rate, and if capital mobility is perfect that is the only option, since sterilized interventions are then ineffective.

If we drop the exchange rate target, we 'release' one instrument, which then becomes available for other purposes. In section 4.3 we argued that an economy needs a nominal anchor in order to tie down expectations of nominal variables. If there is no exchange rate target, it would thus seem a good idea to target another nominal variable. Milton Friedman's (1953) advocacy of flexible exchange rates combined with a target for the money supply is well known. Another alternative is to target the price level. Under the name of inflation targeting[100] this is now practised by several countries (New Zealand, Sweden, Canada, the United Kingdom among others) (see Leiderman and Svensson, 1995; Gerlach, 1999).

The ultimate goal for economic policy is presumably to maximize some welfare function. Relative to this the exchange rate, the money supply and the price level are intermediate targets. They are not of interest in themselves, only because pursuing them is believed to contribute towards fulfilling more fundamental goals. Targeting a price level path with low inflation may be justified because low inflation promotes the use of paper money to save transaction costs – and, more importantly, because it helps fix expectations about nominal variables. In that way we avoid some expectational errors which would otherwise lead to the misuse of resources (for example, to unemployment). However, conflicts easily arise between an intermediate target and the ultimate goal. The reason is that the welfare function usually has more arguments than the number of policy instruments available. It is then necessary to optimize to find the best policy. An intermediate target acts as an extra, self-imposed constraint on the optimization.

Why bother with intermediate targets? Why not just maximize the ultimate welfare function? By definition this should give the best result. However, the ultimate welfare function is a complex entity. Welfare depends on more than monetary policy. Politicians usually disagree on the welfare function and on how different policies affect it. If the politicians in spite of this can agree on setting an intermediate target for monetary policy, they can achieve at least two advantages: First, because a consensus policy is more likely to survive changing political constellations, policy becomes more predictable. Losses owing to expectational errors are thus reduced. Secondly, if decisions on the use of instruments are delegated to the central bank, this facilitates quicker and better informed reactions to changing circumstances. In democracies it is often seen as a precondition for delegation that the central bank is given a clearly stated goal to which it can be held accountable. Thus, an intermediate target may clear the way for quicker and better informed decisions about instrument use. These advantages must be weighed against the eventual welfare gains from a more flexible policy. A good candidate for an intermediate target would have to be 'compatible' with the different ultimate welfare functions – i.e. it must not have too harmful side effects. One such side effect could be excessive output volatility.[101]

There is an additional argument related to the 'time-consistency problem' (see Kydland and Prescott, 1977; Barro and Gordon, 1983). In order to influence private behaviour the authorities may want to tie themselves to a certain course of action irrespective of the private response. In practice it may be impossible to make a credible commitment to the first-best optimal policy which follows from maximizing the ultimate welfare function. The choice may then be between committing to a simple intermediate target or keeping the freedom to optimize, but without being able to influence private behaviour through commitment. In section 10.2 we shall see how a fixed exchange rate (and other intermediate targets) can be defended in this way.

The choice of exchange rate regime can be discussed at two levels. At one level, we can compare the merits of alternative intermediate targets for monetary policy. At another level, we can discuss the wisdom of tying monetary policy to an intermediate target, such as the exchange rate, instead of just pursuing the ultimate goals. Throughout the book we have often made comparisons of the first kind. They have usually been between a fixed exchange rate and a regime with a fixed money supply. This is also the most common comparison in the literature. However, Friedman's money growth rule fell into disrepute in many places when instabilities in money demand were detected in the 1980s. Recent policy discussions have focused on inflation targets, and a closer look at that alternative is warranted. Section 10.1 thus discusses the merits of an exchange rate target versus a price level target. The main emphasis is on how output variability is affected by the choice of intermediate target. Section 10.2 discusses the more fundamental questions of whether the government should commit to an intermediate target and whether such a commitment will be credible. This necessitates a discussion of why fixed exchange rates break down, sometimes as a result of speculative attacks. The basis for the discussion is the time-consistency literature. Section 10.3 contains some final comments on the usefulness of exchange rate flexibility.

Throughout, we assume that the interest rate is the only instrument at the central bank's disposal. This reflects the view that sterilized interventions are usually rather ineffective in today's world. It would be foolhardy to base the choice of policy regime on the presumption that a fixed exchange rate can be maintained through sterilized interventions. They may be used as a supplementary tool, but that is not the subject of the present chapter.

10.1 Exchange rate versus price level targets and output stability

Which policy gives the greater stability in output: a price level target or an exchange rate target? If one chooses a price level target, how does output volatility depend on the weights given to home and foreign goods in the price index? These are the main questions of the present section.[102]

The framework of analysis is this: a stationary environment free from autocorrelation is assumed. Thus, this period's expectations of the levels of all exogenous variables next period are constant. Wages are set before this period's realizations of the exogenous shocks are known. This means that aggregate supply responds positively to an increase in the price level. Aggregate demand depends on the real interest rate and on the real exchange rate. The output level and the price of home goods are determined by the intersection of supply and demand. The central bank uses one instrument, the interest rate. Capital mobility is assumed to be so high that sterilized foreign exchange interventions are of little use. After the exogenous shocks have been observed, the central bank adjusts the interest rate to achieve either price stability or a constant exchange rate. The bank has full knowledge of the structure of the economy. Thus, its policy is always successful. The policy is assumed to be credible in the sense that expectations are based on that the central bank sticks to its target.

The model is kept as simple as possible. The conclusions hold also if there is trend growth in the real variables or in the price level target (for example, if the target implies 3 per cent inflation per year instead of 0). At the end of the section we discuss briefly how the results can be generalized.

The model

We look at a small country. As in the Mundell–Fleming models there are two commodities, one home good and one foreign good. All variables are measured in logs (except the interest rate) and relative to their unconditional expectations.

The short-run aggregate supply function is

$$y = \beta(p - Ep - w + u) \tag{10.1}$$

where y is output, p the price of home goods, Ep this period's expectation of next period's price, w an exogenous wage shock ('cost-push shock'), u an exogenous labour augmenting productivity shock and β a positive constant. The term $Ep + w$ can be interpreted as this period's wage level measured as a deviation from its unconditional expectation. Thus, wages are set on the basis of the expected price level.

Aggregate demand is given by

$$y = -\alpha[i - (Ep - p)] + \gamma(e + p_* - p) + v \tag{10.2}$$

where i is the domestic nominal interest rate. Thus, $i - (Ep - p)$ is the *ex ante* real interest rate. e is the exchange rate and p_* the price of imported goods. The real exchange rate is then $e + p_* - p$. v is an exogenous demand shock and α and γ are positive constants. Since there is no autocorrelation and no lags, Ep is the same as the unconditional expectation of p. Since we measure all variables relative to their expected values, and since there is no autocorrelation, Ep is zero. The real interest rate can thus be written $i + p$. A high price level this period means that we can expect a lower price level next period, and this raises the real interest rate. At this point the assumption of no autocorrelation in the shocks is crucial.

The equilibrium condition for the foreign exchange market is

$$i = i_* + (Ee - e) + z = r_* + (Ep_* - p_*) + (Ee - e) + z \tag{10.3}$$

which says that the domestic interest rate is equal to the foreign interest rate, i_*, plus the expected rate of depreciation, $Ee - e$ and a stochastic risk premium, z. Ee is the exchange rate expected this period to prevail next period. The foreign nominal interest rate is equal to the foreign real interest rate, r_*, plus the expected foreign rate of inflation, $Ep_* - p_*$. Because there is no autocorrelation, and because of the way e and p_* are measured, $Ee = Ep_* = 0$. This means that if we have a depreciated exchange rate today, it is expected to appreciate till next period. If capital mobility is perfect, z is always zero. z may alternatively be interpreted as a 'credibility shock', a stochastic shock to exchange rate expectations. The model does not require perfect capital mobility, but the central bank must not intervene by buying or selling foreign currency.

A fixed exchange rate means that $e = 0$ always. A price level target must be defined relative to some price index. Let the consumer price index be $q = a'p + (1 - a')(e + p_*)$, where a' is the weight on home goods. Targeting the consumer price index means setting $q = 0$. More generally, we can write the policy target as

$$ap + (1 - a)(e + bp_*) = 0 \tag{10.4}$$

where a and b are parameters which define the target. This formulation encompasses both a fixed exchange rate $(a = b = 0)$ and alternative price level targets $(0 \leq a \leq 1, \ b = 1)$. If $a = 1$, the target is producer prices. If $a = 0$ and $b = 1$, the target is import prices. Since the purpose of setting a target is to preserve some degree of nominal stability, we consider only rules where $0 \leq a \leq 1$ and $0 \leq b \leq 1$.

Equations (10.1)–(10.4) determine the four endogenous variables y, p, e and i. The exogenous stochastic shocks are w, u, v, r_*, z and p_*.

Solution

Since the model is linear, it is straightforward to solve for the endogenous variables as functions of the shocks. One way of proceeding is to form an aggregate demand curve relating y and p by combining (10.2), (10.3) and (10.4) and eliminating i and e. Then we combine this curve with the aggregate supply curve (10.1) in order to find y and p.

The policy target (10.4) can be rewritten with e on the left-hand side as

$$e = -bp_* - \frac{a}{1-a}p \tag{10.5}$$

By inserting this in the interest parity condition (10.3), we get the central bank reaction function

$$i = r_* + z - (1-b)p_* + \frac{a}{1-a}p \tag{10.6}$$

The aggregate demand curve is found by substituting (10.5) and (10.6) in (10.2). This gives

$$y = -\frac{\alpha + \gamma}{1-a}p - \alpha(r_* + z) + (1-b)(\alpha + \gamma)p_* + v \tag{10.7}$$

Aggregate demand is a declining function of p, r_* and z, as should be expected. If we have a price level target, $b = 1$ and a foreign nominal shock (p_*) has no effect. If the exchange rate is fixed ($b = 0$), an increase in p_* raises the demand for home goods. There are two reasons for this. One is that an increase in p_* raises the real exchange rate. The other is that an increase in p_* reduces the interest rate, i, as can be seen from the central bank reaction function (10.6).

The aggregate demand curve (10.7) is illustrated in figure 10.1 together with the supply curve (10.1) (marked S). Alternative targets for monetary policy change the slope of the demand curve, while they leave the supply curve unaffected. The price elasticity of aggregate demand in (10.7) is inversely proportional to $1 - a$. Thus, the higher the weight on home goods in the policy target is, the more elastic aggregate demand is. A fixed exchange rate ($a = 0$) always gives the lowest demand elasticity. In figure 10.1 a price level target always means a flatter demand curve than an exchange rate target. Thus, the demand curve marked D_e is for an exchange rate target, while D_p is for a price level target. While a changes the price elasticity of aggregate demand, and nothing else, b determines only the effect on aggregate demand of an imported inflation shock.

By equating aggregate supply and demand ((10.1) and (10.7)) we find (assuming $a \neq 1$) the equilibrium values:

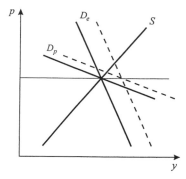

Figure 10.1 The effect of a demand shock.

$$p = \mu\left[-\alpha(r_* + z) + (1 - b)(\alpha + \gamma)p_* + v + \beta(w - u)\right] \qquad (10.8)$$

$$y = \beta\mu\left[-\alpha(r_* + z) + (1 - b)(\alpha + \gamma)p_* + v - \frac{\alpha + \gamma}{1 - a}(w - u)\right] \qquad (10.9)$$

where

$$\mu = \frac{1}{\beta + (\alpha + \gamma)/(1 - a)} = \frac{1 - a}{(1 - a)\beta + (\alpha + \gamma)}$$

is the inverse of the sum of the price elasticities of demand and supply.

When the solution for p is inserted in (10.5) and (10.6), we find that:

$$e = -p_* + \mu\left[\frac{a}{1 - a}[\alpha(r_* + z) - v - \beta(w - u)] + (1 - b)(\beta + \alpha + \gamma)p_*\right] \qquad (10.10)$$

$$i = \frac{(1 - a)(\beta + \alpha) + \gamma}{(1 - a)\beta + \alpha + \gamma}(r_* + z)$$
$$+ \mu\left[\frac{a}{1 - a}[v + \beta(w - u)] - (1 - b)(\beta + \alpha + \gamma)p_*\right] \qquad (10.11)$$

Note that if the exchange rate is fixed ($a = 0$, $b = 0$), the solutions for e and i come out as $e = 0$ and $i = r_* - p_* + z = i_* + z$, as they should. Note also that the unconditional expectations of p, y, e and i are all zero in accord with our assumptions. Furthermore, the solution of the model for $a = 1$ is the same as the limiting form of (10.8)–(10.11) as a approaches 1. In particular, $a = 1$ yields $p = 0$ and $y = \beta(u - w)$.

The effects of shocks

Depending on the origin of the shocks, we distinguish between demand shocks (v, r_*, z and p_*) and supply shocks (u and w).

Demand shocks

The four variables v, r_*, z and p_* all shift the aggregate demand curve while they leave the aggregate supply curve unchanged. One may look upon v as representing a genuine demand shock, r_* and z as foreign exchange shocks and p_* as an imported nominal shock. While an increase in v raises aggregate demand directly, an increase in r_* or z raises the domestic interest rate and, thus, indirectly reduces demand. As already explained, p_* has no effect on aggregate demand if $b = 1$ – i.e. if there is a price level rule. If $0 \leq b < 1$, an increase in p_* has a positive effect on aggregate demand because it leads to a real depreciation and a reduced interest rate.

The effect of an increase in v is shown in figure 10.1. The demand curve shifts to the right. Measured horizontally the size of the shift is independent of the monetary target. The flatter the demand curve, the weaker the effect on both output and the price of home goods. Relative to an exchange rate target, a price level target reduces the effects of demand shocks on p and y. The higher the weight on home goods (a), the more subdued the response.

The reason for the damped effect can be seen from (10.11). When $a > 0$, a positive demand shock induces the central bank to increase the interest rate. This in turn leads to an appreciation, as can be seen from (10.10). A higher interest rate and an appreciation both have a negative effect on aggregate demand. The effects of other demand shocks are similar, except that imported nominal shocks have no effect when there is a price level rule.

The output effects of demand shocks can be neutralized completely by setting $a = 1$ – i.e. by stabilizing producer prices. In this case a positive demand shock induces a fall in the consumer price index since the exchange rate appreciates and foreign goods become less expensive. A fall in the consumer price index will be the result whenever $a > a'$.

If $0 \leq a < 1$, a high supply elasticity β increases the output effect of a genuine demand shock, while high demand elasticities α and γ reduce it. Foreign exchange shocks produce stronger output effects the higher α is.

Supply shocks

An increase in u or a decrease in w shifts the supply curve to the right, as illustrated in figure 10.2. The shift is, of course, the same irrespective of monetary target. As we see, the output effect is strongest when the demand curve is relatively flat. Relative to an exchange rate target, a price level target increases the effect of a supply shock on y and reduces the effect on p. The greater the weight on home goods (a), the stronger the output response and the smaller the price response.

When there is a price level target, the central bank responds to a positive supply shock by lowering its interest rate to stimulate demand and thereby stabilize

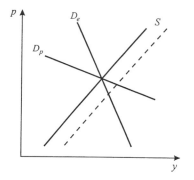

Figure 10.2 The effect of a supply shock.

the price level (cf. (10.11)). This reduction in the interest rate induces the depreciation that can be seen in (10.10), and which also stimulates demand.

High price elasticities in demand and supply increase the effect of supply shocks on output. High price elasticities combined with a high weight on home goods, a, produce the strongest output effects of supply shocks.

Exchange rate volatility

When a price level rule is in operation, an increase in domestic producer prices, p, has to be offset by an appreciation and vice versa. This follows directly from (10.4). As a consequence a price level target may produce a high volatility of both the real and the nominal exchange rate. As can be seen from (10.10), a high a increases the response of the nominal exchange rate to all kinds of shocks except p_*. The same can be shown to hold for the real exchange rate by combining (10.8) and (10.10).

If β is high and there are strong supply shocks, a price level rule may produce particularly strong exchange rate volatility. A high β means that the short-run marginal cost of production is fairly constant, and that the supply curve is relatively flat. Monetary policy, which works through aggregate demand, is then unable to have much effect on p. A negative supply shock must then be balanced by a large reduction in import prices, and this requires a large appreciation. The effects on the real exchange rate will be even stronger, since p and e move in opposite directions.

This points to a potential problem with a price level rule, which is not revealed in a model with only one production sector. High volatility in the real exchange rate may mean large and frequent redistributions of employment between sectors which produce mainly for the domestic and mainly for the foreign market. Lower volatility at the aggregate level may be bought with higher volatility at the sectoral level. Røisland and Torvik (1999) extend the model to include traded and non-traded goods.

Some conclusions

We started by asking: 'Which policy gives the greater stability in output: a price level target or an exchange rate target?' We can conclude:

- Supply shocks have a stronger effect on output when the central bank pursues a price level target.
- Demand shocks have a stronger effect on output when the central bank pursues an exchange rate target.
- Pure nominal shocks from abroad have a positive demand effect when the exchange rate is fixed, no real effect when there is a price level target.

A fixed exchange rate makes sense only if the foreign price level is relatively stable. If p_* is highly volatile, a fixed exchange rate will give too much volatility in both output and the price level. Given that p_* is fairly stable, it seems that the most important criterion for choosing between alternative targets is output stability. Suppose the alternatives under consideration are targeting the exchange rate and targeting the consumer price index. The circumstances favouring a price level target are then

- A high volatility of demand shocks.
- A low volatility of supply shocks.

In addition to the variances of the shocks the elasticities α, β and γ are of some importance:

- *A high real exchange rate elasticity γ means a flat aggregate demand curve.* This increases the output effects of all supply shocks and reduces the output effects of all demand shocks (except p_*). A high γ is thus an argument in favour of a fixed exchange rate, since with a high γ it is relatively more important to dampen the effects of supply shocks.
- *A high interest rate elasticity α has much the same effect,* since it also increases the price elasticity of aggregate demand, albeit in a more indirect way. However, shocks which originate in the foreign exchange market (r_* and z) have stronger effects on output when α is high. Thus, a high α favours a fixed exchange rate if the variances of r_* and z are low, while it may favour a price level target if the variances of r_* and z are high. If the foreign exchange market is an important source of disturbances, and if the real interest rate has a strong effect on aggregate demand, a fixed exchange rate is bad. The reason is that the disturbances from the foreign exchange market are reflected one to one in the real interest rate. It is better to allow foreign exchange shocks to be reflected partly in the interest rate and partly in the exchange rate.
- *A high price elasticity of supply β increases the output effects of all kinds of shocks in both policy regimes,* as is evident from (10.9). The output effects of

demand shocks are increased because of a flatter aggregate supply curve. The output effects of supply shocks are increased because their direct impact (the size of the shift) is greater. This is more important than the slope of the supply curve. Furthermore, the relative weights on the different kinds of shocks in (10.9) are independent of β, since β does not appear inside the brackets. By comparing the values of $\beta\mu$ for $a = a'$ and $a = 0$ one can show that a high β favours a fixed exchange rate.[103]

Small countries tend to have higher shares of imports in their consumer price indices – i.e. $1 - a'$ tend to be higher. As we have seen, this means that the aggregate demand curve under consumer price targeting is steeper and closer to the aggregate demand curve under exchange rate targeting. Price level targeting is more similar to exchange rate targeting, and the alternatives matter less for output stability. However, in small countries the real exchange rate elasticity, γ, also tends to be greater. As explained above, a high γ favours an exchange rate target. This may be part of the reason why small countries more often fix their exchange rates.

Some countries with price level targets make exceptions for certain supply shocks (for example, changes in food prices owing to bad harvests) which are allowed to affect the price level.

Some output variability may be desirable

Above we took for granted that minimum output variability is desirable. However, even if wages are fully flexible, real shocks (u, v, z, or r_*) may have output effects. When the level of employment is given, a productivity shock has a direct effect on output. Other real shocks change the wedge between consumer and producer real wages, and this may change labour supply. Following Aizenman and Frenkel (1986), one may define the optimal output level as the level which would prevail if the nominal wage were fully flexible. However, disequilibrium variations in employment are not the same as equilibrium variations. The distribution of employment between individuals is likely to be different and less desirable. It is not the same thing to respond to a change in the real wage and to be laid-off or called in for compulsory overtime. Still it may be of interest to compare the output variations to what we would get if we had continuous market clearing.

We shall look at the simplest case where labour supply is constant. Then the aggregate supply function with flexible wages is[104]

$$y = \frac{\beta}{1 + \beta} u \qquad (10.12)$$

If this is the desired level of output, it is not obvious that actual output (10.9) responds too strongly to productivity shocks. That depends on the relative size of the coefficients in front of u in the two equations. By comparing these, we find that the output response to productivity shocks is too great if $(\alpha + \gamma)/(1 - a) > 1$ – i.e. if the price elasticity of aggregate demand is greater than one. If a positive output response to a positive productivity shock is desired, this clearly reduces the advantage of a fixed exchange rate compared to a price level target. If $(\alpha + \gamma)/(1 - a') < 1$, even a consumer price target may stabilize output too much when there are productivity shocks.

Note that the argument does not apply to cost-push shocks (w).

Some further remarks

Before we conclude this section, some further points deserve to be mentioned:

1. Above we assumed that there was *no autocorrelation in the shocks*. Rødseth (1996b) shows that we get similar results if the shocks are permanent instead of transitory. The main difference is that a positive permanent productivity shock raises permanent income, and thus shifts both the demand and supply curve to the right. The output response then depends less on which target is used for monetary policy.

2. Implementation of the price level rule requires *much more information than the fixed exchange rate*. As can be seen from (10.11), setting the right interest rate when $a \neq 0$ requires information on all shocks and all parameters of the model. When the exchange rate is fixed, the right interest rate can be found simply by watching the foreign exchange market. (The interest rate may cause pain, especially if the commitment to the fixed rate is not credible, but that is another story.) Poor economic statistics and scant knowledge of the structure of the economy is an extra argument for fixing the exchange rate. The more judgement that is needed, the greater is also the danger to fall prey to wishful thinking when setting instruments.

3. The central bank can respond only to information that is *available at the time the interest rate is set*. i_* and e can be observed continuously, and z can be inferred from the equilibrium condition for the foreign exchange market. Suppose that the shocks u, v and p_* have two components, one that is known by the central bank at the beginning of the period, and one that is not observed until the end. These components are independent. The period's price and output levels are not known until the end of the period. Then the interest rate can respond only to the observed components of u, v and p_*. In this case, the difference in output stability between the two regimes relates only to the components of these shocks that are known by the central bank when it sets interest rates. When Svensson (1996) comes out unequivocally in favour of inflation targeting, one reason is that because of the lag structure in his model the central bank is not able to respond to supply shocks.

4. In the above model it does not make any difference whether one targets *the price level or the rate of inflation*. The reason is that the target is always met. The path for the price level is the same in both cases. However, if some shocks are not known until after the instruments have been set, a useful distinction can be made: with a *price level target* the aim for the whole future path of the price level is set in advance. If the target is missed in one period, the aim is still to bring the price level back to the pre-set path in the future. With an *inflation target* one does not care about past mistakes. If the target is missed in one period, there is no attempt to bring the price level back to any pre-assigned path. The policy is directed only towards influencing current and future inflation. Suppose the target is zero inflation. In spite of that, inflation in period 1 is 5 per cent. With a price level target the central bank should then aim for a 5 per cent deflation in period 2, with an inflation target it should aim for 0. Since expectations are forward-looking and nominal wage rigidity lasts only for one period, the choice between inflation and price level targeting does not have any consequences for output stability in the above model. It would thus seem that the choice between the two should be determined by what kind of price stability one wants. Is it important to be able to predict the price level far into the future, or is it more important to have a stable inflation rate from period to period? However, one can imagine other circumstances where the choice is important – for example, if there is an element of backward-looking expectations, or if wage rigidity is more pronounced.

5. In practice there are *lags between a change in the interest rate and its effect on output and prices*. These lags create further problems for the implementation of a price level rule. However, they also change output variability under fixed exchange rates. Only further investigations can tell how such lags change the conclusions. Ball (1998), on the basis of a model with lags, warns against inflation targets with a short horizon. The argument is that the interest rate affects the exchange rate and the price of imports fairly quickly, domestic output somewhat later and prices on domestically produced goods with an even longer lag. Quick stabilization of price must therefore take place mainly through variations in the exchange rate and import prices, and this creates instability in output.

6. In our model, if a positive demand shock hits and the exchange rate is fixed, the *price level increases this period and is expected to fall next period*. The expected deflation raises the real interest rate. This is the opposite of the Walters effect that was discussed in section 6.5. As we saw there, the Walters effect may destabilize demand in the short run. The reason why there is no Walters effect in the above model is that shocks have their full effect on the price level in the first period. If there are lags in the effects of demand shocks on prices, the Walters effect may be important. Simulations in Leitemo and Røisland (1999) indicate that this may work in favour of an

inflation target. However, it remains a fact that if the exchange rate is fixed and prices rise above their long-run equilibrium levels, prices have to come down again. The expectation that this will happen must raise real interest rates at certain horizons. Walters may be criticized for focusing too much on short-run real rates.

7. *The volatility of demand may depend on fiscal policy*. Fiscal stabilization, to the extent that it is successful, reduces the volatility of aggregate demand. This speaks in favour of targeting the exchange rate.

8. *For overall output volatility the correlation between shocks is important*. Suppose real demand shocks in this country and in the rest of the world are positively correlated. Then, if the foreign central bank acts to stabilize the price level abroad, it is also likely that r_* is positively correlated with the demand shock v. This reduces the overall volatility of aggregate demand. Thus, as discussed in chapter 9, symmetric shocks make a fixed exchange rate more attractive, asymmetric shocks make it less attractive.

9. In a multicountry world the following problem may arise: *the average price level of a country's competitors and trading partners is not stable*. However, there is one large country with reasonably stable prices. One can fix the exchange rate either to the large country or to a basket of currencies where each country is weighted according to its importance as competitor and trading partner. If the former alternative is chosen, variations in the exchange rate between the large country and the other trading partners become an extra source of demand shocks. If the latter alternative is chosen, one has to put up with imported nominal shocks. One can optimize the weight on the different countries in order to minimize the problems. However, as long as not all trading partners have stable prices, one cannot get rid of the disturbances completely. There is then an extra argument for targeting the price level.

10. Obviously, neither a fixed exchange rate nor a consumer price target is the optimal policy if one can *choose the response of interest rates to shocks freely*. It would be better to respond to supply shocks as if the exchange rate were fixed, and to respond to demand shocks as if the price level were fixed. Given a preference function that values both output stability and price stability (as in section 10.2), an optimal policy can be derived. Ball (1998) and Svensson (1998) give interesting examples of optimal rules in models which also take account of lags. However, one can also ask a more limited question: suppose we are going to target a price index. Which index should we choose in order to minimize output variability? Rødseth (1996b) shows that the circumstances favouring a high level of a are the same as were mentioned above as favouring a consumer price target relative to an exchange rate target. If there are no supply shocks, lowest output variability is obtained by stabilizing the producer price index. If the volatility of supply is relatively high, the best choice is to stabilize the import price index. If p_* is uncorrelated with all other

shocks, it is obviously always better to stabilize import prices than the exchange rate.

11. Rødseth (1996a) shows that stabilizing the quantity of money may be preferable to stabilizing the price level, but only if the demand function for money is stable and the interest elasticity of the demand for money is not too high. A money supply target always reduces the output effect of supply shocks relative to a price level target. If the interest rate elasticity of money demand is not too high, it also dampens the output effect of demand shocks. Another alternative is to target nominal GDP (see Bean, 1983).

12. It is one thing to compare output volatility for given shocks and given parameters of the behavioural relations. It is another matter whether *these parameters and the distribution of the shocks change with the different policy regimes.* In chapter 8 we referred to arguments to the effect that high exchange rate volatility would make aggregate demand less responsive to the exchange rate. In our model, this means a lower γ. Some will argue that a successful fix can reduce the volatility of z. Such effects make the comparison of alternative targets even more difficult.

10.2 Credibility and speculative attacks

One reason for targeting the exchange rate is to gain credibility in the fight against inflation. Higher credibility means lower expected inflation. In this section we examine the nature of the credibility problem. Why does it arise? How and when can fixing the exchange rate help? Why does it sometimes fail? The latter question inevitably brings us into a discussion of speculative attacks.

In the literature the credibility problem is usually described as a time-consistency problem (Kydland and Prescott, 1977; Barro and Gordon, 1983). A shortsighted government has an incentive to surprise the public with higher than expected inflation in order to increase employment. The public anticipates this and expected inflation increases to the point where the government is not willing to raise inflation further. The result is higher inflation without higher employment. We shall begin this section by presenting a formal model of the time-consistency problem. Then we present an extension of the model due to Obstfeld (1994) (see also Obstfeld, 1996 and Obstfeld and Rogoff, 1996) which explains why fixed exchange rate regimes break down and why speculative attacks occur. We conclude with some more general remarks on the credibility problem and speculative crises.

The credibility problem

As a background we can think of the extremely open economy of chapter 5. Foreign prices are stable. The law of one price means that the domestic price level is determined by the exchange rate. Time is divided into discrete periods. Wages are set at the beginning of each period on the basis of the expected rate of inflation. Output y (in logs) is then determined by the supply function:

$$y = \bar{y} + (\pi - \pi_e) - s \qquad (10.13)$$

Here $\bar{y}$ is equilibrium output, π the rate of inflation, π_e the inflation expected by the public when setting wages and s a supply shock with expectation zero. Although written differently, the supply function is the same as in section 10.1 except for one simplification – namely, that the supply elasticity is equal to one. This is done to simplify the algebra, and is not important for the conclusions. The supply shock s is the same as $w - u$ in the previous model.

The government behaves as if it minimizes the loss function

$$L = \frac{1}{2}(y - \tilde{y})^2 + \frac{1}{2}\xi\pi^2 \qquad (10.14)$$

L increases in the deviation of output from the output target $\tilde{y}$ and in the deviation of inflation from its target which, without loss of generality, is set to zero. $\xi > 0$ is the weight on inflation relative to output. The output target deviates from equilibrium output by $\kappa = \tilde{y} - \bar{y} > 0$. The reasons for that need not concern us here.

The government chooses π through its monetary policy. Implicitly this means choosing the exchange rate. The government minimizes (10.14) with respect to π given (10.13), which can be inserted for y. The first-order condition is

$$(y - \bar{y}) + \xi\pi = \pi - \pi_e - z - \kappa + \xi\pi = 0$$

When this is solved for π, we find the optimal policy:

$$\pi = \frac{\kappa + \pi_e + s}{1 + \xi} = \pi_{opt} \qquad (10.15)$$

which inserted in (10.13) gives

$$y = \bar{y} + \frac{\kappa - \xi\pi_e - \xi s}{1 + \xi} = y_{opt} \qquad (10.16)$$

The government responds to negative supply shocks and to high expected inflation by raising inflation, but not by enough to prevent a fall in output.

Suppose the public has model-consistent expectations. Then, by taking expectations of (10.15), we get

$$\pi_e = E\pi_{opt} = \frac{\kappa + \pi_e}{1 + \xi}$$

or

$$\pi_e = \frac{\kappa}{\xi} \qquad (10.17)$$

That the output target is above the equilibrium output (i.e. that $\kappa > 0$) gives the government an incentive to create higher inflation than expected. However, this incentive is checked by the desire to keep inflation close to zero (represented by ξ). The result is that the public has reason to expect higher inflation the higher κ is, and the lower ξ is.

With model-consistent expectations from (10.17) plugged into the solutions for inflation and output (10.15) and (10.16), we get

$$\pi = \frac{\kappa}{\xi} + \frac{s}{1+\xi} \tag{10.18}$$

$$y = \bar{y} - \frac{\xi s}{1+\xi} \tag{10.19}$$

Note that the expected level of output is equal to $\bar{y}$. Thus, on average the government does not get higher output, only higher inflation. Note also that we get a unique rational expectations equilibrium here not only for the rate of inflation, but also for the absolute price level, since last period's price level is predetermined. Thus, in this model the fact that the rate of inflation is an argument of the preference function of the government provides a sufficient nominal anchor for expectations.

When we insert the latest expressions for π and y in the loss function, we get

$$L_A = \frac{1}{2}\left(\kappa + \frac{\xi s}{1+\xi}\right)^2 \frac{1+\xi}{\xi} = \frac{1}{2}\left(\frac{1+\xi}{\xi}\kappa^2 + 2\kappa s + \frac{\xi}{1+\xi}s^2\right)$$

which has expected value

$$EL_A = \frac{1}{2}\left(\frac{1+\xi}{\xi}\kappa^2 + \frac{\xi}{1+\xi}\sigma_{ss}\right) \tag{10.20}$$

where σ_{ss} is the variance of s.

The policy derived above is called the *optimal discretionary policy*, since the government chooses π freely after wages have been set. An alternative is the *optimal policy with commitment*. Then we assume that the government is able to commit itself *before* wages are set to follow a certain policy rule *after* wages are set. The optimal policy rule is then the rule that minimizes the *expected* loss given the supply function and given rational expectations. A policy rule in this context is a function that relates π to s. Because of the linear-quadratic nature of the model, it is sufficient to consider linear policy rules: $\pi = c_0 + c_1 s$. Finding the optimal policy then means finding the optimal values of the constant coefficients c_0 and c_1. Given the policy rule, $\pi_e = E\pi = c_0$. Since increasing c_0 only increases inflation without any benefits in the form of employment, the optimal value of c_0 is obviously zero. The optimal value of c_1 can then be found by inserting $\pi = c_1 s$ and $\pi_e = 0$ in the loss function (10.14), taking expectations and minimizing with respect to c_1. In this way one finds that the optimal policy with commitment is $\pi = s/(1+\xi)$, and the concurrent expected loss is

$$EL_B = \frac{1}{2}(\kappa^2 + \frac{\xi}{1+\xi}\sigma_{ss}) \tag{10.21}$$

This is obviously less than EL_A as long as $\kappa > 0$. If $\kappa = 0$, the two policies coincide. Note that the two policies respond to s in the same way.

A problem is that after wages have been set, the best the government can do is still to follow the discretionary policy. At least this is true for a government which, like the one above, is concerned only with the present. Thus, the government has an incentive to violate the pre-set policy rule. This is the *time consistency problem*. It means that it can be difficult to make a credible commitment. The optimal policy with commitment may in practice not be an available option. This is where a fixed exchange rate comes in. The government may actually be able to commit to a fixed rate. This can never be as good as the optimal policy with commitment, but may still be better than the available alternative if that is the discretionary policy.

In the simple environment assumed, a rigidly fixed exchange rate means $\pi = 0$. Like the optimal policy with commitment, the fixed exchange rate rule has no inflationary bias ($E\pi = 0$). Unlike the optimal policy, the fixed exchange rate is independent of s. It is an example of a *fixed rule*, while the optimal rule is a *contingent rule*. Since $\pi_e = \pi = 0$, $y = \bar{y} - s$. The value of the loss function is

$$L_C = \frac{1}{2}(\kappa + s)^2$$

which has expected value

$$EL_C = \frac{1}{2}(\kappa^2 + \sigma_{ss}) \tag{10.22}$$

This is obviously greater than EL_B. The outcome of a comparison to L_A is more ambiguous. Fixing the exchange rate removes the inflationary bias and, hence, reduces the loss related to κ. However, since π does not respond to s, the loss related to σ_{ss} is increased. The effect of a supply shock on output is stronger. Thus, fixing the exchange rate is an advantage if the inflationary bias is high or the variance of the supply shock low.

Why fixed exchange rates collapse: Obstfeld's model

The problem with a fixed exchange rate is, as we just saw, that the government is unable to respond to shocks. If a large shock hits, the government must be tempted to change the parity. One question is then whether it is able to make such a strong commitment that it does not fall to the temptation. A usual technique for committing to a policy is to make strong verbal statements designed to increase the loss of prestige if the policy is abandoned. Another method is to increase the administrative costs of changing the policy. Observations indicate that such methods often work, and that often it is costly for politicians to abandon a fixed exchange rate (see Edwards, 1989, p. 2). However, in practice the commitment to a fixed exchange rate is hardly ever unlimited.

One way of representing an imperfect commitment is as a fixed cost, c, which is added to the loss function when the parity is changed. The interpretation is that the loss of prestige is related to the fact that there is a parity change, and not to the size of the eventual change. The modified loss function can then be written

$$\tilde{L} = \frac{1}{2}(y - \tilde{y})^2 + \frac{1}{2}\xi\pi^2 + C(\pi) = L + C(\pi) \tag{10.23}$$

where

$$C(\pi) = \begin{cases} 0 & \text{when } \pi = 0 \\ c & \text{when } \pi \neq 0 \end{cases}$$

By making commitments the government induces itself to minimize $\tilde{L}$ instead of L. Note that since the cost of a parity change is fixed, the government sets $\pi = \pi_{opt}$ if it changes the parity.

In order to find out whether the government will stick to the fixed exchange rate, it is now necessary to compare the levels of $\tilde{L}$ achieved with $\pi = 0$ and with $\pi = \pi_{opt}$ for given levels of π_e and s. If we insert the two values of π in (10.23), we find

$$\tilde{L}_{fix} = \frac{1}{2}(\kappa + \pi_e + s)^2 \quad \text{for} \quad \pi = 0 \tag{10.24}$$

$$\tilde{L}_{opt} = \frac{1}{2}\frac{\xi}{1+\xi}(\kappa + \pi_e + s)^2 + c \quad \text{for} \quad \pi = \pi_{opt} \tag{10.25}$$

$\tilde{L}_{opt} > \tilde{L}_{fix}$ if, and only if,

$$(\kappa + \pi_e + s)^2 > (1 + \xi)c \tag{10.26}$$

In view of (10.15) the condition can also be written

$$\pi_{opt}^2 > c/(1 + \xi)$$

Thus, the fixed exchange rate is abandoned if the deviation between the optimal discretionary policy and the fixed rate policy is too great.

The inequality (10.26) is illustrated in figure 10.3. It defines a band for π_e and s within which the exchange rate will be held constant. The limits of the band are the two roots of the equation $(\kappa + \pi_e + s)^2 = (1 + \xi)c$, which are

$$\bar{s} = -\kappa - \pi_e + \sqrt{(1 + \xi)c} \tag{10.27}$$

$$\underline{s} = -\kappa - \pi_e - \sqrt{(1 + \xi)c} \tag{10.28}$$

The policy is then to devalue if $s > \bar{s}$, revalue if $s < \underline{s}$, and keep the exchange rate fixed if $\underline{s} \leq s \leq \bar{s}$. In other words, devalue when inflationary expectations are high or there is a strong negative supply shock, revalue when inflationary expectations are low or there is a strong positive supply shock.

The size of eventual parity changes is given by π_{opt}. Thus,

$$\pi = \begin{cases} 0 & \text{if } \underline{s} \leq s \leq \bar{s} \\ \frac{\kappa + \pi_e + s}{1 + \xi} & \text{otherwise} \end{cases} \tag{10.29}$$

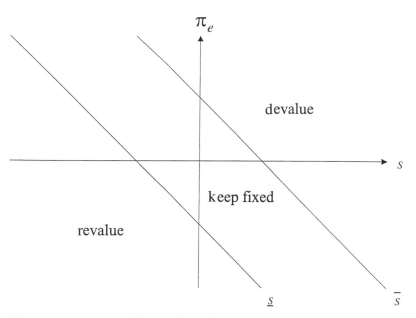

Figure 10.3 How parity changes depend on expectations and supply shocks.

As in the case above, we can now ask what level of inflation private agents should rationally expect. In general, a rational (model-consistent) expectation is a level of π_e which solves the equation

$$\pi_e = \mathrm{E}\pi = \int_{-\infty}^{\infty} \pi\psi(s)ds \qquad (10.30)$$

where $\psi(s)$ is the probability density of s and π is given by (10.29). The shape of the equation and the number of solutions depend on ψ. What is interesting is that there may be solutions that yield lower inflationary expectations than when there are no commitments, and that there may be multiple solutions.

In order to illustrate what can happen we follow Obstfeld (1994) in assuming that s is distributed uniformly on the interval $[-a, a]$.[105] This allows us to find simple expressions for $\mathrm{E}\pi$. We assume that $a > \sqrt{(1+\xi)c}$. This means that the possible occurrences of s cover a wider range than the band between $\underline{s}$ and $\bar{s}$. This ensures that there is some level of π_e for which both devaluations and revaluations are possible. The condition is not essential, but sets an upper limit on the level of commitment.

The interval of possible outcomes for s is $[-a, a]$. The interval where the government sticks to the fixed exchange rate is $[\underline{s}, \bar{s}]$. The location of these two intervals relative to each other determines which parity changes are possible ex ante. There are five different cases that we need to distinguish:

1. $a < \underline{s}$ Revaluation certain
2. $-a < \underline{s} < a < \bar{s}$ Revaluation possible, devaluation excluded

3. $-a < \underline{s} < \overline{s} < a$ Both revaluation and devaluation possible
4. $\underline{s} < -a < \overline{s} < a$ Revaluation excluded, devaluation possible
5. $-a > \overline{s}$ Devaluation certain.

If we insert for $\underline{s}$ and $\overline{s}$, we can alternatively write the conditions for the five cases in terms of constraints on π_e:

1. $\pi_e < -a - k - \sqrt{(1+\xi)c}$
2. $-a - k - \sqrt{(1+\xi)c} < \pi_e < -a - k + \sqrt{(1+\xi)c}$
3. $-a - k + \sqrt{(1+\xi)c} < \pi_e < a - k - \sqrt{(1+\xi)c}$
4. $a - k - \sqrt{(1+\xi)c} < \pi_e < a - k + \sqrt{(1+\xi)c}$
5. $a - k + \sqrt{(1+\xi)c} < \pi_e$

If the public has sufficiently negative inflationary expectations, the government is certain to revalue. With somewhat higher expectations the government revalues only if the realization of the supply shock is sufficiently favourable. Devaluation is excluded. Somewhat higher expected inflation again opens the possibility for devaluation, and if expected inflation is high enough, a devaluation is certain.

In order to find out how $E\pi$ depends on π_e, we can now calculate $E\pi$ in the five different cases. The result is:

$$E\pi = \begin{cases} \frac{\kappa + \pi_e}{1+\xi} & \text{cases 1, 3 and 5} \\ \frac{\kappa + \pi_e}{1+\xi} - \frac{1}{4a(1+\xi)}[(k+\pi_e+a)^2 - (1+\xi)c] & \text{case 2} \\ \frac{\kappa + \pi_e}{1+\xi} + \frac{1}{4a(1+\xi)}[(\kappa+\pi_e-a)^2 - (1+\xi)c] & \text{case 4} \end{cases} \tag{10.31}$$

In cases 1 and 5 a parity change is certain, and the expected rate of inflation is, of course, the same as under discretion. The expectation is the same also in case 3. This is the symmetric case where both devaluations and revaluations are possible. In case 2 there is an extra term which is positive in view of the constraints that define the case. In case 4 there is a similar extra term which is negative. At the edges of the intervals the extra terms drops out, so Ep is a continuous function of π_e. In figure 10.4 the straight line $(\kappa + \pi_e)/(1 + \xi)$ shows how $E\pi$ depends on π_e when there is no commitment. The thick curve which follows this line in intervals 1, 3 and 5 shows how $E\pi$ depends on π_e when there is a commitment.

In order to get an intuitive understanding of the shape of the curve, try this: in interval 1 a revaluation is certain in spite of the 'commitment'. The rational expectation is the same as if there had been no commitment. It increases with π_e. As soon as we enter region 2, the commitment begins to bite. Because π_e is still low, a revaluation would have been certain had there been no commitment. Hence, the effect of the commitment is to prevent some revaluations. This means that $E\pi$ rises above what it would have been without commitment. If π_e increases further, it means that more instances of small revaluations, which would have happened without commitment, are now prevented. Hence, the distance between $E\pi$ with and without commitment increases to begin with. However, somewhere in region 2 π_e becomes so high that a

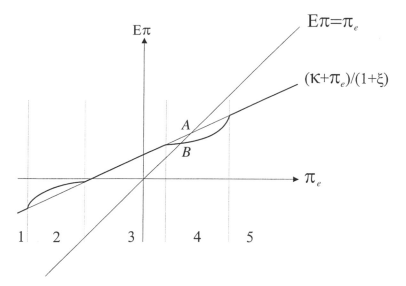

Figure 10.4 Expectational equilibrium with limited commitment to a fixed exchange rate.

devaluation would have been possible without commitment. After that point a higher π_e means that the commitment is more likely to prevent devaluations, and the devaluations that may be prevented also become larger. This means that the distance between $E\pi$ with and without commitment is reduced again. The curve approaches the straight line again. As π_e increases, we must sooner or later get into an interval where revaluations are unlikely anyway and the main effect of the commitment is to prevent devaluations. That brings the rational expectation below what it would have been without commitment. For very large π_e the commitment again has no effect whatsoever, and we are back to the straight line. That there is an intermediate region (case 3) where the two curves coincide is an artifact of the uniform distribution of s. With other distributions the curves may intersect just once.

In figure 10.4 the equilibrium with rational expectations is where the 45° line intersects with the curve for rational expectations. Without commitment the equilibrium is at A, as before. As figure 10.4 is drawn, this is in interval 4. With commitment there is a single rational expectations equilibrium at B. As we can see, the fixed exchange rate helps to bring down expected inflation. This happens without any loss in expected output, since only unexpected inflation matters. However, there is a cost in the form of increased output volatility, because the central bank no longer acts to dampen the effect of small shocks. Since the equilibrium is in region 4, devaluations sometimes happen (when there are strong negative shocks), revaluations never happen.

Are there other possible equilibria than those in figure 10.4? That $\kappa > 0$ means that the rational expectation curves always intersect the vertical axis above the origin. This means that any equilibrium has to be in the first quadrant. That excludes intervals 1 and 2, which are always on the negative side. Thus, the inflationary bias of the government excludes equilibria where devaluations never happen. It is never possible to achieve full credibility for the fixed exchange rate as long as $a > \sqrt{(1 + \xi)c}$. Without commitment there is a unique equilibrium in interval 3, 4 or 5. If this is in interval 3, it is obviously also the only equilibrium with commitment. In this case the commitment has no effect on π_e. Such an equilibrium will arise if either κ or c is low. In that case, the commitment does not bring down expected inflation. However, it still prevents a response to small shocks, and hence increases the loss by creating too much output variability.

More interesting cases can be found if the equilibrium without commitment is in interval 5. Figure 10.5 shows a case where commitment leads to multiple equilibria. A is an equilibrium both with and without commitment, B and C only with commitment. If the public's expectations are focused on B or (even better) on C, fixing the exchange rate helps in bringing down expected inflation. In C and B devaluations are possible, but may happen only rarely. However, if the public suddenly shifts its focus from these favourable equilibria to A, a devaluation is certain. The reason is that inflationary expectations at this level, if not accommodated, produce such a strong recession that the government prefers to break its commitment. According to this theory speculative attacks may happen out of the blue, without any forewarning, and without being triggered by any shock or structural change. A change in sentiment is enough. Perhaps a speculative attack on one country can be the trigger which releases spec-

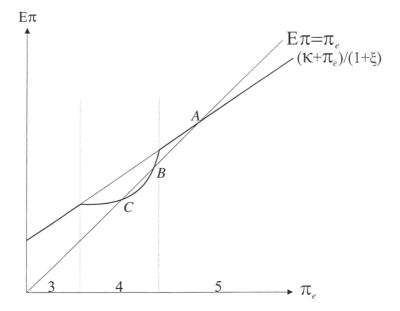

Figure 10.5 Multiple equilibria with rational expectations.

ulative attacks elsewhere. Eichengreen, Rose and Wyplosz (1996) estimate that a devaluation in one country increases the likelihood of devaluations in others by about 8 per cent. Thus, devaluations appear to be contagious. However, the estimated effect can alternatively be explained as a result of common shocks.

Figure 10.6 shows another possibility. Whether there is commitment or not, the only equilibrium is point A in interval 5. Devaluation is certain in spite of the professed commitment. This shows only that fixing the exchange rate is a meaningless exercise if the commitment is not sufficiently strong relative to the inflationary bias.

General discussion

As an explanation for why countries fix their exchange rates, the above model has some appealing features. Fixing the exchange rate is a tool that the government can use to protect itself against an inflationary bias. That some commitment is possible seems obvious, given the great efforts countries sometimes go to in defending their exchange rates. An important lesson is that commitment can be useful even if devaluations happen from time to time. Experience has shown that few countries manage to keep exchange rates fixed for very long periods (Obstfeld and Rogoff, 1995b), but this does not necessarily mean that fixed exchange rates are a bad idea. On the contrary, unlimited commitment to a fixed rate may be harmful, since it means one may have to endure the consequences of severe shocks without any accommodation. In the above model there exists an optimal level of commitment – i.e. an optimal level of c from the

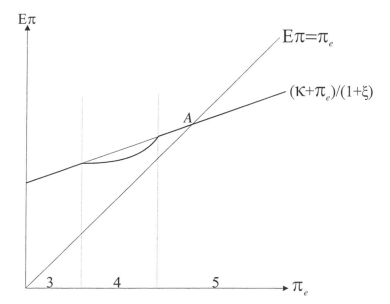

Figure 10.6 An equilibrium where devaluation is certain.

point of view of minimizing L (compare Rogoff, 1985b, on 'The optimal degree of commitment to an intermediate target'), but this may, of course, be difficult to achieve.

A fixed rule, even if it has escape clauses, is never the best conceivable policy. In the above model the optimal rule with full commitment is a state contingent rule where government policy responds to shocks. As emphasized by McCallum (1995) and Fischer (1990), a government may overcome the time-consistency problem. Blinder (1997) argues that the time-consistency problem is not so important in practice; this does not preclude that fixed exchange rates can help in some cases, but then they should also be compared with other techniques for commitment (see Walsh, 1998, ch. 8, or Obstfeld and Rogoff, 1996, section 9.5).

The model also has appeal in the way it explains why fixed exchange rates break down. Basically they break down when the conflict between the fixed exchange rate and the government's ultimate targets become too strong. Self-fulfilling expectations play a role in prompting the breakdown. Eichengreen (1996) claims that the main reason why it has proved more difficult to maintain fixed exchange rates in recent years than during the classical gold standard is that governments no longer enjoy the same 'protection from pressure to trade exchange rate stability for other goals' (p. 4). Eichengreen ascribes the change to universal suffrage, which made the electorate more sensitive to unemployment. Another possible conflict discussed by him and by Obstfeld (1994) is between keeping the exchange rate fixed and avoiding a financial crisis.

The details of the way the model explains speculative attacks may be questioned. The primary speculators in the model are the wage-setters. When there are multiple equilibria, it is their focus on the equilibrium with high inflation which induces the government to devalue. Investors play a more passive role. This does not fit well with some of the most recent speculative episodes that one attempts to explain – for example, the European crisis in 1992–3, the Mexican crisis in 1994 and the Asian crisis in 1997. In none of these cases was the crisis accompanied by a jump in the wage level that has been related to shifts in expectations. Nor am I aware of any suggestions that the crises were prompted by supply shocks.

Given the strong evidence against continuous purchasing power parity (PPP) cited in section 8.1, this assumption is a weakness of the Obstfeld model. The assumption means that exchange rate targeting and price level targeting are formally equivalent. If the level of commitment is the same, the government fails to meet its commitment in exactly the same circumstances. Speculative attacks owing to multiple equilibria also occur in the same circumstances. One may ask whether it is easier to come close to the optimal degree of commitment with one target than the other. In practice, although not in the model, monetary policy has a more immediate effect on the exchange rate than on the price level, and this may make it easier for the government to demonstrate from day to day its commitment to an exchange rate target (see Herrendorf, 1999).

The same logic as in Obstfeld's model may be applied to the model of section 10.1. One then finds that a price level rule more easily breaks down when there is a supply shock, an exchange rate rule when there is a demand shock. Any fixed rule is bound to break down if it is subjected to enough stress.

In the introduction to this chapter it was indicated that there may be other reasons than the time-consistency problem for committing to an intermediate target. More specifically, reasons may be found in the nature of the political decision mechanism. Optimality in the strictest sense requires that all instruments are set simultaneously taking account of all available information. The concept requires that there is a well defined preference function. Real political systems make decisions sequentially and on the basis of limited information, and consistent aggregation of preferences is problematic. There is a danger that an inflationary bias arises not because of biased preferences, but because the political system is unable to make the necessary decisions to prevent inflation. Setting intermediate targets may be one way of reducing this kind of decision making problems. In other political environments the same problem may by solved by delegating all monetary policy decisions to trusted central bankers. Much has been said about the need for a nominal anchor in order to focus expectations, but there may also be a need for a nominal anchor to focus the political decisions process. Setting the rules governing the value of money before money is allocated in the budget may improve the budget decisions. Thus, the use of intermediate targets, such as a fixed exchange rate, should not be condemned before one has taken the political context into account.

10.3 The benefits of having one's own currency

The use of money reduces transaction costs, and the greatest cost reduction is achieved if the same money is used all over the world. Hence it may be legitimate to ask why most nations have their own currencies. There are some obvious answers to this. There is no world government that can impose a single currency. Each country has an incentive to create its own currency in order to capture seigniorage revenue. Also a common money is an advantage only if monetary policy is conducted in a sensible manner. Countries may distrust each other in this respect. In any case there is room for disagreement about what the best monetary policy is. These are formidable obstacles that make monetary unification unlikely without a considerable degree of political unification. Suppose, however, that these difficulties could be overcome. Are there then any advantages to having separate currencies for different countries? We already answered that question with 'yes' in the introduction to this chapter when we said that exchange rate flexibility can be useful. This has also been shown in various places throughout the book. At the end, though, it is time to summarize some of the arguments and to mention some issues that have so far been neglected.

Separate currencies make it possible for countries to choose average inflation rates independently. A high inflation rate means a high nominal interest rate. Thus, up to a point a higher inflation rate also means higher seigniorage revenue to the government. This 'inflation tax' is an alternative to other taxes for financing government expenditure. A high inflation rate entails a real cost because people reduce their real money balances and, thus, incur higher transaction costs. But the alternative taxes also create distortions that have real costs. In an optimum these costs should be balanced against each other on the margin. If the optimal inflation rate varies, countries may benefit from having different average inflation rates. It has been suggested that countries with an inefficient system for tax collection and a large underground economy can benefit from a relatively high inflation rate.

In this book output and employment in long-run equilibrium has always been independent of the inflation rate. Thus, a permanent increase in the inflation rate does not give any benefits in the form of reduced unemployment. This proposition can be questioned. An old, but somewhat heterodox view, is that there is a positive relationship between the rate of inflation and the equilibrium rate of unemployment when inflation is close to zero (see Tobin, 1972; Holden, 1994; Akerlof, Dickens and Perry, 1996). In this view, equilibrium unemployment may be lower if the inflation rate is 1 per cent per year rather than 0. An example of what the relationship between inflation and unemployment in long-run equilibrium may look like according to this view is shown in figure 10.7. This relationship is called a long-run Phillips curve. Since the 1970s the opinion that the long-run Phillips curve is vertical has dominated the theoretical literature.

A possible explanation for the long-run Phillips curve in figure 10.7 is an asymmetry that may arise in ongoing employment relationships. It is a fact that wage contracts are most often made in nominal terms with no automatic index clauses. If the wage is to be changed, one of the parties must take the initiative. Presumably both parties are interested in the real, not the nominal wage. Normally there is a conflict between them. The employer wants a higher real wage than the employee. Assume that both parties have some bargaining power, either collectively or individually. When inflation is high

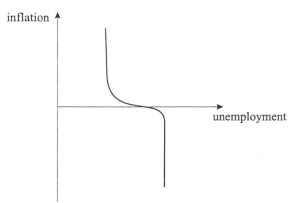

Figure 10.7 A long-run Phillips curve.

and the nominal wage is constant, the real wage is gradually eroded, and the initiative to increase the nominal wage must come from the employees or their unions. If there is a strong deflation, the initiative to cut the nominal wage must come from the employers. Depending on the relevant labour law, the party which has to take the initiative may be at a disadvantage (see Holden, 1994). One reason is that the other party benefits from delays as long as the relationship continues without changes in the nominal wage. There may also be other costs of taking the initiative (reduced goodwill, etc). The upshot is that, everything else being equal, workers are in a better bargaining position when deflation is high, employers when inflation is high. The stronger bargaining position of workers under deflation means that unemployment is pushed up. Thus, the equilibrium unemployment rate is higher when there is deflation than when there is inflation. That there is an intermediate range near zero where the equilibrium unemployment rate depends positively on inflation can be explained if equilibrium relative wages change over time. In the intermediate range some nominal wages need to be cut, some to be raised. The share of cases where the initiative has to come from the workers increases with the rate of inflation.

In our connection the point is that the long-run Phillips curve may differ from country to country. One reason is that labour law differs. In some countries it is easier for employers to cut wages than in others. Another is that in countries with high productivity growth there is less need for downward adjustment of nominal wages. Some countries may thus need higher average inflation rates than others in order to achieve the minimum level of unemployment.

These theories get empirical support from the fact that when inflation is low, there tends to be a spike in the distribution of wage increases at zero. They are also consistent with the macroeconomic history of the twentieth century, where periods of deflation have been characterized by high unemployment, although this may also be explained as a disequilibrium phenomenon. It is difficult to reach definite conclusions since there are comparatively few episodes of zero or negative inflation.

More recently a new reason for the non-neutrality of monetary policy in long-run equilibrium has been proposed. When we studied wage bargaining in earlier chapters, we assumed that each wage contract encompassed a group that was so small that it had no reason to take account of the eventual reaction of the monetary authorities to the wage contract. If wage bargaining is more centralized, the parties may take account of how the central bank responds to their wage contract (see Soskice and Iversen, 1998; Bratsiotis and Martin, 1999; Cukierman and Lippi, 1999; Holden, 1999). This means that countries with a different bargaining structure may benefit from central banks that operate under different rules.

So much for the benefits nations may have from choosing their average inflation rates. As we have seen in the preceding chapters, exchange rate flexibility may also be used to ease the adjustment to various types of exogenous shocks. The condition for this is that nominal wages (or prices) are to some extent rigid in the short run. Devaluation can then be used to achieve a necessary cut in real wages (or reduction in relative wage costs) with a lower level of unemployment than would otherwise have been required. Dornbusch (1996), Gylfason (1990) and Eichengreen (1992) give a number of examples where devaluations appear to have been successful. However, even if there are examples where devaluations have helped, they cannot be expected to help always and everywhere. As we have seen, devaluations may sometimes be contractionary. Dornbusch argues that devaluations are most useful when used rarely and only in response to exceptional shocks. If they are used too often, the economy becomes indexed or dollarized, and devaluations use their force. If they are used in response to events that are not exceptional, credibility is lost. Expectations of new devaluations may then push up inflation and interest rates, and there may be a lot of turbulence in the foreign exchange market.

The case for devaluations is thus probably strongest when the economy is hit by a 'permanent' shock that requires a 'permanent' structural change in the economy. The most obvious case is when the shocks require a permanent reduction in the real wage (or the wage level relative to abroad). More common are perhaps cases where a shock makes a large section of the traded goods industry obsolete or uncompetitive or where changes in international markets significantly reduce the revenues that a country obtains from its natural resources. Then, a period of high profitability may be needed to induce enough investment in new industries. In section 7.4, we saw examples of how a devaluation could help in this. Not only may countries benefit from devaluations in such cases. Because of speculative pressures it may also be difficult to avoid devaluing. The case for devaluations as a tool of structural adjustments is strengthened if the short-run Phillips curve is convex (meaning that wages increase more rapidly than they decrease) or, more generally, if employers are in a weak bargaining position if they want to cut nominal wages. It is then particularly difficult to achieve reductions in real wages without devaluations.

Countries which experience similar shocks in the other direction (e.g. resource discoveries) need an increase in real wages. They can achieve this either by revaluing, or by going through a period of high employment and rapid nominal wage increases. Usually the latter alternative also means a relatively high inflation rate because of price increases on non-traded goods. With a revaluation, inflation can be avoided. The benefits from revaluing may in this case seem small compared to the benefits from devaluing mentioned above. This may help to explain why devaluations are more frequent than revaluations. A stronger case for revaluations can be built if expectations are backward-looking. Once an inflation has got started, it may then be difficult to stop without going through a period of relatively high unemployment. Hence, revaluations may in this case be used to avoid higher future unemployment. For the same reasons, backward-looking expectations also weaken the case for devaluations, except perhaps when they can be used to avoid deflation.

Another matter is whether exchange rate flexibility can also help in the adjustment to temporary shocks – or, in other words, help to smooth the business cycle. As we saw in section 10.1, the right kind of exchange rate flexibility can obviously do so when there is short-run nominal wage rigidity. When capital mobility is high, exchange rate flexibility is necessary if one wants to set interest rates in such a manner that they contribute to dampen local cyclical swings in output. However, in the case of supply shocks there is a conflict between dampening the swings in output and in inflation. Since the exchange rate and the interest rate cannot be set independently of each other, this restricts what can be achieved. It may be difficult to work out what the right policy is, and actual experience does not seem to indicate that countries with floating exchange rates have on average achieved greater stability (see Flood and Rose, 1995). There are some promising experiments with inflation targeting going on (see Leiderman and Svensson, 1995), but it may be too early to judge their success.

One issue is that the short-run variations in the exchange rate and the interest rate that are supposed to dampen cyclical swings may have relatively small effects on aggregate demand. In chapter 8 we reviewed some arguments about pricing to market and investments in market shares which indicated that variations in the exchange rate which are expected to be reversed shortly may have little effect on both prices and trade flows. When capital mobility is high, the average returns over long periods on assets denominated in different currencies should be expected to be roughly the same. If aggregate demand mainly depends on expected long-term interest rates, then short-run local variations in interest rates will have little effect. Thus, the debate on how useful exchange rate flexibility is for cyclical stabilization is still open. Some degree of cyclical stabilization may also be achieved within a wide target zone for the exchange rate, or with a policy which targets the long-run path of the exchange rate but allows deviations in the short run.

In any case there are potentially important macroeconomic advantages to having a separate currency. These advantages can be achieved only if exchange rate policy is to some extent flexible. However, there are also some countervailing effects to consider. One is the extra 'noise' that easily arises from foreign exchange markets where it is genuinely difficult for agents to form rational expectations. Another is the extra discipline it may enforce on governments and on wage- and price-setters if one can commit to a non-inflationary policy. As discussed in section 10.2, a fixed exchange rate can be used to borrow credibility from other countries in the fight against inflation. However, this solution supposes that there are other countries that have solved the credibility problem in a more direct way. As discussed in chapter 9, exchange rates may also be used for 'beggar-thy-neighbour' purposes.

The weight of the different arguments for exchange rate flexibility has changed with increasing capital mobility. When sterilized interventions were more effective, monetary policy could (within limits) pursue two targets at the same time. The conflict between exchange rate stability and counter-cyclical policies was less acute. Disturbances from the foreign exchange market were easier to handle. Adjustable fixed rates have become less attractive, because of the difficulties that are created by speculative capital movements. The policy response has gone in two directions. Some countries have chosen currency boards and other measures to strengthen their commitment to fixed rates, and have renounced the exchange rate as a policy instrument. Such regimes may nevertheless remain vulnerable, and the logical conclusion of such policies is a desire for monetary union. Others have gone in the direction of more exchange flexibility, often by replacing fixed rates with an inflation target. A third alternative figuring in the public debate is to reduce capital mobility (see Haq, Kaul and Grunberg, 1996). So far, this has not had much practical effect. The debate about exchange rate policy is not likely to end soon.

Exercises

1. Compare the relationship between domestic and foreign interest rates under exchange rate and price level targeting. When does an increase in the foreign interest rate have the same effect on the domestic interest rate in the two regimes, and why?
2. What are the implications of the model in section 10.2 for the domestic interest rate? What will the time series of deviations from uncovered interest rate parity look like? What are the implications for tests of interest rate parity?
3. Discuss which equilibria may arise in the Obstfeld model if $\kappa = 0$. Is there any advantage in fixing the exchange rate in this case?

APPENDIX A

Differential equations in two variables

In this book we frequently use systems of two differential equations in two unknown time functions. This appendix gives a brief review of the qualitative theory for such systems, first for linear and then for non-linear systems. The discussion is confined to so-called 'autonomous' systems where time does not appear as a separate argument in the equations, since this is all we need for the book.

Homogeneous linear systems

Let the two unknown time functions be $x_1(t)$ and $x_2(t)$. We shall first look at the equation system

$$\dot{x}_1 = a_{11}x_1 + a_{12}x_2$$
$$\dot{x}_2 = a_{21}x_1 + a_{22}x_2 \tag{A.1}$$

where the *a*s are constant coefficients. The coefficient matrix is defined as

$$A = \begin{bmatrix} a_{11} & a_{12} \\ a_{21} & a_{22} \end{bmatrix} \tag{A.2}$$

The system is called 'homogeneous' because there are no constant terms in the equations. This means that the stationary state of the system is $(x_1 = 0, x_2 = 0)$. At this point $\dot{x}_1 = \dot{x}_2 = 0$, and the system is at rest. We shall later see that the results can be generalized easily to the more interesting case where the equations contain constant terms.

A solution of the system (A.1) is a pair of functions $(x_1(t), x_2(t))$ that satisfies (A.1) for all t. In general, there is an infinity of solutions to (A.1). However, the number of solutions is reduced to one if we demand that the solution passes through a particular point (x_1^0, x_2^0) at time t_0. x_1^0 and x_2^0 are called initial values. In fact, one can prove that for a given set of initial values the system (A.1) has one and only one solution.

One method of solution requires us to solve the quadratic equation

$$\begin{vmatrix} a_{11} - \lambda & a_{12} \\ a_{21} & a_{22} - \lambda \end{vmatrix} = 0 \tag{A.3}$$

This is called the *characteristic equation* for (A.1). By computing the determinant in (A.3) and reorganizing terms, we find that it can be written

$$\lambda^2 - \text{tr}(A)\lambda + |A| = 0 \tag{A.4}$$

where $\mathrm{tr}(A)$ is the sum of the elements on the main diagonal ($\mathrm{tr}(A) = a_{11} + a_{22}$). The solution to this second-order equation is

$$\lambda = \frac{\mathrm{tr}(A) \pm \sqrt{(\mathrm{tr}(A))^2 - 4|A|}}{2} \tag{A.5}$$

Here we can distinguish between three different cases depending on whether $\Delta = (\mathrm{tr}(A))^2 - 4|A|$ (the discriminant) is positive, zero or negative:

1. $|A| < \frac{1}{4}(\mathrm{tr}(A))^2$:   Two different real roots, λ_1 and λ_2 given by (A.5).
   The solution is

   $$x_1 = C_1 e^{\lambda_1 t} + C_2 e^{\lambda_2 t}$$
   $$x_2 = \gamma_1 C_1 e^{\lambda_1 t} + \gamma_2 C_2 e^{\lambda_2 t} \tag{A.6}$$

   where[106]

   $$\gamma_1 = (\lambda_1 - a_{11})/a_{12}, \quad \gamma_2 = (\lambda_2 - a_{11})/a_{12}$$

   C_1 and C_2 are constants which depend on the initial values (x_1^0, x_2^0) and can be found by inserting these and $t = t_0$ in (A.6). We then get two ordinary linear equations with two unknowns C_1 and C_2.

2. $|A| = \frac{1}{4}(\mathrm{tr}(A))^2$:   One real root, $\lambda_1 = \lambda_2 = \mathrm{tr}(A)/2 = \alpha$.
   In this special case the solution of (A.1) is

   $$x_1 = (C_1 + C_2 t)e^{\alpha t}$$
   $$x_2 = (\gamma_1 C_1 + \gamma_2 C_2 + \gamma_1 C_2 t)e^{\alpha t} \tag{A.7}$$

   where

   $$\gamma_1 = (\alpha - a_{11})/a_{12}, \quad \gamma_2 = 1/a_{12}$$

   The Cs are constants which are determined by the initial values.

3. $|A| > \frac{1}{4}(\mathrm{tr}(A))^2$:   No real roots.
   The solution to (A.1) is in this case

   $$x_1 = e^{\alpha t}[C_1 \cos(\beta t) + C_2 \sin(\beta t)]$$
   $$x_2 = e^{\alpha t}[(\gamma_1 C_1 + \gamma_2 C_2)\cos(\beta t) - (\gamma_2 C_1 - \gamma_1 C_2)\sin(\beta t)] \tag{A.8}$$

   where $\alpha = \mathrm{tr}(A)/2$ (as before),

   $$\beta = \frac{1}{2}\sqrt{4|A| - (\mathrm{tr}(A))^2},$$

   and

   $$\gamma_1 = (\alpha - a_{11})/a_{12}, \quad \gamma_2 = \beta/a_{12}$$

   The Cs are constants which are determined by the initial values.

In the last case, where there are no real roots, the characteristic equation has two complex roots. From (A.5) the roots of the characteristic equation are

$$\lambda = \frac{1}{2} \text{tr}(A) \pm \frac{1}{2} \sqrt{4|A| - (\text{tr}(A))^2} \sqrt{-1} = \alpha \pm \beta \sqrt{-1}$$

Thus, the two complex roots are written $\lambda_1 = \alpha + \beta\sqrt{-1}$ and $\lambda_2 = \alpha - \beta\sqrt{-1}$, where α is called the real and β the imaginary part. When the roots are real, the roots themselves are also said to be the real parts, while the imaginary part is said to be zero. It is possible to express the solutions in the different cases in a more compact way by using complex numbers, but there is no need for that here. That (A.6), (A.7) and (A.8) are actually solutions of (A.1) can be shown by computing the time derivatives of the proposed solutions.

We define the equation system as *stable* if for arbitrary initial values (x_1^0, x_2^0) x_1 and x_2 tend towards the stationary state $(0,0)$ as t goes to infinity. From (A.6) it is obvious that if we have two distinct real roots, λ_1 and λ_2, stability requires that they are both negative. If $\lambda < 0$, then $e^{\lambda t}$ goes to 0 when t goes to infinity. If one root is positive, the corresponding exponential function will go to infinity and the system will explode. In the special case where there is only one real root, a negative root ($\alpha < 0$) is obviously necessary for stability, since otherwise the exponential term in (A.7) explodes. $\alpha < 0$ is also sufficient, because when $\alpha < 0$, $e^{\alpha t}$ goes sufficiently fast towards zero that $te^{\alpha t}$ does not explode. If we look at (A.8), we also see that when there are no real roots, stability requires a negative α. The sin and cos functions are bounded. They just repeat themselves over time and cannot cause an explosion. Thus, *the system* (A.1) *is stable if and only if both roots of the characteristic equation have negative real parts.*

The condition for stability can also be given in terms of the trace and determinant of the coefficient matrix. The system (A.1) is stable if, and only if,

$$\text{tr}(A) < 0 \quad \text{and} \quad |A| > 0 \tag{A.9}$$

The justification for this is seen from (A.5), and from the definition of α. In cases 2 and 3 it is obvious that $\text{tr}(A) < 0$ is both necessary and sufficient for stability, since $\text{tr}(A) < 0$ is equivalent to $\alpha < 0$ which again is equivalent to both roots having negative real parts. Adding $|A| > 0$ does no harm, since cases 2 and 3 can arise only if $|A| > 0$. In case 1 an inspection of (A.5) shows that (A.9) is the right condition as it is both necessary and sufficient for both roots to be negative.[107]

We are also interested in whether or not the paths for x_1 and x_2 are cyclic. Case 3, where there are no real roots, obviously leads to cycles, since the sin and cos functions in the solution (A.8) are cyclic. When there are two real roots, the solutions are exponential curves without cycles. Nor can there be cycles in case 2. The necessary and sufficient condition for cycles is thus the same as the condition for no real roots:

$$|A| > \frac{1}{4} (\text{tr}(A))^2 \tag{A.10}$$

Cycles are possible both when the stationary state is stable, and when it is unstable.

Above we discussed stability given an arbitrary starting point. If we have some free-dom in choosing the starting point, we are in a better position to get to the stationary state. Suppose we have two real roots and that $\lambda_1 > 0$ and $\lambda_2 < 0$. The solution is then unstable. However, as we can see from (A.6), if we can choose (x_1^0, x_2^0) in such a way that $C_1 = 0$, it does not matter that $\lambda_1 > 0$. The system approaches the stationary solution in any case. If the initial value for one of the variables is given, while the other can be chosen freely, we can always find an initial value which makes $C_1 = 0$.

In general, if we have one positive and one negative real root, and the initial value of one variable is given, we can always find an initial value for the other variable which gets us onto a path which approaches the steady state as time goes to infinity. Such a path is called a *saddle path*. The condition for such saddle path stability (or for one positive, one negative real root) is from (A.5)

$$|A| < 0 \qquad\qquad\qquad (A.11)$$

In figure A.1 we have shown how tr(A) and $|A|$ together determine the qualitative properties of the solution. All the relevant cases can be read from figure A.1. The dots along the border lines indicate that the borderline case belongs to the region where the dots are.

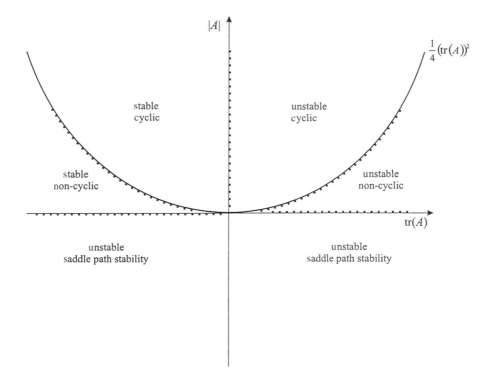

Figure A.1 Regions of stability and instability.

A linear system with constant terms

A linear system with constant terms (a non-homogeneous system) can be written

$$\dot{y}_1 = a_{11}y_1 + a_{12}y_2 + b_1$$
$$\dot{y}_2 = a_{21}y_1 + a_{22}y_2 + b_2$$
(A.12)

Here the *y*s are the unknown time functions, while the *a*s and *b*s are constant parameters. The stationary state of the system $(\bar{y}_1, \bar{y}_2)$ is the solution of

$$\dot{y}_1 = a_{11}\bar{y}_1 + a_{12}\bar{y}_2 + b_1 = 0$$
$$\dot{y}_2 = a_{21}\bar{y}_1 + a_{22}\bar{y}_2 + b_2 = 0$$
(A.13)

Define the transformed variables

$$x_1 = y_1 - \bar{y}_1$$
$$x_2 = y_2 - \bar{y}_2$$
(A.14)

Note that since $\bar{y}_1$ and $\bar{y}_2$ are constants, $\dot{x}_1 = \dot{y}_1$ and $\dot{x}_2 = \dot{y}_2$. Furthermore, by subtracting (A.13) from (A.12) we find

$$\dot{y}_1 = a_{11}(y_1 - \bar{y}_1) + a_{12}(y_2 - \bar{y}_2)$$
$$\dot{y}_2 = a_{21}(y_1 - \bar{y}_1) + a_{22}(y_2 - \bar{y}_2)$$
(A.15)

which is the same as

$$\dot{x}_1 = a_{11}x_1 + a_{12}x_2$$
$$\dot{x}_2 = a_{21}x_1 + a_{22}x_2$$
(A.16)

In this way we have transformed the non-homogeneous system (A.12) to the homogeneous system (A.1). Obviously the two systems are equivalent and their stability conditions are the same. Since x_1 is the deviation of y_1 from $\bar{y}_1$, if x_1 tends to zero as times goes to infinity, y_1 tends to $\bar{y}_1$, and similarly for y_2.

Non-linear systems

The non-linear system which corresponds to (A.12) is

$$\dot{y}_1 = \phi_1(y_1, y_2)$$
$$\dot{y}_2 = \phi_2(y_1, y_2)$$
(A.17)

The matrix of the derivatives of the ϕ functions is

$$A = \begin{bmatrix} \phi_{11} & \phi_{12} \\ \phi_{21} & \phi_{22} \end{bmatrix}$$
(A.18)

where

$$\phi_{ij} = \frac{\partial \phi_i}{\partial y_j} \quad i, j = 1, 2$$

This matrix is called the *Jacobian* of the system.

A central concept is local stability around a stationary state $(\bar{y}_1, \bar{y}_2)$ defined by $\phi_1(\bar{y}_1, \bar{y}_2) = \phi_2(\bar{y}_1, \bar{y}_2) = 0$. 'Local stability' means that if we start from any point sufficiently close to the stationary state, the solution to (A.17) will approach the stationary state as time goes to infinity. The theory of local stability is based on linear approximations around the stationary solution. The right-hand sides in (A.17) are replaced by their linear approximations as follows:

$$\dot{y}_1 = \phi_1(\bar{y}_1, \bar{y}_2) + \phi_{11}(\bar{y}_1, \bar{y}_2)(y_1 - \bar{y}_1) + \phi_{12}(\bar{y}_1, \bar{y}_2)(y_2 - \bar{y}_2) \qquad \text{(A.19)}$$
$$\dot{y}_2 = \phi_2(\bar{y}_1, \bar{y}_2) + \phi_{21}(\bar{y}_1, \bar{y}_2)(y_1 - \bar{y}_1) + \phi_{22}(\bar{y}_1, \bar{y}_2)(y_2 - \bar{y}_2) \qquad \text{(A.20)}$$

since $\phi_1(\bar{y}_1, \bar{y}_2) = \phi_2(\bar{y}_1, \bar{y}_2) = 0$, this yields

$$\dot{y}_1 = \phi_{11}(\bar{y}_1, \bar{y}_2)(y_1 - \bar{y}_1) + \phi_{12}(\bar{y}_1, \bar{y}_2)(y_2 - \bar{y}_2) \qquad \text{(A.21)}$$
$$\dot{y}_2 = \phi_{21}(\bar{y}_1, \bar{y}_2)(y_1 - \bar{y}_1) + \phi_{22}(\bar{y}_1, \bar{y}_2)(y_2 - \bar{y}_2) \qquad \text{(A.22)}$$

This is equivalent to the linear systems we have studied earlier. It is thus not surprising that there is strong similarity with the qualitative theory for linear equations. The conditions for stability, for cycles and for saddle path stability are the same as above except that we have to replace the coefficient matrix with the Jacobian evaluated at the stationary state.

APPENDIX B

The homogeneous production function

Suppose the production function is

$$Y = F(N, K) \tag{B.1}$$

which is homogeneous of degree one in N and K and has standard neo-classical properties. Define the capital intensity as $k = K/N$. Because of the homogeneity, we can write

$$Y = F(N, K) = NF(1, K/N) = Nf(k) \tag{B.2}$$

where $f(k)$ is defined by the last equality. $f(k)$ is called the *per capita* production function. This is increasing and concave ($f' > 0, f'' < 0$). Short-run profit maximization implies that the marginal product of labour should equal the real wage, or

$$f(k) - kf'(k) = \omega \tag{B.3}$$

Implicitly this defines k as a function of ω – i.e. $k = h(\omega)$. Differentiation of (B.3) shows that $h' = -1/kf'' > 0$. What this means is just that an increase in the real wage lowers the demand for labour in the short run.

Since $K/N = h(\omega), N = [h(\omega)]^{-1}K = n(\omega)K$. Because of the homogeneity property, we have

$$Y = F(N, K) = F(N/K, 1)K = F(n(\omega), 1)K = y(\omega)K$$

In terms of the firm's output, its real profits are

$$\Pi = Y - \omega N = y(\omega)K - \omega n(\omega)K$$

or

$$\Pi = \pi(\omega)K$$

where

$$\pi(\omega) = y(\omega) - \omega n(\omega)$$

$\pi(\omega)$ is the profit per unit of capital – or, in other words, capital's rate of return.

From standard duality theory $d\Pi/d\omega = -N$. Since $\Pi = \pi(\omega)K$, we also have $d\Pi/d\omega = \pi'(\omega)K$. Together with $N = n(\omega)K$, this gives us

$$\pi'(\omega) = -n(\omega)$$

which also shows that the rate of return on capital depends negatively on the real wage. Furthermore, $\pi(\omega) = f'(k)$. Recall that $\pi(\omega) = y(\omega) - \omega n(\omega) = f(k)/k - \omega/k$, which after insertion of the first-order condition $\omega = f(k) - kf'(k)$ yields $\pi(\omega) = f'(k)$. This means that $\pi(\omega)$ is equal to the marginal productivity of capital.

Notes

1 This became a standard term after the influential text by Dornbusch (1980).
2 May I suggest for a starter De Grauwe (1989, or later editions), Goldstein *et al.* (1992) or Obstfeld (1995b)?
3 Obstfeld and Rogoff (1996) gives an excellent introduction to the intertemporal general equilibrium approach based on explicit utility maximization.
4 The last chapters in Blanchard and Fischer (1989) are an example.
5 Modern portfolio models of the foreign exchange market originate from Tobin's general equilibrium approach to financial markets (Tobin, 1969), and were developed by, among others, Black (1973); Kouri and Porter (1974); Girton and Henderson (1976); Herring and Marston (1977).
6 By differentiating (1.18) with (1.25) inserted we find

$$\frac{dE/E}{dE_e/E_e} = \frac{\kappa E_e}{\gamma E + \kappa E_e} \tag{B.4}$$

which is between zero and one, increases with κ and goes to one when κ goes to infinity.
7 For an example from the Asian crisis of 1997, see Furman and Stiglitz (1998).
8 It will be recalled from section 1.2 that $W_i = (B_i + EF_i)/P$ for $i = g, p$. When all variables involved are differentiable functions of time, one can find $\dot{W}_i$ by differentiating this expression, which yields

$$\dot{W}_i = \frac{1}{P}(\dot{B}_i + E\dot{F}_i) + e\frac{EF_i}{P} - pW_i \quad i = g, p$$

A government surplus has to be invested in one of the financial assets. Thus $D_g = (\dot{B}_g + E\dot{F}_g)/P$. Similarly, $D - D_g = (\dot{B}_p + E\dot{F}_p)/P$ and $-D = (\dot{B}_* + E\dot{F}_*)/P$, since the two other sectors also have to invest their surpluses in the available financial assets. Equation (1.26) follows from this derivation and a similar derivation for the foreign sector, but it is somewhat more general, since it holds also when there are discrete jumps in the portfolio composition.
9 The connection between (1.32) and (1.6) is this: (1.32) can also be written $i = (1 + e_e)(1 + i_*) - 1$ where $e_e = (E^e_{t+1} - E_t)/E_t$. This yields $i = 1_* + e_e + e_e i_*$. When the period is short, it may be permissible to neglect the last term. In continuous time we simply have $i = i_* + e_e$.
10 See Copeland and Weston (1988).
11 This branch of the theory of finance was first applied to the question of the currency composition of portfolios in the mid-1970s with contributions from Solnik (1974); Grauer, Litzenberger and Stehle (1976); Kouri (1977); Frankel (1979), among others. For a survey, see Branson and Henderson (1985). Dornbusch (1983) integrated the approach in a macro model.
12 There is more on this in section 8.1.

13 Hodrick (1987, ch. 5) surveys some empirical applications of mean–variance models to the foreign exchange market.

14 See, however, Adam–Müller (1997) and the references therein on the hedging decisions of exporters.

15 A complete analysis of this case requires that one also takes account of uncertainty about foreign currency prices, of the effect of the exchange rate on domestic costs over time, of the possibility of changing the levels of inputs and outputs in response to exchange rate changes and of the owner's interest in the consumption value of profits.

16 We get the same result in section 2.1 if we assume $R = 1$ and measure the risk premium by $i - i_* - \mu_e + \sigma_{ep}$, as suggested in section 2.3.

17 There is a large literature which tests whether the foreign exchange market uses other types of information efficiently (see, for example, Levich, 1985; Hodrick, 1987).

18 Early examples of such models are Kouri and Porter (1974); Girton and Henderson (1976); Herring and Marston (1977).

19 We could have used the equilibrium condition for the money market and got the same result, but then we would have to take account of that the money supply is endogenous.

20 Kouri (1977) and Branson and Henderson (1985) analyse the demand for money in the same framework as here, and get the same separation result. However, they use a different s function, and thus obtain a different m function. Their formulation seems to imply that, for some unexplained reason, saved transaction costs are proportional to wealth.

21 Giovannini and Turtelboom (1994) survey the literature on currency substitution. Sometimes the term 'currency substitution' is used as synonymous with 'capital mobility between currencies'; this usage should be avoided.

22 The original version of Gresham's law actually dealt with the circulation of coins with different metal content and, thus, described a slightly different phenomenon.

23 McKinnon and Pill (1998) shows what can happen when banks do not hedge their foreign currency positions and discuss how this exacerbated the Asian crisis of 1997.

24 For an overview of the system, see Osband and Villanueva (1993); for a historical survey, see Schwartz (1993).

25 In addition to the monetary approach to exchange rate determination there is also the monetary approach to the balance of payments under fixed exchange rates, see the collection by Frenkel and Johnson (1976). The monetary approach to fixed rates can be seen as a special case of the portfolio approach. The focus in the present chapter is on the monetary approach to floating rates because of its contribution to the theory of exchange rate expectations.

26 There is an apparent inconsistency here. The differential equation (4.3) assumes that $E(t)$ is differentiable and, hence, continuous. However, we should think of $E(t)$ for $t > 0$ as the expected time path of the exchange rate given today's information. While the actual time path for the exchange rate can jump at any time, the expected future path is always continuous as long as the interest rate differential is finite. If a discrete depreciation is expected at some point in time, then everybody rushes to buy foreign currency before the depreciation. But this surge in the demand for foreign currency means that the jump in the exchange rate occurs immediately. The investors know that new information will arrive in the future, and that this will lead to future jumps in E. However, they cannot foresee when these jumps happen.

27 See exercise 3.

28 A survey of the literature on exchange rate dynamics which is exploited in this section is given in Obstfeld and Stockman (1985).

29 Equation (4.10) is sometimes called the *fundamental* solution. The other solutions are said to include bubbles. Let the fundamental solution given by (4.10) be $e_*(t)$. It is easy to show that all solutions to (4.9) are related to the fundamental solution by $e(t) = e_*(t) + ce^{(1/\eta)t}$ where c is a constant. There is one such solution for every real number c. The component $ce^{(1/\eta)t}$ is called a *bubble*. The bubble is completely unrelated to the underlying exogenous variables in the model. Within the model, however, the bubble is consistent with rational expectations. If everybody believes that the exchange rate will follow a path with a bubble, then it will. Therefore, it is called a 'rational bubble' to distinguish it from bubbles which are created by less rational expectations.

30 For this to be strictly true, we must use the same basket of goods to measure P and P_*.

31 An alternative definition of seigniorage is often used, namely that the seigniorage in a given time period is the same as the increase in the money supply in that period. In long-run equilibrium the two definitions sometimes give the same result.

32 Whether this is a good description of what Hume actually said is the subject of some controversy (see Samuelson, 1980; Cesarano, 1998). Hume may actually have described the price–specie–flow mechanism that is the subject of section 6.6.

33 Other useful sources are Frenkel and Razin (1996), Turnovsky (1997) and the brief and instructive article by Sachs (1982).

34 From the homogeneity of the production function it follows that labour demand and output supply can actually be written $N = n(\omega)K$, and $Y = y(\omega)K$ – i.e. they are proportional to K (see appendix B, p. 359). Since in the present section we make no use of this fact, the more general functional forms are retained. Homogeneity is used when asserting that $N_K > 0$.

35 The supply side in this section is adapted from Kouri (1979), which we return to in chapter 7.

36 When $\pi(\omega) > \rho_*$, Tobin's q is greater than 1. The theory of investment here is equivalent to Tobin's q theory.

37 For a survey of the economic theory of trade unions, see Oswald (1985); for an influential example of an application to macroeconomics, see Layard, Nickell and Jackman (1991).

38 More recently the Nash bargaining solution has also been given a justification in non-cooperative bargaining theory. Then the reference utility is the utility achieved during a conflict – e.g. during a strike. This interpretation may also be used, although it is then a bit harder to argue for the relevance of outside wages and unemployment.

39 General references to this section are Buiter and Marston (1985) and Blanchard *et al.* (1990). For an application to the Maastricht criteria for public debt, see De Grauwe (1997, ch. 8).

40 Strictly speaking, when inflation is constant, seigniorage is a constant share of GDP only if money demand is proportional to GDP.

41 There may be a third option: a one-time wealth tax.

42 Unless they can convince their own governments to use force as in nineteenth-century 'gun-boat diplomacy'.

43 In chapter 6, output depends on domestic demand. An increase in investment demand there raises output which again leads to increased savings. If investment is a major driving force in the business cycle, this tends to produce a high short-run correlation between savings and investment.

44 The Marshall–Lerner condition was named after Alfred Marshall and Abba Lerner. It was derived independently by several authors in the first half of the twentieth century. It formed an important part of the so-called 'elasticities approach' to the foreign exchange market. In this approach the supply of foreign currency to the central bank was simply taken to be X (or, more exactly, the foreign currency value of X). A classical work in the elasticities approach is Bickerdike (1920).

45 Meade (1951) is an example of earlier work in the same direction.

46 The supply of foreign currency to the central bank was usually written as $X(R, Y, Y_*) + k(r)$, where $k(r)$ represented capital movements.

47 By definition $T = G + S_g$, where S_g is the government surplus corrected for (expected) price changes. T tells how much revenue the government detracts from the private sector in order to spend on government consumption or asset accumulation. T here differs from T in chapter 5, where it represented net taxes only.

48 The same ambiguity arises in the end-of-period version of the stock approach (see Frenkel Gylfason and Helliwell, 1980). There a finite period length is assumed and the portfolio equilibrium is modelled after this period's flows have been added to the stocks. I have used the beginning-of-period formulation because it leads to greater theoretical clarity and because we use continuous time in the dynamic models later.

49 The income effect is affected by our assumption about tax policy. If tax payments from the private sector had been kept constant, the first term would have been $+C_Y \rho_* F_p$. The income and the wealth effect then have the same sign.

50 Some readers will be familiar with another diagram where there are three curves, IS, LM and BOP, BOP standing for balance of payments equilibrium. Our BOP curve is the FX equation (6.20). In the traditional diagrams there are three endogenous variables in a two-dimensional figure, E being hidden behind the scene. I find this rather confusing and prefer to eliminate one endogenous variable before the diagram is drawn. Hence the $ISFX$ curve instead of the IS and BOP curves.

51 If e_e is exogenous and capital mobility is perfect, it is hard to tell a reasonable story about how the exchange rate is determined in the very short run.

52 If homogeneity is not assumed, the real exchange rate should be included in the consumption function as an extra argument. This is known as the Harberger–Laursen–Metzler effect after Harberger (1950) and Laursen and Metzler (1950). They argued that because a real depreciation worsens the terms of trade, it has a negative effect on real income and consumption. However, this argument confuses different measures of real income and consumption. If there is an effect, it could go either way, as the intertemporal analysis in Persson and Svensson (1993) shows.

53 One may argue that for forward-looking consumers the relevant price index is not P_c but an index which also contain future prices. Intertemporal general equilibrium models of open economies take account of such effects.

54 *A priori* the Walters effect can make the multiplier process explosive in the same way as the investment accelerator can. In combination, the income effect on consumption and the Walters effect on real interest rates may mean that when output goes up by one unit, aggregate demand goes up by more than one unit. Formally this would show up in our model as a change of sign in the IS curve. However, the model loses its meaning in this case. If the multiplier process is unstable, we need to model the short-run dynamics of output and the impact of capacity constraints, etc. in greater detail than has been done here.

55 For other examples see Turnovsky (1977, ch. 12) and Aoki (1981, ch. 10).

56 See Krugman (1992, ch. 1) for an example from the debate about the US current account deficit in the 1980s that may motivate the discussion here.

57 Risager (1988) and Aoki (1981) present similar dynamic models with real investment. However, Risager lacks the foreign debt dynamics, while Aoki has a different wage equation.

58 The stationarity condition (6.37) implies that $X = i_* W_*'$. Insert this in (6.42) and the rest is straightforward.

59 The condition $\phi_{22} < 0$ is stricter than the condition $C_W > i_*(1 - C_Y)$ which we applied in chapter 5. $\phi_{22} < 0$ is equivalent to $C_W > i_*(1 - C_Y)[1 - (1/X_Y)]$. The reason that we get a stricter condition here is that an increase in F_* reduces Y. This has a negative effect on savings which needs to be overcome by the wealth effect if the current account shall be improved.

60 This presumes that a real depreciation improves the current account measured in foreign goods – i.e. that it improves X/R, not just X. If $X = 0$ initially, an improvement in X and in X/R is obviously the same thing. The analysis of section 6.1 can be repeated for X/R. Obviously, we shall have a positive effect of R on X/R if the quantity effects are sufficiently strong.

61 The problem is formally similar to the ones that were studied in sections 5.5 and 5.7. Readers who are already convinced that the solution is the saddle path from C to F can go straight on to the subsection headed 'A monetary expansion'.

62 It is a useful exercise to check these results by drawing the phase diagram.

63 Gärtner (1993) contains a further discussion of the robustness of the overshooting phenomenon.

64 For simplicity we have taken the real interest rate to be equal to the foreign interest rate. Taking account of the Walters effect, it may be replaced by $\rho_* + \gamma(Y - \bar{Y})$. As long as the IS equation is stable, this does not change the results.

65 For a model where the division between t- and n-goods is endogenous see Dornbusch, Fischer and Samuelson (1977).

66 Models with t- and n-goods have a long history in economics (see Dornbusch, 1980, ch. 6, and the references therein). Many of the models in this chapter seem to have been developed independently by a large number of authors concerned with practical economic problems in small open economies around the globe (Argentina, Australia, Canada, Scandinavia).

67 We use the homogeneity assumption only when the capital stock is changed.

68 The homogeneity of the production functions implies that output supply and labour demand are proportional to the capital stock of the industry (see appendix B, p. 359). Thus, we may alternatively write $Y_i = y_i(\Pi_i)K_i$, $i = n, t$.

69 When $\sigma > 0$ private savings are always positive in the present model. This means that a current account deficit can arise only when government savings are negative. This can easily be remedied by including a constant term in the consumption function or by adding (exogenous) investment. This does not change the substantial conclusions in other respects.

70 The first models with traded and non-traded goods and real wage rigidity were presented in the late 1970s in articles by a large number of authors writing in parallel (see, for example, Helpman, 1977; Rødseth, 1979). The latter also gave a treatment of indirect taxes.

71 The slope of the demand curve is $dY_n/d\Pi_n = m_n c_{nn}$ which can be compared to (7.16). When deriving this and other multipliers, remember that $dN_i/dY_i = 1/\Phi_{iN} = \Pi_{i,} i = n, t$ from the production function and the first-order condition.

72 An example of a Phillips curve amended to a two-sector model is Calmfors (1979).

73 Section 6.6 contains a similar derivation.

74 If wage increases are expansionary, as they could be when the marginal propensity to spend out of profits is small, $N_\omega > 0$ and the wage equation is unstable.

75 See, however, Wissén (1982), who provides an analysis based on some simplifying assumptions.

76 We have no initial value for P_n. Instead we have a final value implied by the stationarity conditions. If expectations are model-consistent, the solution must be a saddle path which P_n jumps onto.

77 In the Scandinavian context the first presentation of the model was in a report to the Norwegian government by the three economists Aukrust, Holte and Stoltz in 1967. Their model included a detailed description of the input–output structure and government determined prices, and was clearly intended as descriptive, not normative (see Aukrust, 1977). The model was popularized and used as a normative device in Edgren, Faxen and Odner (1973); for a survey see Lindbeck (1979). The model has several predecessors around the world.

78 As we have seen before, an exogenous real interest rate determines both the real wage and the factor intensities in long-run equilibrium. The factor shares are then also determined.

79 With the symbols from appendix B (p. 359) the ratio of capital to labour income is $r = \rho k/\omega$. The elasticity of this with respect to ρ can be written $El_\rho r = (1 + El_{(\rho/\omega)} k) El_{(\rho/\omega)}$. By definition $El_{(\rho/\omega)} k = -\sigma$, σ being the elasticity of substitution. Thus, $El_\rho r = (1 - \sigma) El_\rho(\rho/\omega)$. The last elasticity is obviously positive. We then see that capital income increases relative to labour income when $\sigma < 1$, decreases when $\sigma > 1$.

80 After Balassa (1964) and Samuelson (1964).

81 Useful surveys are Dornbusch (1987); Froot and Rogoff (1995); Rogoff (1996); and Goldberg and Knetter (1997).

82 This was documented in pioneering studies by Isard (1977) and Kravis and Lipsey (1977). Evidence against the law of one price has also been accumulated by the different projects for international comparisons of national accounts in real terms (see Summers and Heston, 1991, for an example).

83 For examples, see Frankel (1993) and Lothian and Taylor (1996).

84 The basic idea is from Phelps and Winter (1970). For applications to open-economy macroeconomics, see Rødseth (1985) and Phelps (1994). For a brief exposition of Phelps' theories and a critical discussion, see Woodford (1994).

85 Or the 'international monetary order', as it is called by McKinnon (1993) in his historical survey. Another good introduction to the history is Eichengreen (1996). A highly readable survey of the post-war period from a European perspective is given in de Grauwe (1989).

86 Another example is the franc bloc. Thirteen African countries have had fixed exchange rates to the French franc since 1948 with only one devaluation (in 1994) (see Eichengreen, 1996, pp. 185–6). For a historical analysis of the Bretton Woods era, see Bordo and Eichengreen (1993).

87 At least this is true in a world-wide key currency system.

88 For a thorough introduction to the European Monetary System (EMS), see Gros and Thygesen (1992).

89 Giovannini (1989), for example, claims that Germany was the leader, Fratianni and von Hagen (1990) rejects this. Gros and Thygesen (1992, section 4.5) gives an assessment of the literature.

90 Some reserves may also be kept in the currency of the other country, since this can be exchanged for gold at their central banks. For practical reasons most interventions may be carried out by exchanging domestic and foreign currency, but in a true commodity standard the central bank always stands ready to buy or sell domestic currency against the commodity in question.

91 The history of two-country models with Keynesian features goes back to Harberger (1950), Laursen and Metzler (1950) and Meade (1951). For a good survey of contributions from before 1980, see Mussa (1979). A main difference between Mussa's model and the one presented here is that the former has static expectations. Good examples of more modern discussions of the same questions, including quantitative models, are McKibbin and Sachs (1991), and Taylor (1993), or the shorter articles by the same authors in Bryant *et al.* (1989).

92 Or rather, a substantial share of total demand is for non-traded goods, but we have not modelled this explicitly here.

93 There is no standard terminology in this area. The words *international multiplier, national multiplier, spillover* and *direct impact* (to be defined later) should therefore not be used without proper definition.

94 The authors claim that current account targeting has also been practised more recently.

95 For more details and results of other policy changes see also McKibbin and Sachs (1991).

96 An in-depth treatment is given in Canzoneri and Henderson (1992) and Currie and Levin (1993). Useful brief surveys are Currie (1990) and McKibbin and Sachs (1991, ch. 7).

97 This survey also includes some reasons for coordination in economies where wages and prices are fully flexible, some of them related to tax distortions.

98 For an overiew of the debate about monetary unions in Europe, see de Grauwe (1997) and Gros and Thygesen (1992). For more sceptical views, see Feldstein (1997). The present section does not attempt an overall assessment. It surveys only a part of the literature that is closely related to the rest of the chapter. Among the issues not covered are the micro-economic gains from monetary union (reduced transaction costs, intensified competition) and the question of whether it is optimal for several countries to have the same inflation rates.

99 Alternatively we may choose two other instruments from the list of five potentially exogenous policy variables in the portfolio model of section 3.1. Because of the way these variables are interlinked, our conclusions do not depend on which pair we pick.

100 Some authors define inflation targeting more broadly as including all cases where the authorities maximize a preference function where inflation is given some weight (see Svensson, 1998, for an example). According to this definition the optimal discretionary policy in section 10.2 is an example of inflation targeting. To me, this definition seems too broad to be useful.

101 The debate about whether monetary policy should be directed towards a specific intermediate target or given more freedom is known as the debate about 'rules' versus 'discretion' (see Fischer, 1990, for a survey).

102 The section is built on Rødseth (1996b), which again builds on an earlier literature on the choice of exchange rate regime (see Genberg, 1989, and the surveys by Alogoskoufis, 1994;

Marston, 1985; Argy, 1990). The treatment here differs from the earlier literature in that the target variable under floating is the price level, not the money supply.

103 If we compute $\beta\mu$ for $a = a'$ and $a = 0$ and take the ratio between the two (with $a = a'$ in the numerator), we get

$$\frac{\beta + \alpha + \gamma}{\beta + (\alpha + \gamma)/(1 - a')}$$

This ratio is increasing in β, which means that a higher β raises the variance of y under a price level target relative to the variance under an exchange rate target.

104 Suppose the aggregate production function is $y = \theta(n + u)$, where n is the deviation of employment from its expected value and θ is the elasticity of output with respect to the input of labour. Then profit maximization yields an aggregate supply function $y = (\theta/(1 - \theta))(p - w + u)$. Thus, the price elasticity of supply is $\beta = \theta/(1 - \theta)$. This means that $\theta = \beta/(1 + \beta)$, and that the production function can be written as $y = (\beta/(1 + \beta))(n + u)$.

105 $\psi(s) = 1/2a$ when $s \in [-a, a]$, $\psi = 0$ otherwise.

106 For (A.1) to be a true system, at least one of a_{12} and a_{21} must be different from zero. If necessary, we can always order the equations in such a way that $a_{12} \neq 0$.

107 Alternatively one may look at it this way: from the theory of second-order algebraic equations it is known that $\lambda_1 + \lambda_2 = \text{tr}(a)$ and $\lambda_1 \lambda_2 = |A|$. Then (A.9) follows directly as a necessary and sufficient condition for both roots to be negative.

Bibliography

Aboudi, R. and Thon, D., 1993. Expected utility and the Siegel Paradox: a generalization, *Journal of Economics*, 57, 69–93

Adam-Müller, A. F. A., 1997. Export and hedging decisions under revenue and exchange rate risk: a note, *European Economic Review*, 41, 1421–5

Aizenman, J. and Frenkel, J. A., 1986. Targeting rules for monetary policy, *Economic Letters*, 21, 183–7

Akerlof, G., Dickens, W. and Perry, G., 1996. The macroeconomics of low inflation, *Brookings Papers on Economic Activity*, 1–59

Alogoskoufis, G., 1994. On inflation, unemployment and the optimal exchange rate regime, in F. van der Ploeg (ed.), *Handbook of International Macroeconomics*, Oxford: Blackwell, 192–223

Aoki, M., 1981. *Dynamic Analysis of Open Economies*, New York: Academic Press

Argy, V., 1990. Choice of exchange rate regime for a smaller economy: A survey of some key issues, in V. Argy and P. De Grauwe (eds.), *Choosing an Exchange Rate Regime: The challenge for smaller industrial countries*, Washington, DC: International Monetary Fund, 6–81.

Artis, M. and Bayoumi, T., 1990. Global financial integration and current account imbalances, in G. Alogoskoufis, L. Papademos, and R. Portes (eds.), *External Constraints on Macroeconomic Policy: The European experience*, Cambridge: Cambridge University Press, 10–40

Aukrust, O., 1977. Inflation in the open economy: a Norwegian model, in L. Krause and W. S. Salant (eds.), *Worldwide Inflation: Theory and recent experience*, Washington, DC: Brookings Institution

Backus, D. K., Gregory, A. W. and Telmer, C. I., 1993. Accounting for forward rates in markets for foreign currency, *Journal of Finance*, 48, 1887–1908

Baille, R. T. and McMahon, P. C., 1989. *The Foreign Exchange Market: Theory and econometric evidence*, Cambridge: Cambridge University Press

Balassa, B., 1964. The purchasing-power parity doctrine: a reappraisal, *Journal of Political Economy*, 62, 584–96

Baldwin, R., 1988. Hysteresis in import prices: the beachhead effect, *American Economic Review*, 78, 773–85

Baldwin, R. and Krugman, P., 1989. Persistent trade effects of large exchange rate shocks, *Quarterly Journal of Economics*, 54, 635–54

Ball, L., 1998. Policy rules for open economies, *Working Papers*, 6760, National Bureau of Economic Research

Barro, R. J., 1974. Are government bonds net wealth?, *Journal of Political Economy*, 82, 1095–1117

Barro R. J. and Gordon, D. B., 1983. Rules, discretion and reputation in a model of monetary policy, *Journal of Monetary Economics*, 12, 101–21

369

Bean, C. R., 1983. Targeting nominal income: an appraisal, *Economic Journal*, 93, 806–19
    1994. European unemployment: a survey; *Journal of Economic Literature*, 32, 573–619
Beenstock M., 1988. An econometric investigation of North–South interdependence, in D. Currie and D. Vines (eds.), *Macroeconomic Interaction between North and South*, Cambridge: Cambridge University Press, 32–62
Bernheim, D. B. and Bagwell, K., 1988. Is everything neutral? *Journal of Political Economy*, 96, 308–38
Bickerdike, C. F., 1920. The instability of foreign exchange, *Economic Journal*, 30, 119–22
Bilson, J. F., 1978. Rational expectations and the exchange rate, in J. A. Frenkel and H. G. Johnson (eds.), *The Economics of Exchange Rates*, Reading, MA: Addison-Wesley, 75–96
Black, S. W., 1973. International money markets under flexible exchange rates, *Studies in International Finance*, 32, Princeton University
Blanchard, O. J., Chouraqui, J.-C., Hageman, R. P. and Sator, N., 1990. The sustainability of fiscal policy: new answers to an old question, *OECD Economic Studies*, 15
Blanchard, O. J. and Fischer, S., 1989. *Lectures on Macroeconomics*, Cambridge, MA: MIT Press
Blinder, A. S., 1997. What central bankers could learn from academics – and vice versa, *Journal of Economic Perspectives*, 11, 3–19
Bordo, M. D. and Eichengreen, B. (eds.), 1993. *A Retrospective on the Bretton Woods System. Lessons for international monetary reform*, Chicago: University of Chicago Press
Branson, W. H. and Henderson, D. W., 1985. The specification and influence of asset markets, in R. W. Jones and P. B. Kenen (eds.), *Handbook of International Economics*, 2, Amsterdam: North-Holland, 749–805
Bratsiotis, G. and Martin, C., 1999. Stabilisation, policy targets and unemployment in imperfectly competitive economies, *Scandinavian Journal of Economics*, 102, 241–56
Bruno, M. and Sachs, J. D., 1985. *Economics of Worldwide Stagflation*, Oxford: Basil Blackwell
Bryant, R. C. *et al.* (eds.), 1988. *Empirical Macroeconomics for Interdependent Economies*, Washington, DC: Brookings Institution
Bryant, R. C., Currie, D. A., Frenkel, J. A., Masson P. R. and Portes R. (eds.), 1989. *Macroeconomic Policies in an Interdependent World*, Washington, DC: International Monetary Fund
Bryant, R. C., Hooper, P. and Mann, C. L. (eds.), 1993. *Evaluating Policy Regimes: New research in empirical macroeconomics*, Washington, DC: Brookings Institution.
Buiter W. H. and Marston R. C. (eds.), 1985. *International Economic Policy Coordination*, London: Cambridge University Press
Calmfors, L., 1979. Real wages, inflation and unemployment in the open economy, in A. Lindbeck (ed.), *Inflation and Employment in Open Economies*. Amsterdam: North-Holland, 41–69
Calvo, G. A., 1996. *Money, Exchange Rates, and Output*, Cambridge, MA: MIT Press
Calvo, G. A. and Rodriguez, C. A., 1977. A model of exchange rate determination under currency substitution and rational expectations, *Journal of Political Economy*, 85, 617–24
Canzoneri, M. B. and Henderson, D. W., 1992. *Monetary Policy in Interdependent Economies*, Cambridge, MA: MIT Press
Cassel, G., 1921. *The World's Money Problems*, New York: E.P. Dutton & Co.
Cesarano, F., 1998. Hume's specie–flow mechanism and classical monetary theory, *Journal of International Economics*, 45, 173–86
Copeland, T. E. and Weston, J. F., 1998. *Financial Theory and Corporate Policy*, Reading, MA: Addison-Wesley

Cukierman, A. and Lippi, F., 1999. Central bank independence, centralization of wage bargaining, inflation and unemployment: theory and some evidence, *European Economic Review*, 39, 1395–1434

Currie, D., 1990. International policy coordination, in D. T. Llewellyn and C. Milner (eds.), *Current Issues in International Monetary Economics*, London: Macmillan, 125–48

Currie, D. and Levin, P., 1993. *Rules, Reputation and Macroeconomic Policy Coordination*, Cambridge: Cambridge University Press

Currie, D. A., Holtham, G. and Hughes Hallett, A., 1989. The theory and practice of international policy coordination: does coordination pay?, Washington, DC: Brookings Institution

de Macedo, J. B., Goldstein, J. A. and Meerschwam, D. M, 1984. International portfolio diversification: short-term financial assets and gold, in J. F. O. Bilson and R. C. Marston (eds.), *Exchange Rate Theory and Practice*, Chicago: University of Chicago Press, 199–238

de Vries, C. G., 1994. Stylized facts of nominal exchange rate returns, in F. van der Ploeg (ed.), *The Handbook of International Macroeconomics*, Oxford: Blackwell, 348–89

Dixit, A., 1989. Hysteresis, import penetration, and exchange rate pass-through, *Quarterly Journal of Economics*, 54, 205–28

Dominguez, K. M. and Frankel, J. A., 1993a. *Does Foreign Exchange Intervention Work?*, Washington, DC: Institute for International Economics

  1993b. Does foreign-exchange intervention matter? The portfolio effect, *American Economic Review*, 83, 1356–69

Dornbusch, R., 1976. Expectations and exchange rate dynamics, *Journal of Political Economy*, 84, 1161–76

  1980. *Open Economy Macroeconomics*, New York: Basic Books

  1983. Exchange rate risk and the macroeconomics of exchange rate determination, in R. Hawkins, R. Levich and C. G. Wihlborg (eds.), *The Internationalization of Financial Markets and National Economic Policy*, Greenwich CT: JAI Press, 3–27

  1987. Purchasing power parity, in J. Eatwell, M. Milgate, and P. Newman (eds.), *The New Palgrave Dictionary*, New York: Stockton Press, 1078–85

  1996. The effectiveness of exchange rate changes, *Oxford Review of Economic Policy*, 12, 26–38

Dornbusch, R., Fischer, S. and Samuelson, P. A., 1977. Comparative advantage, trade and payments in a Ricardian model with a continuum of goods, *American Economic Review*, 67, 823–39

Dumas, B., 1994. Partial equilibrium versus general equilibrium models of the international capital market, in F. van der Ploeg (ed.), *The Handbook of International Macroeconomics*, Oxford: Blackwell, 301–47

Eaton, J. and Fernandez, R., 1995. Sovereign debt, in G. Grossman and K. Rogoff (eds.), *Handbook of International Economics*, III, Amsterdam: Elsevier, 2031–77

Edgren, G., Faxen, K.-O. and Odner, C.-E., 1973. *Wage Formation and the Economy*, London: Allen & Unwin

Edison, H. J., 1993. The effectiveness of central bank intervention: a survey of the literature after 1982, *Special Papers in International Economics*, 18, International Finance Section, Princeton University

Edison, H. and Klovland, J. T., 1987. A quantitative reassessment of the purchasing power parity hypothesis: evidence from Norway and the United Kingdom, *Journal of Applied Econometrics*, 2, 309–33

Edwards, S., 1989. *Real Exchange Rates, Devaluation, and Adjustment: Exchange rate policy in developing countries*, Cambridge, MA: MIT Press

Eichengreen, B., 1984. International policy coordination in historical perspective: a view from the interwar years, in W. B. Buiter and R. C. Marston (eds.), *International Economic Policy Coordination*, Cambridge: Cambridge University Press, 139–78

   1992. *Golden Fetters: The Gold Standard and the great depression, 1919–1939*, Oxford: Oxford University Press

   1996. *Globalizing Capital. A history of the international monetary system*, Princeton: Princeton University Press

Eichengreen, B., Rose, A. and Wyplosz, C., 1996. Contagious currency crises: first tests, *Scandinavian Journal of Economics*, 98, 463–84

Feldstein, M., 1997. The political economy of the European economic and monetary union: political sources of an economic liability, *Journal of Economic Perspectives*, 11, 23–42

Feldstein, M. and Horioka, C., 1980. Domestic savings and international capital flows, *Economic Journal*, 90, 314–29

Fischer, S., 1990. Rules versus discretion in monetary policy, in B. M. Friedman and F. H. Hahn, *Handbook of Monetary Economics*, Amsterdam: North-Holland, 1155–84

Fleming, J. M., 1962. Domestic financial policies under fixed and under flexible exchange rates, *International Monetary Fund: Staff Papers*, 9, 369–79

Flood, R. P. and Rose, A. K., 1995. Fixing exchange rates, a virtual quest for fundamentals, *Journal of Monetary Economics*, 36, 3–37

Frankel, J. A., 1979. The diversifiability of exchange rate risk, *Journal of International Economics*, 9, 379–93

   1982. In search of the exchange rate risk premium: a six-currency test assuming mean variance optimization, *Journal of International Money and Finance*, 1, 255–74

   1988. Ambiguous policy multipliers in theory and in empirical models, in R. C. Bryant *et al.* (eds.), *Empirical Macroeconomics for Interdependent Economies*, Washington, DC: Brookings Institution, 17–26

   1993. *On Exchange Rates*. Cambridge, MA: MIT Press

Frankel, J. A. and Froot, K. A., 1990. Chartists, fundamentalists, and trading in the foreign exchange market, *American Economic Review*, 80, 181–5

Fratianni, M. and von Hagen, J., 1990. Asymmetries and realignment in the EMS, in P. De Grauwe and L. Papademos (eds.), *The European Monetary System in the 1990's*, Brussels: Centre for European Policy Studies, 86–116

Frenkel, J. A., 1976. A monetary approach to the exchange rate: doctrinal aspects and empirical evidence, *Scandinavian Journal of Economics*, 78, 200–24

Frenkel, J. A. and Johnson, H. G. (eds.), 1976. *The Monetary Approach to the Balance of Payments*, London: George Allen & Unwin

   1978. *The Economics of Exchange Rates*, Reading, MA: Addison-Wesley

Frenkel, J. A. and Razin, A., 1996. *Fiscal Policies and Growth in the World Economy*, Cambridge, MA: MIT Press

Frenkel, J. A., Goldstein, M. and Masson, P. R., 1989. Simulating the effects of some simple coordinated versus uncoordinated policy rules, in R. C. Bryant, D. A. Currie, J. A. Frenkel, P. R. Masson and R. Portes (eds.), *Macroeconomic Policies in an Interdependent World*, Washington, DC: International Monetary Fund, 203–71

Frenkel, J. A., Gylfason, T. and Helliwell, J. F., 1980. A synthesis of monetary and Keynesian approaches to short-run balance of payments theory, *Economic Journal*, 90, 582–92

Friedman, M., 1953. *Essays in Positive Economics*, Chicago: Chicago University Press

Froot, K. A. and Frankel, J. A., 1989. Forward discount bias: is it an exchange risk premium?, *Quarterly Journal of Economics*, 104, 139–61

Froot, K. A. and Rogoff, K., 1995. Perspectives on PPP and long-run real exchange rates, in G. Grossman and K. Rogoff (eds.), *Handbook of International Economics*, III, Amsterdam: Elsevier, 1647–88

Froot, K. A. and Thaler, R. H., 1990. Anomalies: foreign exchange, *Journal of Economic Perspectives*, 4, 179–92

Furman, J. and Stiglitz, J., 1998. Economic crises: evidence and insights from East Asia, *Brookings Papers on Economic Activity*, 1–135

Garber, P. M. and Svensson, L. E. O., 1995. The operation and collapse of fixed exchange rate regimes, in G. M. Grossman and K. Rogoff (eds.), *Handbook of International Economics*, III, Amsterdam: Elsevier, 1865–1911

Gärtner, M., 1993. *Macroeconomics under Flexible Exchange Rates*, New York: Harvester Wheatsheaf

Genberg, H., 1989. Exchange rate management and macroeconomic policy: a national perspective, *Scandinavian Journal of Economics*, 91, 439–69

Gerlach, S., 1999. Who targets inflation explicitly?, *European Economic Review*, 43, 1257–77

Giovannini, A., 1989. How do fixed-exchange-rate regimes work? Evidence from the gold standard, Bretton Woods and the EMS, in M. Miller, B. Eichengreen and R. Portes (eds.), *Blueprints for Exchange-rate Management*, New York: Academic Press, 13–41

Giovannini, A. and Turtelboom, B., 1994. Currency substitution, in F. van derPloeg (ed.), *Handbook of International Macroeconomics*, Oxford: Blackwell, 390–436

Girton, L. and Henderson, D. W., 1976. Financial capital movements and central bank behavior in a two country short-run portfolio balance model, *Journal of Monetary Economics*, 2, 33–61

Goldberg, P. K. and Knetter, M. M., 1997. Goods prices and exchange rates: what have we learned?, *Journal of Economic Literature*, 35, 1243–72

Goldstein, M. and Kahn, M. S., 1985. Income and price effects in foreign trade, in R. W. Jones and P. B. Kenen (eds.), *Handbook of International Economics*, Amsterdam: North-Holland, 1041–1105

Goldstein, M., Isard, P., Masson, P. R. and Taylor, M. P., 1992. Policy issues in the evolving international monetary system, *Occasional Paper*, 96, Washington, DC: International Monetary Fund

Goodhart, C. A. E., 1994. What should central banks do? What should be their macroeconomic objectives and operations?, *Economic Journal*, 104, 1424–36

Grauer, F. L. A., Litzenberger, R. H. and Stehle, R., 1976. Sharing rules and equilibrium in an international capital market with uncertainty, *Journal of Financial Economics*, 3, 233–56

Grauwe, Paul De, 1989. *International Money: Post-war trends and theories*, Oxford: Clarendon Press
  1997. *The Economics of Monetary Integration*, Oxford: Oxford University Press

Gregorio, J. De, Giovannini, A. and Wolf, H. C., 1994. International evidence on tradables and nontradables inflation, *European Economic Review*, 38, 1225–44

Gros, D. and Thygesen, N., 1992. *European Monetary Integration*, London: Longman

Gylfason, T., 1990. Exchange rate policy, inflation, and unemployment: the Nordic EFTA countries, in V. Argy and P. D. Grauwe (eds.), *Choosing an Exchange Rate Regime: The challenge for smaller industrial countries*, Washington, DC: International Monetary Fund, 163–92

Gylfason, T. and Helliwell, J. F., 1983. A synthesis of Keynesian, monetary and portfolio approaches to flexible exchange rates, *Economic Journal*, 93, 820–31

Haliassos, M., 1994. On perfect foresight models of a stochastic world, *Economic Journal*, 104, 477–91

Hamada, K., 1979. Macroeconomic strategy and coordination under alternative exchange rate systems, in R. Dornbusch and J. A. Frenkel (eds.), *International Economic Policy*, Baltimore, MD: Johns Hopkins University Press, 292–324

Haq, M. u., Kaul, I. and Grunberg, I. (eds.), 1996. *The Tobin Tax: Coping with financial volatility*, Oxford: Oxford University Press

Harberger, A. C., 1950. Currency depreciation, income, and the balance of payments, *Journal of Political Economy*, 58, 47–60

Helpman, E., 1977. Nontraded goods and macroeconomic policy under a fixed exchange rate, *Quarterly Journal of Economics*, 91, 469–80

Herrendorf, B., 1999. Transparency, reputation and credibility under floating and pegged exchange rates, *Journal of International Economics*, 49, 31–50

Herring, R. J. and Marston, R. C., 1977. *National Monetary Policies and International Financial Markets*, Amsterdam: North-Holland

Hicks, J. R., 1939. *Value and Capital: An inquiry into some fundamental principles of economic theory*, Oxford: Clarendon Press

Hodrick, R. J., 1987. *The Empirical Evidence on the Efficiency of Forward and Futures Foreign Exchange Markets*, London: Harwood

Holden, S., 1994. Wage bargaining and nominal rigidities, *European Economic Review*, 38, 1021–39

  1999. Wage setting under different monetary regimes, *Memorandum*, 12, Department of Economics, University of Oslo

Hooper, P. and Marquez, J., 1995. Exchange rates, prices, and external adjustment in the United States and Japan, in P. B. Kenen (ed.), *Understanding Interdependence*, Princeton: Princeton University Press, 107–68

Isard, P., 1977. How far can we push the law of one price?, *American Economic Review*, 67, 942–8

Johansen, L., 1982. A note on the possibility of an international equilibrium with low levels of activity. *Journal of International Economics*, 13, 257–65

Knetter, M., 1989. Price discrimination by US and German exporters, *American Economic Review*, 79, 198–210

  1993. International comparisons of price-to-market behavior, *American Economic Review*, 83, 198–210

Kouri, P. J. K., 1977. International investment and interest rate linkages under flexible exchange rates, in R. Z. Aliber (ed.), *The Political Economy of Monetary Reform*, London: Macmillan, 74–96

  1979. Profitability and growth in a small open economy, in A. Lindbeck (ed.), *Inflation and Employment in Open Economies*, Amsterdam: North-Holland, 129–42

Kouri, P. J. K. and Porter, M. G., 1974. International capital flows and portfolio equilibrium, *Journal of Political Economy*, 82, 443–67

Kravis, I. B. and Lipsey, R. E., 1977. Export prices and the transmission of inflation, *American Economic Review*, 67, 155–63

Kreinin, M. E., 1977. The effect of exchange rate changes on the prices and volume of foreign trade, *International Monetary Fund: Staff Papers*, 24, 297–329

Krugman, P. 1979. A model of balance-of-payments crises, *Journal of Money, Credit, and Banking*, 11, 311–25

    1981. Consumption preferences, asset demands, and distribution effects in international financial markets, *Working Paper*, 651, National Bureau of Economic Research

    1989. *Exchange-rate Instability*, Cambridge, MA: MIT Press

    1991. Target zones and exchange rate dynamics, *Quarterly Journal of Economics*, 106, 669–82

    1992. *Currencies and Crises*, Cambridge, MA: MIT Press

    1995. What do we need to know about the international monetary system?, in P. B. Kenen (ed.), *Understanding Interdependence: The macroeconomics of the open economy*, Princeton: Princeton University Press, 511–29

Krugman, P. R. and Miller M. (eds.), 1992. *Exchange Rate Targets and Currency Bands*, Cambridge: Cambridge University Press

Kydland, F. E. and Prescott, E. C., 1977. Rules rather than discretion: the inconsistency of optimal plans, *Journal of Political Economy*, 85, 619–37

Laursen, S. and Metzler, L., 1950. Flexible exchange rates and the theory of employment, *Review of Economics and Statistics*, 18, 281–99

Layard, R., Nickell, S. and Jackman, R., 1991. *Unemployment*, Oxford: Oxford University Press

Leiderman, L. and Svensson, L. E. O., 1995. *Inflation Targets*, London: Centre for Economic Policy Research

Leitemo, K. and Røisland, Ø., 1999. Choosing a monetary policy regime: Effects on the traded and non-traded sectors, *Memorandum*, 4, University of Oslo, Department of Economics

Levich, R. M., 1985. Empirical studies of exchange rates, in R. W. Jones and P. B. Kenen (eds.), *Handbook of International Economics*, II, Amsterdam: North-Holland, 979–1040

Lewis, K., 1989. Changing beliefs and systematic rational forecast errors with evidence from foreign exchange, *American Economic Review*, 79, 621–36

    1995. Puzzles in international financial markets, in G. Grossman and K. Rogoff (eds.), *Handbook of International Economics*, III, Amsterdam: North-Holland, 1914–71

Lindbeck, A., 1979. Imported and structural inflation and aggregate demand: the Scandinavian model reconsidered, in A. Lindbeck (ed.), *Inflation and Employment in Open Economies*, Amsterdam: North-Holland, 13–40

Lizondo, J. S. and Montiel, P. J., 1989. Contractionary devaluations in developing countries, *International Monetary Fund: Staff Papers*, 36, 182–227

Lothian, J. R. and Taylor, M. P., 1996. Real exchange rate behavior: the recent float from the perspective of the past two centuries, *Journal of Political Economy*, 104, 488–509

Lucas, R. E., 1982. Interest rates and currency prices in a two-country world, *Journal of Monetary Economics*, 10, 335–59

MacDonald, R. and Taylor, M. P., 1992. Exchange rate economics: a survey. *International Monetary Fund: Staff Papers*, 39, 1–56

Marston, R. C., 1985. Stabilization policies in open economies, in R. W. Jones and P. B. Kenen (eds.), *Handbook of International Economics*, Amsterdam: North-Holland, 859–916

    1987. Real exchange rates and productivity growth in the United States and Japan, in S. W. Arndt and J. D. Richardson (eds.), *Real-financial Linkages among Open Economies*, Cambridge, MA: MIT Press

1988. Exchange rate policy reconsidered, in M. Feldstein (ed.), *International Economic Cooperation*, Chicago: University of Chicago Press, 79–136

1990. Pricing to market in Japanese manufacturing, *Journal of International Economics*, 29, 217–36

1993. Three parity conditions in international finance, in H. Frisch and A. Wörgötter (eds.), *Open-economy Macroeconomics*, London: Macmillan, 257–71

Masson, P. R. and Knight, M., 1990. Economic interactions and the fiscal policies of major industrial countries, in A. S. Courakis and M. P. Taylor (eds.), *Private Behaviour and Government Policy in Interdependent Economies*, Oxford: Clarendon Press, 282–334

Mayer, T, 1993. *Truth versus Precision in Economics*, Aldershot: Edward Elgar

McCallum, B. T., 1995. Two fallacies concerning central-bank independence, *American Economic Review*, 85, 207–11

McKibbin, W. J. and Sachs, J. D., 1989. Implications of policy rules for the world economy, in R. C. Bryant, D. A. Currie, J. A. Frenkel, P. R. Masson and R. Portes (eds.), *Macroeconomic Policies in an Interdependent World*, Washington, DC: International Monetary Fund, 151–94

1991. *Global Linkages*, Washington, DC: Brookings Institution

McKinnon, R. I., 1963. Optimum currency areas, *American Economic Review*, 53, 717–25

1993. The rules of the game: international money in historical perspective, *Journal of Economic Literature*, 31, 1–44

McKinnon, R. I. and Pill, H., 1998. International overborrowing: a decomposition of credit and currency risks, *World Development*, 26, 1267–82

Meade, J. E., 1951. *The Theory of International Economic Policy, I: The balance of payments*, Oxford: Oxford University Press

Mishskin, F. S., 1984. Are real interest rates equal across countries? An empirical investigation of international parity conditions, *Journal of Finance*, 39, 1345–57

Mundell, R. A. 1961. A theory of optimum currency areas, *The American Economic Review*, 51, 657–64

1963. Capital mobility and stabilization policy under fixed and flexible exchange rates. *Canadian Journal of Economics and Political Science*, 29, 472–85

1968. *International Economics*, London: Macmillan

Muscatelli, A. and Vines, D., 1989. Macroeconomic interactions between the north and south, in R. C. Bryant, D. A. Currie, J. A. Frenkel, P. R. Masson and R. Portes (eds.), *Macroeconomic Policies in an Interdependent World*, Washington, DC: International Monetary Fund, 381–412

Mussa, M., 1979. Macroeconomic interdependence and the exchange rate regime, in R. Dornbusch and J. A. Frenkel (eds.), *International Economic Policy*, Baltimore, MD: Johns Hopkins University Press, 160–204

1986. Nominal exchange rate regimes and the behavior of real exchange rates: evidence and implications, *Carnegie–Rochester Conference Series on Public Policy*, 25, 117–213

Naug, B. and Nymoen, R., 1996. Pricing to market in a small open economy, *Scandinavian Journal of Economics*, 98, 329–50

Obstfeld, M., 1994. The logic of currency crises, *Cahiers économiques et monétaires*, 43, 189–213

1995a. International capital mobility in the 1990s, in P. B. Kenen (ed.), *Understanding Interdependence*, Princeton: Princeton University Press, 201–61

1995b. International currency experience: new lessons and lessons relearned, *Brookings Papers on Economic Activity*, 119–220

1996. Models of currency crises with self-fulfilling features, *European Economic Review*, 40, 1037–47

Obstfeld, M. and Rogoff, K., 1995a. The intertemporal approach to the current account, in G. M. Grossman and K. Rogoff (eds.), *Handbook of International Economics*, III, Amsterdam: Elsevier, 1731–99

1995b. The mirage of fixed exchange rates, *Journal of Economic Perspectives*, 9(4), 73–96

1996. *Foundations of International Macroeconomics*, Cambridge, MA: MIT Press

Obstfeld, M. and Stockman, A. C., 1985. Exchange-rate dynamics, in R. W. Jones and P. B. Kenen (eds.), *Handbook of International Economics*, II, Amsterdam: North-Holland, 917–77

Osband, K. and Villanueva, D., 1993. Independent currency authorities: an analytic primer, *International Monetary Fund: Staff Papers*, 40, 202–16

Oswald, A. J., 1985. The economic theory of trade unions: an introductory survey, *Scandinavian Journal of Economics*, 87, 160–93

Oudiz, G. and Sachs, J., 1985. International policy coordination in dynamic macroeconomic models, in W. H. Buiter and R. C. Marston (eds.), *International Economic Policy Coordination*, Cambridge: Cambridge University Press, 274–318

Persson, M., Persson, T. and Svensson, L. E. O., 1987. Time consistent fiscal and monetary policy, *Econometrica*, 55, 1419–31

Persson, T. and Svensson, L. E. O., 1993. Current account dynamics and the terms of trade: Harberger–Laursen–Metzler two generations later, *Journal of Political Economy*, 93, 43–65

Persson, T. and Tabellini, G., 1995. Double-edged incentives: institutions and policy coordination, in G. M. Grossman and K. Rogoff (eds.), *Handbook of International Economics*, III, Amsterdam: Elsevier, 1973–2030

Phelps, E. S., 1994. *Structural Slumps: The modern equilibrium theory of unemployment, interest, and assets*, Cambridge, MA: Harvard University Press

Phelps, E. S. and Winter, S. G., 1970. Optimal price policy under atomistic competition, in E. S. Phelps (ed.), *Microeconomic Foundations of Employment and Inflation Theory*, New York: Norton, 309–37

Reinhart, C. M., 1995. Devaluation, relative prices, and international trade, *International Monetary Fund: Staff Papers*, 42, 290–312

Risager, O., 1988. Devaluation, profitability and investment, *Scandinavian Journal of Economics*, 90, 125–40

Rødseth, A., 1979. Macroeconomic policy in a small open economy, *Scandinavian Journal of Economics*, 81, 48–59

1985. Dynamics of wages and trade in a fixed-exchange-rate economy, *Scandinavian Journal of Economics*, 87, 120–36

1996a. Exchange rate versus price level targets, *Memorandum*, 7, University of Oslo, Department of Economics

1996b. Exchange rate versus price level targets and output stability, *Scandinavian Journal of Economics*, 98, 559–77

Rogoff, K., 1985a. Can international monetary policy coordination be counterproductive?, *Journal of International Economics*, 18, 199–217

1985b. The optimal degree of commitment to an intermediate monetary target, *Quarterly Journal of Economics*, 18, 1169–89

1996. The purchasing power parity puzzle, *Journal of Economic Literature*, 34, 647–68

Røisland, Ø. and Torvik, R., 1999. Exchange rate versus inflation targeting: a theory of output fluctuations in traded and non-traded sectors, *Arbeidsnotat*, 1, Norges Bank

Sachs, J., 1982. The current account in the macroeconomic adjustment process, *Scandinavian Journal of Economics*, 84, 147–59

Samuelson, P. A., 1964. Theoretical notes on trade problems, *Review of Economics and Statistics*, 46, 145–54

   1980. A corrected version of Hume's equilibrating mechanism for international trade, in J. S. Chipman and C. P. Kindleberger (eds.), *Flexible Exchange Rates and the Balance of Payments*, Amsterdam: North-Holland, 141–58

Sargent, T. J., 1986. *Rational Expectations and Inflation*, New York: Harper & Row

Schwartz, A. J., 1993. Currency boards: their past, present, and possible future role, *Carnegie–Rochester Conference Series on Public Policy*, 39, 147–87

Sibert, A., 1989. The risk premium in the foreign exchange market, *Journal of Money, Credit, and Banking*, 21, 49–65

Siegel, J. J., 1972. Risk, information and forward exchange, *Quarterly Journal of Economics*, 86, 303–9

Sinn, H.-W., 1989. Expected utility and the Siegel paradox, *Journal of Economics*, 50, 257–68

Solnik, B. H., 1974. An equilibrium model of the international capital market, *Journal of Economic Theory*, 8, 500–24

Soskice, D. and Iversen, T., 1998. Multiple wage-bargaining systems in the single European currency area, *Oxford Review of Economic Policy*, 14, 110–24

Stockman, A., 1990. Exchange rates, the current account, and monetary policy, in W. Haraf and T. Willet (eds.), *Monetary Policy for a Volatile Global Economy*, Washington, DC: American Enterprise Institute

Stulz, R. M., 1984. Currency preferences, purchasing power risks, and the determination of exchange rates in an optimizing model, *Journal of Money, Credit, and Banking*, 16, 302–16

Summers, R. and Heston, A., 1991. The Penn World Table (mark 5): an expanded set of international comparisons, 1950–1988, *Quarterly Journal of Economics*, 106, 327–68

Svensson, L. E. O., 1991. The simplest test for target zone credibility, *International Monetary Fund: Staff Papers*, 38, 655–65

   1992. An interpretation of recent research on exchange rate target zones, *Journal of Economic Perspectives*, 6, 119–44

   1994. Monetary independence in spite of fixed exchange rates, *Journal of Monetary Economics*, 33, 157–99

   1996. Inflation forecast targeting: implementing and monitoring inflation targets, *European Economic Review*, 41, 1111–46

   1998. Open-economy inflation targeting, *Seminar Paper*, 638, Institute for International Economic Studies, Stockholm

Takagi, S., 1991. Exchange rate expectations: a survey of survey studies, *International Monetary Fund: Staff Papers*, 38, 156–83

Taylor, J. B., 1989. Policy analysis with a multicountry model, in R. C. Bryant, D. A. Currie, J. A. Frenkel, P. R. Masson and R. Portes (eds.), *Macroeconomic Policies in an Interdependent World.*, Washington, DC: International Monetary Fund, 122–42

   1993. *Macroeconomic Policy in a World Economy*, New York: Norton

Taylor, M. P., 1995. The economics of exchange rates, *Journal of Economic Literature*, 33, 13–47

Tobin, J., 1969. A general equilibrium approach to monetary theory, *Journal of Money, Credit, and Banking*, 1, 15–29

   1972. Inflation and unemployment, *American Economic Review*, 62, 1–18

   1980. *Asset Accumulation and Economic Activity*, Oxford: Basil Blackwell

1982. The commercial banking firm: a simple model. *Scandinavian Journal of Economics*, 84, 495–530

Tobin, J. and de Macedo, J. B., 1980. The short-run macroeconomics of floating exchange rates: an exposition, in J. S. Chipman and C. P. Kindleberger (eds.), *Flexible Exchange Rates and the Balance of Payments*, Amsterdam: North-Holland, 5–28

Turnovsky, S. J., 1977. *Macroeconomic Analysis and Stabilization Policy*, Cambridge: Cambridge University Press

1997. *International Macroeconomic Dynamics*, Cambridge, MA: MIT Press.

Varian, H. R., 1993. *Intermediate Microeconomics*, New York: Norton

Walsh, C. E., 1998. *Monetary Theory and Policy*, Cambridge, MA: MIT Press

Walters, A., 1986. *Britain's Economic Renaissance*, Oxford: Oxford University Press

Wissén, P., 1982. *Wages and Growth in an Open Economy*, Stockholm: The Economic Research Institute

Woodford, M., 1994. Structural slumps, *Journal of Economic Literature*, 32, 1784–1815

Index